PHONOLOGY OF CATALAN

PUBLICATIONS OF THE PHILOLOGICAL SOCIETY
XXVIII

PHONOLOGY OF CATALAN

MAX WHEELER
University of Liverpool

PREMI NICOLAU D'OLWER, 1975
de l'Institut d'Estudis Catalans

Published for the Society by
BASIL BLACKWELL · OXFORD
1979

© 1979, Fundació Palma Guillén

ISBN 0 631 11621 4

Set in Great Britain by Preface Ltd., Salisbury
Printed and bound by Billing & Sons Ltd.,
London, Guildford and Worcester

On the recommendation of a committee consisting of Ramon Aramon i Serra and Pere Bohigas, nominated by the Secció Filològica of the INSTITUT, Jordi Rubió, nominated by the Secció Històrico-Arqueològica of the INSTITUT, Antoni M. Badia i Margarit, nominated by the Societat Catalana d'Estudis Històrics, and Jordi Carbonell, nominated by the Board of Trustees of the Fundació Palma Guillén, the INSTITUT D'ESTUDIS CATALANS at its plenary session held on 11 April, 1975, agreed unanimously to award the XIII Nicolau d'Olwer Prize to Max W. Wheeler for his work *Some Rules in a Generative Phonology of Modern Catalan*.

At its plenary session held on 12 March 1976, the INSTITUT, in agreement with the Fundació Palma Guillén, resolved to authorize the publication of this work.

Contents

	Page
Preface	ix

Introduction
 1. Broad aims: Generative Phonology — xi
 2. Type of language studied: *català comú* — xi
 3. Scope of study — xii
 4. Survey of previous work on Catalan phonology — xiv
 5. Use of distinctive features — xx
  6.1. Phonetic transcriptions — xxi
  6.2. Glosses — xxi

Chapter I. Non-verbal morphology and vowel epenthesis
 1. Morphological classes "Masculine" and "Feminine" — 1
 2. Outline of epenthesis of final unstressed vowels — 2
  2.1. Epenthesis of [ə] in F words — 2
  2.2. Epenthesis of [ə] after consonant groups — 3
  2.3. Epenthesis of [u] in M plurals — 3
  2.4. Final [i], [u], [ə] in M words: stem or affix? — 3
  2.5. Final [i], [u], [ə] in M words: empty morphs. Truncation rules. — 4
  2.6. Final /+u/ subject to glide formation
 3. Epenthesis of [ə] in F words in detail — 7
  3.1. Rule for final [ə] in F words — 8
  3.2. Exceptions to epenthesis of [ə] in F word stems — 9
  3.3. Exceptions to epenthesis of F [ə] in adjective suffixes — 9

Contents

- 3.4. Exceptions to epenthesis of F [ə] in words ending in c̦ — 10
- 3.5. [±female] distinguished lexically — 10
- 4. Epenthesis of [ə] after consonant groups — 11
  - 5.1. Plural formation; epenthesis of [u] in M plurals — 22
  - 5.2. Exceptions to plural formation and epenthesis of [u] — 23
- 6. Epenthesis of [ə], [d] in verb forms — 27
- 7. Epenthesis of [ə] in initial position — 30

Chapter II. Stress assignment
- 1.1. Phonetic aspects of stress — 33
- 1.2. Vowel reduction: unstressed vowels — 33
- 1.3. Words with two stresses — 34
- 1.4. Unstressed words — 34
- 1.5. Syllables which may bear stress — 34
- 1.6. Predictability of stress position: Major and Minor rule — 35

- 2.1. Initial form of Major stress rule — 35
- 2.2. Modification to allow unstressed adjective suffixes — 37
- 2.3. An alternative solution to unstressed adjective suffixes — 38
- 2.4. Preferred solution to unstressed adjective suffixes — 39

- 3.1. Major stress rule modified for monosyllables — 39
- 3.2. Major stress rule modified for further verb forms — 39
- 3.3. Major stress rule modified for different stress pattern of related nouns and verbs — 40
- 4. Minor stress rule — 41
- 5. Ordering of stress rules relative to epenthesis and truncation rules — 43
  - 6.1. Unstressed words: boundary adjustment? — 43
  - 6.2. Review of boundary markers and readjustment rules — 44

Contents

6.3.	Environment for Word-boundary insertion	46
7.1.	Compound words: two stresses	47
7.2.	Compound words: one stress	48
8.1.	Scope of stress rules	50
8.2.	Left limit of stress rules	51
8.3.	Stressed bound prefixes	53
9.	Vowel reduction	55

Chapter III. Verb morphology
Introduction   59
1. Verbal syntax   62
   1.1.1. Base rules; readjustment rules   63
   1.1.2. Further readjustment rules. Matthews'
       condition   64
   1.1.3. Syntactic features   68
   1.1.4. Perf and Progr   68
   1.2.1. The /ba/ preterite auxiliary   68
   1.2.2. The future and conditional   69
   1.2.3. Affix shift   70
   1.2.4. The future auxiliary rule   70
   1.2.5. Perfect tense readjustment   71
  1.3. Sample derivations   72
  1.4. Morphosyntactic features incorporated
      within stems   77

  2.1. Person affixes   78
   2.2.1. Conjugation classes. Phonetic forms of
       paradigms. Thematic infixes   78
   2.2.2. Frequency of conjugation classes   79
   2.3.1. Extension of truncation rule   83
   2.3.2. Thematic vowel of class II   83

  3.1. Proposed infixes and rules to generate them   84
   3.2.1. Environment for /g/-insertion   87
   3.2.2. The /g/-insertion rule   91
  3.3. Absence of /+u/ in 1sg pres ind   92

4. Tense and person affixes
  4.1. Rule for /+ɛ/ in IIA verbs   93
  4.2. Rule for /+e/ infix   94

Contents

- 4.3. Rule for /+i/ in the imperfect and preterite 1sg — 95
- 4.4. Rule for /+r/ in the infinitive — 95
- 4.5. Rules for /+b/ and /+j/ in the imperfect — 96
- 4.6. Rule for /+s/ in the past subjunctive — 97
- 4.7. Rule for /+nt/ in the gerund — 97
- 4.8. Rule for /+d/ in the participle. Athematic participles and rules for them — 98
- 4.9. Remaining verb affix vowels. Irregular imperatives — 102
- 4.10. Person morphs. Perfect tenses final vowel-deletion rule — 104

- 5.1. Future and conditional — 105
- 5.2. Additions to the Stress-assignment rule. Sample derivations — 108, 111

- 6. Suppletive stems
  - 6.1. Verbs with suppletive stems nos. 1–12 — 112
  - 6.2. Generalizations and modifications suggested by these suppletive stems — 118
  - 6.3. Further cases of suppletion — 123

- 7.1. More rules for verb forms. Stem-stressed imperfects and rules for /j/ and /i/ — 129
- 7.2. Further rules for the systematic phonetic representations of class II verbs — 133
- 7.3. Further thoughts on *dur* and *dir* — 138

Chapter IV. Unstressed pronouns
1. Syntactic context of unstressed pronouns — 141
2. Position of unstressed (clitic) pronouns — 142
   - 2.1. Clitic raising — 143

   - 3.1. General differences between Standard and Barcelona colloquial — 143
   - 3.2. No one-to-one correspondence between realizations of unstressed pronouns in the two dialects — 144
     - 3.2.1. Different realizations of semantic dative in 3rd person pronouns — 144

Contents

      3.2.2. Agreement of participle with preceding unstressed pronouns   145
      Table 1: Pronoun forms   147
      Explanatory notes to Table 1   156
4. Rules for unstressed pronouns in Barcelona colloquial
    4.1. Subcategorization of *Pro*. Rule for linear ordering   157
    4.2. Imperatives: adjustments to verb forms   157
    4.3. Rules limiting pronoun sequences to not more than one [1]   159
    4.4. Rule switching /i/ of /li/ to sequence-final position   160
    4.5. Realization of *ho + hi*   161
    4.6. Insertion of /+z/ in plural pronouns. Consonant deletion in or next to gerunds   162
    4.7. Primary syllabification of pronoun sequences   163
    4.8. Deletion of final /+r/ of infinitives. The vowel of *lo*. Optional preverbal *me, te, se*   165
    4.9. Initial and final [ə] in pronoun sequences   167
    4.10. Sample derivations   169
5. Rules for unstressed pronouns in Standard
    5.1. Subcategorization of *Pro*. Linear ordering. Degemination of /l + l/. Realization of *ho + hi*   175
    5.2. Insertion of /+z/ in plural pronouns. Feminine /+ə/. Insertion of [u] in *vos, nos, los*   177
    5.3. Syllabification of pronoun sequences. Remaining rules   178
    5.4. Sample derivations   180
6. The definite article   187
    7.1. An inadequacy of the analysis offered   187
    7.2. Alternative rules (ordered lexical-insertion rules) for pronouns in Barcelona colloquial   187

Contents

Chapter V. Problems in underlying representations
1. The representation of phonetic [r]   191
2. The glides [j] and [w]   194
3. Labiovelar phonemes /k^w/ and /g^w/   199
4. The phoneme /v/   200
5. Affricates   202
    5.1. [ts]   203
    5.2. Distribution of affricates   203
    5.3. Possible diphonemic examples for [dʒ]   204
    5.4. Affrication rule   204
    5.5. Badia's arguments for monophonemic solutions   205
6. Geminate obstruents   207
7. Geminate sonorants   209
8. The vowel [ə]   213

Chapter VI. Between underlying representations and the input to the phonological rules
    1.1. Purpose of lexical (underlying) representations   216
    1.2. Nature of the output of the phonological rules   216
    1.3. Feature specifications: the requirements for inputs to phonological rules. Stanley's condition   216
    1.4. Purpose of marking conventions. Distinction between 'redundant' and 'unmarked'   218

    2.1. Minimal specifications of Catalan segments in maximally distinctive positions   221
       2.1.1. Markedness hierarchy of Catalan segments   223
    2.2. Context-free redundancy (CFR) rules   223
    2.3. Markedness and marking rules   230
       2.3.1. Suggestions for relative markedness of segments   230
       2.3.2. Marking rules formulated   232
    2.4. Linking. Linking conventions   233
3. Morpheme-structure rules
       3.1.1. Function of morpheme-structure rules   239

3.1.2.	Form of morpheme-structure rules. Directionality	241
3.2.	Possible segment sequences in Catalan	242
3.2.1.	Vowel sequences	242
3.2.2.	Morpheme-initial single segments	242
3.2.3.	Morpheme-initial two-consonant sequences: plosive + liquid	242
3.2.4.	Morpheme-initial two-consonant sequences: /+sC/	243
3.2.5.	'Exceptional' two-consonant initial sequences	244
3.2.6.	Morpheme-initial three-consonant sequences	244
3.3.	MS rules for morpheme-initial sequences	246
3.4.1.	Sequence redundancy (SR) rules: preferred syllable structure	248
3.4.2.	Restrictions on initial groups	249
3.5.	Medial and final groups. MS base rule	250
3.5.1.	Medial and final groups resembling initial groups	252
3.5.2.	Other two-consonant sequences. Examples of three-consonant and four-consonant sequences	254
3.5.3.	Rule for C_d	262
3.5.4.	Sequence redundancy in medial/final groups	262
3.5.5.	Further SR rules	266

Chapter VII. Further phonological rules
1. Word-final /n/-deletion 270
2. Word-final /r/-deletion 275
  2.1. A solution to oxytone exceptions to the Major stress rule 278
3. Deletion of final /s/ and /z/ 279
4. Deletion of final stops 280
  4.1. Deletion of anterior stops after non-continuant sonorants 280

Contents

      4.1.1. 'Reciprocal rules' and their relation to stop deletion — 281
      4.1.2. 'Reciprocal rules' as context-free redundancy rules — 283
   4.2. Deletion of coronal stops after continuants. A new notation for 'before or after' environments — 283
   4.3. Deletion of velar stops after nasals — 286
5. Vowel sandhi: contacts between vowels across word boundaries — 287
6. Assimilation of point of articulation — 294
   6.1. Assimilation to labials — 298
   6.2. Alveolar assimilation — 299
   6.3. Partial palatal assimilation — 300
   6.4. Velar assimilation — 301
   6.5. Dental assimilation — 302
   6.6. The relation of assimilation to stop deletion — 303
   6.7. Further investigation of velarization of /l/ — 306
   6.8. Sample derivations — 308
7. Affrication of final /ʒ/ — 309
8. Voicedness assimilation — 310
   9.1. Lateral assimilation — 314
   9.2. Nasal assimilation — 315
10. Spirantization of /b/, /d/, /g/ — 316
11. Affrication — 321
12. Long tense consonants = geminates — 324

Bibliography — 325

Preface

This book is a corrected version, without substantial alteration, of a doctoral thesis entitled *Some Rules in a Generative Phonology of Modern Catalan*, which I completed in December, 1974, and which was approved by the Board of the Faculty of Mediaeval and Modern Languages, University of Oxford, in June, 1975. It was awarded the 1975 "Nicolau d'Olwer" prize by the Institut d'Estudis Catalans, Barcelona, to whom I express my gratitude. I am also very grateful to the Provost and Fellows of the Queen's College, Oxford, whose award to me of a Laming Travelling Fellowship enabled me to study in Barcelona. I must also thank the Council of the Philological Society for having accepted this work for publication.

Among individuals I should like to thank first Dr Roy Harris, my supervisor, for his useful criticism and advice during the preparation of the thesis. To Professor Antoni Badia i Margarit and Professor Antoni Comas of the University of Barcelona I am indebted for their encouragement and assistance during my stay there. I wish to express my gratitude to Dr Ramon Aramon i Serra of the Institut d'Estudis Catalans for his encouragement, interest, and generosity, and for his valuable advice on a number of matters; to Montserrat Martí i Bas who was unfailingly generous with all sorts of advice and help in getting to know Catalan and Catalonia; and to Joan

Mascaró for his comments on various aspects of the work and profitable discussion of several phonological issues.

I want, too, to thank all my Catalan friends and acquaintances, in whose company I acquired what skill I have in their language, and whose speech, whether they knew I was observing it or not, furnished some of the data for this book. And last but not least, I am grateful to Professor Anna Morpurgo-Davies, who first taught me linguistics, and persuaded me to pursue the subject.

Liverpool, Max W. Wheeler
August, 1976

Introduction

1. In this work I attempt to analyse a part of the phonological system of contemporary Catalan in terms of what has come to be known as Generative Phonology, — more precisely, the formal and methodological approach which deals with the phonological component of a Transformational Generative Grammar. I have been guided to some extent by a number of recent works which apply the theory of Generative Phonology to particular languages, for example, French (Schane, 1968), Spanish (Harris, 1969), Italian (Saltarelli, 1970b), Russian (Lightner, 1972) and Ancient Greek (Sommerstein, 1973). The general theory and practice is expounded by Harms (1968) and Schane (1973), but most fundamentally in Chomsky & Halle's monumental "The Sound Pattern of English" (1968) on which subsequent work in Generative Phonology, including the present attempt, is founded.

A Generative Phonology aims to give an account of the "competence" of a native speaker/hearer in the sounds of his language, and includes everything that has to do with the phonetic realization of lexical and grammatical formatives. It therefore includes morphology within its domain, in so far as the surface phonetic form of underlying formatives or of elements introduced transformationally can be accounted for by rule.

2. The language to be studied here is contemporary Standard Catalan (*català comú*), or more precisely, that

kind of Catalan spoken by educated people in Barcelona. It is defined by Cerdà (1972:13), for whose study it is also the object of investigation as: "el catalán que se aprende allí donde se enseñe, propio de las personas cultas y del lenguaje cuidado, universitario y modernamente litúrgico, en particular". It is to a great extent that kind of language whose norms are enshrined in normative grammars, of which the most authoritative are those of Badia (1962) and Fabra (1968a). In the field of pronunciation at least, what is recommended by normative grammars differs little from what is heard among educated Catalans, except in the case of unstressed pronouns. Consequently, it is only when I discuss these, in chapter IV, that I refer other than in passing to pronunciations which normative grammar labels "incorrect". The forms and rules I present, then, aim to represent part of the linguistic competence of an idealized speaker/hearer belonging to the class of people I have mentioned. To put it another way, I claim that if anyone were to speak according to the rules I present, he would be said by native speakers to be speaking correctly and grammatically.

3. The scope of this work is as follows: I should like to think I have included all the important rules of inflectional morphology, — of the noun and adjective in chapter I, of the verb in chapter III, and of the unstressed pronouns in chapter IV. I include also the rules for word stress (chapter II); morpheme structure rules (chapter VI); problems in assigning underlying representations ("phonemicization") — (chapter V); and relatively low level phonological rules, some of which are discussed at the various places where they become relevant to another issue, and the remainder of which are dealt with in chapter VII. Two substantial areas of Catalan phonology are not covered. They are: sentence intonation, about

Introduction

which relate to synchronic material, present the results of phonetic experiments with the simple equipment available at that time, basically the kymograph and the artificial palate. The experimental circumstances mean that the investigations are restricted to words pronounced in isolation, and sometimes to single sounds. Even so, bearing this limitation in mind, Barnils's descriptive studies are fundamental in presenting the "typical" realizations of Catalan phonemes, and also some of the sequentially conditioned allophones, as well as establishing some negative conclusions, e.g. that Catalan vowels are not perceptibly nasalized (79–88) and that sonorants are not voiceless in whole or in part when adjacent to voiceless consonants (59–66).

The study of Lacerda & Badia (1948) is limited to the pronunciation of sixteen different words by one subject. The experimental data were recordings on Lacerda's chromograph of each of the words pronounced three times in a declarative manner and three times in an interrogative manner. The experimental results, which one can only describe as excessively detailed, enable one to observe minutely the change in the pattern of air vibration through time as each word is pronounced, and also the smallest movements of the fundamental frequency, corresponding to the intonation. The instrument used has been superseded by the sound spectrograph, of which the spectrograms are a great deal easier to interpret and much more informative; these facts, added to the very greatly restricted scope of the experiment and the artificiality of the conditions implicit in the articulating of isolated words, mean that the experimental study is now of very little value. The "subjective" analysis (21–36) represents the relative length and pitch of the syllables of the fifteen words of more than one syllable which were investigated. The limited scope and artificial conditions of the study make this perceptual evidence no more than suggestive. A much more substantial study of Catalan rhythm and intonation is still needed.

Badia's chapter "Sonidos del catalán" (1951: 83–117) is a very valuable description of the phones of Catalan and their distribution, including those (particularly of consonants) in syntactic phonetic environments. There is a useful transcription (114–7) of a continuous text; this contains a number of archaisms prevalent in the literary style of the turn of the century when the text was written and which do not correspond to the normal speech of the present day. There also appears to be a degree of uncertainty in the transcription as to the style of pronunciation to be represented. The attempt to pick a middle path between a declamatory style and a rapid style occasionally leads to selections from both. As with Arteaga's texts (1915), however, this one is useful in exemplifying syntactic phonetic phenomena. A number of errors in this chapter are corrected by Coromines (1971: 246 -8). (The first version of these corrections appeared in 1958). The description of Catalan sounds is repeated with different examples in Badia, 1962: I, 59 –106.

Cerdà (1970; greatly expanded in Cerdà, 1972) discusses the results of articulatory and acoustic experiments on two subjects to establish the nature and relationship of the Catalan vowels. The articulatory evidence consists of palatograms and measurements taken from cineradiographic films, shot from the side, of the subjects pronouncing chosen phrases. The acoustic evidence consists of the pronunciation of these phrases displayed on sound spectrograms. Among other things, the evidence reveals, as one might expect, the partial overlap of the realizations of structurally adjacent vowel phonemes. Measurements revealing allophonic variation are presented but are not systematically related to classes of immediate phonetic environments, except in the case of allophonic variation dependent upon stress.

Badia (1973a: 115–137) reviews what is known of Catalan pronunciation, and includes some interesting observations on diphthongs, especially rising diphthongs, concerning their realization and distribution.

Phonological studies of Catalan – those which examine the function of sounds – begin with the valuable article of Fabra (1897). Many of the important phonological rules of Catalan, such as glide formation, vowel reduction, word-final voicing neutralization, external vowel sandhi, and weak pronoun forms are discussed with awareness of the importance of paradigmatic alternation. The concept of underlying forms more basic than their variant surface realizations seems implicit. Even more valuable, because more detailed, is Fabra's monograph (1913) on unstressed words in the colloquial dialect of Barcelona. Many of the variant realizations of unstressed pronouns are discussed, with which topic I deal here in chapter IV. Fabra's "Converses filològiques" (1954, - the latest edition, revised) are also useful in exemplifying "incorrect" forms, especially of pronouns.

The first consciously phonemic treatment of Catalan is a short article by Alarcos Llorach (1953). He establishes the phoneme inventory of Catalan with a few examples, denying phonemic status to [ə], [j], and [w] which he regards as allophones of vowels in the phoneme inventory. He also interprets the phonetic affricates [ts], [dz], [tʃ], [dʒ] as phonemic sequences of stop + fricative. In much of the article he is engaged in classifying the phonemes according to a primitive and non-binary version of the Jakobsonian distinctive feature system. Alarcos also refers to some of the conditioned neutralizations such as those of unstressed vowels, and of word-final consonants. He does not consider morphological alternations. A very short article by Di Pietro (1965) states baldly what the phonemes are in his view, without argument. He adds nothing to what Alarcos had already said.

Substantial contributions to our knowledge of Catalan

phonology have been made by Badia i Margarit in several works. A problem for users of these works is that Badia does not make clear the theoretical basis of his phoneme. Normally he ignores morphological or paradigmatic alternations, though these *are* considered in discussing the status of [ə] (Badia, 1965b). He establishes (1965a) the consonant phonemes by extensive commutation. A strict requirement of identity of commutation frames, in phonetic terms, leads him to include sequences of more than one word on occasion, ignoring the possible phonological effects of word boundaries. There are unfortunately no examples of geminates contrasting with single consonants. This work concludes with a discussion in which [ŋ] is denied phonemic status, and in which, after lengthy argument, the unit phoneme affricates /tʃ/, /dz/, /dʒ/ are accepted. Badia (1973a) reviews and summarizes the previous work, and adds useful discussions of diphthongs and glide formation; discussing nominal morphology (1973b) he admits implicitly a morphophonological view of the phoneme, accepting that word-final [p], [t], [k], [f], [s], [tʃ] in masculine words can realize not only /p/, /t/, /k/, /f/, /s/, and /tʃ/ but also /b/, /d/, /g/, /v/, /z/, and /dʒ/ or /ʒ/, as revealed in other forms of the paradigms. Badia's other contributions to phonology discuss questions which concern only marginally the subject of this present work, in particular (1966; 1970a, b, c) free variation between /e/ and /ɛ/, /o/ and /ɔ/, and /s/ and /z/ in certain specified lexical items (that is, variation of the English [iːkənɔmiks]/ [ekənɔmiks] or [niːðə]/[najðə] type). From my point of view these alternatives are always a matter of alternative underlying representations; the examples I use of words having this kind of alternation will always be of the pronunciation which is regarded as "more correct".

The first application of Generative Phonology to Catalan is by Saltarelli (1970a). This article deals with

Introduction

algueres, a dialect very different from the Standard, and is so short as to be of no great value. A much more substantial study, with subject matter and approach similar to those of this work, is that of Lleó (1970). Naturally many of her correct observations and solutions are repeated here, though with my own examples and arguments. A number of her solutions, however, seem to me to be erroneous, sometimes, as in the case of verb morphology, as a result of her not examining the question as a whole. On other issues, such as glide formation, plural formation in masculines, final stop and /n/ deletion, her conclusions are based on incomplete evidence, which ignores possible counterexamples. Still, Lleó's work is a valuable first step in the direction in which this work attempts to go, taking, I hope, a broader and deeper look.

It is appropriate here to mention one unpublished work: Mascaró (1972) covers much of the ground I cover here in chapter VII, though my solutions differ from his in a number of relatively minor ways. Rather than any disagreement of substance, it is my different use of features and an attempt to be more comprehensive which explain the rather different appearance of the rules of this area of grammar in my work.

A few other recent articles refer briefly to issues of Catalan phonology. Vogt (1971) and Phelps (1972) discuss how the vowel-reduction rule (see below, II §9) should be formulated. Neither considers the case of a non-labial non-high vowel before [ə] or [á] which is [e] and not [ə] as it would be elsewhere. This "exception" indeed makes the reduced formulation of the vowel-reduction rule much more difficult anyway. Brasington (1972) mentions the Catalan final /n/–deletion rule as it occurs in verbs and non-verbs, in a paper discussing classes of exceptions to phonological rules. Brasington (1973) discusses some problems of Catalan final stop deletion in the environment before /+s/ (see below, VII §4.1.1), and mentions the vowel-reduction rule to which, he claims, a reciprocal redundancy rule may link.

5. The use of distinctive features in what follows is in accordance with the conclusions to which I come in my article (Wheeler, 1972). These can be summarized briefly as they affect this work as follows:
  (a) Abbreviations by Greek-letter variables are not appropriate in the formulation of natural classes. This conclusion was also arrived at by Zwicky (1970) and Daniels (1971).
  (b) To avoid the possibility of formulating false generalizations some features should be assigned to a "second rank", that is, apply only to certain subclasses of [+segment]. Hence [anterior], [coronal], and [distributed] are relevant only to [−syllabic] segments, and [low] only to [+syllabic] segments.
  (c) [syllabic] is required in addition to [vocalic].
  (d) I adopt the suggestion I made (1972:99−100) to introduce the feature [labial] and dispense with [grave] and [round]. The feature [labial] is also suggested in this sense by Wang (1968:701) and Smith (1973:197).
  (e) The feature [strident] is dispensed with. This conclusion is also reached by Hill & Nessly (1973:105).
  (f) Apico-alveolar consonants are [−anterior] (and [−distributed]) as opposed to lamino-alveolars which are [+anterior]. My arguments (1972:97) based on Harris (1969) are misleading. He only suggests (192) that apico-alveloar [s] (which is the phonetic realization of Catalan /s/, as of Castilian Spanish /s/) is [−anterior, −distributed], without extending this specification to the other alveolar consonants of Spanish, whose apical articulation Harris does not elsewhere contrast with laminal articulation. In fact, the

normal pronunciation of [n], [l], [ɾ], [r], [s], [z] in Catalan is apico-alveolar, as it is in Castilian; see the palatograms of Barnils (1933: 21–36). Since apical articulations are [−distrib] (Chomsky & Halle, 1968:312), the appropriate way to distinguish interdentals from apico-alveolars is for the former to be [+anterior] and the latter [−anterior]. This enables the following classes to be established in this region:

	dentals	lamino-alv.	apico-alv.	palato-alv.	palatals
coronal	+	+	+	+	—
anterior	+	+	—	—	—
distrib.	—	+	—	+	+

A table of the feature specification of Catalan underlying segments is overleaf.

6.1. The phonetic transcriptions use the symbols of the International Phonetic Alphabet, except that stress is indicated by an acute accent for primary stress, or a grave accent for secondary or weaker stress, placed over the vowel of the stressed syllable, and that palatalization is indicated by ´ placed after a consonant. Phonetic transcriptions quoted from other works are transliterated with IPA symbols. The transcriptions are in general fairly broad except where particular allophonic details are being discussed; their purpose is to illustrate or clarify the points at issue.

6.2. Glosses are provided for Catalan words, to assist in their identification, except where the English gloss would have the same orthographic form as the word glossed, ignoring accents. Glosses are also omitted when a word is mentioned again shortly after a previous glossed occurrence.

Distinctive feature specification of Catalan phonemes

	i	e	ɛ	a	ɔ	o	u	j	w	l	ʎ	r	n	m	ɲ	p	b	t	d	k	g	kʷ	gʷ	f	v	s	z	ʃ	ʒ
syllabic	+	+	+	+	+	+	+	−	−	−	−	−	−	−	−	−	−	−	−	−	−	−	−	−	−	−	−	−	−
vocalic	+	+	+	+	+	+	+	−	−	+	+	+	−	−	−	−	−	−	−	−	−	−	−	−	−	−	−	−	−
conson	−	−	−	−	−	−	−	−	−	+	+	+	+	+	+	+	+	+	+	+	+	+	+	+	+	+	+	+	+
obstruent	−	−	−	−	−	−	−	−	−	−	−	−	−	−	−	+	+	+	+	+	+	+	+	+	+	+	+	+	+
contin	−	−	−	−	−	−	−	+	+	+	+	−	−	−	−	−	−	−	−	−	−	−	−	+	+	+	+	+	+
nasal	−	−	−	−	−	−	−	−	−	−	−	−	+	+	+	−	−	−	−	−	−	−	−	−	−	−	−	−	−
labial	−	−	−	−	−	−	−	−	+	−	−	−	−	+	−	+	+	−	−	−	−	+	+	+	+	−	−	−	−
voiced	+	+	+	+	+	+	+	+	+	+	+	+	+	+	+	−	+	−	+	−	+	−	+	−	+	−	+	−	+
low	−	−	+	+	+	−	−	−	−	−	−	−	−	−	−	−	−	−	−	−	−	−	−	−	−	−	−	−	−
high	+	−	−	−	−	−	+	+	+	−	−	−	−	−	−	−	−	−	−	+	+	+	+	−	−	−	−	−	−
back	−	−	−	+	+	+	+	−	+	−	−	−	−	−	−	−	−	−	−	+	+	+	+	−	−	−	−	−	−
anterior										+	−	+	+	+	−	+	+	+	+	−	−	−	−	+	+	+	+	−	−
coronal								−	−	+	+	+	+	−	−	−	−	+	+	−	−	−	−	−	−	+	+	+	+
distrib								+	−	−	+	−	−	+	+	+	+	+	+	+	+	+	+	−	−	−	−	+	+

xxii

CHAPTER I

Non-verbal morphology and vowel epenthesis

1. Before plunging into the strictly phonological aspects of this question it will be convenient to expound the significance of the morphological classes conventionally called "masculine" and "feminine" which I shall abbreviate as M and F respectively. Every noun in the surface structure is marked either M or F. If it is F, an attributive or predicative adjective which can have a form with a final [ə] does so. Thus *roba bruta* [rɔ́βə βrútə] 'dirty clothes', but *un mitjó brut* [um midʒó βrút] 'a dirty sock', because *roba* is F, while *mitjó* is M. A noun phrase containing a F noun is conveniently called a F NP and is pronominalized by special F forms, e.g. subject *ella*, verbal direct object *la*, and may be preceded by F articles *la* or *una*. Nouns referring to male beings, i.e. having a semantic marker [+male] are M; those referring to female beings, i.e. having a semantic marker [+female] are F. So in the grammar of Catalan there are these redundancy rules:

(1) N[+female] → [+F]

(2) N[+male] → [+M]

The only complications occur in the case of nouns referring to certain animals, where the above rules do not apply, the morphological class being specified in the lexicon. Normally these words are semantically unmarked for sex. Thus *una sargantana* (F) 'a lizard' — sex unspecified —; a specifically male lizard is *una sargantana mascle*, i.e. to *sargantana* (F) is added *mascle* (M) 'male being'. The proper way of generating such a noun phrase is not obvious, and anyway falls outside the domain of phonology; suffice it to say that such nouns, in addition to being marked [+M] or [+F] in the lexicon, will also have to be marked as exceptions to rules (1) and (2). [+M] or [+F] must be stated non-redundantly in the lexicon for all nouns referring to non-sexual beings, as also for those which must be unmarked for sex, e.g. *persona* (F) 'person', *criatura* (F) 'baby'. Observe that the feature [+male] added to those of 'baby' would require the lexical item *nen*, for example, not *criatur (M) nor *criatura mascle*. In fact of course we can make the morphological class marker a binary feature [±F], and the members of only one class need be marked in the lexicon, the other marker being supplied by a marking rule. If we suppose that the F words are marked in the lexicon, the rule would be:

(3) $N[uF] \rightarrow [-F]$ (= [+M])

I shall take for granted that the syntactic transformation rules can be formulated to extend the features M and F to adjectives, pronouns and articles, since my purpose here is merely to point out that these features are supplied by rule in such cases.

2. Now I should explain in what cases it is necessary to generate final unstressed vowels by rules, and how other final unstressed vowels are to be dealt with.

2.1. In the first place, the vast majority of words in the morphological class F end in [ə] in the singular and in [əs] in the plural. This is clearly to be dealt with by a rule which adds a final [ə] to those stems. See below, § 3.

Non-verbal morphology and vowel epenthesis 3

2.2. In the second place there are several consonant groups which do not occur word-finally at the phonetic level, being always followed by [ə]. See §4 for detailed discussion. This "epenthetic" [ə] can be supplied by rule.

2.3. Thirdly, [u] appears in the masculine plural (i.e. the termination is [us]) of words ending in a sibilant (/s/, /z/, /ʃ/, /ʒ/) or a sibilant followed by a stop. This phenomenon is wholly predictable on phonetic and independently required morphological criteria. See §5.1. for details.

2.4. There remain to be considered nouns and adjectives which in the M singular end in [i], [u], or [ə]. (Verbal endings are dealt with in chapter III.) We can leave aside cases a) where final [i] or [u] is a part of the stem which appears throughout the paradigm and derivatives, or b) where [i] (there are no examples with [u] in M words) is a formative suffix. Such cases are:

(a) *custodi* 'custody', cf. *custodiar* 'to guard'
estalvi 'safe' (M), cf. *estàlvia* 'safe' (F), *estalviar* 'to save'
divorci 'divorce', cf. *divorciar* 'to divorce'
canvi 'change', cf. *canviar* 'to change'
tebi 'tepid' (M), cf. *tèbia* id. (F)
continu 'continuous' (M), cf. *contínua* id. (F), *continuar* 'to continue'
vacu 'vacuous' (M), cf. *vàcua* id. (F), *vacuïtat* 'vacuity'
vidu 'widower', cf. *vídua* 'widow', *enviduar* 'to be widowed'

(b) i) /+i/ adjective suffix from concrete nouns:
ferri (M) *ferria* (F) 'of iron', cf. *ferro* 'iron'
corinti (M) *coríntia* (F) 'Corinthian', cf. *Corint* 'Corinth'

4 Non-verbal morphology and vowel epenthesis

faringi (M) *faríngia* (F) 'pharyngeal', cf. *faringe* 'pharynx'
ii) /+i/ abstract noun suffix, mostly from verbs:
murmuri 'murmur', cf. *murmurar* 'to murmur'
equilibri 'balance', cf. *equilibrar* 'to balance'
suïcidi 'suicide', cf. *suïcidar-se* 'to commit suicide'
domini 'dominion', cf. *dominar* 'to dominate'
adulteri 'adultery', cf. *adúlter* 'adulterous'

In the examples in a) the final vowel is a part of the stem in the underlying representation; in b) it is characterized as a word-forming suffix, as is /+u/ which appears in a few F abstract nouns, e.g.

pèrdua 'loss' /pɛrd+u+ə/, cf. *perd* 'loses'
vàlua 'value' /bal+u+ə/, cf. *val* 'is worth'

It is also possible that cases of final [ə] in M words where there is no paradigmatic evidence for its absence in related forms is part of the stem, e.g.

plaga 'joker' [pláɣə] /plaga/
prevere 'priest' [prəβérə] /prabera/

2.5. We are left then with M words ending in a final vowel which is not part of the stem as revealed by paradigmatic evidence, nor an identifiable suffix, nor a support vowel required because the previous consonant or group may not end a word at the systematic phonetic level. There are a reasonable number with [ə], some with [u], and apparently a very few with [i].

There is rarely any synchronic justification, phonological or morphological, for final [ə]; compare the following relationships:

reprotxe [rəprɔ́tʃə] 'reproach' is to *reprotxar* 'to reproach' as
esquitx [əskítʃ] 'splash' is to *esquitxar* 'to splash';

Non-verbal morphology and vowel epenthesis 5

infame 'infamous' (M) is to *infàmia* 'infamy' as
blasfem 'blasphemous' is to *blasfèmia* 'blasphemy';
vague [báɣə] 'vague' (M) is to *vaga* [báɣə] id. (F)
and *vaguetat* 'vagueness' as
cec [sék] 'blind' (M) is to *cega* [séɣə] id. (F) and
ceguetat 'blindness'.

Others are, for example:

còmode 'comfortable' (M), cf. *comoditat* 'comfort'
discorde 'disagreeing' (M), cf. *discòrdia* 'disagreement
mite 'myth', cf. *mitologia* 'mythology'.

[u] sometimes appears after groups of consonants which anyway require a support vowel, especially after /rr/, thus:

ferro [férru] 'iron', cf. *ferrar* 'to shoe' (horse, etc.)
carro [kárru] 'cart', cf. *carret* 'little cart'
ganxo 'hook', cf. *ganxet* 'crochet hook'
flonjo 'soft, flabby' (M), cf. *flonja* id. (F)
guerxo 'cross-eyed' (M), cf. *guerxa* id. (F),

and also:

toro [tɔ́ru] 'bull', cf. *torejar* 'to fight bulls'
maco 'attractive' (M), cf. *maca* id. (F)
esbarjo 'recreation', cf. *esbargir-se* 'to relax'
suro 'cork', cf. *surar* 'to float'.

Two examples with [i] are:

bienni [biénni] 'biennium', cf. *biennal* 'biennial'
municipi [munisípi] 'town', cf. *municipal*

Now in the case of final [u] and [i] at any rate, comparison with the examples in §2.4. shows that here we cannot have either stem-final vowels in the underlying representation, nor lexical suffixes, for these are not deleted when a vowel follows. The evidence against the

6 *Non-verbal morphology and vowel epenthesis*

possibility of deletion of stem final [ə] is less clear. [ə] at the systematic phonetic level may be the reflex of underlying /e/, /ɛ/, or /a/, which are subject to the Vowel-reduction rules (see II §9.). In e.g. *proteic* [pɾutɛ́jk] /prutɛ+ik/ 'proteinic' we have an example of stem-final /ɛ/ which is not deleted before +V in the suffix /+ik/; similarly *arcaic* [ərkájk] /arka+ik/ 'archaic' provides an example of /a/ which is not deleted. However, the underlying forms of these stems may be rather /prutɛj+/, /arkaj+/ respectively, with a rule deleting /j/ before /i/, which is required anyway, cf. III §4.5., §7.1. Compare *heroi* [əɾɔ́j] 'hero', *heroic* [əɾɔ́jk] /arɔj+ik/, *heroina* [əɾuínə] /arɔj+in+ə/ 'heroine'.

In verbs such as *obeir* [uβəí] 'to obey', *obeeix* [uβəéʃ] 'obeys', *agrair* [əɣɾəí] 'to thank', *agraeix* [əɣɾəéʃ] 'thanks', the stem vowels are never stressed, thus no evidence is provided in favour of /e/, /ɛ/, or /a/ specifically as the underlying stem-final segment. I shall proceed on the assumption that in fact stem-final /a/ is deleted before +V, becoming [ə] elsewhere when not stressed; this will account for the [-ə] ~ ø alterations given above, thus I suggest that the underlying representation of the M words in question is /rapɾɔtʃa/, /infama/, /baga/, /kɔmɔda/, /mita/ and so on.

I suggest *obeir*, *agrair*, etc. have stems ending in /e/ or /ɛ/. Note that there are also no first conjugation verbs in *–aar*, such as would have 1sg. present in [-áu], though there are verbs with 1sg. present in [-ɛ́u] (e.g. *creo* 'I create') and in [-éu] (e.g. *menyspreo* 'I scorn'). It seems more appropriate for the majority case – the nouns and M adjectives in [-ə] – to have the less marked vowel /a/, and that it should be the less marked vowel which is deleted before +V. So the rule in question is:

(4) $\begin{bmatrix} +\text{syllab} \\ +\text{back} \\ -\text{labial} \end{bmatrix} \rightarrow \emptyset \ / \underline{\quad} + \ [+\text{syllab}]$

Non-verbal morphology and vowel epenthesis

N.B. this rule will deal with verb forms such as *fem, feu* (from *fer* 'to make') and *estem, esteu* (from *estar* 'to be') if from /fa+ε+m/, /fa+ε+w/, /sta+ε+m/, /sta+ε+w/, cf. *fas, fa, fan; estàs, està, estan.*
For the [−u] and [−i] cases, e.g. *toro, bienni,* we need a rule introducing /+u/ or /+i/ in a specific environment to words carrying the appropriate morphological class marker − let us call them [+U] and [+I] respectively. Thus

(5)   ø → +u /   [+U]___(+C)   #

(6)   ø → +i /   [+I]___(+C)   #

(Ordering with respect to rule (9) − see below − is indeterminate if we have a Truncation rule +V → ø /___+V.) However, these class markers can be avoided provided we allow the words concerned to end in the lexicon in some way other than just /u/ or /i/, which, as we have seen, are normally carried throughout the paradigm. A likely possibility is underlying /+u/, /+i/, i.e. /tɔr+u/, /bi+εnn+i/ in the lexicon, since we shall anyway require a Truncation rule of the form

(7) $\begin{bmatrix} V \\ -\text{Affix} \end{bmatrix}$ → ø / +___+V

to account for verbal inflexions. In the case of the derivatives in /+i/ and /+u/ as mentioned in §2.4., these final vowels will be [+Affix] as a result of a difference in bracketing: *toro* will be [[N tɔr+u]N, *bienni* [[N[Af bi+]Af εnn+i]N; but *pèrdua* will be [[N[Vpεrd]V[Af+u]Af]N; and *ferri* [A[N fεrr+u]N[Af +i]Af]A.

2.6. In a small number of examples of final /+u/ in M words an additional but natural rule of glide formation is required in order to account for the phonetic form.

8 Non-verbal morphology and vowel epenthesis

Consider:

déu [déw] 'god', cf. *dea* [déə] 'goddess'
plebeu [pləβéw] 'plebeian' (M), cf. *plebea*
[pləβéə] id. (F)
ateu [ətéw] 'atheist' (M), cf. *atea* [ətéə] id. (F)
hebreu [əβréw] 'Hebrew' (M), cf. *hebrea* [əβréə]
id. (F)
europeu [əwɾupéw] 'European' (M), cf. *europea*
[əwɾupéə] id..(F)
impiu [impíw] 'impious' (M), cf. *impia* [impíə]
id. (F)

It is not the case that all unstressed /u/s become [w] after a stressed vowel, though counter-examples to this general principle are not numerous. We have for example, *período* [pəɾíuðə] 'period', *trio* [tɾíu], *caos* [káus] 'chaos' *paleozoic* [pəlèuzɔ́jk], *harmònium* [əɾmɔ́nium], *Màrius* [máɾius]; see below, chapter V §2. There are two possible explanations: either that it is only non-affix /+u/ which is subject to glide formation, or that in *període*, etc. the underlying vowel is not /u/ but /ɔ/ or /o/, both of which are later reduced to [u] by the Vowel-reduction rule. Underlying /ɔ/ is revealed by such related items as *periòdic* [pəɾiɔ́ðik], *caòtic*[kəɔ́tik] 'chaotic' and so on. Since with the second proposal the correct output can be achieved by means of rule ordering alone, it is to be preferred to the first, which requires a restriction on the rule itself. Thus the following rule applies before Vowel reduction, but after Stress assignment:

(8) $\begin{bmatrix} -\text{cons} \\ +\text{high} \end{bmatrix} \rightarrow [-\text{syllab}] / \begin{bmatrix} +\text{syllab} \\ +\text{stress} \end{bmatrix} \underline{\quad} \text{X}]_{N,A}$

3.1. The form of the rule to generate feminine final [ə] is very simple:

(9) ø → + [+syllab]/[+F]___ (+C) #

Non-verbal morphology and vowel epenthesis   9

The morpheme boundary '+' before the segment introduced is needed to present the correct environment for the application of (4), (7), and the Stress-assignment rule. (+C) allows for the presence of plural /+s/. The features realizing [+syllab] as [ə] will be supplied by linking conventions; see below, VI § 2.4. Examples are:

/os/ → /os+ə/ óssa 'female bear'
+F

/altr/ → /altr+ə/ altra 'other' (F)
+F

/ʒustisi/ → /ʒustisi+ə/ justícia 'justice'
+F

3.2. There is a small but not inconsiderable number of exceptions to rule (9), e.g. llum (F) 'light', dent (F) 'tooth', mà (F) 'hand', mercè (F) 'favour', crisi (F) 'crisis' among nouns; among adjectives we have gran 'large' (F), breu 'short' (F), sublim 'sublime' (F), pitjor 'worse' (F), miop 'short-sighted' (F). All such lexical items must be marked [−rule (9)], that is, they are just exceptions to the general rule.

3.3. The adjectival endings −ar, −al, −el, −il are exceptions also, but only when they are suffixes, thus:

      escolar (M and F) 'school (adj.)', cf. escola 'school'
      central (M and F), cf. centre
      cruel (M and F), cf. cruent 'bloody'
      mòbil (M and F) 'mobile', cf. movem 'we move'
but: car (M), cara (F) 'dear', clar (M), clara (F) 'clear', etc. and
      mal (M), mala (F) 'bad', paral·lel (M), paral·lela (F) 'parallel'.

This can be expressed by a redundancy rule of the form:

10 Non-verbal morphology and vowel epenthesis

(10) $\left[+\begin{bmatrix} +\text{syllab} \\ -\text{labial} \\ \langle+\text{back}\rangle_b \end{bmatrix} \right] \begin{bmatrix} +\text{vocal} \\ +\text{cons} \\ \langle+\text{cont}\rangle_a \end{bmatrix}] A$
      1   2   3   4   ⇒

$$1 \begin{bmatrix} 2 \\ -\text{rule (9)} \end{bmatrix} \begin{bmatrix} 3 \\ -\text{rule (9)} \end{bmatrix} 4$$

condition: if a, then b.

[−labial] is mentioned to prevent application to words like *crèdul* (M), *crèdula* (F) 'credulous' which have a /+ul/ suffix. Without using the device of conditions on angle brackets one would have to have two rules, presumably one for /−r/, the other for /−l/.

3.4. A third group of exceptions to rule (9) consists of some adjectives ending in /s/ which is spelt ç and which is preceded by a vowel; these have [ə] before [s] in the feminine plural, but have no final [ə] in the singular. Thus

feliç (M and F sg.) 'fortunate', *feliços* (M pl), *felices* (F pl).

It would be possible to take a hint from the orthography and suppose that the final underlying consonant is not /s/ but /ts/, and that the morphological difference is related to this − there are no adjectives ending phonetically in [ts]. But there is no independent motivation for such a solution. So a more appropriate way is to mark these adjectives lexically, let us say [+Z]. Then a rule ordered before (9) will be

(11) $\begin{bmatrix} +Z \\ -\text{Plural} \end{bmatrix} \rightarrow [-\text{rule (9)}]$

3.5. The last group of exceptions consists of those in which rules (1) and (9) are insufficient, e.g.

Non-verbal morphology and vowel epenthesis 11

oncle (M) 'uncle' but *tia* (F) 'aunt'
porc (M) 'pig' but *truja* (F) 'sow'
abat (M) 'abbot' but *abadessa* (F) 'abbess'
príncep (M) 'prince' but *princesa* (F) 'princess'

This is, of course, a lexical rather than a phonological question. Restrictions on rule (1), not on rule (9), are required in these cases. The lexical entries might read something like this for *porc/truja* : /pɔrk/ [*m* —female] (where *m* = marked, and indicates a non-deletable semantic feature) with a cross-reference to /truʒ/ [*m* —male]; for *abat/abadessa* a lexical rule;

⟦$_N$ abad   ⟧$_N$
   [+female]
1   2   3   ⇒   1   2   + ⟦$_{Af}$ εs   ⟧$_{Af}$ 3
                                      [+F]

These suggestions are naturally no more than tentative, since little is known about how precisely to deal with lexical insertion.

4. Now we come to epenthesis of [ə] after consonant groups not yet supported by a vowel supplied by the rules already given. (See above, §2.2.) In fact these epenthesis rules are not crucially ordered with respect to the feminine [—ə] rule (9). If (9) applied first, the environment for epenthesis would not occur in F words; if it applied afterwards, (9)'s structural description would not be met, since the epenthetic [ə] is not [+F]. That is, in words like *altra* 'other' (F) [áltrə] it is immaterial whether [ə] is introduced by (9) or by epenthesis after a consonant group since the result is the same. The environment for epenthesis is almost entirely phonetic; morphological considerations help to clarify a few examples, however. Naturally, in consequence of the point just made about F words, the noun and adjective

12 *Non-verbal morphology and vowel epenthesis*

examples which follow are all [−F]. The discussion also includes a few verb forms which are subject to the same rules. Morpheme structure constraints exclude /k^w/, /g^w/, /ʃ/, and /ʒ/ except as the last consonant of a group; /ɲ/ and /ʎ/ (except geminate /ʎʎ/) do not appear in consonant groups at all within morphemes. The relevant groups will be presented below with examples before I proceed to consider the formulation of the rule.

/C₁ r#/ groups:

/jr/: *aire* 'air', *caire* 'edge', *drapaire* /drap+ajr/ 'rag-and-bone man'. /j+r#/ in the infinitive of conjugation II verbs will have been converted to /w+r#/ before this rule applies − see the examination of verb morphology, chapter III § 7.2.

/wr/ : *lliure* 'free', *centaure* 'centaur'.

/lr/ : *folre* 'lining' (unique example); /l+r#/ in the infinitive of conjugation II verbs is converted to /ld+r#/ before this rule applies.

/rr/ : *esquerre* 'left', *terra* (M) 'floor',[1] cf. also *corre* 'runs' (3sg present indicative) from UR /korr/. (N.B. /rr+r#/ gives /rr+ər/, thus *córrer-hi* [kórəri] /korr+r#i/ 'to run there'.)

/nr/ : no examples, but observe that /n+r#/ in the infinitive of conjugation II verbs results in /nd+r#/ before the epenthesis of [ə] applies; compare /lr/ above. It does not seem likely, though, that the absence of examples here is due to the epenthesis of /d/ between /n/ and /r/ when + is not present, for the forms *honra* (F) [ónrə] 'honour', *conreu* [kunréw] 'cultivation', *Enric* [ənrík]

---

[1] An exception to epenthesis here is *cigar*; underlying /rr/ is demonstrated by derivatives, e.g. *cigarreta* 'cigarette'. The popular, "incorrect", form for *cigar* is *cigarro* which is phonologically regular.

'Henry' exist. The absence of examples for /nr#/ is thus fortuitous.

/mr/ : again no examples. /m+r#/ in the infinitive of conjugation II verbs does not give *[mbrə] as might be expected, but [mər] : esprémer /sprem+r/ 'to squeeze', témer /tem+r/ 'to fear', except in Barcelona colloquial where we have *fumbre* [fúmbrə] beside *fúmer* [fúmər-] /fum+r/, a pro-verb of no specific meaning. Cf. also *somriure* [sumríwrə] /som+rij+r/ 'to smile'. There is thus no reason for supposing that in general it is /mr#/ rather than /nbr#/ that is realized as [mbrə], as in *cogombre* [kuyómbrə] 'cucumber', and I suppose /mr#/ to be excluded by morpheme structure rules. As long as the rule changing /m+r#/ to /m+ər/ applies earlier, this epenthesis rule is not required to include or exclude /mr#/ specifically.

*/ɲr/: As mentioned above, this sequence, along with all sequences containing /ɲ/ is excluded by morpheme structure rules. In the infinitive of conjugation II verbs /ɲ+r#/ becomes /ɲ+ər/ e.g. *estrènyer* /strɛɲ+r/ 'to squeeze'. The case is parallel to that of /mr/ above.

/pr/ : *aspre* 'rough', *estupre* 'rape'.
/br/ : *pobre* 'poor', *novembre* 'November'.
/tr/ : *catre* 'camp bed', *ceptre* 'sceptre', *claustre* 'cloister'.
/dr/ : *lladre* 'thief', *tendre* 'tender' (A).
/kr/ : *mediocre*, *pollancre* 'black poplar'.
/gr/ : *sogre* 'father-in-law', *congre* 'conger eel'.
/fr/ : *llefre* 'gooey', *sofre* 'sulphur'.
*/vr/ : as the presence of underlying /v/ is revealed only by an adjacent formative boundary, there are no examples of the sequence outside infinitives of conjugation II verbs, e.g. *deure* [déwrə] /dɛv+r#/ 'to owe', *moure* [mɔ́wrə] /mɔv+r#/ 'to move'.
/sr/, /zr/ : The opposition between /s/ and /z/ is

14 *Non-verbal morphology and vowel epenthesis*

neutralized before consonants. There are no examples of the sequence within morphemes before #. The only examples of /s+r#/ are *ésser* /es+r#/ 'to be', *tòrcer* 'to twist', *vèncer* 'to conquer'; these have an epenthetic vowel before /r/ as occurs with /m+r#/, /ɲ+r#/. Rule ordering can prevent the generation of incorrect outputs.
*/ʃr/, */ʒr/: As stated above, these sequences are excluded by morpheme-structure rules. In infinitives we have e.g. *conèixer* [kunéʃər-] /kunɛʃ+r#/ 'to know', *créixer* [kréʃər-] /kreʃ+r#/ 'to grow', with epenthesis before /r/ as we have seen in some other cases.

/Cl#/ groups:

/jl/ : *rail* is the only example of this consonant group I can find anywhere. It is obviously an Anglicism, and is likely to be regarded as [+foreign] and to be an exception to phonological rules. In any case, an alternative form *raïl* [rəíl] /rail/ occurs, which may be the appropriate naturalization of the word.

/wl/ : *retaule* 'altar-piece', *acaule* 'stemless'.

/rl/ : No example found, though the sequence is not excluded by morpheme structure rules, cf. *perla* (F) 'pearl'.

$\begin{bmatrix} -\text{cont} \\ +\text{coron} \end{bmatrix} \begin{bmatrix} +\text{vocal} \\ +\text{cons} \\ -\text{cont} \end{bmatrix}$ (= /tl/ which is not distinct

from /dl/, /nl/, /ll/ and is usually realized as [ll].) On the one hand we have e.g. *afil·le* 'aphyllous, i.e. leafless'; on the other hand, e.g. *tranquil* [trəŋkíl] 'peaceful', cf. *tranquil·la* id. (F) [trəŋkíllə], *nul* (M), *nul·la* (F) 'null', *rebel* 'rebellious', cf. *rebel·lar* [rəβəllá] 'to rebel'. An underlying final /a/ would be acceptable in the case of *afil·le* and similar words; then, rather than complicate the rule so as to exclude this group from epenthesis in the

Non-verbal morphology and vowel epenthesis   15

case of *tranquil*, etc., /tl#/ could be reduced by an earlier rule:

(12) $\begin{bmatrix} -\text{cont} \\ +\text{coron} \end{bmatrix} \to \emptyset \,/\,\underline{\quad} \begin{bmatrix} +\text{vocal} \\ +\text{cons} \\ -\text{cont} \end{bmatrix} (C) \,\#$

Alternatively, *afil·le* etc. would end in /tl/ but be marked as exceptions to rule (12); they would then undergo epenthesis of final [ə] in the normal way. It is not obvious that one of these groups of words rather than the other is e.g. [−popular], i.e. consists of words introduced from Latin or Greek and not handed down with the common stock, so as to motivate the different treatment, for [ll] is in any case found largely in [−popular] words. The solution requiring *afil·le* to have underlying final /a/ is perhaps to be preferred since the position of these words is no different from the other cases of M words in [−ə].

$\begin{bmatrix} -\text{syllab} \\ +\text{nasal} \end{bmatrix} \begin{bmatrix} +\text{vocal} \\ +\text{cons} \\ -\text{cont} \end{bmatrix}$ (= /nl/, /ml/, /ɲl/) : These appear
to be excluded by morpheme structure rules.

/pl/ : *amplc* 'broad', *exemple* 'example'.
/bl/ : *deixeble* [dəʃébblə] 'disciple', *amable* 'kind';
for discussion about the status of /bl/ see chapter V, §6.
/kl/ : *miracle* [miráklə], *oncle* 'uncle', *cercle* 'circle'.
/gl/ : *segle* [ségglə] 'century', *angle* [áŋglə].
/fl/ : *rifle, girofle* 'clove'. N.B. */vl/ is not distinct from /wl/, /bl/; see on */vr/ above.
/sl/, /zl/ : No examples found. The sequence is probably to be excluded by MS rules; *gusla* (F) 'Yugoslav one-stringed fiddle' is doubtless to be regarded as [+foreign].

/tʎ/ : *batlle* [báʎʎə] 'mayor', *motlle* [móʎʎə] 'mould'. There are no other /ʎ/ groups.

16 *Non-verbal morphology and vowel epenthesis*

/Cn#/ groups:

/jn/ : *badaine* 'narrow chisel' (sole example).
/wn/ : *faune* 'faun' (sole example).
/ln/ : No example, though the sequence occurs, uniquely, in *alna* (F) 'ell'. Since the related /lm#/ and /rn#/ have no epenthetic [ə] it will be appropriate to allow the rule to exclude /ln/ along with them from the environment of [ə] epenthesis.
/rn/ : No epenthesis : *infern* [iɱfɛ́rn] 'hell', *torn* 'lathe'.

$$\begin{bmatrix}+\text{conson}\\+\text{labial}\end{bmatrix}\begin{bmatrix}-\text{syllab}\\+\text{nasal}\\+\text{coron}\end{bmatrix}(= /\text{pn}/ \text{ which is not distinct}$$

from /mn/, /bn/, /fn/, /vn/) : *solemne* 'solemn', *himne* 'hymn'.

$$\begin{bmatrix}-\text{vocal}\\+\text{coron}\end{bmatrix}\begin{bmatrix}-\text{syllab}\\+\text{nasal}\\+\text{coron}\end{bmatrix}(= /\text{tn}/ \text{ which is not distinct}$$

from /nn/, /dn/, /sn/, /zn/) : *perenne* [pərɛ́nnə] 'perennial', *equidna* (M) [əkínnə] 'echidna'.
/kn/ (not distinct from /gn/) : *regne* [réŋnə] 'reign', *benigne* [bəníŋnə] 'benign'.

/Cm#/ groups :

/jm/ : No examples, though the sequence is not excluded by MS rules, cf. *esblaimar-se* [əzβləjmársə] 'to turn pale'.
/wm/ : *guilleume* 'small joiner's plane', *trauma, neuma* 'neum'.
/lm/ : No epenthesis : *salm* [sálm] 'psalm', *elm* [ɛ́lm] 'helmet'.
/rm/ : No epenthesis : *eixarm* [əʃárm] 'magical cure', *ferm* 'firm' (A).

$\begin{bmatrix} +\text{conson} \\ +\text{labial} \end{bmatrix} \begin{bmatrix} -\text{syllab} \\ +\text{nasal} \\ +\text{labial} \end{bmatrix}$ (= /pm/ which is not distinct
from /bm/, /mm/, /fm/, /vm/) : *summe* [súmmə]
'supreme'.

$\begin{bmatrix} -\text{vocal} \\ -\text{cont} \\ +\text{coron} \end{bmatrix} \begin{bmatrix} -\text{syllab} \\ +\text{nasal} \\ +\text{labial} \end{bmatrix}$ (= /tm/ which is not distinct from
/nm/, /dm/) : *ritme* [rímmə] or [rídmə] 'rhythm',
logaritme 'logarithm'.
/km/ (not distinct from /gm/) : *dogma* [dóŋmə] or
[dógmə], *borborigme* 'tummy-rumble'.
/sm/ (not distinct from /zm/) : *socialisme*
'socialism', *blasme* 'blame'.

/Cz#/ groups :

/jz/ : No example, though the sequence occurs, e.g.
faisà 'pheasant'.
/wz/ : No examples, though the sequence occurs, e.g.
causa (F) [káwzə] 'cause'.
/lz/ : *salze* 'willow', *colze* 'elbow'.
/rz/ : *catorze* 'fourteen' (sole example).
/nz/ : *bronze*, *quinze* 'fifteen', and several other
examples. Counter-examples are *fons* [fóns] /fon+z/
'bottom' (cf. *fonament* 'foundation', *enfonsar* [əɱfunzá]
'to send to the bottom'), *dins* /din+z/ 'inside' (cf.
endinsar [əndinzá] 'to put in', *dintre* 'inside'). Note
that both of these have + before the /z/. Also *brunz*
[brúns] 'buzzes' (V) (cf. *brunzir* [brunzí] 'to buzz')
which, however, is perhaps not genuinely from the
dialect studied, where the more usual form is *brunzeix*
'buzzes'. One would hope that the relative simplicity
of the alternative rules might indicate whether *fons* etc.
or *bronze* etc. are the exceptions.
/mz/ : No examples of the sequence occur.

18 Non-verbal morphology and vowel epenthesis

/pz/, /bz/ : No examples; the sequences are possibly to be excluded by MS rules.
/tz/ (not distinct from /dz/) : *dotze* 'twelve', *setze* 'sixteen'.
/kz/, /gz/ : No example, though the sequence is not excluded by MS rules, cf. *èczema* [ɛ́gzəmə].

/Cʃ#/, /Cʒ#/ groups:

/jʃ/, /jʒ/ : Excluded by MS rules.
/wʃ/: No examples, though the sequence is not excluded by MS rules, cf. *rauxa* (F) [ráwʃə] 'whim'.
/lʃ/ : The only example, without epenthesis, is the Valencian city of *Elx* [élʃ]; therefore not strictly a word native to the dialect being studied.
/rʃ/ : No example, though the sequence is possible, cf. *xarxa* (F) [ʃárʃə] 'net'.
/nʃ/ : No example, other than the Anglicism *ponx* [pónʃ] 'punch', though the sequence is possible, e.g. *ganxo* 'hook'.

$$[+obstr] \begin{bmatrix} +obstr \\ +cont \\ +distr \\ -voice \end{bmatrix}$$ (= /tʃ/ which is not distinct from

/pʃ/, /ʃʃ/, etc.) : Though final [ə] after /tʃ/ is common, e.g. *reprotxe* 'reproach', *cotxe* 'car', there are also counterexamples without epenthesis, e.g. *esquitx* 'splash', *tatx* 'sample'.
/wʒ/ : *greuge* 'grudge', *auge* 'apogee'.
/lʒ/ : No example, though the sequence occurs elsewhere, cf. *nostàlgic* [nustálʒik].
/rʒ/ : *conserge* [kunsérʒə] 'concierge', *marge* 'margin'.
/nʒ/ (not distinct from /mʒ/, /ɲʒ/) : *canonge* 'canon', *diumenge* 'Sunday'.

Non-verbal morphology and vowel epenthesis 19

[+obstr] $\begin{bmatrix} +\text{obstr} \\ +\text{cont} \\ +\text{distr} \\ +\text{voice} \end{bmatrix}$ (= /tʒ/ which is not distinct from

/pʒ/, /kʒ/ etc.) : Though there are many words which have final [ə], e.g. *viatge* 'journey', *rellotge* 'clock', there are also several without, e.g. *lleig* [ʎétʃ], cf. *lletja* (F) [ʎédʒə] 'ugly', *trepig* [trəpítʃ] 'footstep', cf. *trepitjar* [trəpidʒá] 'to tread'.

/Ct#/ groups :

/mt/ : Although there are numerous cases of final [ə], e.g. *comte* [kómtə] 'earl', *compte* [kómtə] 'account', *assumpte* [əsúmtə] 'matter', there is one counter-example, viz. *exempt* [əgzémt]. There is no morphological explanation for this anomaly, since *exempt* is to *eximir* 'to exempt', as *presumpte* [prəzúmtə] 'presumptive', is to *presumir* 'to presume'. One must conclude that either all members of the majority class have underlying final /a/, or *exempt* is uniquely marked [−epenthesis].

/pt/ (not distinct from /bt/) : *apte* 'apt', *concepte* 'concept'.

/kt/ (not distinct from /gt/) : *compacte* 'compact', *projecte* 'plan'.

/ft/ : No example, though the sequence occurs, cf. *nafta* (F) 'naphtha'.

I have now mentioned all two-consonant sequences which, when not followed by another formative, are followed by [ə]. Other groups either occur finally without a supporting vowel, or are excluded by MS rules from all positions, or are not found at the end of a morpheme. The purpose of the rule which follows is to represent the fact that occurence of [ə] is wholly predictable, in the environments mentioned. I believe the simplest form of the rule is as follows:

Non-verbal morphology and vowel epenthesis

(13) $\emptyset \rightarrow [+\text{syll}] / \left/ \left\{ \begin{matrix} \begin{bmatrix} \langle -\text{obstr}\rangle_b \\ -\text{syll} \end{bmatrix} \begin{bmatrix} \langle +\text{distr}\rangle_a \\ +\text{cont} \\ +\text{voice} \\ -\text{syll} \end{bmatrix} \\ \begin{bmatrix} -\text{cont} \\ +\text{obstr} \end{bmatrix} [-\text{cont}] \\ [-\text{vocal}] \begin{bmatrix} -\text{obstr} \\ -\text{syll} \end{bmatrix} \end{matrix} \right\} - \left\{ \begin{matrix} \# \\ +C \end{matrix} \right\} \right.$ i, ii

iii

iv

condition: if a, then b.

N.B. the rule as expressed also accounts for the internal epenthetic [ə] in *corregut* [kurəyút] 'run' (ptcp.) /korr+g+u+d/. The sequences represented by the different parts of the rule are these:

i) = $\left\{ \begin{matrix} j \\ w \\ l \\ \Lambda \\ r \\ n \\ m \\ \textipa{\textltailn} \end{matrix} \right\}$ 3 ii) = $C \left\{ \begin{matrix} r \\ z \end{matrix} \right\}$ iii) = $\left\{ \begin{matrix} p \\ b \\ t \\ d \\ k \\ g \\ k^w \\ g^w \end{matrix} \right\}$ $\left\{ \begin{matrix} l \\ \Lambda \\ n \\ m \\ \textipa{\textltailn} \\ p \\ b \\ t \\ d \\ k \\ g \\ k^w \\ g^w \end{matrix} \right\}$ iv) = $\left\{ \begin{matrix} j \\ w \\ n \\ m \\ \textipa{\textltailn} \\ p \\ b \\ t \\ d \\ k \\ g \\ k^w \\ g^w \\ f \\ v \\ s \\ z \\ \textipa{S} \\ 3 \end{matrix} \right\}$ $\left\{ \begin{matrix} j \\ w \\ l \\ \Lambda \\ r \\ n \\ m \\ \textipa{\textltailn} \end{matrix} \right\}$

The device of conditions on angle-brackets is offered by Harms (1968:74). It seems to me that here and elsewhere where sequences of more than one matrix are concerned,

Non-verbal morphology and vowel epenthesis 21

(cf. for example, in morpheme-structure rules), some such device is needed to indicate which sequences can occur and which not, that is simpler than disjunctive bracketing with { }. However, the decision, in the case of a sequence of two items, whether to make the first depend on the second or vice versa seems from the point of view of the present theory to be arbitrary. I have in this case made the first depend on the second because, a) the number of distinct systematic units which may appear in the second position is smaller, and contains some (/l/, /r/) which require only that the preceding segment be [−syllabic], and b) elsewhere in the language regressive feature determination is found much more widely than progressive.

Here the function of the features in angle-brackets is to account for the difference with respect to epenthesis between /tz#/ (→ [−ə]) and /tʒ#/ (↛ [−ə]). The consequence of omitting those features would be that epenthesis would become "normal" in the case of *viatge, rellotge*, i.e. the final vowel need not after all be mentioned in the underlying representation; on the other hand, cases such as *lleig, trepig* would have to be marked lexically [−rule (13)]. Another possibility would be for /tz/ words to have underlying /−a/ (i.e. *dotze* /dotza/ 'twelve', *setze* /setza/ 'sixteen', etc.) as in the case of /tʒa/ [−dʒə], supposing the absence of /tz/ without a following vowel, paralleling *lleig*, to be fortuitous. Then the first line of the rule would most appropriately be restricted to deal with sequences of sonorant plus voiced fricative or /r/, thus:

$$(13') \quad \emptyset \to [+\text{syll}] \; / \; \left\{ \begin{matrix} \begin{bmatrix} -\text{obstr} \\ -\text{syll} \end{bmatrix} \begin{bmatrix} +\text{cont} \\ +\text{voice} \\ -\text{syll} \end{bmatrix} \\ \begin{bmatrix} -\text{cont} \\ +\text{obstr} \end{bmatrix} [-\text{cont}] \\ [-\text{vocal}] \begin{bmatrix} -\text{obstr} \\ -\text{syll} \end{bmatrix} \end{matrix} \right\} - \left\{ \begin{matrix} \# \\ +C \end{matrix} \right\}$$

22   *Non-verbal morphology and vowel epenthesis*

5.1. As mentioned above, § 2.3. [u] appears in the M plurals of words ending in /s/, /z/, /st/, /sk/, /ʃ/ and /ʒ/ (including /tʃ/ and /tʒ/). For example:

pas 'step', plural: *passos* [pásus]
pis /piz/ 'flat', plural: *pisos* [pízus]
test 'flower-pot', plural: *testos* [téstus]
mixt [míkst] 'mixed', M plural: *mixtos* [míkstus]
fosc 'dark', M plural: *foscos* [fóskus]
calaix [kəláʃ] 'drawer', plural: *calaixos* [kəláʃus]
esquitx [əskítʃ] 'splash', plural: *esquitxos* [əskítʃus]
lleig [ʎétʃ] /ʎetʒ/ 'ugly', M plural: *lletjos* [ʎédʒus]
boig [bɔ́tʃ] /bɔʒ/ 'mad', M plural: *bojos* [bɔ́ʒus]

Some apparent exceptions to this rule are discussed below. [u] is not found in the plural of F words, even in those which are exceptions to rule (9). Thus *pols* (F) 'powder', plural: *pols; falç* (F) 'sickle', plural: *falçs* [fáls] ; *post* (F), plural: *posts* [póts] ; *ics* (F) '(letter) x', plural: *ics*. These M plurals in [us] are obligatory after /s/, /z/, and /ʃ/; they are usual after /sk/, /st/, though, for example, *discs* 'records', *tests* 'pots' are correct. I have found no example of a word ending in /sp/; *cresp* 'curly' appears in Fabra, 1968b, but I was told by an informant that the word is not used in Barcelona, and he did not know what the plural might be. After /ʒ/ the commonest or most popular words have [us], while rarer or more learned words tend to have zero; (this is best regarded as /+s/ which is deleted after, or coalesces with, [ʃ], [ʒ]). Thus *assaigs* [əsátʃ] /asaʒ+s/ 'essays', *desigs* [dəzítʃ] /dazitʒ+s/ 'desires' cf. Badia, 1973b:202.

Elsewhere in the language the plural consists merely of [s] added to the singular. Note that voicedness is neutralized in final consonants and groups of final consonants, so that the voicedness of underlying forms is revealed only elsewhere in the paradigm; in addition /ʒ/

Non-verbal morphology and vowel epenthesis   23

and /tʒ/ are both realized as [tʃ] before a pause. The details of this will be discussed later. I shall now give this [u]–insertion rule for reference before considering the apparent exceptions. I assume a rule of the following form has already applied:

(14) [+Plural] → +s /___ #]N,A,Pro,Det

The phonetic character of (15) is thus more clearly seen:

(15) ∅ → $\begin{bmatrix} +\text{syllab} \\ +\text{labial} \end{bmatrix}$ / $\begin{bmatrix} +\text{obstr} \\ +\text{cont} \\ +\text{coron} \\ -F \end{bmatrix}$ ($\begin{bmatrix} +\text{obstr} \\ -\text{cont} \end{bmatrix}$) + ___ $\begin{bmatrix} +\text{obstr} \\ +\text{cont} \\ +\text{coron} \end{bmatrix}$ #

If this rule is ordered after rule (13) accounting for [ə]-epenthesis in phonetic environments, it will be possible to put merely C in the parenthesized matrix, since only [+obstr, −cont] segments will remain to fit the other conditions, /sm/ etc. having become [smə] etc. The additional consonant groups after which such a formulation of the rule would insert [u], such as /sn/, /ʃt/, /sd/, do not occur at all, that is, they are excluded from well-formedness by morpheme-structure rules.

5.2. Now I shall consider the exceptions to (15), all of which, ending in [s] in the singular, are phonetically unchanged in the plural:

(a) *tipus* [típus] 'type'
llapis [ʎápis] 'pencil'
òmnibus [ɔ́mniβus]
dimecres 'Wednesday'
divendres 'Friday'
index [índəks]
apèndix [əpɛ́ndiks] 'appendix'
atlas [álləs]
(b) *parallamps* 'lightning conductor'

24 Non-verbal morphology and vowel epenthesis

  escanyapobres 'money-lender'
  tocadiscos 'record player'
  siscents 'SEAT 600' (a popular car)
(c) *temps* [téms] 'time'
  fons [fóns] 'bottom'
  plus [plús] 'bonus'
  esfinx [əsfíŋs] 'sphinx'
  linx [líŋs] 'lynx'
  dilluns [diʎúns] 'Monday'
  dimarts [dimárs] 'Tuesday'
  dijous [diʒóws] 'Thursday'
  reps 'rep' (cloth)

Those of list (a) all have the stress falling on a syllable before the last. This rule is recognized by traditional normative grammars; thus Fabra (1968a:28): "Els noms en *s*, *ç*, o *x* no prenen la terminació *os* si són plans, esdrúixols o femenins". However, another interpretation is possible, as I shall show. Those of list (b) are compounds of transparent form, in which the final [s] has already been introduced by the plural /+s/ rule (14) at a different level. It is correct to say, as does Vallès (1931:61) : "Són invariables per al plural . . . els compostos que ja tenen en plural el seu segon element", but a broader generalization can be made. Nouns of this group will have to have their internal syntactic structure recorded in the lexicon in order to avoid duplicating the rules generating their phonetic representation, and the semantic markers of the items of which they are composed. They must of course be lexicalized to account for the additional semantic information they convey, for not everything which conducts lightning is a lightning conductor, nor is every person or thing that plays records a record player. Thus *tocadiscos* may appear as

$$[_N[_S[_{NP}\text{ Pro}, -\text{Plur}]_{NP}[_{VP}[_V\text{ tɔk }{}^{-\text{Past}}_{+I}]_V$$
$$[_{NP}[_N\text{disk }^{+\text{Plur}}_{-F}]_N]_{NP}]_S]_N$$

Note that nouns of this form are all M, thus ⟦N⟦S X⟧S⟧N → [−F] even though the N dominated by S is itself feminine. Group (c) consists of a small closed class of which this list is intended to be exhaustive. As I said above, in group (b) the final [s] represents the formative +Plural; let me now present some evidence that final [s] which occurs in the other groups is not a part of the root of the words mentioned:

temps, cf. *temporada* [təmpuɾáðə] 'season', *temporal* [təmpuɾál], *tempesta* [təmpéstə] 'storm', *tempura* [təmpúɾə] 'stormy weather': so underlying /tenp+s/ = *temps*.

fons, cf. *fonar* [funá] 'to put a bottom into/on', *fonament* [funəmén] 'foundations', *fonamental* [funəməntál] 'fundamental', but also *enfonsar* [əɱfunzá] 'sink, plunge, send to the bottom' which shows that /fon+z/ is more appropriate than */fon+s/.

apèndix, cf. *apendicle* [əpəndíklə] 'small appendix', *apendicular* [əpəndikulár] 'appendicular'; so /apɛndik+s/ = *apèndix*.

índex, cf. *indicar* [indiká] 'to indicate', *indicatiu* [indikətíw] 'indicative', so, possibly, /indak+s/ = *índex*.

tipus, cf. *tipografia* [tipuɣɾəfíə] 'typography', *típic* [típik] 'typical'.

Note that the [u] of *tipus* is fundamentally of the same kind as that of *toro, maco*, etc. cf. § 2.4, 2.5. Thus the underlying representation of *tipus*, will be /tip+u+s/. This analysis will apply to *òmnibus* and to *cactus*, and in fact to all words which are directly transferred to Catalan from the Latin second declension nominative singular. The other words in groups (a) and (c) do not appear to possess any paradigmatic relations, but a tenuous indication that we are on the right track may be the orthography of *atles* [álləs] 'atlases', which is to *atlas* as e.g. F plural

cames [kámǝs] 'legs' is to *cama* [kámǝ] 'leg'. What I
suggest then is that in all words such as those in groups
(a) and (c) the final [s] is preceded by a morpheme
boundary. *Enfonsar* [ǝɱfunzá] is the only clear example
in which this meaningless morph reappears elsewhere in
the paradigm, and it is seen to be /z/ rather than /s/. It
would be possible to conclude that *all* the additional [s]'s
being discussed here, and perhaps also the plural morph,
belonged to /z/, but one example alone is very weak
support for such a conclusion whose consequence is that
the matrix in question should everywhere be marked
[+voice] rather than be left unmarked for voicedness.

We have now to consider which rule to modify to
achieve the correct result. Modification of (15) would
require imposing a condition excluding + (formative
boundary). There is no straightforward way of doing this,
since all rules are normally interpreted as if (+) occurred
between each matrix, i.e. it is easy to require the presence
of + in a rule, but not to require its absence, on the
grounds that ordinary phonological rules generally apply
across + as well (cf. Chomsky & Halle, 1968:67, 364). One
example favours a solution along these lines, though
apparently in a rather improbable way. *Aquest* (M)
[ǝkέst] 'this' (Pro, A) has the plural *aquests* (M) [ǝkέts],
being a unique type of exception to (15). The reduction
of /sts/ to [ts] is required anyway, cf. *post* (F) [pɔ́st],
plural: *posts* [pɔ́ts], *host* (F) [ɔ́st] 'host (army)', plural:
hosts [ɔ́ts]. If the UR of *aquest* were /akɛ+st/ a modification of rule (15) excluding + from the relevant
position would allow the correct output. This UR
is favoured by the related forms *aqueix* [ǝkέʃ] 'this/
that' (2nd person) (?/akɛ+ʃ/) and *aquell* [ǝkέʎ] 'that'
(?/akɛ+ʎ/). Thereby plural /+s/ would in fact be added
to all the words in question by (14); (15) would fail to
apply, and geminate [ss] (/+s+s/) would be reduced to [s]
by the rule reducing all geminates in appropriate

environments. In view of the difficulty of formally excluding + from the environment of (15) a possible procedure would be to introduce an exception feature to (14) by means of a [−next rule] device; thus:

(16) [+Plural] → [−next rule, i.e. (14)] / + $\begin{bmatrix} +\text{obstr} \\ +\text{cont} \\ -\text{distr} \end{bmatrix}$ #

Aquest would be lexically marked [−rule (15)]. Or even, including *aquest* within the scope:

(17) [−F] → [−next rule, i.e. (15)]

/ + $\begin{bmatrix} +\text{obstr} \\ +\text{cont} \\ +\text{coron} \end{bmatrix}$ (C) + $\begin{bmatrix} +\text{obstr} \\ +\text{cont} \\ +\text{coron} \end{bmatrix}$ #

which puts the exceptionality back where it strictly belongs.

6. For completeness, I will describe here some other cases of vocalic epenthesis. The following conjugation II infinitives have been mentioned briefly above, §4; observe too some 2nd singular present indicative forms which must be accounted for by an epenthesis rule:

témer [témər−] /tem+r/ 'to fear', *tems* /tem+s/ 'you fear'
esprémer [əsprémər−] /sprem+r/ 'to squeeze'
atènyer [ətɛ́ɲər−] /atɛɲ+r/ 'to attain'
plànyer [pláɲər−] /plaɲ+r/ 'to pity', *planys* /plaɲ+s/ 'you pity'
empènyer [əmpɛ́ɲər−] /anpɛɲ+r/ 'to push'
estrènyer [əstrɛ́ɲər−] /strɛɲ+r/ 'to squeeze'
ésser [ésər−] /es+r/ 'to be'
tòrcer [tɔ́rsər−] /tɔrs+r/ 'to twist', *torces* [tɔ́rsəs] /tɔrs+s/ 'you twist'

vèncer [bɛ́nsər–] /bɛns+r/ 'to defeat', vences
[bɛ́nsəs] /bɛns+s/ 'you defeat'
cf. also cuses [kúzəs] /kuz+s/ 'you sew', cosir
'to sew'
conèixer [kunɛ́ʃər–] /kunɛʃ+r/ 'to know',
coneixes [kunɛ́ʃəs] /kunɛʃ+s/ 'you know'
aparèixer [əpəɾɛ́ʃər–] /a+parɛj+r/ 'to appear',
apareixes [əpəɾɛ́ʃəs] /a+parɛʃ+s/ 'you appear'
créixer [kɾéʃər–] /kreʃ+r/ 'to grow', creixes
[kɾéjəs] /kreʃ+s/ 'you grow'
néixer [néʃər–] /neʃ+r/ 'to be born', neixes
[néʃəs] /neʃ+s/ 'you are born'
cf. also fuges [fúʒəs] /fuʒ+s/ 'you run away',
fugir 'to run away'
córrer [kórər–] /korr+r/ 'to run', corres [kórəs]
/korr+s/ 'you run'

The last example, though it resembles the others in the list, is in fact already accounted for by the rule already given, (13), the infinitive morph /+r/ and the second person singular /+s/ corresponding to the +C condition to the right of the environment position. In order to avoid rule (13) incorrectly introducing a final [ə] after these cases of underlying /C+r/, the present rule must be ordered before (13). In brief the environment is this:

$$\begin{Bmatrix} m \\ ɲ \\ s \\ ʃ \end{Bmatrix} \underline{\quad} +r, \begin{Bmatrix} s \\ z \\ ʃ \\ ʒ \end{Bmatrix} \underline{\quad} +s$$

Now /m, ɲ, s, ʃ/ are not a natural class, nor do they belong to one which excludes the stops. An alternative arrangement, e.g.

$$\begin{Bmatrix} s, z \\ ʃ, ʒ \end{Bmatrix} \underline{\quad} + \begin{Bmatrix} r \\ s \end{Bmatrix}, \quad \begin{Bmatrix} m \\ ɲ \end{Bmatrix} \underline{\quad} +r$$

would not express the generalization much better.

Non-verbal morphology and vowel epenthesis 29

However, the fact is that /l+r/, /n+r/ are not just required to be excluded here so as to be considered for the application of (13); rather they are subject to a different rule, of /d/ epenthesis, as mentioned in §4 above. So if /l+r/, /n+r/ were altered to /ld+r/, /nd+r/ respectively by an earlier rule, it would be necessary here only to exclude obstruent stops before /+r/, there being no examples of */ʎ+r/ or */f+r/ while /v+r/ will already have been converted to /w+r/, cf. III (96). Córrer with /r+r/ would be correctly accounted for by such a rule, and there is no counter-example, though in any case it is already adequately generated by (13). The evidence for /d/ epenthesis is briefly this:

absoldre /ab+sɔl+r/ 'to absolve', *absolem* /ab+sɔl+ɛ+m/ 'we absolve', *absolent* /ab+sɔl+e+nt/ 'absolving'; *absoldria* /ab+sɔl+r+ij+a/ 'I would absolve'
caldre /kal+r/ 'to be necessary', *calia* /kal+ij+a/ 'it was necessary', *calent* /kal+ɛ+nt/ 'it being necessary'; *caldrà* /kal+r+a/ 'it will be necessary'
ofendre /ufɛn+r/ 'to offend', *ofenem* /ufɛn+ɛ+m/ 'we offend', *ofenent* /ufɛn+e+nt/ 'offending'; *ofendria* /ufɛn+r+ij+a/ 'I would offend'
respondre /raspɔn+r/ 'to reply', *responem* /raspɔn+ɛ+m/ 'we reply', *responent* /raspɔn+e+nt/ 'replying'; *respondria* /raspɔn+r+ij+a/ 'I would reply'

There are numerous similar verbs; see below, chapter III. I find Lleó's arguments with respect to these verbs (1970: 26–7, 56) unconvincing. She proposes that they have underlying stem-final /d/, which is deleted by a rule special to these verbs except before /r/, in order to account for the non-deletion of final /n/ in the 3rd singular present indicative; thus *respon* [rəspɔ́n] 'replies' /raspɔnd/ but *ve* [bé] 'comes' /ben/ from *venir* 'to come'. However she needs a /d/–epenthesis rule anyway for the future of *venir: vindré* 'I shall come', etc. In fact the difference in treatment of final /n/ has nothing to do with the presence of [d] in the infinitives of these verbs; there are clear cases also in non-verbs of final /n/ not subject to deletion which cannot derive from /nd/ or /nt/, cf. below VII §1, and Brasington, 1972.

The /d/–epenthesis rule is thus as follows:

$$(18) \quad \emptyset \rightarrow \begin{bmatrix} +\text{coron} \\ +\text{obstr} \\ -\text{cont} \\ +\text{voice} \end{bmatrix} / \begin{bmatrix} +\text{coron} \\ -\text{obstr} \\ -\text{cont} \end{bmatrix} \underline{\quad} + \begin{bmatrix} +\text{coron} \\ -\text{obstr} \\ +\text{cont} \\ -\text{syll} \end{bmatrix}$$

and the [ə]–epenthesis rule under discussion is:

$$(19) \quad \emptyset \rightarrow [+\text{syll}]$$

$$/ \left[\begin{Bmatrix} \langle -\text{obstr} \rangle \\ +\text{cont} \end{Bmatrix}_a \\ +\text{cons} \right] \underline{\quad} + \begin{bmatrix} +\text{coron} \\ +\text{cont} \\ \langle -\text{obstr} \rangle_b \\ +\text{cons} \end{bmatrix} X]\!]_{V, \text{Aux}}$$

condition: if a, then b.

The $]\!]_{V, \text{Aux}}$ limitation is because /ʒ+s/, /s+s/ occur in nouns and adjectives without epenthesis, cf. §5 above, where /+s/ represents the formative +Plural. Some other restriction on rule (19), e.g. specification of [–Plural] could be used with the same effect. The correct order of these rules is thus (18), then (19), then (13).

7. To complete this section dealing with the introduction of vowels by rule, I would like to bring forward evidence for [ə] being supplied by rule before initial /s/ followed by consonant. Consider the following series of derivatives; the root word appears first:

> *estel* [əstél] /stɛl/ (or /stɛtl/ ? cf. *tranquil/tranquil·la*, §4) 'star', *constel·lar* [kunstəllá] /kɔn+stɛtl+a+r/ 'to decorate with stars'

Non-verbal morphology and vowel epenthesis

espirar [əspirá] /spir+a+r/ 'to breathe, blow',
inspirar [inspirá] /in+spir+a+r/ 'to breathe in',
transpirar [trənspirá] /trans+spir+a+r/ 'to transpire'
estrat [əstrát] /strat/ 'stratum', *substrat* [supstrát] /sub+strat/ 'substratum'
estrènyer [əstɾéɲə] /strɛɲ+r/ 'to squeeze',
constrènyer [kunstɾéɲə] /kən+stɾɛɲ+r/ 'to constrain'
espuma [əspúmə] /spum+a/ 'scum', *despumar* [dəspumá] /das+spum+a+r/ 'to remove scum from'
escriure [əskɾíwɾə] /skriv+r/ 'to write',
circumscriure [sirkumskɾíwɾə] /sirkum+skriv+r/ 'to circumscribe', *transcriure* /trans+skriv+r/ 'to transcribe', *inscriure* /in+skriv+r/ 'to inscribe', *proscriure* /pru+skriv+r/ 'to proscribe'
estar [əstá] /sta+a+r/ 'to be', *està* [əstá] /sta+a/ 'is', *estan* [əstán] /sta+a+n/ 'they are'.

The evidence provided by the last example is of a different kind; the point is that if /asta/, say, were the correct UR for the root of this verb, the Stress-assignment rule would assign the feature [+stress] to the first vowel in the present tense forms, giving *[ástə] *[ástən] whereas, exceptionally from a superficial point of view, forms of this verb have the final syllable stressed. If the UR is /sta/ as I propose, the stress pattern follows regularly from the normal application of the Stress-assignment rule to monosyllables. (The Truncation rule (4) applies before Stress assignment).

There are of course no cases of initial [sC] phonetically. However, not in all cases of [əsC–] is the [ə] epenthetic, for the prefix /as+/ 'away' accounts for several, e.g. *esfullar* [əsfuʎá] 'to take off leaves', cf. *fulla* 'leaf', *espolsar* [əspulsá] 'to dust', cf. *pols* 'dust'. The

32 *Non-verbal morphology and vowel epenthesis*

rule is therefore as follows:

(20) $\emptyset \rightarrow [+\text{syll}] \ / \ \# \underline{\qquad} \begin{bmatrix} -\text{syll} \\ +\text{cont} \end{bmatrix} [-\text{syll}]$

N.B. In the underlying representations of Catalan, as in English, /s/ is the only continuant which may occur before another consonant at the beginning of a morpheme. It follows from what was said above about *estar* that (20) follows the Stress-assignment rule.

CHAPTER II

Stress assignment

1.1. Stress in Catalan is chiefly manifested at the phonetic level by the relative intensity and the quality of the vowel in each syllable; consequently it is convenient to refer to "stressed or unstressed vowels" abbreviating "vowels in stressed or unstressed syllables". For the greater relative intensity of stressed vowels see Cerdà, 1970:70–82; this is coupled, it seems, with a tendency to greater length, cf. Lacerda & Badia, 1948: passim; Cerdà, 1972:51, 55. Stressed vowels are from the series [i e ɛ a ɔ o u]; unstressed vowels are from the series [i ə u] with a few exceptions in specific phonetic environments which will be discussed later.

1.2. In most cases where there is an unstressed vowel at the systematic phonetic level it is clear from paradigmatic evidence that a vowel of the stressed series is present in the UR and is "reduced" – several oppositions being neutralized – by a rule affecting vowels to which stress has not been assigned. A few examples will suffice to illustrate this widespread and well-known phenomenon of vowel-reduction. (Cf. Cerdà, 1970:76–84; Fabra, 1897:6–8; Barnils, 1933 [1911]: 3–20; Roca, 1971: 103–6.) The examples also show that the position of stress is not inherent in lexical formatives.

menjo [ménʒu] 'I eat'   *mengem* [mənʒém] 'we eat'
pesco [pésku] 'I fish'   *pesquem* [pəském] 'we fish'

mano [mánu] 'I command'   manem [mənέm] 'we command'
dono [dónu] 'I give'   donem [dunέm] 'we give'
poso [pɔ́zu] 'I put'   posem [puzέm] 'we put'
jugo [ʒúɣu] 'I play'   juguem [ʒuɣέm] 'we play'
fico [fíku] 'I put in'   fiquem [fikέm] 'we put in'

1.3. Two positive degrees of stress can be seen in compounds such as *ràpidament* [ràpiðəmén] 'quickly', *gratacels* [grὰtəsέls] 'sky-scraper'. These compounds appear to manifest at word level the principle of stress reduction by which the greatest degree of stress occurs in the last stressed syllable of a tone group (Cerdà, 1972: 55–6). The formulation of the general stress-reduction rule awaits further analysis of syntax and intonation patterns, but examples of the above kind will be discussed here to make more comprehensive the treatment of stress at the level of the conventional "word"; see §7.

1.4. There is a small number of unstressed words: the articles, the "weak" pronouns, the prepositions *a, amb, de, en,* and *per,* and a few others, cf. Fabra, 1913. These "enclitic" words receive no stress themselves, but, unlike other affixes, have no effect on the assignment of stress to the word to which they are attached; thus:

mà [má] 'hand'
la mà [ləmá] 'the hand'
a la mà [ələmá] 'in the hand'
per a la mà [pərələmá] 'for the hand'

donar [duná] 'to give'
donar-nos [dunárnus] 'to give us'
donar-nos-en [dunárnuzən] 'to give us some'

1.5. With the exception of the cases just mentioned (§ §1.3–4), each word has one stressed syllable which may be the last (*mots aguts*), e.g. *regular* [reɣulár], *bisturí*

Stress assignment 35

[bisturí] 'scalpel'; the penultimate (*mots plans*), e.g. *estimada* [əstimáðə] 'beloved', *anàvem* [ənáβəm] 'we were going'; or the antepenultimate (*mots esdrúixols*) e.g. *càtedra* [kátəðrə] 'university chair', *harmònium* [ərmɔ́nium].

1.6. The position of the stressed vowel can always be predicted by rule within verbs, but in other cases, e.g. where there is no bound suffix, it is not always possible to predict on phonetic, morphological or syntactic grounds which vowel will be stressed, though in the great majority of cases it is the vowel preceding the last segment (discounting such morphs as /+s/ plural). The exceptions to this principle consist of (a) a smallish number of words terminating in a stressed vowel (other than those clearly having underlying final /n/ or /r/ which are deleted in word-final position, the underlying consonant being revealed elsewhere in the paradigm, cf. VII § § 1 and 2). For example, *sofà* [sufá], plural *sofàs* [sufás], *consomé* [kunsumé] 'consommé', *monestir* [munəstí] 'monastery'. A solution to stress assignment for these words is proposed in VII § 2.1. (b) A relatively small proportion of the total vocabulary in which the vowel preceding that which would be stressed by the general rule is stressed, e.g. *mànig*a [mániɣə] 'sleeve', *pròsper* [prɔ́spər] 'favourable', *filòleg* [filɔ́lək] 'philologist'. Such words, I propose, carry a morphological class marker which triggers a minor rule; let the marker be [+E]. Then we have the following rule:

(1) $[+E] \rightarrow \begin{bmatrix} +\text{minor stress rule} \\ -\text{major stress rule} \end{bmatrix}$

or something with the same effect.

2.1. Let us now consider the stress rule in detail, stage by stage; the basic form of the major rule is as follows:

(2) $[+syll] \rightarrow [+stress] / \underline{\hspace{1em}} C_o \begin{Bmatrix} \begin{bmatrix} +syll \\ +high \end{bmatrix} +V \\ [+segment] \end{Bmatrix} (+C) \#$

condition: the braces apply disjunctively.

The second line within the braces deals with the majority of cases; thus:

> *mosques* [móskəs] /mosk+ə+s/ 'flies'
> *parc* [párk] /park/ 'park'
> *paraula* [pəráwlə] /parawl+ə/ 'word'
> *comunisme* [kumunízmə] /kumun+ism+ə/ 'communism'
> *barrets* [bərɛ́ts] /barrɛ́t+s/ 'hats'
> *tanca* [táŋkə] /tank+ə/ 'closes'
> *pateixen* [pətéʃən] /pat+eʃ+ə+n/ 'they suffer'
> *captaires* [kəptájrəs] /kapt+ajr+ə+s/ 'beggars'
> *barrejàvem* [bərəʒáβəm] /barrɛʒ+aβ+ə+m/ 'we mixed' (imperfect)

The first line within the braces accounts for the feminine forms in final [-ə] of adjectives and nouns having stems ending in unstressed [i] or [u], e.g.

> *fèrria* [fɛ́riə] /fɛrr+i+ə/ 'of iron'
> *carícia* [kərísiə] /karisi+ə/ 'caress'
> *necessària* [nəsəsáriə] /nasas+ari+ə/ 'necessary'
> *conspícua* [kunspíkuə] /kɔn+spiku+ə/ 'conspicuous'
> *pèrdua* [pɛ́rðuə] /pɛrd+u+ə/ 'loss'

For words in [-íə] I propose that the UR terminates in /ij+ə/. Certain verb forms indicate that /ij/ is a permissible underlying sequence, and that a rule deleting /j/ after /i/ is required anyway, see below, III §4.5, §7.1. Thus *fotografia* 'photography' has as its UR /fotɔ+graf+ij+ə/

Stress assignment

to which stress is assigned regularly by line two of (2); /j/-deletion follows, giving [futuɣrəfíə]. Similarly *mania* /manij+ə/ [mənía], *badia* /badij+ə/ [bəðíə] 'bay'. The imperfect and conditional suffixes in [−íə] can also be accounted for in this way; there, underlying /+i+ə/ is ruled out since non-affix /+i/ is deleted before +V by the truncation rule I (7). So, for example *sentia* /sent+ij+ə/ [səntíə] 'I heard' (imperfect).

2.2. It might be possible to extend rule (2) so as to deal with stress assignment in the presence of the unstressed adjectival suffixes —all have [i] or [u], that is, [+high]; the suffixes are:

[ik] e.g. *bàsic* [bázik] 'basic' (M), cf. *base*
esfèrica [əsfɛ́rikə] 'spherical' (F), cf. *esfera* 'sphere'
proteic [prutɛ́jk] 'proteinic' (M), cf. *proteïna* 'protein'
[id] e.g. *fluida* [flújðə] 'fluid' (F), cf. *fluir* 'to flow',
fluidesa [fluiðɛ́zə] 'fluidity'
vàlid [bálit] cf. *valer* 'to be valid',
proteid [prutɛ́jt]
[il] e.g. *mòbil* [mɔ́βil] 'mobile', cf. *movem* [muβɛ́m] 'we move'
[ul] e.g. *grànul* [gránul] 'granule', cf. *grans* 'grains'
càpsula [kápsulə] 'capsule', cf. *capsa* 'little box'
glòbul [glɔ́βul] 'globule', cf. *globus* 'globe'

The rule might then be:

(3)   [+syll] → [+stress]

$$/ \underline{\quad} C_0 \left\{ \begin{bmatrix} +\text{syll} \\ +\text{high} \end{bmatrix} \left(\begin{bmatrix} -\text{cont} \\ -\text{nasal} \end{bmatrix} \right) (+V) \atop [+\text{segment}] \right\} (+C) \#$$

The glide-formation rule (I (8)) will generate *proteic* [prutέjk] etc., but *fluïdesa* [fluiðέzə]. There is, however, with this form of rule no well motivated way of distinguishing these suffixes from the stressed [ík], [íd], [íl] etc., e.g. *mentida* [məntíðə] 'lie', cf. *ment* 'lies', *hostil* [ustíl] 'hostile', cf. *host* 'army', *bonic* [buník] 'pretty', cf. *bona* (F) 'good'. It would be possible to analyse the unstressed suffixes as /+i+k/, /+i+d/, /+i+l/, /+u+l/, and restrict the rule accordingly, but this would be an entirely ad hoc solution with no independent justification.

2.3. An alternative would be to propose that the UR of these unstressed suffixes was /+jk/, /+jd/, /+jl/, /+wl/. Stress would be assigned to the correct vowel by rule (2), and a subsequent rule –well motivated on general phonological grounds – would convert glides to vowels between consonants, i.e.

(4)   [–cons] → [+syll] / [+cons]──────[+cons]

(2) and (4) correctly generate the systematic phonetic representation of all the examples except *fluïdesa* [fluiðέzə] in which [i] is syllabic, though it follows a vowel. No general rule will deal with this kind of example as we have *buida* [bújðə] /bujd+ə/ 'empty' (F) and *buidesa* [bujðέzə] /bujd+ɛz+ə/ 'emptiness' with [j] in both forms. Parallel cases to *fluïdesa* are *heroïcitat* [əruisitát] 'heroism' (but *heroic* [ərɔ́jk]); *laïcitzar* [ləisidzá] 'to laicize' (but *laic* [lájk]); and *trapezoïdal* [trəpəzuiðál] (but *trapezoide* [trəpəzɔ́jðə] 'trapezoid') cf. Fabra, 1968a: 6. These examples could be dealt with by an additional rule.

(5)   j → i / $\begin{bmatrix} V \\ -\text{stress} \end{bmatrix}$+──────

though this requires the suffix *–oide* to be analysed, somewhat artificially, as /+ɔ+jd+a/. All suffixes containing

Stress assignment

an underlying vowel would become stressed by the general rule, with the exception of two or three which must still be marked for recessive stress, e.g. *–ívol, –ívola* (which could however be /+ibwl/ with rule (4)); *–íssim, –íssima* (which could be /+isjm/) and *–íac, –íaca.*

2.4. The remaining and most realistic possibility is that, having the form /+ik/, /+id/, /+il/, /+ul/, – and /+ɔida/ for *–oide,* these suffixes are marked as exceptions to rule (2) and trigger off the minor Recessive Stress rule (see below, §4, rule (10)). The Glide-formation rule I (8) will then account for the occurrences of [j] at the systematic phonetic level.

3.1. Rule (2) as it stands does not account for stress on monosyllables ending in a vowel, e.g. *fa* [fá] 'does', *he* [é] 'I have', *no* [nó] 'not'. To account for these it is sufficient to put parentheses round the [+segment] in the environment of the rule. In fact, the disjunctive braces can be entirely replaced with parentheses which normally apply disjunctively:

(6) [+syll] → [+stress]

$$/ \underline{\quad} C_0 ([+\text{segment}])\begin{bmatrix}+\text{syll}\\+\text{high}\end{bmatrix}+V)(+C) \#$$

3.2. Rule (6) is still too general. Though it correctly stresses many verb forms, it is not yet precise enough to deal accurately with, e.g.

tanquem /tank+ɛ+m/ [təŋkɛ́m] 'we close'
tanqueu /tank+ɛ+w/ [təŋkɛ́w] 'you close'
tancar /tank+a+r/ [təŋká] 'to close'
tancat /tank+a+d/ [təŋkát] 'closed'

Rule (6) would wrongly accent these forms on the first syllable, though it deals correctly with *tanco* /tank+u/

[tánku] 'I close' and other root-stressed forms. We should make (6) more precise so as to admit only /+s/ and /+n/ instead of +C at the right of the environment; thus:

(7)   [+syll] → [+stress]

$$/\underline{\quad}C_0 \; ([+segm])\left(\begin{bmatrix}+syll\\+high\end{bmatrix}+V\right)\left(+\begin{bmatrix}-vocal\\+coron\\-distr\end{bmatrix}\right)\#$$

Further specific modifications will be proposed below (III, §5.2) to deal with some other verb forms ending in a consonant, and the apparently anomalous stress pattern of the future tense will also be dealt with in III §5.1.

3.3. The inclusion of the parenthesis ($\begin{bmatrix}+syll\\+high\end{bmatrix}+V$), while correct for nouns and adjectives (see above, §2.1) is wrong for verbs. That the distinction is one of syntactic category alone can be shown by the following forms:

estalvia /stalbi+a/ [əstəlβíə] 'saves', cf. *estàlvia* /stalbi+ə/ [əstálβiə] 'safe' (F)
varies /bari+a+s/ [bəríəs] 'you (sg) vary', cf. *vàries* /bari+ə+s/ [báriəs] 'varied' (F pl)
evacua /a+baku+a/ [əβəkúa] 'evacuates', cf. *vàcua* /baku+ə/ [bákuə] 'vacant'

There are no verb forms accented on the pattern [$-\acute{V}C_0$iə] or [$-\acute{V}C_0$uə]; hence the parenthesis in question must be restricted so as to apply only to non-verbs, or specifically to nouns and adjectives since the pattern does not occur elsewhere; so:

(8)   [+syll] → [+stress]

$$/\underline{\quad}C_0 \; ([+segm])\left\langle\left(\begin{bmatrix}+syll\\+high\end{bmatrix}+V\right)\right\rangle\left(+\begin{bmatrix}-vocal\\+coron\\-distr\end{bmatrix}\right)\# \; \rbrack \langle N,A\rangle$$

Stress assignment   41

This is the Major Stress-assignment rule, which deals with
the stress pattern of the great majority of words. A
solution to the problem of oxytone polysyllabic words
ending in a vowel will be put forward below, VII §2.

4. The minor stress rule is required to account for all
the remaining exceptions to (8), which are stressed on the
syllable preceding that to which stress would be assigned
by (8). I propose that forms subject to the Minor Stress
Rule are marked with the class marker [+E] which triggers
rule (1). Note that no verb roots are exceptions to (8); the
only verb forms with recessive stress are those in the
present subjunctive of *saber* 'to know' and *cabre* 'to fit':
sàpiga etc., and *càpiga* etc. which are anomalous on other
grounds too. So we can state a rule

(9)   ⟦ᵥ X ⟧ᵥ → [−E]

That this is an effective rule of the grammar rather than a
blank-filling rule applying to lexical formatives is shown by
the fact that roots can be identical except that the N/A
form is [+E] and the V form [−E], e.g.

fórmula [fórmulə] /formul+ə/, cf. *formula* [furmúlə]
          [+E]
⟦ᵥ⟦N formul⟧N +a⟧ᵥ (before application of (9))
   [+E]
'formulates'
invàlida (F) [imbáliðə] /in+bal+id+ə/ 'invalid' (A),
                                           [+E]
cf. *invalida* [imbəlíðə]
⟦ᵥ⟦A⟦Af in⟧Af⟦ᵥ bal⟧ᵥ⟦Af id⟧Af⟧A +a ⟧ᵥ
                                      [+E]
(before (9) applies) 'invalidates'
càrrega [károyə] /karrɛg+ə/ 'load', cf. *carrega*
                                           [+E]
[kəréɣə] /karrɛg+a/ 'loads' (V)

mànec [mánək] /manɛg/ 'handle', cf. *emmanega*
[+E]
[əmmənɛ́ya] /an+manɛg+a/ 'puts a handle on'
The form of the Minor Stress Rule is:

(10)   [+syll] → [+stress]

$$/ \text{---} C_0 \begin{bmatrix} V \\ +E \end{bmatrix} [+\text{segm}] \ ([+\text{segm}])(+C) \ \#\|$$

The sequence V[+segm] ([+segm]) permits correct stress on *harmònium* (see above, I § 2.6), *harmòniums* and also *mùltiple* (see below). [+E] is placed under one particular segment in the formulation of the rule so as to bring under the domain of the rule sequences with [+E] suffixes (see § 2.2 above), even though these may be affixed to stems otherwise [−E]. More examples appear below. Within morphemes, of course, by convention class markers are assigned to every matrix in the sequence of segments, cf. Chomsky & Halle, 1968: 173–5, 373–80.

Examples:

−CCCV[+segm]+C :
  pàncreas [páŋkreəs] /pankrea+s/
                     [+E]
−CCV[+segm] [+segm] +C:
  índexs [índəks] /indak+s+s/ 'indices'
                 [+E]
−CV[+segm] [+segm] +C:
  harmòniums [ərmóniums]/ərmɔn+ium+s/
                       [+E]
  hipòtesis [ipótezis] /ipɔ+tɛ+zi+s/ 'hypotheses'
                 [+E]
−CCV[+segm] [+segm] :
  càrrega [károyə] /karrɛg+ə/ 'load'
              [+E]
  múltiple [múltiplə] /multi+pl/
             [+E]

Stress assignment

demòcrata [demɔ́krətə] /damɔ+krata/ 'democrat'
[+E]
–CV[+segm]+C : *àrabs* [árəps] /arab+s/ 'Arabs'
[+E]
–CV[+segm] : *àrea* [área] /are+ə/
[+E]
–V[+segm] : *fluid* [flújt] /flu+id/ (rule I (8) applies).
[+E]

5. How are the Stress-assignment rules ordered with respect to the epenthesis and truncation rules discussed in chapter I (viz. (4), (7), (9), (13), (15), (19), (20))? I (4) must precede Stress assignment to give *còmoda* 'comfortable' (F); Stress assignment must apply at the stage /kɔmɔd+ə/ not at the stage /kɔmɔda+ə/ since then
    [+E]   [+E]
III (10) would stress the wrong vowel. Similarly I (7) applies before III (8) and III (10). I (9) precedes Stress assignment to account for the stress of e.g. *idea* [iðéə]. I (19) must follow Stress assignment to account for *témer* [témə] 'to fear' rather than *[təmá] and I (20) also follows Stress assigment to give *estan* [əstán] 'they stay' (see I §7.). The ordering of I (15) is not critical. It is clear that the epenthesis and truncation rules preceding Stress assignment are morphological rules – those whose structural descriptions include reference to morphological classes – while those that follow are rules with "phonetic" environments. The main epenthesis rule I (13) must anyway follow I (19)–see I §6. Naturally, the rules supplying verb morphs (see chapter III) will also precede Stress assignment.

6.1. How is the Stress-assignment rule to be prevented from applying in the case of the unstressed words mentioned in §1.4? In Chomsky & Halle, 1968:83–108, various kinds of boundaries are used to limit the applicability of stress rules; I shall attempt something similar, using word boundary # and formative boundary +.

6.2. Before proceeding any further, I would like to try and elucidate the question of boundary markers and readjustment rules. Chomsky & Halle's discussion of boundaries is inconsistent and confusing (1968:5n, 8, 9, 12–14, 29, 66–7, 85–7, 364–70). Consider these statements:

(i) "The formative boundary is characterized by the features $\begin{bmatrix} +\text{formative boundary} \\ -\text{segment} \end{bmatrix}$; it indicates the point at which a given formative begins and ends. It is therefore part of the representation of every formative in the lexicon" (364).

(ii) "There can be no rule in the grammar that introduces or deletes the feature [+formative boundary] (except as part of a longer string of units)" (364).

(iii) "The boundary # is automatically inserted at the beginning and end of every string dominated by a major category, i.e. by one of the lexical categories "noun", "verb", "adjective", or by a category such as "sentence", "noun phrase", "verb phrase" which dominates a lexical category" (366).

(iv) "... the language-specific rules that replace certain occurrences of # by +, i.e. that convert $\begin{bmatrix} -\text{FB} \\ +\text{WB} \end{bmatrix}$ (where FB stands for "formative boundary" WB for "word boundary") to [+FB] in certain contexts" (368–9).

(v) "In our formulation, formative boundary *never is preceded or followed by a boundary* but must be bounded on both sides by segments" (66n, C & H's italics).

Of these statements (ii) appears to be inconsistent with (iv) as it stands; (i) and (iii) together are inconsistent with (v)

Stress assignment

unless (ii) is false; for if /kab/ is a formative and a noun (Catalan *cap* 'head'), then (i) gives us /+kab+/, (iii) gives ⟦$_N$ # +kab+ # ⟧$_N$, (ii) forbids the deletion of +, but ⟦$_N$ # +kab+ # ⟧$_N$ contradicts (v).
Clearly some of these formulations must be discarded. Let us suppose that the conventions for introducing # and +, − (i) and (iii) −, are basically correct as far as they go. We must ignore (v) which seems to follow from a different view of +, regarding it not as a boundary but as a juncture. ⟦$_N$ # +kab+ # ⟧$_N$ is now well-formed but carries superfluous information. A readjustment rule of the following form will remove superfluous + :

(11) $+ \rightarrow \emptyset \Big/ \left\{ \begin{array}{l} \underline{}(\rrbracket) \, \# \, \rrbracket \\ \llbracket \, \# \, (\llbracket) \underline{} \\ \underline{} + \end{array} \right\}$

Thus:

⟦$_A$#⟦$_N$#+ferr+#⟧$_N$ ⟦$_{Af}$ +i+⟧$_{Af}$#⟧$_A$ *ferri* 'of iron', after (11): ⟦$_A$#⟦$_N$# fɛrr #⟧$_N$⟦$_{Af}$+i ⟧$_{Af}$#⟧$_A$

⟦$_N$#⟦$_{Af}$ +damɔ+⟧$_{Af}$⟦$_{Af}$ +krata+⟧$_{Af}$#⟧$_N$ *demòcrata* 'democrat' with (11):

⟦$_N$#⟦$_{Af}$ damɔ⟧$_{Af}$⟦$_{Af}$ +krata⟧$_{Af}$ # ⟧$_N$

This rule is not strictly essential, since, by convention, absence of + between any units in the structural description of a rule is interpreted as if (+) were there, but it could be seen as a kind of constraint preventing rules which specify + from applying to certain sequences to which they otherwise would apply. Statement (ii) can be held to be valid except as provided for in (11). It then becomes unnecessary to talk of *replacing* # by + (statement (iv)). To achieve the sequences ⟦$_V$kep̄+d⟧$_V$, ⟦$_A$ long+ər⟧$_A$ (English 'kept', 'longer'; Chomsky & Halle, 1968:370) it is sufficient to delete category markers (before #–insertion), or to delete #, or, if necessary, to delete both categories and #.

Statements (i) and (iii) in fact need to be extended somewhat; it seems as though not just every formative in the lexicon must have +, but also every morpheme introduced by a morphological readjustment rule. Thus the nominal plural [−s] must be /+s/, and the feminine [−ə] must be /+ə/; all the verb endings likewise must have +. It would be possible to regard this as a convention – that every sequence of segments introduced by a rule with non-phonetic features to the left of the arrow (e.g. [+Plural], [+PRET], [+SUBJ]) or with similar features or morphological class markers (e.g. [+F], [+III]) in the environment, should be preceded (in the case of suffixes) by +. For the present, however, for the sake of clarity, I shall mention + explicitly in such rules.

6.3. As far as statement (iii) is concerned, in Catalan not only nouns, verbs and adjectives require word boundaries, but also all adverbs, simple and compound, e.g. *ara* 'now', *on* 'where', *bé* 'well', *ràpidament* [ràpiðəmén] 'quickly', *potser* 'perhaps'; all prepositions except *a* 'to, at', *en* 'in', *amb* 'with', *de* 'of' and *per* 'for' which are unstressed; and conjunctions except *que* 'that', and *i* 'and', which are unstressed. Some pronouns are stressed, e.g. demonstratives *aquest* 'this one', *això* 'that'; subject pronouns *jo* 'I', *vosaltres* 'you (pl.)'; and personal pronouns after prepositions : *per a mi* [pərəmí] 'for me', *amb ells* [əmbéʎs] 'with them'. Unstressed pronouns *me, te, se, nos, vos, lo, los, la, les, li, ne, hi, ho* and *que* (see chapter IV) occur, I believe, in syntactically specifiable contexts.

I suggest therefore that word boundaries should be automatically inserted before and after adverbs and

Stress assignment

pronouns; in the case[1] of stressed prepositions and conjunctions one solution is to give them word boundaries in the lexicon, for there are not many which are not derived from other lexical categories – these last, of course, retain the categorization and word boundaries of the formatives from which they are derived, e.g. *durant* 'during' ⟦$_{Prep}$⟦$_V$# dur+a+nt #⟧$_V$⟧$_{Prep}$ (cf. *durar* 'to last'), and perhaps *com* 'as' ⟦$_{Conj}$⟦$_{Ad}$ # kɔm #⟧$_{Ad}$⟧$_{Conj}$ (cf. *com* 'how'). Alternatively, insert # by convention with Prep, Conj also, deleting # by special rule for *a, amb, de, en, per, i,* and *que*. The non-derived stressed prepositions are *contra* 'against', *des* 'since', *entre* 'between', *envers (vers, devers)* 'towards', *fins* 'up to', *malgrat* 'in spite of', *segons* 'according to', *sense* 'without', *sobre* 'over', *sota* 'under', *ultra* 'beyond', *vora* 'near'. The stressed conjunctions are: *car* 'for', *mentre* 'while', *o* 'or', *puix* 'since', *però* 'but', *si* 'if', *sinó* 'but'.

7.1. Compound words whose parts are themselves lexical category items, have, with a few exceptions, a stressed vowel in each part, the rightmost stress of the whole being the primary stress. Here are a few examples of compound words with irrelevant structure omitted:

parallamps [pàrəʎáms] ⟦$_N$#⟦$_V$#par+a#⟧$_V$
 ⟦$_N$#ʎanp+s⟧$_N$#⟧$_N$ 'lightning conductor', cf. *para* 'stops', *llamp* 'lightning'
capgirar [kàbʒirá] ⟦$_V$#⟦$_N$#kab#⟧$_N$⟦$_V$#ʒir+a+r#⟧$_V$#⟧$_V$ 'to turn upside down', cf. *cap* 'head', *girar* 'to turn'
aiguardent [àjɣwərðén] ⟦$_N$#⟦$_N$#ajg^w +ə#⟧$_N$
 ⟦$_A$#ardent#⟧$_A$#⟧$_N$ 'aguardiente, liquor', cf. *aigua* 'water', *ardent* 'burning'

---

[1] The right answer may be to assume different kinds of boundary according to the category, as proposed by Stanley, 1971: § 7.

48 Stress assignment

centcames [sèŋkámǝs] ⟦_N#⟦_A#sent#⟧_A
⟦_N#kam+ǝ+s#⟧_N#⟧_N 'centipede', cf. cent 'a
hundred', cames 'legs'
proppassat [prɔ̀ppǝsát] ⟦_A#⟦_Ad#prɔp#⟧ _Ad
⟦_A#pas+a+d#⟧_A#⟧_A 'last (of dates, days, etc.)'
cf. prop 'near', passat 'passed'
vaivé [bàjβé] ⟦_N#⟦_V#ba#⟧_V⟦_Conj+i⟧_Conj
⟦_V#ben#⟧_V#⟧_N 'vicissitude', cf. va 'goes', i 'and',
ve 'comes'
sobretot [sòβrǝtót] ⟦_Ad#⟦_Prep#sobr#⟧_Prep
⟦_A#tot#⟧⟧_A#⟧_Ad 'especially', cf. sobre 'over',
tot 'all'
capvespre [kàbbéspɾǝ] ⟦_N#⟦_N#kab#⟧_N
⟦_N#bespr#⟧_N#⟧_N 'dusk', cf. cap 'end', vespre
'evening'.

Obviously the full internal structure of many of these
compounds is rather complex; many of them, e.g.
parallamps are derived from sentences, but only the
relevant surface structure need concern us here. If we
suppose for the sake of argument that the tone group
corresponds to the surface structure sentence, then the
stress-reduction rule which applies cyclically is of the form:

(12)   Within ⟦... ⟧ reduce all stresses except the right-
       most by 1.

Interpreting [+stress] —the output of the Stress-
assignment rules— as [1 stress], we have the kind of
derivation shown opposite:

7.2. There are some exceptions consisting of
compound words with one stress only, and with vowel
reduction in the first part of the compound, e.g.

paraigua [pǝɾájɣwǝ] 'umbrella', cf. *para* 'stops', *aigua*
'water'
trespeus [tɾǝspéws] 'tripod', cf. *tres* 'three', *peus* 'feet'
només [numés] 'only', cf. *no* 'not', *més* 'more'
potser [putsé] 'perhaps', cf. *pot* 'may', *ser* 'to be'

[S[VP[AuxV *va*] AuxV[V *instal·lar*] V[NP[D *un*] D[N[V *para*] V[N *llamps*] N[A[P *de*] P[N *coure*] N] A] NP] VP] S

S–A:	*va*	*instal·lar*	*un*	*para*	–	*llamps*	*de*	*coure*
(12)	1	1	1	1		1	1	1
(12)'	2	1	2	3		2	1	1
(12)"	3	2	3	4		3	2	1

'he installed a copper lightning-conductor'

també [təmbé] 'also', cf. *tan* 'as', *bé* 'well'

We must suppose that forms like these undergo either a special deletion of the word boundary following the first part so that it never becomes stressed, or a special deletion of secondary stress.

8.1. The scope of the Stress-assignment rules (8) and (10) has been defined only by placing #⟧ to the right of the environment. There is no reason to suppose they apply cyclically. The rules inserting inflectional morphs (see §5 above, and chapter III) insert segments before the final # of the lexical formative to which they are added, i.e. morphological rules apply in the environment ⟦ # X___ # ⟧ as required for correct stress assignment. Words which are composed of a lexical formative and one or more lexical affixes will have by convention an internal structure of the form ⟦ # ⟦$_{Af}$ Y+⟧$_{Af}$⟦#X #⟧ ⟦$_{Af}$+Z⟧ # ⟧. In such words we do not want stress assigned to the innermost X #⟧ sequence, but to the whole compound. Here are some examples of suffixed compounds taken from this chapter, with internal boundaries and structure specified; (rule (11) has applied):

comunisme ⟦$_N$#⟦$_A$# kumun #⟧$_A$⟦$_{Af}$ +ism⟧$_{Af}$#⟧$_N$
   'communism'
captaires ⟦$_N$#⟦$_V$ #kapt# ⟧$_V$⟦$_{Af}$ +ajr⟧$_{Af}$ +s#⟧$_N$
   'beggars'
fèrria ⟦$_A$#⟦$_N$#fɛrr+u#⟧$_N$⟦$_{Af}$ +i⟧$_{Af}$ +ə#⟧$_A$ 'of iron' (F)
pèrdua ⟦$_N$#⟦$_V$# pɛrd#⟧$_V$⟦$_{Af}$+u⟧$_{Af}$ +ə#⟧$_N$ 'loss'
bàsic ⟦$_A$#⟦$_N$#baz#⟧$_N$⟦$_{Af}$ +ik⟧$_{Af}$#⟧$_A$
                              [+E]
fluidesa ⟦$_N$#⟦$_A$#⟦$_V$# flu # ⟧$_V$⟦$_{Af}$+id⟧$_{Af}$ #⟧$_A$
                                        [+E]
   ⟦$_{Af}$ +ɛz⟧$_{Af}$ +ə#⟧$_N$ 'fluidity'
laicitzar ⟦$_V$#⟦$_A$#⟦$_{Stem}$ laj⟧$_{Stem}$⟦$_{Af}$ +ik⟧$_{Af}$#⟧$_A$
                                                            [+E]

Stress assignment

⟦$_{Af}$ +itz⟧$_{Af}$ +a+r#⟧$_V$ 'to laicize'

The deletion of internal # can most simply be achieved by a readjustment rule

(13)   # → ø / ___ ⟧⟦ +

provided that it applies after (11). After (13) has applied, the sequence bounded by the innermost brackets no longer meets the structural description of the stress rules. Stanley, 1971: §7, does not use + in these cases but "weakens" #. "The principles for weakening # would depend on the class of associated affix, and there would be as many different weakened versions of # (each of which would be regarded as a distinct boundary type) as there are affix classes. Further, I would suggest that each time # between a prefix and what follows (or between a suffix and what precedes) is weakened in this way, the occurrence of # on the other side of the stem that is paired with this weakened # be simply eliminated." In our case, if we have just one weakened boundary, +, this principle would give us e.g.

fluidesa ⟦$_N$#⟦$_A$⟦$_V$ flu+⟧$_V$⟦$_{Af}$ id⟧ + ⟧$_A$⟦$_{Af}$ εz⟧ $_{Af}$+ə#⟧$_N$
                                                        [+E]

and (see §8.2):

desfâ ⟦$_V$#⟦$_{Af}$ das⟧$_{Af}$⟦$_V$ +fa⟧$_V$#⟧$_V$ 'undoes'

8.2. The question of the left limit of the Stress-assignment rules is more complicated. In the following examples the stress must be prevented from falling on the first syllable:

refa [rəfá] ⟦$_V$#⟦$_{Af}$ ra+⟧$_{Af}$⟦$_V$# fa # ⟧$_V$#⟧$_V$ 'redoes'

desfâ [dəsfá] ⟦$_V$#⟦$_{Af}$ das+ ⟧$_{Af}$⟦$_V$ # fa #⟧$_V$#⟧$_V$ 'undoes'

that is, rule (8) must apply to the sequence ⟦ # fa #⟧ and not to ⟦ # ra+fa # ⟧ or ⟦# das+fa #⟧ for these would give *[ráfə], *[dásfə]. Should the left limit be ⟦ or # ? There are cases in which for other reasons than Stress assignment initial # must apparently be deleted when a prefix precedes. Consider examples such as were cited in I §7.

constel·lar ⟦$_V$#⟦$_{Af}$ kɔn+⟧$_{Af}$⟦$_V$ #stɛtl+a+r#⟧$_V$#⟧ $_V$
    'to decorate with stars'
inspirar ⟦$_V$#⟦$_{Af}$ in+⟧$_{Af}$⟦$_V$ #spir+a+r#⟧$_V$#⟧$_V$ 'to breathe in'
substrat ⟦$_N$#⟦$_{Af}$ sub+⟧$_{Af}$⟦$_N$ #strat#⟧$_N$#⟧ $_N$
    'substratum'
constrènyer ⟦$_V$#⟦$_{Af}$ kɔn+⟧$_{Af}$⟦$_V$ #strɛɲ+r#⟧$_V$#⟧ $_V$
    'to constrain'
proscriure ⟦$_V$#⟦$_{Af}$ pru+⟧$_{Af}$⟦ $_V$ #skriv+r#⟧$_V$#⟧ $_V$
    'to proscribe'
restablir ⟦$_V$#⟦$_{Af}$ ra+⟧$_{Af}$⟦$_V$ #stabbl+i+r#⟧$_V$#⟧ $_V$ 'to reestablish'

In these cases # must be deleted following the prefix to prevent application of the initial [ə]—epenthesis rule I (20). It would seem that (13) can be generalized so as to delete # which is preceded or followed by +. The left boundary of Stress assignment would be ⟦. However, there are counter-examples to those just cited, in which initial epenthesis takes place:

preestablir [prɛəstəbblí] 'to pre-establish'
inestable [inəstábblə] ⟦$_A$#⟦$_{Af}$ in+⟧$_{Af}$⟦$_A$ #sta+bbl#⟧ $_A$#⟧ $_A$
    'unstable'
inescrutable alongside *inscrutable*, both 'inscrutable'

Such counter-examples are very few in the case of unstressed prefixes; of these three *preestablir* may in fact have the stressed prefix *pre–*, cf. *pre-romá* [prɛ̀rumá] 'pre-Roman', in which case epenthesis is less anomalous. *Inescrutable* may have an additional prefix, /in+as+skrut+a+bbl/; or, more probably, it is less grammatical than *inscrutable* (hence to be accounted for

Stress assignment 53

by a different rule); *inestable* may perhaps not be synchronically related to *estar* 'to remain, stay', but have the form /in+ast+a+bbl/.

Even so, it does not seem that the rule can be so general as to delete # after all cases of +, since unstressed forms other than prefixes do not prevent epenthesis before /sC−/. Alongside *substrat* we have *l'estrat* ⟦$_D$ l+⟧ D⟦$_N$#strat#⟧ N 'the stratum' and *per estrats* ⟦$_P$ par+⟧ P⟦$_N$#strat+s#⟧ N 'through strata'. At present, then it seems that the rule must be

(14)   # → ø / X+⟧$_{Af}$⟦ ___

and that Stress assignment indeed applies with ⟦ as the left limit; that is, (8) and (10) are more precisely (15) and (16):

(15)   [+syll] → [+stress]

$$/ \left[\!\!\left[X \underline{\quad} C_0 ([+segm]) \left\langle \left(\begin{bmatrix}+syll\\+high\end{bmatrix}+V\right)\right\rangle \left(+\begin{bmatrix}-vocal\\+coron\\-distr\end{bmatrix}\right)\# \right]\!\!\right] \langle N, A \rangle$$

(16)   [+syll] → [+stress]

$$/ \ [\!\![X \underline{\quad} C_0 \begin{bmatrix} V \\ +E \end{bmatrix} [+segm]([+segm])(+C)\#]\!\!]$$

8.3. There are also a number of prefixes which receive secondary stress just as do the compounds mentioned in §7.1, but which do not appear as free forms, e.g. *anti−*, *arxi−* 'archi−', *circum−*, *ex−*, *inter−*, *meta−*, *post−*, *paleo−*, *pseudo−*, *semi−*, *sots−*, 'under', and several others, e.g.

ex-president [èksprəziðén]
paleolític [pəlèulítik] 'palaeolithic'
post-palatal [pòspələtál]

pseudo-profeta [psɛ̀wðuprufɛ́tə] 'pseudo-prophet'
semicercle [sɛ̀misérklə] 'semicircle'
sots-secretari [sòtsəkrətári] 'under-secretary'

If these prefixes are classed as affixes, no # will be inserted round them, and stress will fail to be assigned. I propose to regard these formatives as members of lexical categories (mostly adjectives or adverbs). In the lexicon, or by a special syntactic rule, their occurrence is limited to certain syntactic environments, e.g.

⟦ $_A$ sɛmi⟧$_A$/⟦$_{N,A}$___⟦X⟧⟧$_{N,A}$
⟦$_{A,Ad}$ sots⟧$_{A,Ad}$ / ⟦$_{N,V}$___⟦X⟧⟧$_{N,V}$

Thus, for example, *semicercle* will have the structure
⟦$_N$ #⟦$_A$ #sɛmi#⟧$_A$⟦$_N$#serkl#⟧$_N$#⟧$_N$.

This approach seems to me well-motivated on both syntactic and phonological grounds. With this structure we should expect [ə] −epenthesis to operate normally in the environment #___sC which begins the second item. Clear evidence on this point is scarce, however: only prefixes ending in a consonant provide clear evidence, for by a general vowel-elision rule (cf. VII §5) [−ə] may be deleted in the environment V##___. We find in fact

interestel·lar 'interstellar', cf. *constel·lar* 'to
    decorate with stars'
paneslavisme 'panSlavism', cf. *iugoslau* 'Yugoslav'
preestablir 'to pre-establish' (see above)

but on the other hand :

interstici 'interstice'
circumscriure 'to circumscribe'
circumspecte 'circumspect'

and vacillation between

superestructura and *superstructura* 'superstructure'.

It looks as though the language applies some rules inconsistently or optionally in this area; one possibility is

Stress assignment

that some prefixes may sometimes be regarded as stressed (hence ending in #), and sometimes as unstressed (hence ending in +), an uncertainty which is especially likely in those prefixes whose vowel quality would not clearly distinguish between an unstressed and a secondarily stressed pattern, e.g. *inter–*, *circum–*, *super–* : either [íntər–], [sírkum–], [súpər–], or [intər–], [sirkum–], [supər–].

9. As mentioned in §1.2 of this chapter, a vowel-reduction rule reduces unstressed labial vowels to [u] and unstressed non-labial, non-high vowels to [ə]. Hence, apart from exceptions to be mentioned presently, unstressed syllables in this dialect of Catalan may have only [ə], [u] or [i]. (For the "naturalness" of rules reducing unstressed vowels in the direction of a target /i, a, u/ system, see Haiman, 1972.) The features of vowels appearing in underlying representations are those which are appropriate when stress is assigned to that vowel by rule, since they are not predictable. The rules of Vowel reduction have the following basic form in this order:

(17) $\begin{bmatrix} +\text{syllab} \\ +\text{labial} \\ -\text{stress} \end{bmatrix} \rightarrow [+\text{high}]$

(18) $\begin{bmatrix} +\text{syllab} \\ -\text{high} \\ -\text{stress} \end{bmatrix} \rightarrow \begin{bmatrix} +\text{back} \\ -\text{low} \end{bmatrix}$

The formulation of (17) assumes the operation of a universal redundancy rule : [+high] → [−low] (see below VI §2.2). As Phelps (1972) rightly points out in answer to a proposal of Vogt (1971), these rules can most simply be collapsed as follows (using [labial] for Phelps's [round]):

(19) $\begin{bmatrix} V \\ \alpha\text{labial} \\ -\text{high} \\ -\text{stress} \end{bmatrix} \rightarrow \begin{bmatrix} \alpha\text{high} \\ -\text{low} \\ +\text{back} \end{bmatrix}$

However, there are some exceptions to (18) which show that (17) and (18) cannot in fact be collapsed in this way. The exceptions avoid producing the sequence $\begin{bmatrix} +\text{back} \\ -\text{labial} \end{bmatrix}$ $\begin{bmatrix} +\text{back} \\ -\text{labial} \end{bmatrix}$ at the surface phonetic level, i.e. there is no *[əə], *[əá], or *[áə]. (see Badia, 1962:I, 64; Roca, 1971:104). Instead we have examples of unstressed [e]; thus:

(20) *cereal* [səreál]
teatre [teátrə] 'theatre'
teatral [teətrál] 'theatrical'
esteàric [əsteárik] 'stearic'
real [reál]
realitat [reəlitát] 'reality'

(21) *israelita* [izrəelítə] 'Israelite', cf. *Israel* [izrəέl]
aeroport [əerupɔ́rt] 'airport', cf. *aeri* [əέri] 'aerial'

This fact can be expressed by (22) which precedes and applies disjunctively with (18):

(22) $\begin{bmatrix} +\text{syllab} \\ -\text{high} \\ -\text{stress} \end{bmatrix} \rightarrow \begin{bmatrix} -\text{back} \\ -\text{low} \end{bmatrix} / \left\{ \begin{array}{l} \underline{} \begin{bmatrix} +\text{syllab} \\ +\text{back} \\ -\text{labial} \end{bmatrix} \\ \begin{bmatrix} +\text{syllab} \\ +\text{back} \\ -\text{labial} \end{bmatrix} \underline{} \end{array} \right\}$

This rule seems eligible for abbreviation through the device suggested by Bach (1968) so that to the right of

Stress assignment

the environment slash we would read:

(23) $\Big/ \begin{bmatrix} +\text{syllab} \\ +\text{back} \\ -\text{labial} \end{bmatrix}$

However, Bach proposes that this device should be interpreted as an abbreviation for

(24) $\left\{ \begin{matrix} \begin{bmatrix} +\text{syllab} \\ +\text{back} \\ -\text{labial} \end{bmatrix} \underline{\quad} \\ \underline{\quad} \begin{bmatrix} +\text{syllab} \\ +\text{back} \\ -\text{labial} \end{bmatrix} \end{matrix} \right\}$

in that order. This would work in our case provided none of the examples of the kind in (20) had /aa/ in the UR, for the ordering of (24) would give [əe]. In fact there appears to be no evidence for the sequence /aa/ in UR's: analysis of the examples does not reveal which of the vowels /e/, /ɛ/, or /a/ may underlie, except that *real* may be related to *res* [rés] 'anything', and may be analysed as /rɛ+al/.

It is very probable that all sequences of more than one identical vowel are to be excluded by morpheme-structure rules, while /a+a/ will suffer truncation by rule I (4). For the moment, then, we can accept the formulation as in (23) provided that in the UR's of words like those in (20) and (21) we have /aɛ/, /ae/, /ea/, or /ɛa/. For another proposal concerning the formulation of such "mirror-image" rules see below, VII §4.2. Rules (18) and (22) can be combined as:

(25) $\begin{bmatrix} +\text{syllab} \\ -\text{high} \\ -\text{stress} \end{bmatrix} \rightarrow \begin{bmatrix} \{\langle -\text{back}\rangle\} \\ +\text{back} \\ -\text{low} \end{bmatrix} \Big/ \Big\langle \begin{bmatrix} +\text{syllab} \\ +\text{back} \\ -\text{labial} \end{bmatrix} \Big\rangle$

Rule (25) is ordered after (17) which "bleeds" it, i.e.
after (17) there are no unstressed, non-high labial vowels
to which (25) could (incorrectly) apply.

CHAPTER III

Verb morphology

Introduction

   This analysis of the morphology of the Catalan verb aims to show how all the forms may be generated of all the verbs normally used in the dialect which is the object of study of this work. In doing this I hope to reveal the true extent of "irregularity" in the Catalan verbal system. In Generative Phonology "irregularity" is revealed by the presence of rules which refer to particular lexical items, or to arbitrary morphological classifications, and by rule features on lexical items, such as those which state that a lexical item is an exception to a named rule or rules, e.g. [−rule (x)], or that it undergoes a "minor rule", e.g. [+rule (y)]. In this view, forms such as the stem alternants in /g/ of §3.2.1. are not regarded as suppletive, and thence irregular, if they are predictable by a phonological rule. Similarly, the apparent irregularities of the strong participles (§4.8) are shown to be almost entirely the phonological consequence of a single irregularity of the whole group — the absence of the thematic vowel.
   This approach to irregularity in morphology relies on the "naturalness condition", according to which morphological and phonological alternations are not to be accounted for by the setting up of arbitrary "phonological" segments in the UR; cf. Hoard, 1972; Matthews, 1972:374−6. I hope to have adhered to this condition by showing good phonological reasons −

Verb morphology

"phonological" in the narrow sense — for the underlying representations I propose.

There are two recent descriptions of Catalan verb morphology: Roca, 1970, and Badia, 1973b. The latter deals only with the type verbs *cantar, perdre, sentir*, and *servir*, i.e. those "regular" verbs with no stem alternants other than those consequent upon Stress assignment and the Vowel-reduction rule. Roca adds to his general discussion a section (242—54) on "irregular verbs" in which he presents their stem-alternants. Both these studies are entirely taxonomic, and shed no more light on the nature of the system, its structure and principles than was done in the pedagogical grammars — in themselves quite adequate — of forty years previously, such as Vallès, 1931:96—138; Renat i Ferris, 1933.

My own analysis is based on two key approaches. The first is a classification of inflectional functions by means of binary features which resemble and may be largely identical to syntactic features. These are [±PERFECT], [±3P] (3P = third person), and so on. The classes these features permit are intended to correspond to natural classes of morpho-syntactic environments, and it is hoped that they reconcile significant generalizations with brevity of statement. The proper criteria for an evaluation measure in this area of grammar are not entirely clear. Matthews (1972:283—6) discusses some formal simplifications achieved by rule ordering which he believes, rightly, I think, do not correspond to significant generalizations. Such would be a rule specifying the plural person markers expressed disjunctively:

$$\emptyset_i \rightarrow \begin{Bmatrix} +m \ / \ \begin{bmatrix} +PL \\ +1P \end{bmatrix} \underline{\quad} \\ +w \ / \ \begin{bmatrix} +PL \\ +2P \end{bmatrix} \underline{\quad} \\ +n \ / \ [\,+PL\,] \underline{\quad} \end{Bmatrix}$$

Verb morphology

where the disjunctive interpretation permits the omission of the feature [+3P]. I have tried to avoid such apparent "simplifications", except in the case of genuinely suppletive stems (§6), where to state in the last line of a disjunctive brace that a certain stem occurs "elsewhere" than in the environments specified for the other stems does not seem inappropriate; my choice of the "elsewhere" stem depends on the formal economy of the rule in question. Significant generalization hardly seems a relevant issue for suppletion. Morphological features seem to me much the neatest way of dealing with the morphology of inflecting languages, in which morphs realize different intersections of functional classes in different cases.

The other key is the Truncation rule III (24) which states in effect that only the rightmost of a sequence of vowel morphs has overt realization. Truncation rules of this kind occur in the verb morphology of several other languages; see, for example, Schane, 1968; Harris, 1969: 67, 102; Lightner, 1972:89, 91; Sommerstein, 1973:56. Such a rule enables one to regard thematic vowel insertion and the insertion of other infix vowels as being much more general than the individual surface forms reveal.

If we suppose that a simple system of verb morphology would be one in which each syntactic function or each bundle of certain functions was realized consistently by one clearly identifiable phonetic form, then it is clear that the Catalan verb system is far from simple. One is moved to speculate on how a language acquires such a non-simple system and on the direction in which it is likely to develop. It is known that the present system in Catalan is the product of substantial restructuring through the ages; it differs markedly from the "classical" fifteenth-century system which itself was the product of the restructuring of the thirteenth-century system derived more or less directly from Common Romance. So it is perhaps surprising that all this restructuring has not led to more simplification of the whole system. It may be that three different and conflicting simplificatory tendencies have continued to operate, even though the effects of the three tendencies together leave the simplicity of the overall pattern much as it was, or even rather reduced. The three tendencies I have in mind are:

(1) a tendency towards the overt expression of the integrity of each morphological class, achieved by extending distinct thematic vowels and other infixes throughout each class.

(2) a tendency towards distinctive overt realization of each syntactic function − a tendency against syncretism.

(3) a tendency towards the same realization of each syntactic function throughout the verb system.

The morphological innovations in the Catalan verb, both in the past and at the present may be explained as the result of the operation of one or other of these tendencies. The radically differing innovations of other dialects may also be interpreted as diverse consequences of these powerful and conflicting tendencies; (see the collection of verb forms in Alcover & Moll, 1929−33.)

1. Before proceeding to a discussion of the phonological realization of verb forms, it is necessary, I think, to give some account of verbal syntax; that is, to explain the syntactic structure of the Catalan verb. The rules I shall give are intended only as a guide, as some form of orientation for the discussion that will follow. They are based on those suggested by G. Ferrater (course of lectures 'Llengua Catalana II', Barcelona University, 1971−2), with the modifications I have thought necessary. There are many other possibilities, on the one hand, because the syntactic analysis of Catalan sentences is only just being begun, and on the other, because there is no consensus within TG theory

Verb morphology

about what this area of syntax should look like. For some alternative approaches in verb morphology see Harris (1969:87–96) and Saltarelli (1970b:69–74) — both of these try out linear sequences of non-phonological formatives as input to the phonological component.

1.1.1. It is proposed that a well-formed verb phrase contains obligatorily Auxiliary (Aux) and Verb (V), the latter dominating a lexical item. (There may be syntactic grounds for believing that the copula *ser* 'to be', and perhaps also *estar* 'to be' and other verbs, should be introduced transformationally, but this need not concern us here, and I shall regard them as lexical verbs for this discussion.) The base rules proposed for the expansion of VP are these (ignoring irrelevant matter); (cf. Stockwell, Schachter & Partee, 1973:28):

(1) VP → Aux, V, (NP), etc.

(2) Aux → Affix, (Perfect), (Progressive)

Perf(ect) corresponds to the compound tenses with *haver* : *he fet* 'I have done', *hauré fet* 'I shall have done', *havia fet, vaig haver fet* 'I had done', and their subjunctives. Progr(essive) corresponds to the periphrases consisting of *estar* or *anar* with the gerund, e.g. *estava fent* 'I was doing', *anava fent* 'I went on doing'.

(3) Affix → Person, Tense

(4) Person → $\begin{bmatrix} \pm 1P \\ \pm 2P \\ \pm 3P \\ \pm PL \end{bmatrix}$

([+1P] = first person, [+2P] = second person, etc. [+PL] = plural, [−PL] = singular.)

(5) Tense → $\begin{bmatrix} \pm INF \\ \pm FUT \\ \pm PRET \end{bmatrix}$

Verb morphology

(6) [−FUT] → [±PERF]
(7) [−INF] → [±IMPER]
(8) [+INF] → [±PART]
(9) [−IMPER] → [±SUBJ]

Readjustment rules:

(10) [+IMPER] → $\begin{bmatrix} -\text{FUT} \\ -\text{PRET} \\ -\text{PERF} \end{bmatrix}$

(11) [+IMPER] → $\begin{bmatrix} +\text{SUBJ} \\ -\text{IMPER} \end{bmatrix} \Big/ \begin{bmatrix} \overline{} \\ -2\text{P} \end{bmatrix}$

(12) [+IMPER] → [−SUBJ]

In rules (5)–(12) the features correspond to the following conventional terms: INF = infinitive, FUT = future, PRET = preterite (= Past), PERF = perfective, IMPER = imperative, PART = participle, SUBJ = subjunctive.

Rule (11) accounts for the fact that other than in the true second person forms, e.g. *vine* 'come!' (sg.), *veniu* 'come!' (pl.), the imperative has forms identical to those of the present subjunctive, e.g. *vingui* 'let him come', *vinguem* 'let us come'.

The table opposite shows to what forms the various possible feature matrices correspond. Second person singular forms, where possible, are used as types.

1.1.2. This classification is based on morphological considerations in the first place, though in major respects it corresponds, I propose, to a likely syntactic or semantic analysis. A few readjustment rules are necessary to meet the condition of completeness in the inflectional/ derivational section of the grammar; cf. Matthews (1972: 197) : "the inflectional rules as a whole must provide at

	INF	FUT	PRET	PERF	IMPER	PART	SUBJ		
venir 'to come'	+	−	−	−	−	−	−	(infinitive)
vindr–	−	+	−	−	−	−	−	(future stem)
venint	−	−	−	−	−	+	−	(gerund)
vingut	−	−	−	+	−	+	−	(participle)
véns	−	−	−	−	−	−	−	(present indicative)
vinguis	−	−	−	−	−	−	+	(present subjunctive)
venies	−	−	−	−	−	−	−	(imperfect)
vingueres/vas venir	−	−	+	+	−	−	−	(preterite)
vinguessis	−	−	+	−	−	−	+	(past subjunctive)
vine	−	−	−	−	+	−	−	(imperative)
vindràs	−	+	−	−	−	−	−	(future)
vindries	−	+	+	−	−	−	−	(conditional)

least one realization for every word which is specified by the syntactic section of the description". *Vinguessis* is [+PERF] because it is morphologically related to the preterite *vingueres*, not to the imperfect *venies*. This feature should perhaps be introduced by a readjustment rule such as:

(14) $\begin{bmatrix} +\text{PRET} \\ +\text{SUBJ} \end{bmatrix} \rightarrow [+\text{PERF}]$

This rule would account for the neutralization of the expression of perfectivity in the past subjunctive. The feature classification of the conditional tense as [+FUT, +PRET] corresponds syntactically and semantically only to one use of the conditional tense, viz. as "future in the past" : *va dir que vindria* 'he said he would come', which corresponds to *diu que vindrà* 'he says he will come'. We assume therefore a readjustment rule resulting in this specification whatever the original features required by semantics and syntax may be for the conditional tense.

Similarly, for morphological reasons the present indicative and subjunctive are classed as [−PERF]; the expression of perfectivity is either neutralized in the present tense, or possibly $\begin{bmatrix} -\text{FUT} \\ -\text{PRET} \\ +\text{PERF} \end{bmatrix}_{\text{Tense}}$ is readjusted to

$\begin{bmatrix} -\text{FUT} \\ -\text{PRET} \\ -\text{PERF} \end{bmatrix}_{\text{Tense}}$ + Perf, resulting in e.g. *he vingut* 'I have come' as the expression of the "present perfect".

Furthermore, the features $\begin{bmatrix} +\text{INF} \\ -\text{FUT} \\ +\text{PRET} \\ +\text{PERF} \\ -\text{PART} \end{bmatrix}$ may be realized by e.g.

Verb morphology

haver vingut 'to have come' in a similar way to what happens in English (see Stockwell, Schachter & Partee, 1973:547). It seems that [+FUT, +PART], and [+INF, −FUT, +PRET, −PERF] have no overt realization, i.e. there is no future participle or past imperfective infinitive. They may be excluded by readjustment or redundancy rules, e.g.

(15) [+PART] → [−FUT]

(16) $\begin{bmatrix} +\text{INF} \\ -\text{FUT} \\ -\text{PERF} \end{bmatrix}$ → [−PRET]

Such gaps may be more properly dealt with in the syntactic component; this is the view of Matthews (1972: 197n1). There remain, defined by rules (6)–(16) theoretical future subjunctive and conditional subjunctive formatives, that is, [−INF, +FUT, −PRET, −IMPER, +SUBJ] and [−INF, +FUT, +PRET, −IMPER, +SUBJ] respectively. These notional formatives are realized by the forms corresponding either to [−FUT] or to [−SUBJ], but which feature is switched depends on the syntactic environment; thus *no va dir que això passaria* 'he did not say that would happen' with the ordinary conditional (*passaria*) where a subjunctive form would elsewhere be the rule after *no va dir;* or *encara que tornis aviat, no podrem anar* 'though you may return soon, we shan't be able to go' where *tornis* is in fact ambiguous with regard to present or future time. The other sense could be rendered 'although you are accustomed to return early, etc.' (present time). In the first example we have [+FUT, +PRET] → [−SUBJ]; in the second, [+SUBJ,−PRET] → [−FUT]. I shall not go further into this syntactic issue; whatever the syntactic approach, before the phonological rules apply no matrix will contain [+FUT, +SUBJ].

68   *Verb morphology*

1.1.3. Symbols such as [+PERF], [−IMPER], [+2P], [+PL] are to be interpreted not as formatives but as syntactic features. They are not therefore linearly ordered within the categories Tense, Person, etc. The arguments for not regarding them as formatives are 1) so that they do not have to be mentioned in environment strings where they are not directly relevant; 2) so that one does not have to make an arbitrary choice which of them to realize as zero when, as is usually the case, they have not each an independent phonetic counterpart. The same view lies behind § 1.4.

1.1.4. Perf and Progr are expanded as follows

$$(17) \quad \text{Perf} \rightarrow [\![_V \text{ av }]\!]_V + \begin{bmatrix} +\text{INF} \\ -\text{FUT} \\ +\text{PRET} \\ +\text{PERF} \\ +\text{PART} \end{bmatrix}_{\text{Tense}}$$
$$\text{IIA}$$

$$(18) \quad \text{Progr} \rightarrow \begin{Bmatrix} [\![_V \text{ sta }]\!]_V \\ \text{I} \\ [\![_V \text{ an }]\!]_V \\ \text{I} \end{Bmatrix} + \begin{bmatrix} +\text{INF} \\ -\text{FUT} \\ -\text{PRET} \\ -\text{PERF} \\ +\text{PART} \end{bmatrix}_{\text{Tense}}$$

/av/, /sta/ and /an/, though dominated by Aux, must themselves belong to the category Verb, in order for them to receive primary stress and combine with Tense and Person suffixes.

1.2.1. A transformational rule is required to introduce the auxiliary verb $[\![_V \text{ ba}]\!]_V$ in the preterite perfect tense, e.g. *vas venir* 'you came'. There is no synchronic reason to relate this morpheme to the lexical verb *anar* 'to go' with which it shares several phonetic

Verb morphology

forms. The rule introducing /ba/ is obligatory in the spontaneous spoken language, as far as the indicative is concerned, and optional in formal styles (i.e. written texts, though these may be uttered orally) where *vas venir* coexists with *vingueres* 'you came'. In the subjunctive the perfect preterite may be realized *vinguessis* or *vagis venir;* here, though, the choice is not purely stylistic, but partly syntactic. A typical use of the compound form is after negative performatives, and negative verbs of thinking, e.g. *no creu que vagis venir* 'he doesn't believe you came'. The rule introducing /ba/ should be ordered before (14) since only underlying [+PERF, +PRET, +SUBJ] can be realized as e.g. *vagis venir;* underlying [−PERF, +PRET, +SUBJ] must become *vinguessis.* The transformation introducing /ba/ is, in tree diagram form:

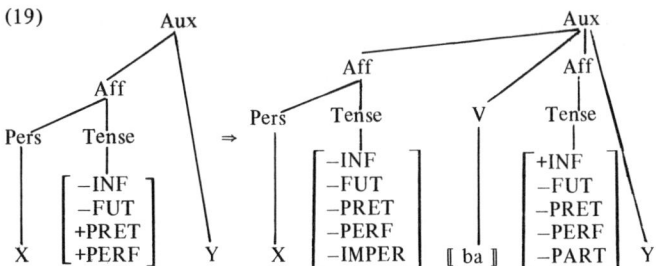

1.2.2. A similar transformation will account for the future and conditional forms *vindràs* 'you will come' and *vindries* 'you would come'. These forms are interpreted here as compounds, consisting of a form of the infinitive, which is in most cases identical with the independent infinitive (though not in the case of *venir*), and the auxiliary *haver.* This type of analysis is argued for in

Spanish, where the structure is similar to that in Catalan, by Harris (1969:91–3). It accounts for the anomalous final stress on the forms of the future tense, e.g. *vindré, vindràs, vindrà, vindran,* as well as for the presence of /r/ in the paradigm; and, of course, the terminations [-é], [-ás], [-á], [ém], [-éw], [-án] are identical to the present indicative of *haver* as in *haver de* 'to have to':

he de venir [éðəβəni] 'I have to come'
has de venir [ázðəβəní] etc.
ha de venir [áðəβəní]
hem de venir [émdəβəní]
heu de venir [éwðəβəní]
han de venir [ándəβəní]

1.2.3. Before expressing this rule, it is convenient to introduce a transformation adjoining Affix to the V which is to the right of it. (Cf. English Affix Shift: Stockwell, Schachter & Partee, 1973:288.) The form of this rule is as follows:

(20) Affix   V
  1   2 ⇒ # 2 + 1

Examples of the operation of the rule are given below.

1.2.4. Now the future-auxiliary rule is as follows, after the application of (20):

(21) ⟦$_V$⟦$_V$ X⟧$_V$⟦$_{Aux}$⟦$_{Af}$ Y$\begin{bmatrix} Z \\ +FUT \end{bmatrix}$⟧$_{Af}$⟧$_{Aux}$⟧$_V$ ⇒

⟦$_V$⟦$_{Aux}$ X⟦$_{Af}$⟦$_{Tense}$ $\begin{bmatrix} +INF \\ +FUT \\ -PRET \\ -PART \end{bmatrix}$ ⟧$_{Tense}$⟧$_{Af}$⟧$_{Aux}$

⟦$_V$ av⟦$_{Af}$ Y$\begin{bmatrix} Z \\ -FUT \\ -PERF \end{bmatrix}$⟧$_{Af}$⟧$_V$⟧$_V$

or, in tree diagram form:

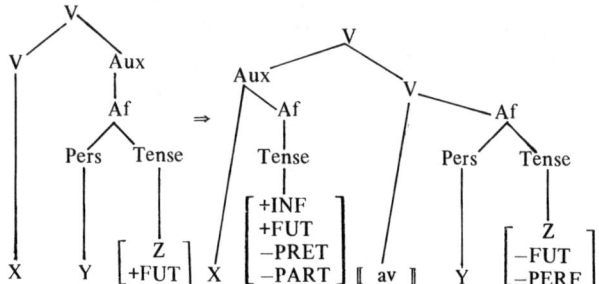

In this rule the lexical verb is removed from direct dominance by V so that it shall not receive word boundaries, and consequently, stress will not be assigned.

1.2.5. A minor readjustment rule is needed to deal with the fact that forms *has, ha, han* of the compound perfect auxiliary are unstressed; we have *has cantat* [əskəntát], 'you have sung. but *hem cantat* [ɛ̀mkəntát] 'we have sung'.

(22) # → ø

$$/ \text{ⅼ}_V \text{ av} \left\{ \begin{matrix} [+3P] \\ \begin{bmatrix} +2P \\ -PL \end{bmatrix} \end{matrix} \right\} \begin{bmatrix} -INF \\ -FUT \\ -PRET \\ -SUBJ \\ -IMPER \end{bmatrix} \underline{\quad\quad} \text{ⅼ}_V \text{ⅼ}_V \begin{bmatrix} +INF \\ +PART \\ +PRET \end{bmatrix}$$

By deleting # the structural description of II (15) (Major Stress Rule) is not met. Observe that this deletion is

72 *Verb morphology*

restricted to where another verb (i.e. past participle) follows. For we have *ha de venir* [áðəβəní] 'he must come', and *vindrà* [bindɾá] 〚bin+r〛〚#a#〛 'he will come', *anirà fent* [ənirə̀fén] 〚an+i+r〛〚[ᵥ #a#]ᵥ〚ᵥ f+e+nt〛ᵥ 'he will go on doing'. Alternatively the structural description of (22) could explicitly refer to the category perfect (i.e. 〚Perf〚ᵥ av ... 〛ᵥ〛Perf). This is preferable since in this form the rule contains the same number of syntactic brackets and fewer features.

1.3. Some sample derivations will illustrate the operation of the rules given so far. The matrices are simplified where possible. Word boundary # is inserted at the boundaries of major categories; cf. II §6.3.

(1)   *anaven llegint* 'they were reading'

(a)

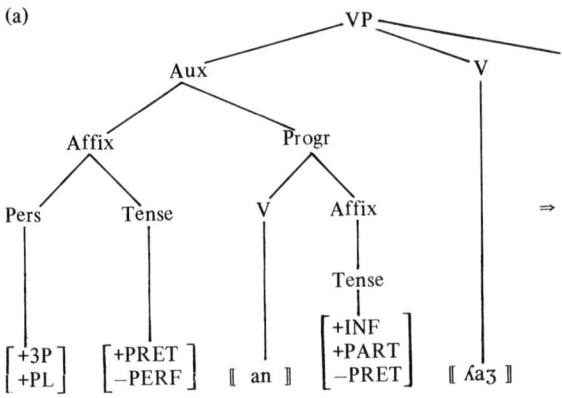

by rule (20) becomes

Verb morphology

(b)

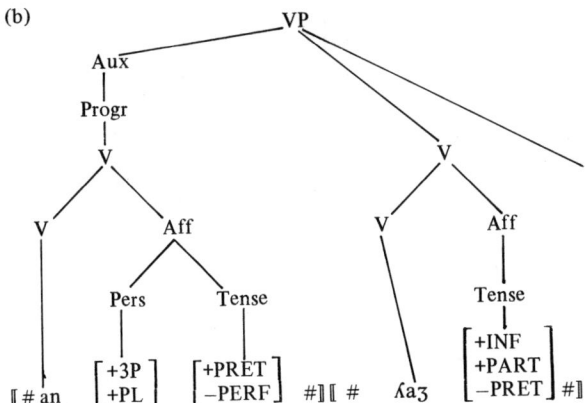

Then by the rules to be given in this chapter:

(c) ⟦ # an +a +ba +n #⟧⟦ # ʎaʒ +i +nt # ⟧
(d) by II (15), (25)
    ⟦ # ən +á +bə +n̄ # ⟧⟦ # ʎəʒ +í +nt #⟧

(2)   *correré* 'I shall run'

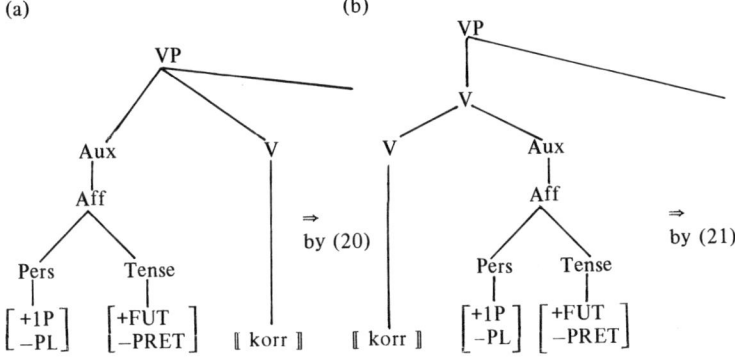

(c)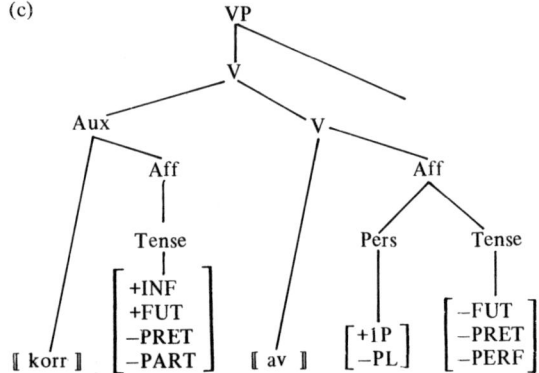

(d) rules of this chap.
⟦ # ⟦ korr + r + ⟧ ⟦ # e # ⟧ # ⟧

(e) by I (13) etc.
⟦ # ⟦ korrə + r + ⟧ ⟦ # é # ⟧ # ⟧

(3) A more complex example: *(quan) vam haver estat parlant (tres hores)* 'when we had been talking for three hours'

(a)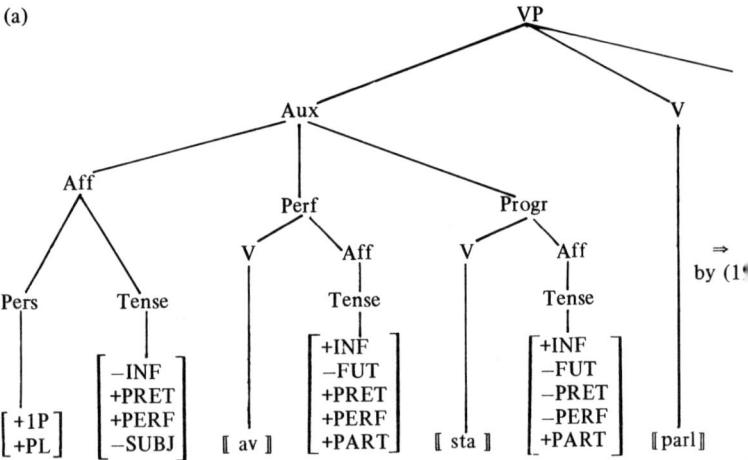

Verb morphology

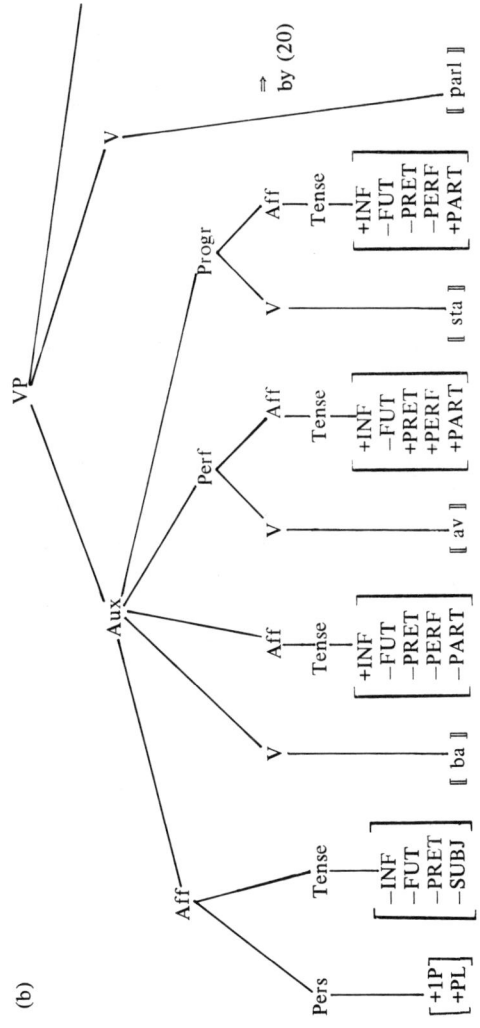

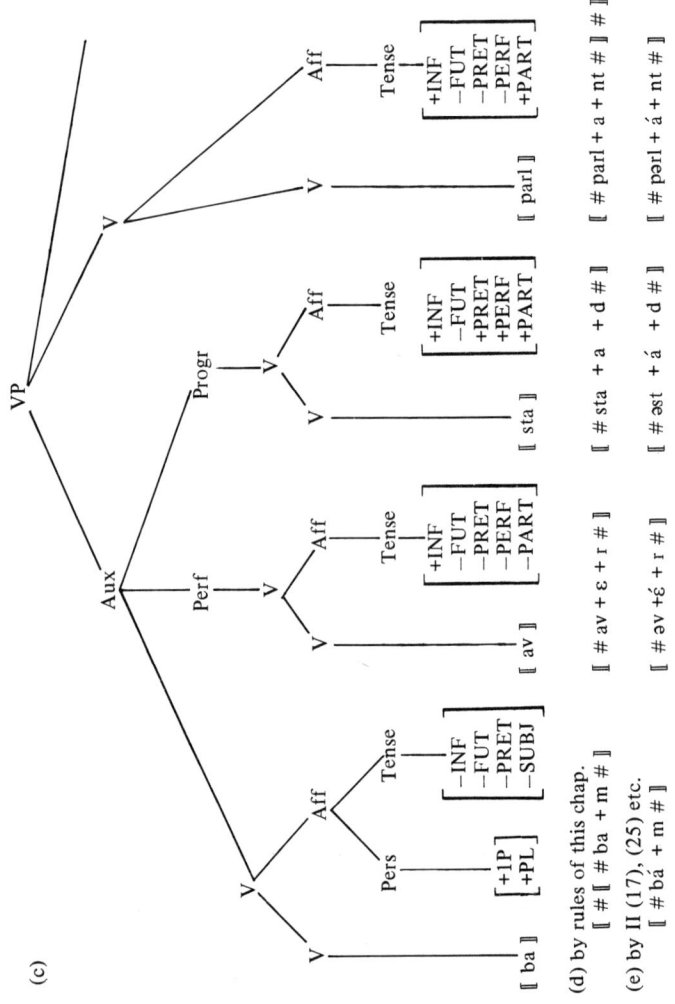

Verb morphology

1.4. From here on, the person and tense markers will be regarded as unordered with respect to the phonological matrices of the verb they are attached to; or, more exactly, they are inherent in every matrix of the sequence. This process can be expressed more formally as follows:

(23) $\quad \llbracket_{V,Aux} [m_1] [m_2] \ldots [m_n] \quad \llbracket_{Pers} \begin{bmatrix} F_1 \\ F_2 \\ \cdot \\ \cdot \\ F_n \end{bmatrix} \rrbracket_{Pers} \llbracket_{Tense} \begin{bmatrix} F'_1 \\ F'_2 \\ \cdot \\ \cdot \\ F'_n \end{bmatrix} \rrbracket_T \rrbracket_{V,Aux}$

$\Downarrow$

$\llbracket_{V,Aux} \begin{bmatrix} m_1 \\ F_1 \\ F_2 \\ \cdot \\ \cdot \\ \cdot \\ F_n \\ F'_1 \\ F'_2 \\ \cdot \\ \cdot \\ \cdot \\ F'_n \end{bmatrix} \begin{bmatrix} m_2 \\ F_1 \\ F_2 \\ \cdot \\ \cdot \\ \cdot \\ F_n \\ F'_1 \\ F'_2 \\ \cdot \\ \cdot \\ \cdot \\ F'_n \end{bmatrix} \ldots \begin{bmatrix} m_n \\ F_1 \\ F_2 \\ \cdot \\ \cdot \\ \cdot \\ F_n \\ F'_1 \\ F'_2 \\ \cdot \\ \cdot \\ \cdot \\ F'_n \end{bmatrix} \quad \emptyset \quad\quad \emptyset \quad \rrbracket_{V,Aux}$

where $m_1, m_2 \ldots m_n$ are feature matrices and $F_1 \ldots n, F'_1 \ldots n$ are morphosyntactic features with $\pm$ variables.

In interpreting the rules which are to be given below, redundancy rules which are the exact converses of (6)–(9) will be assumed, i.e. [± PERF] → [–FUT], etc. Otherwise, strictly speaking, the operation of the rules would be indeterminate in the case of surface structures whose matrices were necessarily unspecified for [PART],

[PERF], [IMPER], or [SUBJ]. This ensures, in effect, that rules do *not* operate on structures which have blanks for those features.

2.1. The category Person is realized in the following manner: 1st person plural by [−m], 2nd person plural by [−w] and 3rd person plural by [−n] throughout the paradigm of all verbs; the 2nd person singular by [−s] except in the imperative of regular verbs; the 3rd person singular by zero throughout; and the 1st person singular by zero, or by alterations of the thematic vowel. These rules will be formalized below; see § 3.2, § 4.10. The [+INF] marker is realized /−r/ in the context $\left[\overline{-\text{PART}} \right]$ (i.e. what is conventionally called the infinitive); by /−nt/ in the context $\left[\overline{-\text{PRET}} \right]$ (the gerund); and by /−d/, in the majority of cases, in the context $\left[\overline{+\text{PRET}} \right]$ (the past participle). All these suffixes are subject to phonological rules which disguise their underlying form somewhat: these are to be discussed in due course; see § § 4.4, 4.7, 4.8, 4.10.

2.2.1. Between the verb stem and the Person or [+INF] suffixes mentioned above there appear various "thematic" vowels or more complex infixes, which vary according to Person, Tense, and morphological "conjugation" class. Conventionally the conjugation classes of Catalan verbs are called I, II and III; II and III are each subdivided into 'a' and 'b' (Fabra, 1968a:41). For convenience I shall maintain the symbols I, II and III, but will call the subdivisions of II and III 'A' and 'B', since I subdivide on different criteria from Fabra.

His IIa (type *perdre*) and IIb (type *témer*) differ only in the infinitive, in a way that is purely automatic. My IIA is the type *valer* 'to be worth', IIB is the type *perdre* 'to lose'; IIIA (= Fabra IIIb) is the type *dormir* 'to sleep' and IIIB (= Fabra IIIa) is the type *servir* 'to serve'. The following tables will facilitate the comparison of the various infixes. The labels on the left are the conventional tense and person names, abbreviated in the usual way. The type verb of conjugation I is *cantar* 'to sing'. In Table 1, the phonetic forms are those before certain low-level rules apply, such as Final-consonant deletion, voicing neutralization.

Table 2 reveals to what extent the traditional classification into three conjugations is justified and also shows that II shares many infixes with either I or III. Only line 7 (1sg pret in [−í]) is common to all three classes. There are a few verbs which have gerunds of class IIA and infinitives of IIB, e.g. *caldre* 'to be necessary', gerund: *calent* [kəlént]; a few share forms of IIB and IIIA, e.g. *viure* 'to live', *escriure* 'to write', *tenir* 'to have', *venir* 'to come'. There is a small group of thoroughly irregular verbs, which have, in addition to forms from various conjugations, suppletive paradigms and athematic forms; they are *ésser* 'to be', *estar* 'to be', *anar* 'to go' and Progr auxiliary, *va−* preterite auxiliary, *haver* perfect auxiliary, *fer* 'to do', *haver-hi* 'to exist'; see below, §6.

2.2.2. The great majority of verbs belong to class I, which thus assumes the character of an unmarked class. G. Ferrater reckoned (lectures 1971−2) that of some 4500 verbs in Fabra, 1968b, known to him, 3500 were of class I, and 700 of class IIIB. For comparison of these proportions with textual frequency, however, I have looked at the first 1000 verbs (excluding the *va−* and *haver* auxiliaries) in the play by Jordi Teixidor: "El retaule del

TABLE 1 Verb conjugation. Phonetic forms

		I	IIA	IIB	IIIA	IIIB
1	1sg pres ind	kánt–u	bál–g	pérð–u	dórm–u	sərβ–έj–u
2	2sg pres ind	kánt–ə–s	bál–s	pérd–s	dórm–s	sərβ–έj–e–s
	2sg imper	kánt–ə	bál	pérd	dórm	sərβ–έj
	3sg pres ind }					
3	3pl pres ind	kánt–ə–n	bál–ə–n	pérð–ə–n	dórm–ə–n	sərβ–έj–e–n
	1pl pres ind	kənt–έ–m	bəl–έ–m	pərð–έ–m	durm–í–m	sərβ–í–m
	2pl imper }					
	2pl pres ind	kənt–έ–w	bəl–έ–w	pərð–έ–w	durm–í–w	sərβ–í–w
4	1, 3sg pres subj	kánt–i	bál–γ–i	pérð–i	dórm–i	sərβ–έj–i
	2sg pres subj	kánt–i–s	bál–γ–i–s	pérð–i–s	dórm–i–s	sərβ–έj–i–s
	3pl pres subj	kánt–i–n	bál–γ–i–n	pérð–i–n	dórm–i–n	sərβ–έj–i–n
5	1pl pres subj	kənt–έ–m	bəl–γ–έ–m	pərð–έ–m	durm–í–m	sərβ–í–m
	2pl pres subj	kənt–έ–w	bəl–γ–έ–w	pərð–έ–w	durm–í–w	sərβ–í–w
6	1, 3sg imperf	kənt–áβə	bəl–íə	pərð–íə	durm–íə	sərβ–íes
	2sg imperf	kənt–áβə–s	bəl–íə–s	pərð–íə–s	durm–s–ei–s	s–ei–βies

1pl imperf	kənt–áβə–m	bəl–iə́–m	pərð–iə́–m	durm–iə́–m	sərβ–iə́–m
2pl imperf	kənt–áβə–w	bəl–iə́–w	pərð–iə́–w	durm–iə́–w	sərβ–iə́–w
3pl imperf	kənt–áβə–n	bəl–iə́–n	pərð–iə́–n	durm–iə́–n	sərβ–iə́–n
7 1sg pret	kənt–í	bəl–ɣ–í	pərð–í	durm–í	sərβ–í
8 3sg pret	kənt–á	bəl–ɣ–é	pərð–é	durm–í	sərβ–í
9 2sg pret	kənt–árɡ–s	bəl–ɣ–éɾə–s	pərð–éɾə–s	durm–íɾə–s	sərβ–íɾə–s
1pl pret	kənt–áɾə–m	bəl–ɣ–éɾə–m	pərð–éɾə–m	durm–íɾə–m	sərβ–íɾə–m
2pl pret	kənt–áɾə–w	bəl–ɣ–éɾə–w	pərð–éɾə–w	durm–íɾə–w	sərβ–íɾə–w
3pl pret	kənt–áɾə–n	bəl–ɣ–éɾə–n	pərð–éɾə–n	durm–íɾə–n	sərβ–íɾə–n
10 1, 3sg past subj	kənt–és	bəl–ɣ–és	pərð–és	durm–ís	sərβ–ís
11 2sg past subj	kənt–ési–s	bəl–ɣ–ési–s	pərð–ési–s	durm–ísi–s	sərβ–ísi–s
1pl past subj	kənt–ési–m	bəl–ɣ–ési–m	pərð–ési–m	durm–ísi–m	sərβ–ísi–m
2pl past subj	kənt–ési–w	bəl–ɣ–ési–w	pərð–ési–w	durm–ísi–w	sərβ–ísi–w
3pl past subj	kənt–ési–n	bəl–ɣ–ési–n	pərð–ési–n	durm–ísi–n	sərβ–ísi–n
12 ptcp	kənt–á–d	bəl–ɣ–ú–d	pərð–ú–d	durm–í–d	sərβ–í–d
13 gerund	kənt–á–nt	bəl–ɛ́–nt	pərð–é–nt	durm–í–nt	sərβ–í–nt
14 inf	kənt–á–r	bəl–ɛ́–r	pɛɾð–ɾ–ə	durm–í–r	sərβ–í–r
15 fut	kənt–ə–ɾ–é	bəl–d–ɾ–é	pərð–ɾ–é	durm–i–ɾ–é	sərβ–i–ɾ–é
	etc.	etc.	etc.	etc.	etc.

81

Verb morphology

TABLE 2 Verb infixes. Possible form before vowel reduction

	I	IIA	IIB	IIIA	IIIB
1					éʃ
2	a	ø ([ə])	ø ([ə])	ø([ə])	éʃ+ə
3	ɛ́	ɛ́	ɛ́	í	í
4	i	i	i	i	éʃ+i
5	ɛ́	ɛ́	ɛ́	í	í
6	ába	ía	ía	ía	ía
7	í	í	í	í	í
8	á	ɛ́	é	í	í
9	ára	éra	éra	íra	íra
10	és	és	és	ís	ís
11	ési	ési	ési	ísi	ísi
12	á	ú	ú	í	í
13	á	ɛ́	é	í	í
14	á	ɛ́	ø	í	í
15	á	ø	ø	í	í

flautista" (1970). They are classified as follows:

```
Class I              417
Class IIIB            57
                     ---
                     474

wholly irregular     239
Class IIB            130
Class IIIA            94
Class IIA             63
                     ---
                     526
```

Verb morphology

(For this calculation I included in class IIA verbs with IIA gerunds but IIB infinitives.) Observe that in this fragment of text at any rate, more than half the verbs are from the closed classes II and IIIA + "wholly irregular".

2.3.1. An examination of Tables 1 and 2 immediately reveals a number of possible generalizations, both in the vertical and in the horizontal direction. For instance, vertically, /a/ is frequent in class I, /i/ in class III; horizontally, /i/ is general in rows 4 and 11, /í/ in row 7, /r/ in row 9, and /s/ in rows 10 and 11. Let us try to reveal some more.

We already have rules in the grammar to delete a vowel which is followed by +V (I (4), (7)). If we extend these rules so as to delete all inflectional suffix (but not lexical affix) vowels before +V, we see that not only can class I have /+a/ throughout, but also that class III can have /+i/ except in row 2 (IIIA), or possibly, /+i/ throughout, with later deletion in just this case. The form of such an extended Truncation rule could be:

(24) $\left[\left\langle \left\{ \begin{matrix} V \\ -\text{back} \\ +\text{labial} \end{matrix} \right\} \right\rangle_a \right] \rightarrow \emptyset \; / \; \langle + \rangle_b \left[\begin{matrix} \underline{\quad\quad} \\ -\text{Affix} \end{matrix} \right] + V$

condition: if a, then b.

2.3.2. Is there a thematic vowel in class II corresponding to the /+a/ of I and the /+i/ of III? There is some evidence that /+u/ which appears phonetically in the past participle (row 12) in the majority of class II verbs is present at some stage in a considerable number of forms. Class II verbs whose stems, as revealed most clearly in the gerund, end in /l/, /n/, /v/, /j/, or /w/ have [g] or [ɣ] following, or instead, before the participle in /+u+d/. Thus:

creient [krəjén] 'believing'; *cregut* [krəɣút] 'believed'

plaent [pləén] 'pleasing'; *plagut* [pləɣút] 'pleased'
(stem: /plaw/)
dolent [dulén] 'hurting'; *dolgut* [dulɣút] 'hurt'
venent [bənén] 'selling'; (*vengut* [bəŋgút]'sold': also
venut)
movent [muβén] 'moving'; *mogut* [muɣút] 'moved'

This /g/ also appears a) in the present subjunctive (rows 4–5), and preterite indicative and subjunctive (rows 7–11); b) in the 1sg present indicative (row 1), instead of the [u] which in verbs of classes I, II, IIIA occurs directly after the stem, and in class IIIB after /+ɛʃ/. These two additional facts give the clue to a possible solution, namely, that /+u/, as the thematic vowel of II, is present in the cases corresponding to rows 4–5 and 7–12; that it causes the insertion of /g/ after certain consonants; and that it is deleted except before a consonant.

3.1. Let me now formalize the position as explained so far. Compare Table 3, which shows the system I propose underlying the infixes of Table 2.

The rules generating the thematic vowels and infixes will be given below. The morphological classes I, IIA, IIB, IIIA, IIIB will be specified in the rules in strict binary feature form in order to make the application of the rules unambiguous. The features assigned to each are these:

$$\begin{matrix} \text{I} & \text{IIA} & \text{IIB} & \text{IIIA} & \text{IIIB} \\ \begin{bmatrix} +\text{I} \\ -\text{II} \\ -\text{III} \end{bmatrix} & \begin{bmatrix} -\text{I} \\ +\text{II} \\ -\text{III} \\ +\text{A} \end{bmatrix} & \begin{bmatrix} -\text{I} \\ +\text{II} \\ -\text{III} \\ -\text{A} \end{bmatrix} & \begin{bmatrix} -\text{I} \\ -\text{II} \\ +\text{III} \\ -\text{B} \end{bmatrix} & \begin{bmatrix} -\text{I} \\ -\text{II} \\ +\text{III} \\ +\text{B} \end{bmatrix} \end{matrix}$$

The subclasses referred to informally as A and B are spelt out differently in each case. IIA and IIIA have nothing in common warranting the same specifications for 'A', nor have IIB and IIIB for 'B'. Some of the

TABLE 3 Proposed underlying verb infixes

	I							IIA									IIB								IIIA						IIIB						
	1	3	4	5	6	7		1	2	3	4	5	6	7		1	3	4	5	6	7		1	4	5	6	7		1	2	4	5	6	7	
1	a					u								u								u		i				u		i	ɛʃ				u	
2	a									u														i						i	ɛʃ					
3	a					ɛ				u				ɛ				u				ɛ		i						i						
4	a			i								i								i				i		i				i	ɛʃ		i			
5	a			i		ɛ						i		ɛ						i		ɛ		i		i				i			i			
6	a			b	a							i	j	a						i	j	a		i		i	j	a		i			i	j	a	
7	a		i	r	(a)					u	e	i	r	(a)				u	e	i	r	(a)		i		i	r	(a)		i		i	r	(a)		
8	a			r	(a)					u	e		r	(a)				u	e		r	(a)		i		i	r	(a)		i		i	r	(a)		
9	a			r	a					u	e		r	a				u	e		r	a		i		i	r	a		i		i	r	a		
10	a	e		s	(i)						e		s	(i)				u	e		s	(i)		i		i	s	(i)		i		i	s	(i)		
11	a	e		s	i					u	e		s	i				u	e		s	i		i		i	s	i		i		i	s	i		
12	a			d				u					d				u		e		d			i		i		d		i		i		d		
13	a			nt					ɛ				nt								nt			i		i		nt		i		i		nt		
14	a			r					ɛ				r								r			i		i		r		i		i		r		
15	a			r									r								r			i		i		r		i		i		r		

86   *Verb morphology*

features in the matrices are obviously to be supplied by redundancy rules (e.g. [+I] → [−II, −III]), just as we have e.g. [+1P] → [−2P, −3P]; the remainder are part of the lexical entry for each verb, or are introduced along with phonological matrices in the Auxiliary rules (17), (18), (19), (21).

For /+i/ (columns IIIA 1, IIIB 1 of Table 3):

(25)   ø → +i / [+III]___]

(26)   +i → ø / [+III]___ $\left(+\begin{bmatrix}-\text{vocal}\\+\text{coron}\\-\text{distr}\end{bmatrix}\right)$ #

As suggested above, § 2.3.1, (26) deletes the thematic /+i/ before /+s/, /+n/ or #. It applies, of course, after the rule introducing the person morphs (rule (65)), but before the Truncation rule (24), otherwise the subjunctive /+i/ (row 4) would be wrongly deleted. Applying before (24) (26) will fail to delete all the /+i/ subjunctive morphs (column 6) since the preceding segment in every case is not [+III].

For /+u/ (columns IIA 1, IIB 1, rows 4−5, 7−12):

(27)   ø → +u / $\begin{bmatrix}+\text{II}\\\left\{\begin{matrix}[+\text{SUBJ}]\\[+\text{PERF}]\\\begin{bmatrix}+\text{Irr Imp}\\+\text{IMPER}\end{bmatrix}\end{matrix}\right\}\end{bmatrix}$ ___]

See below, § 4.9, for an account of the feature [+Irr Imp].

For /+εʃ/ (column IIIB 2):

(28)   ø → +εʃ / $\begin{bmatrix}+\text{III}\\+\text{B}\\-\text{INF}\\-\text{FUT}\\-\text{PRET}\\\left\{\begin{matrix}+\text{3P}\\-\text{PL}\end{matrix}\right\}\end{bmatrix}$ ___]

Verb morphology 87

For /+a/ (column I 1):

(29) ø → +a / [+I]___]

The rule for the /+u/ morph of the 1sg pres ind (row 1) is:

(30) ø → +u / $\begin{bmatrix} -\text{IMPER} \\ -\text{PRET} \\ -\text{SUBJ} \\ +1\text{P} \\ -\text{PL} \end{bmatrix}$ X___]

3.2.1. I shall now specify more precisely the environment for /g/-insertion. The cases are these (separate mention is not made of compound verbs formed from these roots):

After /j/: verbs with underlying root-final /j/ are, I suggest, those with root-accented imperfects of the type *creia* [kréjə] 'I believed', most of which have a phonetic [j] in the gerund. In the examples which follow the numbers refer to the rows of Tables 1–3. Final underlying voiced stops are represented [g], [d] etc. for clarity; usually, they become unvoiced at the end of a word. Internal voiced stops are likewise represented at a stage before spirantization to [ɣ], [ð] etc.

riure 'to laugh' 6[réjə], 13[riént], 1[ríg], 10[rigés], 12[rigúd]
caure 'to fall' 6[kéjə], 13[kəjént], 1[kájg], 10[kəjgés], 12[kəjgúd]
creure 'to believe' 6[kréjə], 13[krəjént], 1[krég], 10[krəgés], 12[krəgúd]
treure 'to take away' 6[tréjə], 13[trəjént], 1[trég], 10[trəgés], (12[trét])
seure 'to sit' 6[séjə], 13[səjént], 1[ség], 10[səgés], 12[səgúd]
jeure 'to lie' 6[ʒéjə], 13[ʒəjént], 1[ʒég], 10[ʒəgés], 12[ʒəgúd]

88   *Verb morphology*

dir 'to say' 6[déjə], 13[diént], 1[díg], 10[digés],
      (12[dít])
dur 'to bring' 6[dújə], 13[duént], 1[dúg], 10[dugés],
      (12[dút])
The underlying form of the following two verbs is not clear; they have partly suppletive conjugations:

veure 'to see' 6[bɛ́jə], 13[bəjént], 1[bɛ́ʒ],
      10[bəjés], 12[bíst]
fer 'to do' 6[fɛ́jə], 13[fént], 1[fáʒ], 10[fés], 12[fét]

Comparable forms are some of *haver* 'to have to' : 1[áʒ], 4[áʒi], *anar* 'to go' 1[báʒ], 4[báʒi] and the auxiliary verbs which resemble them. *Fer* is presumably athematic (i.e. [−rules (25), (27), (29)]) in some of these forms.

ser/ésser 'to be' has: 1[sóg], 4[síɡi], 12 (vulgar) [siɡúd]. One could propose arbitrarily that the stem in rows 4−5 is /sij/, in which case the occurring forms would be accounted for as those of *riure* with UR /rij/.

After /w/ : I suggest that the following verbs have underlying final /w/, which appears at the surface in forms corresponding to row 2 of the tables. Observe that these verbs differ systematically from the /−j/ verbs above, and from the /−v/ verbs below.

plaure 'to please' 6[pləíə], 13[pləént], 1[plág],
      10[pləgés], 12[pləgúd]
cloure 'to close' 6[kluíə], 13[kluént], 1[klóg],
      10[klugés], (12[klóz])
coure 'to cook' 6[kuíə]. 13[kuént], 1[kóg],
      10[kugés], 12[kugúd]
raure 'to scrape' 6[rəíə], 13[rəént], 1[rág],
      10[rəgés], 12[rəgúd]

After /v/: these verbs differ systematically from those in /−w/ above, and form those in /−b/, which regularly

Verb morphology

have no /g/—insertion (e.g. *rebre* 'to receive'). /v/ between vowels will be realized as [β] by a later rule.

deure 'to owe' 6[dəvíə], 13[dəvént], 1[dɛ́g], 10[dəgés], 12[dəgúd]
moure 'to move' 6[muvíə], 13[muvént], 1[mɔ́g], 10[mugés], 12[mugúd]
ploure 'to rain' 6[pluvíə], 13[pluvént], 10[plugés], 12[plugúd]
heure 'to get' 6[əvíə], 13[əvɛ̨nt], 1[ɛ́g], 10[əgés], 12[əgúd]
haver 'to have to' 6[əvíə], 13[əvént], (1[é] or [áʒ]), 10[əgés], 12[əgúd]
haver (Aux vb.) 6[əvíə], 13[əvént], (1[é]), 10[əgés], 12[əgúd]
beure 'to drink' 6[bəvíə], 13[bəvént], 1[bɛ́g], 10[bəgés], 12[bəgúd]
escriure 'to write' has forms from IIB and III; the following IIB forms are relevant here: 6[əskɾivíə], 1[əskɾíg], 10[əskɾigés]
viure 'to live' has forms with [sk] where [g] might be expected, e.g. 6[bivíə], (13[bivínt]), 1[bísk], 10[biskés], 12[biskúd] N.B. the verbs *créixer* 'to grow', *néixer* 'to be born', and *merèixer* 'to deserve' like *viure* have participles in [—skúd] and optionally e.g. 5[kɾəskɛ́m], 7[kɾəskí], 8[kɾəské], 9[kɾəskéɾəs], 10[kɾəskés], 11[kɾəskésis], etc. It is doubtful to me if this /—sk—/ is in any way synchronically related to the /g/— insertion under discussion. See below, and §6.

After /ʃ/ : in addition to those verbs just mentioned there are *conèixer* 'to know' and *parèixer* 'to seem', which have the following forms:
conèixer 13[kunəʃént], 1[kunɛ́g], 10[kunəgés], 12[kunəgúd]

Verb morphology

parèixer 13[pərəʃént], 1[pərɛ́g], 10[pərəgés], 12[pərəgúd]

N.B. 4[kunɛ́gi], [pərɛ́gi], but [krɛ́ʃi], [néʃi], mərɛ́ʃi].

After /l/ : [g] appears in forms corresponding to rows 1, 4, 5, 7–12, with isolated exceptions, e.g.

resoldre 'to resolve' 13[rəzulént], 1[rəzɔ́lg], 10[rəzulgés], (12[rəzɔ́lt])
valer 'to be worth' 13[bəlɛ́nt], 1[bálg], 10[bəlgés], 12[bəlgúd]
soler 'to be accustomed to' 13[sulɛ́nt], 1[sɔ́lg], 10[sulgés], 12[sulgúd]
voler 'to want' 13[bulɛ́nt], (1[búʎ]), 10[bulgés], 12[bulgúd]

Similar forms with *moldre* 'to grind', *caldre* 'to be necessary'. *doldre* 'to hurt'.

After /r/: There is only one example, *córrer* 'to run' which normally has [g] only in rows 7–12, and optionally in 5[kurəgɛ́m].

córrer 13[kurént], 1[kóru], 10[kurəgés], 12[kurəgúd]

After /n/: There are numerous examples, e.g.

vendre 'to sell' 13[bənént], 1[béŋg]
10[bəŋgés], 12[bəŋgúd], (also [bənúd])
venir 'to come' has 3, 13, 14 from class III.
13[bənínt]; 1[bíŋg], 10[biŋgés], 12[biŋgúd]
fondre 'to melt' 13[funént], 1[fóŋg], 10[fuŋgés], (12[fóz])

Likewise: *encendre* 'to light', *atendre* 'to attend', *estendre* 'to extend', *pretendre* 'to pretend', *prendre* 'to take', *ofendre* 'to offend', *romandre* 'to remain', *dependre* 'to depend', *tondre* 'to shear', *respondre* 'to reply'.

Verb morphology

After /b/: We have [g] only in the verbs *saber* 'to know', and *cabre* 'to fit', and then only in the present subjunctive (+ irregular imperative for *saber*) which is irregular in other respects. Vulgar Barcelona speech extends the stems [sapig], [kapig] to cases 10–14. 7–9 are, of course, not used in that dialect.

saber 13[səbɛ́nt], (vulgar [səpigɛ́nt]), 4[sápigə],
Imperative [sápigəs], [səpigɛ́w]
cabre 13[kəbɛ́nt], (vulgar [kəpigɛ́nt]), 4[kápigə]

After /d/: Class II has only two verbs in stem-final /d/, viz. *perdre* 'to lose' and *poder* 'to be able'. The latter has forms with [g] in 1, 4, 5, 7–12.

poder 13[pudɛ́nt], 1[púg], 10[pugés], 12[pugúd]

In addition *ser/ésser* 'to be', as mentioned above, has [g] forms in 1, 4, 5 + Imperative, and vulgarly in 12. 1[sóg], 4[sígi], 12[sigúd]. *Estar* 'to be, stay' has [g]- forms (the stem is /stig/) in 1, 4,5 + Imperative, 7–11; elsewhere it has forms from the stem $\genfrac{}{}{0pt}{}{/\text{sta}/}{[+I]}$ $-/-a/$ is deleted before +V by (24).

Though there are exceptions and problems, it is clear that [g]–insertion occurs in class II verbs in forms corresponding to rows 1, 4, 5, 7–12 and some irregular imperatives, and nowhere else. In rows 1 and 12 the /+u/ morph is required anyway, and the rule to introduce it as a thematic vowel in 12 can be extended to the other cases without otherwise distorting the output.

3.2.2. On the question whether the [g]–insertion rule should be formally limited to class II verbs the evidence is scanty. There are some 25 or so different verbs (excluding compounds) of class IIIA. A few have a stem-final consonant which might require [g]–insertion before /+u/ in 1sg pres ind., such as *acudo* 'I come along', *pudo* 'I stink', which like the IIA verb *poder* 'to be able' have stems ending in /d/. As we have seen only two class II verbs in /–ʃ/ have [g]–insertion: *conèixer* (1sg pres ind. *conec*) and *parèixer* (1sg pres ind. *parec*). Class IIIA verbs in /–ʃ/, e.g. *cruixo* 'I crackle', *reixo* 'I succeed' resemble the more general class II type in having [u] after [ʃ] like *mereixo*. The class IIIA verb *lluir* 'to shine' has, in the present indicative singular the forms 1 *lluo* [ʎúu], 2 *lluus* [ʎú(w)s], 3 *lluu* [ʎú(w)], and imperfect *lluïa* etc. [ʎuíə]. This verb appears to have underlying root-final /w/; it does not have [g] at all. It looks, therefore, as though /g/–insertion ought not to be extended to class III verbs. This can be achieved by ordering the rules thus: (25), (30), (31), (24). Then IIIA verbs do not meet the structural description of (31) when it applies, having for row 1 the form ⟦X+i+u⟧.

So the most general form of the /g/–insertion rule seems to be as follows, applying to all verbs with stem-final /j/, /w/, /v/, /l/, /n/ after thematic infix (27) and [+1P, –PL] suffix (30) have applied.

$$(31) \quad \emptyset \rightarrow + \begin{bmatrix} -\text{syllab} \\ -\text{labial} \\ +\text{back} \\ +\text{voiced} \end{bmatrix}$$

$$/[+\text{syll}] \left\{ \begin{bmatrix} -\text{syll} \\ +\text{cont} \\ -\text{coron} \end{bmatrix} \begin{bmatrix} -\text{cont} \\ -\text{distr} \end{bmatrix} \right\} \underline{\quad} + \begin{bmatrix} +\text{syll} \\ +\text{back} \end{bmatrix} \rrbracket V$$

3.3. Then we need a rule to delete [u] after /+g/ in the 1sg pres ind. (row 1). This rule must precede Truncation (24) which deletes /+a/ before +V, otherwise /+u/ would be wrongly deleted in class I verbs with stem-

Verb morphology 93

final velars, e.g. *amago* 'I hide' /amag+a+u/. The rule must follow those introducing the remaining affixes, or all /+u/'s supplied by (27) will be deleted. Class II verbs ending in /ʒ/ in row 1 also have no [−u] termination, e.g. *veig* 'I see', *vaig* 'I go', *haig* 'I have to', though class III verbs have, e.g. *fujo* 'I run away'. So rule (32) has the following form, if, like (31), it is ordered before (24).

$$(32) \quad \begin{bmatrix} +syll \\ +back \\ +high \end{bmatrix} \rightarrow \emptyset \bigg/ \begin{bmatrix} +high \\ +obstr \\ \{+voice\} \\ \{-cont\} \end{bmatrix} + \underline{\qquad}]\!]_V$$

[−cont] is included only to account for the absence of [−u] in the irregular *visc* 'I live'. That this form has underlying /sk/ and not, for example, /s+g/ is indicated by the presence of the stem /bisk/ in rows 4, 5 and 7−12. Rule (31) as formulated does not account for the [g] appearing in the verbs *córrer, saber, cabre, poder, ser, conèixer*, and *parèixer*. For these verbs see below § 6.

4.1. There now follow the rules introducing the remaining tense and person affixes, as in table 3. I try to make the rules as general as possible, bearing in mind that apparently incorrect outputs of some rules will subsequently be corrected by rules that we shall require in any case.

$$(33) \quad \emptyset \rightarrow +\varepsilon \bigg/ \begin{bmatrix} +II \\ +A \\ +INF \\ -FUT \\ -PRET \end{bmatrix} X \underline{\qquad}]\!]$$

This rule accounts for the distinctive forms of conjugation IIA, (cf. Badia, 1951:312): the infinitive in [ɛ́(r)] and the gerund in [ɛ́n(t)], e.g. of *valer* 'to be worth' [bəlɛ́], [bəlɛ́n]; and similar forms with *voler* 'to want', *saber* 'to know', *soler* 'to be accustomed to', *haver* 'to have (to), *poder* 'to be able', and optionally *doler* 'to hurt' (alternative to *doldre*), *caler* 'to be necessary' (alternative to *caldre*), and *caber* 'to fit' (alternative to *cabre*); a few verbs have [ɛ] only in the gerund: *devent* [dəβέn] from *deure* 'must', (but [dəβέn] from *deure* 'to owe'), *havent* [əβέn] from *heure* 'to get'.

In some dialects, including vulgar Barcelonese, (27) is extended so as to apply in the infinitive and the gerund, so (31) applies before (33) inserting /g/; similarly, in these dialects the /g/–stems of the anomalous words mentioned at the end of the last section occur before /+ɛ/ in the gerund and infinitive, giving e.g. *valer* [bəlɣέ], [bəlɣέn], *voler* [bulɣέ], [bulɣέn], *saber* [səpiɣέ], [səpiɣέn], *poder* [puɣέ], [puɣέn], *cabre* [kəpiɣέ], [kəpiɣέn]. Note that the /+ɛ/ is not inserted in the future and conditional tenses, so we have *valdré* 'I shall be worth', *voldré, podré*, etc. from /bal+r+e/, /bɔl+r+e/, /pɔd+r+e/, etc. That is, (33) does not apply in the environment [+INF, + FUT]_____.

4.2. For /+e/, in class II preterite indicative, class I and II past subjunctive, and class IIB gerunds, we have:

$$(34) \quad \emptyset \rightarrow +e \; / \; \left\{ \begin{bmatrix} \begin{bmatrix} -\text{INF} \\ +\text{PERF} \\ \begin{Bmatrix} \begin{bmatrix} +\text{SUBJ} \\ -\text{III} \end{bmatrix} \\ +\text{II} \end{Bmatrix} \end{bmatrix} \end{bmatrix} \\ \begin{bmatrix} +\text{PART} \\ -\text{PRET} \\ +\text{II} \\ -\text{A} \end{bmatrix} \end{array} \right\} X\underline{\quad}]\!]$$

Verb morphology 95

N.B. X (which stands for any number of segments or none) is to take account of morphs already introduced.

4.3.

$$(35) \quad \emptyset \rightarrow +i \left/ \begin{bmatrix} +\text{PRET} \\ -\text{SUBJ} \\ \left\{ \begin{bmatrix} -\text{PERF} \\ -\text{I} \end{bmatrix} \right\} \\ \left\{ \begin{bmatrix} +\text{PERF} \\ +1\text{P} \\ -\text{PL} \end{bmatrix} \right\} \end{bmatrix} \right. X \underline{\quad}]\!]$$

(i)

(ii)

Part (i) accounts for the first vowel of the [-íə] ending of the imperfect tense in classes II and III (column 4, row 6): [bəlíə], [pərðíə], [durmíə], [sərβíə], etc. Part (ii) accounts for the final vowel of the 1sg preterite forms (column 4, row 7): *cantí, valguí, perdí, dormí, serví,* etc. These forms occur rarely in Standard Catalan, even in the formal (written) styles, where the other persons of this tense are frequently used. No forms of this tense are uttered spontaneously in ordinary speech.

4.4.

$$(36) \quad \emptyset \rightarrow +r \left/ \left\{ \begin{bmatrix} +\text{PERF} \\ -\text{SUBJ} \end{bmatrix} \right\} X \underline{\quad}]\!] \right.$$
$$[-\text{PART}]$$

N.B. If we had # rather than]] at the right of the environment, /+r/– insertion would fail in the future tense forms, since after (21) these infinitives will not receive #, no longer being V's. (36) introduces /r/ into the preterite and the infinitive, (column 5, rows 7–9, 14, 15). In the preterite it appears phonetically as [ɾ] in 2sg and throughout the plural, that is, when a vowel follows. Thus: [kəntárəs], [kəntárəm], [kəntárəw], [kəntárən]; [bəlɣérəs], [bəlɣérəm], [bəlɣérəw],

[bəlyérən]; [sərβírəs], [sərβírəm], [sərβírəw],
[sərβírən].
There are two reasons for introducing it into the other
persons, though it is never realized phonetically there;
firstly, for greater generality, and secondly to account for
oxytone stress on the phonetic final vowel. This stress is
normal in words ending in a consonant, even when this
is later deleted, cf. VII § 2. The /r/ in the infinitive is
found phonetically in most IIB forms; thus *perdre*
[pérðrə] /pɛrd+r/ 'to lose', *vendre* [bę́ndrə] /bɛn+r/
'to sell', *jeure* [ʒéwrə] /ʒɛj+r/ 'to lie'. In infinitives of
other classes it is pronounced when followed by an
unstressed pronoun. Thus *cantar-nos* [kəntárnus]
/kant+a+r#nus/ 'to sing to us', *valer-ho* [bəlérụ]
/bal+ɛ+r#u/ 'to be worth it', *servir-ne* [sərβírnə]
/sarb+i+r#n/ 'to serve some'. Likewise, /r/ is realized
phonetically in the future and conditional tenses of all
verbs, which, as I proposed above § 1.2.2, are formed
from the infinitive with the auxiliary /av/. Thus *cantarà*
[kəntərá] /kant+a+r+a/ 'he will sing', *valdrà* [bəldrá]
/bal+r+a/ 'it will be worth', *dormirem* [durmirém]
/dɔrm+i+r+ɛ+m/ 'we shall sleep', etc.

4.5.

(37) $\emptyset \rightarrow +b \Big/ \begin{bmatrix} +\text{PRET} \\ -\text{PERF} \\ +\text{I} \end{bmatrix} X \underline{\qquad}]$

This /+b/ corresponds to the [–β–] of *cantava*
[kəntáβə] 'I was singing' etc. (Class I, column 5, row 6
of Table 3.)
For the imperfects of the other classes I propose the
following rule:

(38) $\emptyset \rightarrow +j \Big/ \begin{bmatrix} +\text{PRET} \\ -\text{PERF} \end{bmatrix} +V \ (+V) \underline{\qquad}]$

Verb morphology

+V (+V) prevents application to class I since (37) has applied; perhaps rather [−I] should be mentioned here. Though it does not appear phonetically, this /+j/ is necessary to prevent deletion of the preceding vowel (/+i/) by the Truncation rule (24). A rule deleting /j/ after /i/ before a vowel is required anyway; see too I §2.5 for a suggestion about rule j → ø /_____ i, of which this would be a generalization. Compare the gerunds of the following verbs with root-final /j/:

caient [kəjén] /kaj+e+nt/ 'falling'
seient [səjén] /sɛj+e+nt/ 'sitting'
creient [krəjén] /krɛj+e+nt/ 'believing'
rient [rién] /rij+e+nt/ 'laughing'
dient [dién] /dij+e+nt/ 'saying'

Similarly, the difference in the position of the stress of some abstract nouns with [iə] suffixes can be accounted for if we assume an underlying /j/ where appropriate; thus:

prudència [pruðɛ́nsiə] /prudent+i+ə/ 'prudence'
llargària [ʎərɣáriə] /ʎarg+ar+i+ə/ 'length'
audàcia [əwðásiə] /awdas+i+ə/ 'boldness'

simpatia [simpətíə] /sinpat+ij+ə/ 'friendliness'
antologia [əntuluʒíə] /antolog+ij+ə/ 'anthology'

/j/ is deleted in these environments after Stress assignment has placed stress on the preceding /i/.

4.6. For the /+s/ of column 5, rows 10−11 (the past subjunctive), e.g. *cantés* [kəntés] 'sing' (1, 3sg), *valguéssim* [bəlɣésim] 'be worth' (1pl), *servissin* [sərβísin] 'serve' (3pl) we have the following rule:

(39) ø → +s / $\begin{bmatrix} +\text{PRET} \\ +\text{SUBJ} \end{bmatrix}$ X_____]]

4.7. And for the gerund:

(40) ø → +nt / $\begin{bmatrix} +\text{PART} \\ -\text{PRET} \end{bmatrix}$ X ___]]

e.g. *cantant* [kəntán] 'singing', *perdent* [pərðén] 'losing', *servint* [sərβín] 'serving'. The /–t/, deleted in the majority of occurrences by a phonological rule (see VII § 4), is pronounced before unstressed pronouns beginning with a vowel: *valent-ho* [bəléntu] 'being worth it', *dormint-hi* [durmínti] 'sleeping there'.

4.8. The rule introducing the /+d/ of the regular participle (column 6, row 12) is:

(41) ø → +d / $\begin{bmatrix} +\text{PART} \\ +\text{PRET} \end{bmatrix}$ X ___]]

Rules (25), (27), (29), (41) as given account (together with the rule neutralizing voicedness in word-final obstruents) for the regular past participles in *–at/–ada*, etc., *–ut/–uda*, etc., and *–it/–ida*, etc. There are a considerable number of athematic participles of classes II and III which must be lexically marked with exception features, e.g. [–rule (25)] or [–rule (27)] / $\begin{bmatrix} \overline{+\text{PART}} \\ +\text{PRET} \end{bmatrix}$.

Disregarding for a moment the suppletive participles, of which, in fact, there are not more than half a dozen or so, we can observe the following combinations of verb stems with the participal /+d/ when (25), (27) have not applied to insert a vowel. Where possible I give the feminine form of the participle, which reveals voicedness in the resulting consonant.

(42) /–j+d/: *treta* 'taken' [trétə] /trɛj+d+ə/
 dita 'said' [dítə] /dij+d+ə/
 duta 'brought' [dutə] /duj+d+ə/
 feta 'made' [fétə] /fej+d+ə/ (Though *fer* has many suppletive stems, /fej/ with final /j/ necessarily also underlies the imperfect tense forms, as we shall see.)

(43) /—v+d/: *escrita* 'written' [əskɾítə] /skriv+d+ə/
cf. *escriure*

(44) /—Vr+d/: *morta* 'dead' [mɔ́rtə] /mɔr+d+ə/
oferta 'offered' [ufɛ́rtə] /ufɛr+d+ə/

(45) /—Vrs+d/: *torta* 'twisted' [tɔ́rtə] /tɔrs+d+ə/ cf.
tòrcer

(46) /—Cr+d/: *soferta* 'suffered' [sufɛ́rtə] /sufr+d+ə/
cf. *sofrir*
coberta 'covered' [kuβɛ́rtə]/kubr+d+ə/
cf. *cobrir*
oberta 'opened' [uβɛ́rtə] /ɔbr+d+ə/
cf. *obrir*

(47) /—Cl+d/: *omplerta* 'filled' [umplɛ́rtə] /onpl+d+ə/
cf. *omplir*
establerta 'established' [əstəbblɛ́rtə]
/stabbl+d+ə/ cf. *establir*
suplerta 'supplied' [suplɛ́rtə[/supl+d+ə/
cf. *suplir*
reblerta 'filled in' [rəbblɛ́rtə]/rabbl+d+ə/
cf. *reblir*
completra 'fulfilled' [kumplɛ́rtə]
/kunpl+d+ə/ cf. *complir*

(48) /—Vl+d/: *resolta* 'resolved' [rəzɔ́ltə] /razɔl+d+ə/
(or /re+sɔl+d+ə/ with s → z/V+____V?)
dissolta 'dissolved' [disɔ́ltə] /dis+sɔl+d+ə/
absolta 'absolved' [əpsɔ́ltə] /ab+sɔl+d+ə/
molta 'ground' [mɔ́ltə] /mɔl+d+ə/

(49) /—ɔn+d/: *postos* (M pl) 'laid' (of eggs) [pɔ́stus]
/pɔn+d+s/ cf. *pondre*
resposta 'replied' [rəspɔ́stə] /raspɔn+d+ə/
cf. *respondre*
composta 'composed' [kumpɔ́stə]
/kɔn+pɔn+d+ə/

100   Verb morphology

(50)   /–en+d/: *encesa* 'lit' [ənsézə] /ansen+d+ə/
       cf. *encendre*
       estesa 'extended' [əstézə] /asten+d+ə/
       cf. *estendre*
       etc.

(51)   /–ɛn+d/: *presa* 'taken' [pɾézə] /prɛn+d+ə/
       cf. *prendre*
       despesa 'spent' [dəspézə] /daspɛn+d+ə/
       cf. *despendre*
       ofesa 'offended' [ufézə] /ufɛn+d+ə/
       cf. *ofendre*
       etc.

(52)   /–ɛɲ+d/: *empesa* 'pushed' [əmpézə] /ampɛɲ+d+ə/
       cf. *empènyer*
       atesa 'reached' [ətézə] /atɛɲ+d+ə/
       cf. *atènyer*

(52a) /–im+d/: *impresa* 'printed' [impɾézə] /inprim+d+ə/
       cf. *imprimir*

(53)   /–on+d/: *fosa* 'melted' [fózə] /fon+d+ə/ cf. *fondre*
       confosa 'confused' [kuɱfózə]
       /kɔn+fon+d+ə/ cf. *confondre*
       tosa 'shorn' [tózə] /ton+d+ə/ cf. *tondre*

(54)   /–an+d/: *romasa* 'remaining' [rumázə]
       /ruman+d+ə/ cf. *romandre*

(55)   /–t+d/: *permesa* 'permitted' [pərmézə]
       /parmɛt+d+ə/ cf. *permetre*
       promesa 'promised' [pɾumézə]
       /prumɛt+d+ə/ cf. *prometre*
       emesa 'emitted' [əmézə] /amɛt+d+ə/
       cf. *emetre*

The phenomena these examples show can be expressed by means of the following partly ordered rules:

Verb morphology

(56) n → s / ɔ____+d #   (examples (49))

(57) $\begin{bmatrix} +\text{syll} \\ \langle -\text{back} \rangle \end{bmatrix}$ $\begin{bmatrix} -\text{vocal} \\ +\text{cons} \\ -\text{labial} \\ -\text{cont} \end{bmatrix}$ + $\begin{bmatrix} -\text{syllab} \\ -\text{labial} \\ +\text{voiced} \\ +\text{anter} \end{bmatrix}$
　　　　1　　　　　　2　　　　　3　　　4

⇒ $[\langle +\text{low}\rangle]$ ø 3 ø $\begin{bmatrix} +\text{obstr} \\ -\text{labial} \\ +\text{voiced} \\ -\text{distr} \end{bmatrix}$
　　　1　　　　　　　　5

Rule (57) accounts for the examples with [z]:(50)–(55), converting front vowels to /ɛ/ before it :(50)–(52a), (55).

(58) ø → r / Cl____+d #   (examples (47))

(59) ø → ɛ / C____r+d #   (examples (46), (47))

(60) $\begin{bmatrix} +\text{obstr} \\ -\text{cont} \\ +\text{coron} \end{bmatrix}$ → [−voiced] / C +____#

(examples (42)–(49))

Rule (60) which unvoices the participial morph /+d/ after a consonant applies after (57) which "bleeds" it.

(61) $\begin{bmatrix} -\text{vocal} \\ \langle +\text{coron} \rangle \end{bmatrix}$ → ø

/ $\langle [+\text{cons}] \rangle$____+ $\begin{bmatrix} +\text{obstr} \\ -\text{cont} \\ +\text{coron} \end{bmatrix}$ #

Rule (61) deals with examples (42), (43) and (45), deleting /j/ and /v/ before /+t/, and /s/ between a consonant and /+t/ (example (45)), leaving the irregular participle *vist* [bíst] 'seen' unaffected, as also the examples in (49).

4.9. There remain three more affix vowels to introduce in verb forms: 1) /+i/ in the subjunctive (column 6), 2) /+a/ in the past indicative (column 6), and 3) /+ε/ in the 1st and 2nd plural present of classes I and II (column 7, rows 3 and 5). As Table 1 shows, [i] occurs phonetically in the singular and 3rd plural present subjunctive. Rule (24), the Truncation rule, means there is no obstacle to letting the rule introduce /+i/ throughout in the present tense, provided that the /+ε/ affix follows in the 1st and 2nd plural of classes I and II. It is not only desirable, but also necessary that the addition of /+i/ be extended throughout the past subjunctive in order for Stress-assignment to apply correctly. For after the application of Truncation (24) /kant+a+s/ *cantes* 'you sing' would not otherwise be distinguishable in a way relevant to Stress assignment from /kant+e+s/ *cantés* '(1 or 3sg past subj.). Stress assignment applies correctly to /kant+e+s+i/ giving /kant+é+s+i/, and /+i/ will be deleted later. So for the subjunctive morph /+i/ we have:

(62) ø → +i / [+SUBJ] X ____ #

[−ə] appears in rows 6 and 9 of Table 1 — throughout the imperfect tense and in the plural and 2sg of the preterite. Note that these persons are just those in which [−i] is phonetically present in the past subjunctive. This suggests that we can have /+a/ inserted throughout the past indicative, and have just one rule deleting final vowels, after the other person/number morphs are introduced, in the [+PERF] tenses. Thus

(63) ø → +a / $\begin{bmatrix} +\text{PRET} \\ -\text{SUBJ} \end{bmatrix}$ X ____ #

The rule introducing /+ε/ (column 7) is:

Verb morphology 103

(64)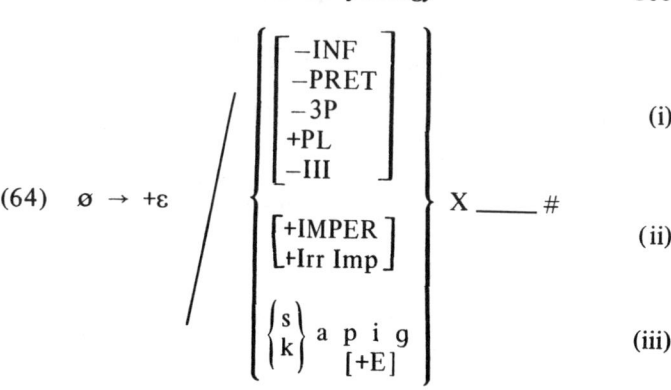

Part (i) of this rule deals with I, II column 7, rows 3 and 5. Part (ii): Normally the imperative forms 2sg and 2pl are identical with the 3sg and 2pl present indicative respectively. In a few verbs of class II, however, the imperative resembles the present subjunctive but without the distinctive [−i−] infix. Thus we have the following, which is a complete list, excluding compounds of these verbs:

dir 'to say' sg [díɣəs], pl [diɣɛ́w]
ser 'to be' sg [síɣəs], pl [siɣɛ́w]
estar 'to be' sg [əstíɣəs], pl [əstiɣɛ́w]
poder 'to be able' sg [púɣəs], pl [puɣɛ́w]
saber 'to know' sg [sápiɣəs], pl [səpiɣɛ́w]
tenir 'to have' sg [tíŋgəs], pl [tiŋgɛ́w], also sg [té], pl [təníw]
veure 'to see' sg [béʒəs], pl [bəʒɛ́w]
voler 'to want' sg [búlɣəs], pl [bulɣɛ́w]

N.B. The two types of imperative of *tenir* are not in free variation; the choice depends on the Deep Structure underlying the subject of the sentence. In terms of a Fillmore (1968) type of case-grammar, *té, teniu* occur with Agentive subjects, *tingues, tingueu* with subjects derived from other cases. All these verbs will

have a morphological class marker [+Irr Imp]
(="irregular imperative").

Part (iii) : The present subjunctive of *saber* 'to know' and *cabre* 'to fit' resembles their irregular imperative forms: of *saber* 1sg [sápiɣə], 2sg [sápiɣəs], 3sg [sápiɣə], 1pl [səpiɣém], 2pl [səpiɣéw] 3pl [sápiɣən]. With these forms and the irregular imperatives which have [ɛ] when stressed, it seems appropriate to introduce /+ɛ/ throughout, which when unstressed is reduced to [ə] by the usual Vowel-reduction rule. All the [-ém] and [-éw] forms are accounted for by part (i) of the rule, so parts (ii) and (iii) are of very little generality.

4.10. Before the final-vowel deletion rule mentioned in §4.9, the person morphs referred to in §2.1 are introduced:

$$(65) \quad \emptyset \rightarrow \begin{Bmatrix} +s \Big/ \begin{bmatrix} +2P \\ -PL \\ \begin{Bmatrix} -IMPER \\ +Irr\ Imp \end{Bmatrix} \end{bmatrix} & (i) \\ \begin{Bmatrix} +m \\ +w \\ _1+n \end{Bmatrix}_1 \Big/ \begin{bmatrix} \begin{Bmatrix} +1P \\ +2P \\ _1+3P \end{Bmatrix}_1 \\ +PL \end{bmatrix} \end{Bmatrix} X\underline{\quad}\#$$

By part (i) of this rule /+s/ is introduced in the imperative only when this is irregular as mentioned above; otherwise the imperative singulars are e.g. *canta* [kántə] 'sing', *val* [bál] 'be worth', *perd* [pért] 'lose', *dorm* [dórm] 'sleep', *serveix* [sərβéʃ] 'serve'.

Now the perfect tense vowel-deletion rule can be formulated thus:

$$(66) \quad V \rightarrow \emptyset \Big/ \begin{bmatrix} -INF \\ +PERF \end{bmatrix} X\underline{\quad}\#$$

Verb morphology

Only the 1sg and 3sg forms meet the structural description of this rule, since in the other persons there is now a consonant before the rightmost #.

5.1. The formation of the future tense and the related conditional is somewhat complex. As mentioned above § 1.2.2, the peculiarities of the future tense, such as suffix accent in all persons, can best be accounted for by supposing that the ending consists of the auxiliary verb /av/ (class IIA), which occurs in a similar form to the future suffix in the compound perfect tense *he cantat* 'I have sung', and in the syntagm *naver de* 'to have to'. In these uses there are some optional forms which are used alongside those resembling the future suffix. The common forms are:

Future		Perfect	
cantaré	[kəntəɾé]	he cantat	[ékəntát]
cantaràs	[kəntəɾás]	has cantat	[əskəntát]
cantarà	[kəntəɾá]	ha cantat	[əkəntát]
cantarem	[kəntəɾɛ́m]	hem cantat	[ɛ́mkəntát]
cantareu	[kəntəɾɛ́w]	heu cantat	[ɛ́wkəntát]
cantaran	[kəntəɾán]	han cantat	[əŋkəntát]

haver de	
he de cantar	[éðəkəntá]
has de cantar	[ázðəkəntá]
ha de cantar	[áðəkəntá]
hem de cantar	[ɛ́mdəkəntá]
heu de cantar	[ɛ́wðəkəntá]
han de cantar	[ándəkəntá]

The unaccented forms of the auxiliary in the Compound Perfect are generated as a result of the boundary adjustment rule (22) which does not affect the present question. In the conditional tense the similarity to the forms of /av/ used elsewhere is not so apparent:

106 Verb morphology

Conditional		haver de (imperfect)	
cantaria	[kəntəría]	havia de cantar	[əβíəðəkəntá]
cantaries	[kəntəríəs]	havies de cantar	[əβíəzðəkəntá]
cantaria	[kəntəría]	havia de cantar	[əβíəðəkəntá]
cantaríem	[kəntəríəm]	havíem de cantar	[əβíəmdəkəntá]
cantaríeu	[kəntəríəw]	havíeu de cantar	[əβíəwðəkəntá]
cantarien	[kəntəríən]	havien de cantar	[əβíəndəkəntá]

Other than as a conditional suffix the imperfect tense of /av/ is regular. Nevertheless the structure Infinitive + Stressed suffix is the same in the conditional tense as in the future. It seems simpler to introduce a special rule reducing /av/ in the conditional than to separate $\begin{bmatrix} +FUT \\ +PRET \end{bmatrix}$ and $\begin{bmatrix} +FUT \\ -PRET \end{bmatrix}$ in the rule (21) and provide a rule similar (but not identical: N.B. [−íə−] in all classes, not [−áβə−]) to the imperfect tense inflection rules.

Starting from the structure displayed in rule (21), I shall now explain the special adjustment rules and other minor rules necessary for the future and conditional tenses. After the application of (23), with *cantar* as a type verb, the structure for the 1sg future (*cantaré* 'I shall sing') is

$$\llbracket_V \# \llbracket_{Aux} \begin{bmatrix} k\ a\ n\ t \\ -PART \\ +FUT \end{bmatrix} \rrbracket_{Aux}$$

$$\llbracket_V \# \begin{bmatrix} a\ v \\ +1P \\ -PL \\ -PRET \\ -SUBJ \end{bmatrix} \# \rrbracket_V \# \rrbracket_V$$

and for the 3pl conditional (*cantarien* 'they would sing') the structure is

Verb morphology 107

$$[_V \# [_{Aux} \begin{bmatrix} k\,a\,n\,t \\ -PART \\ +FUT \end{bmatrix}]_{Aux}$$

$$[_V \# \begin{bmatrix} a\,v \\ +3P \\ +PL \\ -PERF \\ +PRET \end{bmatrix} \#]_V \#]_V$$

To deal with the special forms of *haver* in the conditional suffix, a possible approach is to delete the stem-final /v/ there.

(67) $\quad v \rightarrow \emptyset \;/\; X\,]_{Aux}\, [_V \# \begin{bmatrix} a \\ +PRET \end{bmatrix}$ ——+Y $\#\,]_V$

that is, /av+i+j+a/ etc. becomes /a +i+j+a/ etc. and the initial /a/ becomes subject to the Truncation rule III (24).

The future endings [–é], [–ás], [–á], [–ém], [–éw], [–án] are also the independent forms of the verb *haver de* 'to have to' and of *haver-hi* (3rd person only *hi ha* [iá] 'there is', etc.). And, with [ás], [á], [án] replaced by unstressed [əs], [ə], [ən], (rule (22)), they are the forms of the perfect auxiliary as in *he cantat* 'I have sung', etc. A suppletion rule is required for the 1sg *he/–é* :

(68) $\begin{bmatrix} av \\ +II \\ +A \end{bmatrix} \rightarrow \begin{bmatrix} e \\ -\text{rule (30)} \end{bmatrix} \Bigg/ \begin{bmatrix} +1P \\ -PL \\ -PRET \\ -SUBJ \end{bmatrix}$

The other forms are perhaps best interpreted as having undergone /v/–deletion in a similar way to what (67) provides for; the remaining /a/ of the root will be deleted before a following vowel by the Truncation rule

108   *Verb morphology*

(24) in the 1st and 2nd plural [ém], [éw]. This can be done by generalizing rule (67) as follows:

(69) $\quad v \rightarrow \emptyset \Big/ \langle X \rrbracket_{Aux} \rangle_b \: \llbracket_V \# \begin{bmatrix} a \\ -INF \\ \langle +PRET \rangle_a \end{bmatrix} \underline{\quad\quad} (+Y) \# \rrbracket_V$

condition: if a, then b.

We now have the following derivations from the verb $\begin{bmatrix} av \\ +II \\ +A \end{bmatrix}$ when [−PRET]:

by (64) and (65)	#av#	#av+s#	#av#	#av+ɛ+m#	#av+ɛ+w#	#av+n#
by (68)	#e#					
by (69)		#a+s#	#a#	#a+ɛ+m#	#a+ɛ+w#	#a+n#
by (24)				#+ɛ+m#	#+ɛ+w#	
by II (15)	#é#	#á+s#	#á#	#+é+m#	#+é+w#	#á+n#

5.2. Before presenting some sample derivations some additions to the Stress-assignment rule are necessary. The rule as given (II (15)) accounts for all the forms in Table 1 except the 1st and 2nd plurals of all the past finite tenses, which have recessive stress, e.g. –àvem, –àveu, –íem, –íeu, –àrem, etc., –éssim, etc. It looks as if an additional line in the rule would account for this, as follows:

(70) $\quad V \rightarrow [+stress] \: / \: + \underline{\quad\quad} C V + \begin{bmatrix} -syllab \\ +labial \end{bmatrix} \#$

applying disjunctively before II (15). The specification of

Verb morphology

+ at the left of the environment would prevent stress being assigned to the root in e.g. /kant+ɛ+m/ *cantem*, /sarb+i+m/ *servim* and giving *[kántəm], *[sárβim]. However, this cannot be right, for recessive stress occurs in the imperfect of /–j/–stem verbs of class II, and falls on the *root*, thus *crèiem* [krέjəm] /krɛj+a+m/ (←/krɛj+i+j+a+m/ by a rule to be discussed) 'we believed'. *vèieu* 'you could see', *duien* [dújən] 'they were bringing', etc. So it seems that the rule must mention past tense specifically. So a revised form of the Major Stress Rule would be:

(71)

$$V \rightarrow [+\text{stress}] \ / \ [\![X \left\{ \begin{array}{l} \begin{bmatrix} +\text{PRET} \\ -\text{INF} \end{bmatrix} \underline{\quad} C V + \begin{bmatrix} -\text{syllab} \\ +\text{labial} \end{bmatrix} \\ \underline{\quad} C_0 \ ([+\text{segm}]) \langle \begin{bmatrix} +\text{syll} \\ +\text{high} \end{bmatrix} + V \rangle \langle + \begin{bmatrix} -\text{vocal} \\ +\text{coron} \\ -\text{distr} \end{bmatrix} \rangle \end{array} \right\} \#]\!]_{<N,A>}$$

This formulation, however, obscures the fact that recessive stress in these past tense forms is basically the same as that provided by the Minor Stress rule II(16); an alternative to the modification of II(15) along the lines of (71) would be a rule assigning the [+E] feature so that the structural description of II(16) would be met. So rather than (70) or (71) we would have

(72) $\quad V \rightarrow [+E] \ / \ \begin{bmatrix} +\text{PRET} \\ -\text{INF} \end{bmatrix} X \underline{\quad} + \begin{bmatrix} -\text{syllab} \\ +\text{labial} \end{bmatrix} \#$

On the other hand, the stress pattern of the preterite tenses can be seen as a generalization of the Major Stress Rule, which effectively, as formulated in II(15), ignores all inflections for the purpose of stress assignment except for word-final /+m/ and /+w/. If the rule is generalized so as to parenthesize word-final (+C), the exceptional forms become the non-finite verb forms and the non-pasts ending in /+m/ or /+w/; in these the inflectional consonant "attracts" stress. The non-finite forms end in /+r/ —the infinitive— by rule (36), /+d/ —the past participle— by rule (41) or /+t/ by rule (60), /+nt/ —the gerund— by rule (40). /+nt/ as two consonants will not meet the structural description anyway. The others could be excluded by indexed angle-brackets requiring some non-occurring segment if the stem is [+INF]; thus:

(73)
$$V \rightarrow [+\text{stress}] / \left[\!\!\left[X \begin{bmatrix} \langle +\text{INF} \rangle_a \\ \langle -\text{PRET} \rangle_c \end{bmatrix} \text{---} C_0 ([+\text{segm}]) \left\langle \begin{bmatrix} +\text{syll} \\ +\text{high} \end{bmatrix} +V \right. \right.$$
$$\left. \left(+ \begin{bmatrix} \langle \begin{bmatrix} -\text{syll} \\ +\text{obstr} \\ +\text{cont} \end{bmatrix} \rangle_b \\ \langle +\text{coron} \rangle_d \end{bmatrix} \right) \right\rangle \# \left.\!\!\right]\!\!\right] \langle N, A \rangle$$

condition: if a, then b; if c, then d.

In the b angle bracket [+obstr, +cont] permits /s/ and thus allows correct stress on feminine plural participles as in *les he perdudes* [ləz é pərðúðəs] 'I have lost them(F)' where the participle has the form /pɛrd+u+d+ə+s/.

The last alternative is for /+r/, /+d/, /+t/ to be excluded from the rightmost parenthesis by strictly phonological features, requiring that the relevant consonant to be ignored for stress assignment should be [−vocal] and either [−obstr] or [+cont]. (The class $\begin{Bmatrix} [-\text{obstr}] \\ [+\text{cont}] \end{Bmatrix}$ is probably a natural class (see Zwicky, 1972) and should be definable without braces. Perhaps [−plosive] would be an appropriate feature, enabling the establishment of a hierarchy such as Zwicky refers to.) Anyway, using phonological features here the rule appears a little simpler:

Verb morphology

(74)

$$V \rightarrow [+\text{stress}] \,/\, \left[\!\!\left[X \left\langle [-\text{PRET}] \right\rangle_c \underline{} C_0 ([+\text{segm}]) \left\langle \begin{bmatrix} +\text{syll} \\ +\text{high} \end{bmatrix} +V \right\rangle_1 \right.\right.$$
$$\left.\left. \left(+ \begin{bmatrix} -\text{vocal} \\ \{\begin{smallmatrix} -\text{obstr} \\ +\text{cont} \end{smallmatrix}\} \\ \langle +\text{coron}\rangle_d \end{bmatrix} \right) \# \right]\!\!\right] \left\langle N,A \right\rangle_1$$

condition: if c, then d.

Sample derivations:

1. *temeries* 'you would fear'

(21), (23)	⟦$_V$#⟦$_{Aux}$	$\begin{bmatrix} t\ e\ m \\ -\text{PART} \\ +\text{FUT} \\ +\text{II} \\ -\text{A} \end{bmatrix}$	⟧$_{Aux}$⟦$_V$#	$\begin{bmatrix} a\ v \\ +2P \\ -\text{PL} \\ +\text{PRET} \\ -\text{PERF} \\ +\text{II} \\ +A \end{bmatrix}$	#⟧$_V$ # ⟧$_V$
(35), (36)		t e m + r		a v + i	
(38), (63), (65)		t e m + r		a v + i+j+a+s	
(69)		t e m + r		a ø + i+j+a+s	
(24)		t e m + r		ø + i+j+a+s	
(74)		t e m + r		+ í+j+a+s	
I(19) + /j/– deletion		t e mə+ r		+ í ø+a+s	
II(25) etc.		t ə mə r		í ə s	

2. *cantarem* 'we shall sing'

(21), (23)	⟦$_V$#⟦$_{Aux}$	$\begin{bmatrix} \text{kant} \\ -\text{PART} \\ +\text{FUT} \\ +\text{I} \end{bmatrix}$	⟧$_{Aux}$⟦$_V$#	$\begin{bmatrix} a\ v \\ +1P \\ +\text{PL} \\ -\text{FUT} \\ -\text{PRET} \\ +\text{II} \\ +A \end{bmatrix}$	#⟧$_V$ #⟧$_V$
(29)		kant + a		a v	
(36)		kant + a +r		a v + ɛ	
(64)		kant + a +r		a v + ɛ	
(65)		kant + a +r		a v + ɛ + m	
(69)		kant + a +r		a ø + ɛ + m	
(24)		kant + a +r		ø + ɛ́ + m	
(74)		kant + a +r		+ ɛ́ + m	
II(25) etc		kənt ə r		ɛ́ m	

Verb morphology

6.1. In order to complete the picture of verb morphology, and to reveal to what extent what are usually called irregularities have been dealt with by the rules already given, I shall now present the various forms of verbs with suppletive conjugations. The verbs with irregular participles (i.e. either [−rule (25)]/[$\overline{\text{+PART}}$ +PRET] or [−rule (27)]/[$\overline{\text{+PART}}$ +PRET] have been discussed already (§4.8), as have those with irregular imperatives (§4.9). There remain 32 verbs and their compounds (cf. Fabra, 1968a:51−60; Badia, 1962:351−84) for whose alternations no well-motivated simplification can obviously be established. I list them below with their suppletive stems disjunctively ordered, i.e. the last line of the brace is the stem that appears "elsewhere", and indicate where appropriate which rules do not apply; it is to be understood that stem alternants to which a conjugation class is not assigned do not undergo rules in which morpheme classes are specifically mentioned. On the right I place a sample of illustrative forms in conventional orthography; the numbers are those of the rows of tables 1−3 to which the forms given correspond.

1. *venir* 'to come'

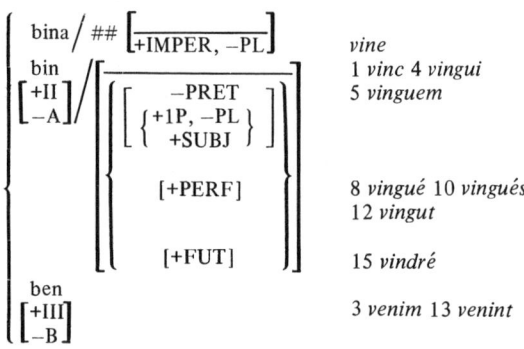

vine
1 *vinc* 4 *vingui*
5 *vinguem*

8 *vingué* 10 *vingués*
12 *vingut*

15 *vindré*

3 *venim* 13 *venint*

The imperative *vine* occurs only in the simple verb; the compounds have the singular imperatives *convén* 'agree', *intervén* or *intervé* 'intervene', *pervén* 'reach', *prevén* 'warn', *provén* 'originate', *revén* 'return', *sobrevén* 'occur suddenly', *subvén* 'subsidize'. I shall return to this question presently.

2. *tenir* (a) 'to hold', (b) 'to have'

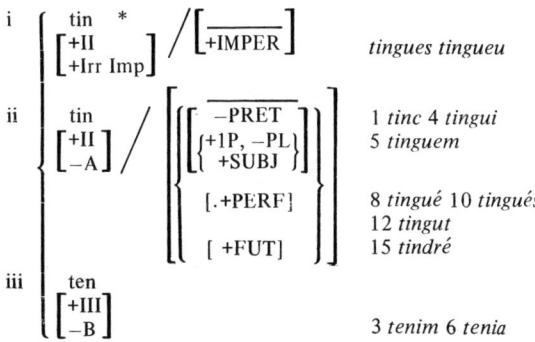

i [tin *, +II, +Irr Imp] / [+IMPER] *tingues tingueu*

ii [tin, +II, −A] / [[−PRET, {+1P, −PL}, +SUBJ]] 1 *tinc* 4 *tingui*
5 *tinguem*

[.+PERF] 8 *tingué* 10 *tingués*
12 *tingut*
[+FUT] 15 *tindré*

iii [ten, +III, −B]
3 *tenim* 6 *tenia*

*obligatory in *tenir* (b) and optional in the compounds. Stem i) gives *tingues*, *tingueu* in the imperative of *tenir* 'to have' (cf. *tingueu paciència* 'have patience'); *tenir* 'to hold' has imperatives *té* or *ten* and *teniu*, and in the compounds we have *detén* 'detain', *mantén* 'maintain', *obtén* 'obtain', *retén* 'retain', *sostén* 'support', or *detingues*, etc.

It is noteworthy that the regular imperatives of *tenir* and *venir*, except for *té* and *intervé* do not undergo deletion of final /−n/, whereas the 3sg pres ind. does in the same phonetic environment (see Brasington, 1972:101−19). *Tenir* and *venir* are the only verbs which undergo final /−n/−deletion at all, though this process is common, but not universal, in nouns and adjectives, (see VII §1). Verbs in general may be marked [−/n/−deletion] and the relevant forms of *tenir* and *venir* [+/n/−deletion].

114   *Verb morphology*

3. *córrer* 'to run'

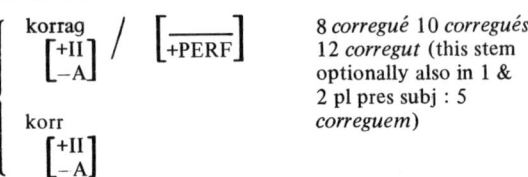

8 *corregué* 10 *coregués*
12 *corregut* (this stem
optionally also in 1 &
2 pl pres subj : 5
correguem)

4. *conèixer* 'to know', *parèixer* 'to seem'

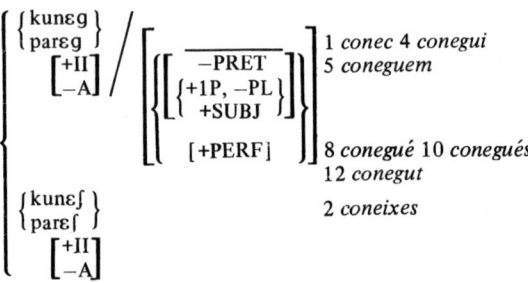

1 *conec* 4 *conegui*
5 *coneguem*

8 *conegué* 10 *conegués*
12 *conegut*

2 *coneixes*

5. *créixer* 'to grow', *néixer* 'to be born', *merèixer* 'to deserve'

{ { kresk
    nesk
    marɛsk } / [+PERF]
  [+II]   [+INF]
  [−A]

  { kreʃ
    neʃ
    marɛʃ }
  [+II]
  [−A] }

12 *crescut*
(optionally also in
all [+PERF] and
1 & 2pl pres subj:
8 *cresqué*
10 *cresqués* 5 *cresquem*)

2 *creixes*

Verb morphology

6. *viure* 'to live'

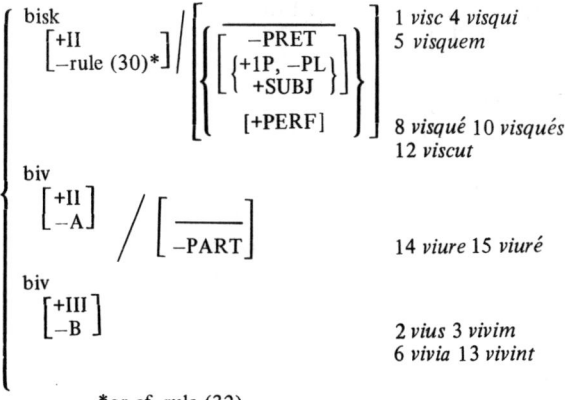

1 *visc* 4 *visqui*
5 *visquem*

8 *visqué* 10 *visqués*
12 *viscut*

14 *viure* 15 *viuré*

2 *vius* 3 *vivim*
6 *vivia* 13 *vivint*

*or cf. rule (32)

7. *escriure* 'to write'

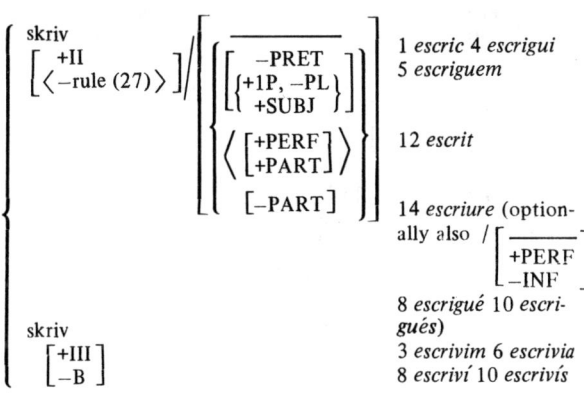

1 *escric* 4 *escrigui*
5 *escriguem*

12 *escrit*

14 *escriure* (optionally also / [̄ ̄ ̄ ̄ ̄ ̄ / +PERF / −INF])
8 *escrigué* 10 *escrigués*
3 *escrivim* 6 *escrivia*
8 *escriví* 10 *escrivís*

8. *voler* 'to want'

$$\left\{\begin{array}{l} \begin{bmatrix} \text{buʎ} \\ [-\text{rule (30)}] \end{bmatrix} \Big/ \begin{bmatrix} \overline{} \\ -\text{PRET} \\ -\text{SUBJ} \\ +1\text{P} \\ -\text{PL} \end{bmatrix} \qquad 1\ vull \\[2em] \begin{bmatrix} \text{bɔl} \\ \begin{bmatrix} +\text{II} \\ +\text{A} \end{bmatrix} \end{bmatrix} \Big/ \begin{bmatrix} \overline{} \\ -\text{PRET} \\ -\text{SUBJ} \end{bmatrix} \qquad 2\ vols\ 3\ volem \\[2em] \begin{bmatrix} \text{bul} \\ \begin{bmatrix} +\text{II} \\ +\text{A} \\ +\text{Irr Imp} \end{bmatrix} \end{bmatrix} \qquad\qquad\qquad \begin{array}{l} 6\ volia\ 10\ volgués \\ 4\ vulgui\ 12\ volgut \end{array} \end{array}\right.$$

or equivalently:

$$\left\{\begin{array}{l} \begin{bmatrix} \text{buʎ} \\ [-\text{rule (30)}] \end{bmatrix} \Big/ \begin{bmatrix} \overline{} \\ -\text{PRET} \\ -\text{SUBJ} \\ +1\text{P} \\ -\text{PL} \end{bmatrix} \qquad 1\ vull \\[2em] \begin{bmatrix} \text{bul} \\ \begin{bmatrix} +\text{II} \\ +\text{A} \\ +\text{Irr Imp} \end{bmatrix} \end{bmatrix} \Big/ \begin{bmatrix} \left\{\begin{bmatrix} -\text{PRET} \\ +\text{SUBJ} \end{bmatrix}\right\} \\ [+\text{IMPER}\ ] \\ [+\text{PERF}\ ] \end{bmatrix} \quad \begin{array}{l} 4\ vulgui\ 5\ vulguem \\ \\ \text{Imper } vulgues \\ 8\ volgué\ 10\ volgués \\ 12\ volgut \end{array} \\[2em] \begin{bmatrix} \text{bɔl} \\ \begin{bmatrix} +\text{II} \\ +\text{A} \end{bmatrix} \end{bmatrix} \qquad\qquad\qquad \begin{array}{l} 2\ vols\ 6\ volia \\ 15\ voldré \end{array} \end{array}\right.$$

Observe that when the root of *voler* is unstressed it is pronounced [bul–] and the UR is not revealed to be specifically /bul/ or /bɔl/.

9. *poder* 'to be able'

$$\left\{\begin{array}{l} \text{pug} \\ \begin{bmatrix} +\text{II} \\ +\text{A} \\ +\text{Irr Imp} \end{bmatrix} \end{array} \Bigg/ \left[\left\{ \begin{bmatrix} \overline{-\text{PRET}} \\ \{+1\text{P}, -\text{PL}\} \\ +\text{SUBJ} \end{bmatrix} \right\} \atop \begin{array}{c} [+\text{IMPER}] \\ [+\text{PERF}] \end{array} \right] \right.$$

1 *puc* 4 *pugui*
5 *puguem*

Imper *pugues*
8 *pogué* 10 *pogués*
12 *pogut*

$$\text{pɔd} \quad \begin{bmatrix} +\text{II} \\ +\text{A} \end{bmatrix}$$

2 *pots* 3 *podem*
13 *podent*

10. *saber* 'to know'

$$\left\{\begin{array}{l} \text{se} \\ [-\text{rule (30)}] \end{array} \Bigg/ \begin{bmatrix} \overline{-\text{PRET}} \\ -\text{SUBJ} \\ +1\text{P} \\ -\text{PL} \end{bmatrix} \right.$$

1 *sé*

$$\begin{array}{l} \text{sapig} \\ \begin{bmatrix} -\text{rule (62)} \\ +\text{rule (64)} \\ +\text{Irr Imp} \\ <+\text{E}> \end{bmatrix} \end{array} \Bigg/ \left[\left\{ \begin{bmatrix} \overline{-\text{PRET}} \\ +\text{SUBJ} \end{bmatrix} \right\} \atop [+\text{IMPER}] \atop \left\langle \left\{ \begin{array}{l} +3\text{P} \\ -\text{PL} \end{array} \right\} \right\rangle \right]$$

4 *sàpiga*
5 *sapiguem*

Imper *sàpigues*

$$\text{sab} \quad \begin{bmatrix} +\text{II} \\ +\text{A} \end{bmatrix}$$

2 *saps* 3 *sabem*
6 *sabia*

118   *Verb morphology*

11. *cabre* 'to fit'

$$\left\{ \begin{array}{l} \text{kapig} \begin{bmatrix} -\text{rule (62)} \\ +\text{rule (64)} \\ \langle +\text{E} \rangle \end{bmatrix} \Big/ \begin{bmatrix} -\text{PRET} \\ +\text{SUBJ} \\ \langle \{ \begin{smallmatrix} +3\text{P} \\ -\text{PL} \end{smallmatrix} \} \rangle \end{bmatrix} & 4 \textit{càpiga } 5 \textit{ capiguem} \\[1em] \text{kab} \begin{bmatrix} +\text{II} \\ +\text{A} \end{bmatrix} \Big/ \begin{bmatrix} \overline{+\text{PART}} \end{bmatrix} & 13 \textit{ cabent } [\text{kəβén}] \\[1em] \text{kab} \begin{bmatrix} +\text{II} \\ -\text{A} \end{bmatrix} & \begin{array}{l} 2 \textit{ caps } 3 \textit{ cabem} \\ 14 \textit{ cabre} \end{array} \end{array} \right.$$

12. *estar* 'to be'

$$\left\{ \begin{array}{l} \text{stig} \begin{bmatrix} +\text{II} \\ -\text{A} \\ +\text{Irr Imp} \end{bmatrix} \Big/ \begin{bmatrix} -\text{PRET} \\ \{ \begin{smallmatrix} +1\text{P}, -\text{PL} \\ +\text{SUBJ} \end{smallmatrix} \} \end{bmatrix} & \begin{array}{l} 1 \textit{ estic } 4 \textit{ estigui} \\ 5 \textit{ estiguem} \end{array} \\[1em] \text{sta } [+\text{I}] & \begin{bmatrix} +\text{PERF} \\ +\text{INF} \end{bmatrix} & 8 \textit{ estigué } 10 \textit{ estigués} \\ & [+\text{IMPER}] & \text{Imper } \textit{estigues} \\[1em] & & \begin{array}{l} 2 \textit{ estàs } 6 \textit{ estava} \\ 12 \textit{ estat } 14 \textit{ estar} \end{array} \end{array} \right.$$

6.2. In the foregoing list of verbs the frequency with which $\left\{ \begin{bmatrix} -\text{PRET} \\ \{ \begin{smallmatrix} +1\text{P}, -\text{PL} \\ +\text{SUBJ} \end{smallmatrix} \} \\ [+\text{PERF}] \end{bmatrix} \right\}$ appears in the conditioning environment of one of the alternating stems, which often terminates in /g/, suggests that a generalization is being missed. Let us suppose that for the twelve types of verb just listed the following are the underlying lexical forms.

Verb morphology

venir : $\begin{cases} \text{bina} \ / \ \#\# \ \begin{bmatrix} \overline{\text{+IMPER}} \\ -\text{PL} \end{bmatrix} \\ \text{bin} \\ \begin{bmatrix} +\text{II} \\ -\text{A} \end{bmatrix} \end{cases}$

tenir :   tin
('hold') $\begin{bmatrix} +\text{II} \\ -\text{A} \end{bmatrix}$

tenir :   tin
('have') $\begin{bmatrix} +\text{II} \\ -\text{A} \\ +\text{Irr Imp} \end{bmatrix}$

córrer :   korr
$\begin{bmatrix} +\text{II} \\ -\text{A} \end{bmatrix}$

conèixer : kunɛj
$\begin{bmatrix} +\text{II} \\ -\text{A} \end{bmatrix}$

créixer : krej̇
$\begin{bmatrix} +\text{II} \\ -\text{A} \end{bmatrix}$

viure :   biv
$\begin{bmatrix} +\text{II} \\ -\text{A} \end{bmatrix}$

escriure : skriv
$\begin{bmatrix} +\text{II} \\ -\text{A} \\ \langle -\text{rule (27)} \rangle \end{bmatrix} \Big/ \begin{bmatrix} \overline{\langle +\text{PERF} \rangle} \end{bmatrix}$

120 *Verb morphology*

$$voler: \begin{Bmatrix} \text{buʎ} \\ [-\text{rule (30)}] \end{Bmatrix} \Big/ \begin{bmatrix} \overline{-\text{PRET}} \\ -\text{SUBJ} \\ +1\text{P} \\ -\text{PL} \end{bmatrix}$$

$$\text{bul} \begin{bmatrix} +\text{II} \\ +\text{A} \\ +\text{Irr Imp} \end{bmatrix}$$

$$poder: \text{puw} \begin{bmatrix} +\text{II} \\ +\text{A} \\ +\text{Irr Imp} \end{bmatrix}$$

$$saber: \begin{Bmatrix} \text{se} \\ [-\text{rule 30})] \end{Bmatrix} \Big/ \begin{bmatrix} \overline{-\text{PRET}} \\ -\text{SUBJ} \\ +1\text{P} \\ -\text{PL} \end{bmatrix}$$

$$\text{sab} \begin{bmatrix} +\text{II} \\ +\text{A} \\ +\text{Irr Imp} \end{bmatrix}$$

$$cabre: \text{kab} \begin{bmatrix} +\text{II} \\ \{\langle +\text{A} \rangle\} \\ -\text{A} \end{bmatrix} \Big/ \begin{bmatrix} \overline{\langle +\text{PART} \rangle} \end{bmatrix}$$

$$estar: \text{stij} \begin{bmatrix} +\text{II} \\ -\text{A} \\ +\text{Irr Imp} \\ \langle -\text{rule (27)} \rangle \end{bmatrix} \Big/ \begin{bmatrix} \overline{\langle +\text{PART} \rangle} \end{bmatrix}$$

We now want to arrange it so that the occurrence of the other stem alternants is triggered by the absence of /+g/. The insertion of /+g/ depends on the presence of /+u/ supplied by rule (27) or rule (30). We can reorder the rules so that /+g/−insertion may come between the insertion of /+u/ and the insertion of /+i/, /+ɛʃ/ and /+a/. In place of rules (25)−(31) we will have:

(75)

(=(27))   ø → +u / $\left/ \begin{bmatrix} \left\{\begin{bmatrix} [+\text{SUBJ}] \\ [+\text{PERF}] \\ [+\text{Irr Imp}] \\ [+\text{IMPER}] \end{bmatrix}\right\} \\ +\text{II} \end{bmatrix} \right.$ ————]

(76)

(=(30))   ø → +u / $\left/ \begin{bmatrix} -\text{IMPER} \\ -\text{PRET} \\ -\text{SUBJ} \\ +1\text{P} \\ -\text{PL} \end{bmatrix} \right.$ X ————]

(77)

replaces (31)   ø → + $\begin{bmatrix} -\text{syllab} \\ -\text{labial} \\ +\text{back} \\ +\text{voiced} \end{bmatrix}$

$$/ \left\{\begin{matrix} \begin{bmatrix} -\text{syll} \\ +\text{cont} \\ -\text{coron} \end{bmatrix} \\ \begin{bmatrix} -\text{syll} \\ -\text{obstr} \\ -\text{distr} \\ \left\{\begin{matrix}+\text{PERF}\\-\text{cont}\end{matrix}\right\} \end{bmatrix} \\ \begin{bmatrix} \left\{\begin{matrix}k\ a\ b\\s\ a\ b\end{matrix}\right\} \\ \left\{\begin{bmatrix}-\text{PRET}\\+\text{SUBJ}\end{bmatrix}\atop[+\text{IMPER}]\right\} \end{bmatrix} \end{matrix}\right\} \text{———} + \begin{bmatrix}+\text{syll}\\+\text{back}\end{bmatrix}]_V$$

This is the /g/-insertion rule. N.B. As required, the mention of [+IMPER] is vacuous in the case of *cabre* since (73) has not introduced /+u/ in the imperative of this verb. This rule gives us the stems /kab+g/ (pres subj) and /sab+g/ (pres subj and imper). If we make rule (64) apply to these forms, giving e.g. /kab+g+ɛ+s/, /sab+g+n/, (74) assigns stress to the right syllable without the necessity for triggering the minor stress rule, and a subsequent minor rule:

(78)   b → pi / a ——— +g

will produce the correct output.

Verb morphology

$$(79) \left\{ \begin{array}{l} \text{biv} \to \text{bisk} \\ \int \to \text{sk} \end{array} \middle/ \left[\begin{array}{l} \text{kre} \\ \text{ne} \\ \text{mar}\varepsilon \\ +\text{PART} \\ +\text{PRET} \end{array} \right] \right\} \Big/ \, [\!\!\![\underline{} + \begin{bmatrix} +\text{syll} \\ +\text{back} \end{bmatrix}]\!\!\!]_V$$

Now a rule ordered after (75) and (79) provides for the stem alternants (of those verbs in §6.1) which occur other than before /+g/.

$$(80) \left\{ \begin{array}{l} \left[\begin{array}{l} \{\text{tin}\} \\ \{\text{bin}\}_1 \\ +\text{II} \\ -\text{A} \end{array} \right] \to \left[\begin{array}{l} \{\text{ten}\} \\ \{\text{ben}\}_1 \\ +\text{III} \\ -\text{B} \end{array} \right] \Big/ \left[\overline{-\text{FUT}} \right] \\[2em] \left[\begin{array}{l} \text{biv} \\ +\text{II} \\ -\text{A} \end{array} \right] \to \left[\begin{array}{l} +\text{III} \\ -\text{B} \end{array} \right] \Big/ \left[\overline{\left\{ \begin{array}{l} +\text{PART} \\ -\text{INF} \end{array} \right\}} \right] \\[1.5em] \text{kun}\varepsilon\text{j} \to \text{kun}\varepsilon\int \\ \text{par}\varepsilon\text{j} \to \text{par}\varepsilon\int \\ \text{skriv} \to \left[\begin{array}{l} +\text{III} \\ -\text{B} \end{array} \right] \\ \text{bul} \to \text{b}\mathrm{\supset}\text{l} \\ \text{puw} \to \text{p}\mathrm{\supset}\text{d} \\ \text{stij} \to \left[\begin{array}{l} \text{sta} \\ +\text{I} \end{array} \right] \end{array} \right\} \Big/ \, [\!\!\![\underline{}]\!\!\!]_V$$

And now the thematic infix rules (25), (28) and (29) must where appropriate operate also before /+u/ inserted by (76) in the 1sg pres ind.; thus:

(81) for (25) $\emptyset \to +\text{i} \, / \, [+\text{III}] \underline{} (+\text{u}) \,]\!\!\!]$

(82) for (28) $\emptyset \to +\varepsilon\int \, / \, \begin{bmatrix} -\text{INF} \\ -\text{FUT} \\ -\text{PRET} \\ \left\{ \begin{array}{l} +3\text{P} \\ -\text{PL} \end{array} \right\} \\ +\text{III} \\ +\text{B} \end{bmatrix} \, X \underline{} (+\text{u}) \,]\!\!\!]$

Verb morphology 123

(83) for (29) ø → +a / [+I] ___ (+u)]

I shall return below (§ 7) to the question of the changes or deletions of consonants before /+g/.

6.3. Further cases of suppletion; (X)* indicates optional forms.

13. *veure* 'to see'

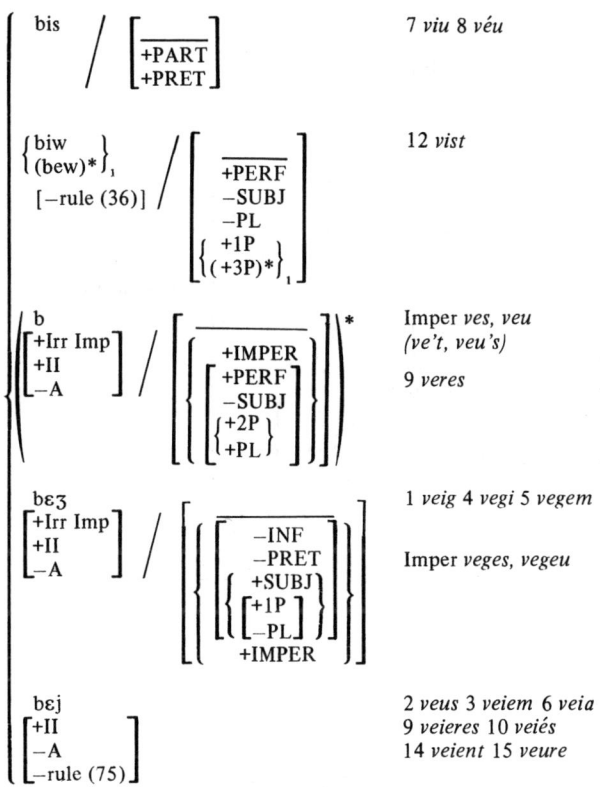

(N.B. [–rule (75)] is specified to prevent /g/–insertion in forms corresponding to rows 8 and 10 of the tables.)

14. *fer* 'to do'

$$\left\{\begin{array}{l}
\begin{Bmatrix}\text{fiw}\\\text{few}\end{Bmatrix}_1 \\
[-\text{rule (36)}]
\end{array}\Bigg/ \begin{bmatrix}\overline{}\\+\text{PERF}\\-\text{SUBJ}\\-\text{PL}\\\begin{Bmatrix}+1\text{P}\\+3\text{P}\end{Bmatrix}_1\end{bmatrix} \quad 7\ \textit{fiu}\ 8\ \textit{féu}\right.$$

$$\begin{array}{l}\text{fa}\textipa{Z}\\[+\text{II}]\end{array} \Bigg/ \begin{bmatrix}\overline{}\\-\text{PRET}\\-\text{SUBJ}\\+1\text{P}\\-\text{PL}\end{bmatrix} \quad 1\ \textit{faig}$$

$$\text{fas} \Bigg/ \begin{bmatrix}\overline{}\\-\text{PRET}\\+\text{SUBJ}\\\begin{Bmatrix}+3\text{P}\\--\text{PL}\end{Bmatrix}\end{bmatrix} \quad \begin{array}{l}4\ \textit{faci}\ (\text{vulgar}\\ [\text{fá}\textipa{Z}\text{i}]\ \text{i.e. with}\\ \text{stem /fa}\textipa{Z}\text{/ as}\\ \text{above)}\end{array}$$

$$\begin{array}{l}\text{fe}\\[+\text{Irr Imp}]\end{array} \Bigg/ \begin{bmatrix}\left\{\begin{matrix}\overline{}\\-\text{PART}\\\begin{bmatrix}+\text{IMPER}\end{bmatrix}\\-\text{PL}\end{matrix}\right\}\end{bmatrix} \quad \begin{array}{l}14\ \textit{fer}\ [\text{fé}]\ \text{Imper}\\ \text{sg}\ \textit{fes}\ [\text{fés}]\end{array}$$

$$\begin{array}{l}\text{fej}\\\begin{bmatrix}+\text{II}\\-\text{A}\\-\text{rule (75)}\end{bmatrix}\end{array} \Bigg/ \begin{bmatrix}\overline{}\\+\text{PRET}\\\begin{Bmatrix}-\text{PERF}\\+\text{INF}\end{Bmatrix}\end{bmatrix} \quad 6\ \textit{feia}\ 12\ \textit{fet}$$

$$\begin{array}{l}\text{fa}\\\begin{bmatrix}+\text{II}\\-\text{A}\end{bmatrix}\end{array} \qquad\qquad\qquad \begin{array}{l}2\ \textit{fas, fa, fan}\ 3\ \textit{fem}\\ /\text{fa+}\varepsilon\text{+m/},\ \textit{feu}\\ /\text{fa+}\varepsilon\text{+w/}\ 5\ \textit{fem}\\ /\text{fa+u+i+}\varepsilon\text{+m/},\ \textit{feu}\\ /\text{fa+u+i+}\varepsilon\text{+w/}\\ 9\ \textit{feres}\ /\text{fa+u+e+r+a+s/}\\ 10\ \textit{fes}\ /\text{fa+u+e+s+i/}\\ 13\ \textit{fent}\ /\text{fa+e+nt/}\end{array}$$

Verb morphology

15. *anar* 'to go'

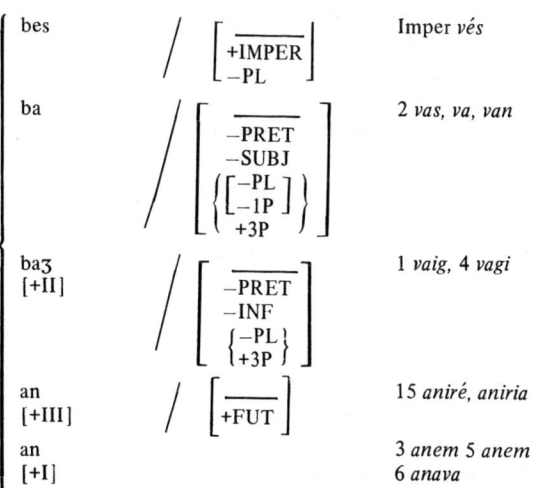

bes	/ [+IMPER, −PL]	Imper *vés*
ba	/ [−PRET, −SUBJ, {[−PL, −1P], +3P}]	2 *vas, va, van*
baʒ [+II]	/ [−PRET, −INF, {−PL, +3P}]	1 *vaig*, 4 *vagi*
an [+III]	/ [+FUT]	15 *aniré, aniria*
an [+I]		3 *anem* 5 *anem* 6 *anava*

16. *va*– (Preterite auxiliary)

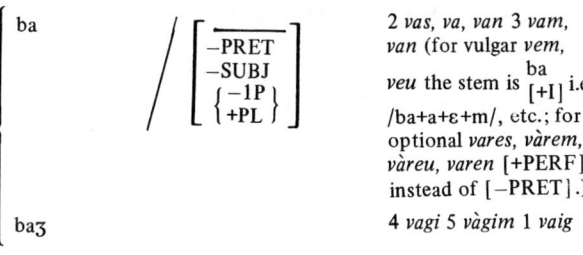

ba	/ [−PRET, −SUBJ, {−1P, +PL}]	2 *vas, va, van* 3 *vam, van* (for vulgar *vem, veu* the stem is $\genfrac{}{}{0pt}{}{ba}{[+I]}$ i.e. /ba+a+ɛ+m/, etc.; for optional *vares, vàrem, vàreu, varen* [+PERF] instead of [−PRET].)
baʒ		4 *vagi* 5 *vàgim* 1 *vaig*

17. *haver* a) Perfect auxiliary, Future auxiliary
    b) 'to have to', 'there is/are'

Some forms of *haver* are accounted for by rules (68)–(69). The remainder are:

$$\left\{ \begin{matrix} \text{a}_3 \Big/ \begin{bmatrix} \overline{-\text{PRET}} \\ \left\{ \begin{matrix} +\text{SUBJ} \\ \begin{pmatrix} +1\text{P} \\ -\text{PL} \end{pmatrix}* \end{matrix} \right\} \end{bmatrix} \\ \text{av} \\ \begin{bmatrix} +\text{II} \\ +\text{A} \end{bmatrix} \end{matrix} \right\}$$

4 *hagi* 5 *hàgim, hàgiu*

1 *haig* (optional, in sense (b))

6 *havia* 13 *havent*

In no. 16 (*va*–) and 17 (*haver*) the stems /baʒ/ and /aʒ/ are given no morphological class marker; consequently, rule (64) will fail to apply supplying /+ɛ/ in the 1st and 2nd plural, and /+i/ introduced by (62) will fail to be deleted by the Truncation rule (24). The recessive stress on *vàgim, vàgiu, hàgim, hàgiu* remains to be accounted for. In effect the angle bracket condition of (74) is ignored in these forms, or, to put it another way, these forms exceptionally behave as if they were [+PRET] for the application of the Stress-assignment rule. *Va*– in fact is introduced by transformation (rule (19)) from a deep structure which is [+PRET], but this is not so with *haver*. Perhaps it is right to specify in the condition on (74) that *va*– and *haver* are exceptions to it.

Verb morphology

18. *ser* (or *ésser*) 'to be'

$$\left\{\begin{array}{l} \text{sig}\begin{bmatrix}+\text{II}\\+\text{Irr Imp}\end{bmatrix} \Big/ \left[\left\{\begin{bmatrix}-\text{PRET}\\+\text{SUBJ}\end{bmatrix}\right\}\atop +\text{IMPER}\right] \quad \begin{array}{l}4\;sigui\;5\;siguem\\ \text{Imper}\;sigues,\;sigueu\end{array}\\[2ex] \text{so} \Big/ \begin{bmatrix}-\text{PRET}\\+\text{PL}\end{bmatrix} \quad 3\;som,\;sou\;3\text{pl}:\;són\\[2ex] \text{et} \Big/ \begin{bmatrix}-\text{PRET}\\+2\text{P}\end{bmatrix} \quad 2\;ets\;(2\text{sg})\\[2ex] \text{es}\begin{bmatrix}+\text{II}\\-\text{A}\end{bmatrix} \Big/ \left[\left\{\begin{bmatrix}-\text{PRET}\\+3\text{P}\end{bmatrix}\atop\left(\begin{bmatrix}+\text{INF}\\-\text{FUT}\\-\text{PRET}\end{bmatrix}\right)\right\}^{*}\right] \quad \begin{array}{l}3\text{sg}:\;és\\ \\ (13\;essent\;14\;ésser)\end{array}\\[2ex] \text{so+g} \Big/ \begin{bmatrix}-\text{PRET}\\+1\text{P}\end{bmatrix} \quad 1\;sóc\\[2ex] \text{er} \Big/ \begin{bmatrix}+\text{PRET}\\-\text{PERF}\end{bmatrix} \quad 6\;era\\[2ex] \left\{\begin{array}{l}\text{fuj}\\ \text{fow}\end{array}\right\}_1 \Big/ \begin{bmatrix}+\text{PERF}\\-\text{SUBJ}\\-\text{PL}\\\{{}^{+1\text{P}}_{+3\text{P}}\}_1\end{bmatrix} \quad 7\;fui\;8\;fou\\[2ex] \text{sta} \Big/ \begin{bmatrix}+\text{PART}\\+\text{PRET}\end{bmatrix} \quad 12\;estat\\[2ex] \text{fo} \Big/ \begin{bmatrix}+\text{PERF}\end{bmatrix} \quad 9\;fores\;10\;fos\;11\;fóssim\\[2ex] \text{se} \qquad\qquad 13\;sent\;14\;ser\;15\;seré \end{array}\right.$$

Verb morphology

19. *eixir* 'to go out' (and *reeixir* 'to succeed')

$$\begin{cases} \text{i}\int \begin{bmatrix} +\text{III} \\ -\text{B} \end{bmatrix} \\ \text{a}\int \begin{bmatrix} +\text{III} \\ +\text{B} \end{bmatrix} \end{cases} \bigg/ \begin{bmatrix} \overline{-\text{PRET}} \\ \begin{Bmatrix} -\text{PL} \\ +3\text{P} \end{Bmatrix} \end{bmatrix} \quad \begin{array}{l} 1 \; ixo \; 2 \; ixes \\ \\ 3 \; eixim \; 6 \; eixia \end{array}$$

20. *deure* 'must'

$$\begin{bmatrix} \text{d}\varepsilon\text{v} \\ +\text{II} \\ \{\langle +\text{A} \rangle\} \\ -\text{A} \end{bmatrix} \bigg/ \begin{bmatrix} \overline{\langle +\text{PART} \rangle} \end{bmatrix} \quad \begin{array}{l} 13 \; devent \; [\text{d}\text{ə}\beta\acute{\varepsilon}\text{n}] \\ \\ 14 \; deure \end{array}$$

21. *caldre* 'to be necessary', *cabre* 'to fit', *doldre* 'to grieve', *heure* 'to get'

$$\begin{cases} \begin{Bmatrix} (\text{kal})^* \\ \text{kab} \\ \text{dɔl} \\ (\varepsilon\text{v})^* \end{Bmatrix} \\ \begin{bmatrix} +\text{II} \\ -\text{A} \end{bmatrix} \\ \begin{Bmatrix} \text{kal} \\ \text{kab} \\ \text{dɔl} \\ \varepsilon\text{v} \end{Bmatrix} \\ \begin{bmatrix} +\text{II} \\ +\text{A} \end{bmatrix} \end{cases} \bigg/ \begin{bmatrix} \overline{-\text{PART}} \end{bmatrix}$$

14 *caldre, cabre, doldre, heure*

13 *calent, cabent, dolent, havent* ([−ɛ́n]); optionally 14 *caler, haver*

22. *cloure* 'to close'

$$\begin{cases} \text{klɔz} \\ \text{klɔw} \\ \begin{bmatrix} +\text{II} \\ -\text{A} \end{bmatrix} \end{cases} \bigg/ \begin{bmatrix} \overline{+\text{PART}} \\ +\text{PRET} \end{bmatrix} \quad 12 \; clos$$

Verb morphology

23. *coure* 'to cook'

$$\left\{\begin{matrix} \text{kuj} \begin{bmatrix} -\text{rule (61)} \\ -\text{rule (94)} \end{bmatrix} \Big/ \begin{bmatrix} \overline{+\text{PART}} \\ +\text{PRET} \end{bmatrix} & 12\ cuit \\ \text{kɔw} \begin{bmatrix} +\text{II} \\ -\text{A} \end{bmatrix} & \end{matrix}\right.$$

24. *estrènyer* 'to squeeze'

$$\text{strɛɲ} \begin{bmatrix} -\text{rule (75)} \\ -\text{rule (57)} \\ +\text{II} \\ -\text{A} \end{bmatrix} \qquad 12\ estret$$

The athematic ([−rule (75)]) participle *estret* does not undergo rule (57), which would give *[əstrɛ́s] but does undergo (60) and (61).

25. *dir* 'to say', *dur* 'to bring'

$$\left\{\begin{matrix} \left\{\begin{matrix}\text{di} \\ \text{du}\end{matrix}\right\} \Big/ \begin{bmatrix}\overline{-\text{PART}}\end{bmatrix} & 14\ dir,\ dur \\ \begin{bmatrix} +\text{II} \\ -\text{A} \end{bmatrix} & \\ \left\{\begin{matrix}\text{dij} \\ [+\text{Irr Imp}] \\ \text{duj}\end{matrix}\right\} \Big/ \left[\left\langle\begin{matrix}\overline{+\text{PART}} \\ +\text{PRET}\end{matrix}\right\rangle\right] & \begin{matrix}\text{Imper } digues \\ 12\ dit,\ dut\end{matrix} \\ \begin{bmatrix} \langle -\text{rule (75)} \rangle \\ +\text{II} \\ -\text{A} \end{bmatrix} & \end{matrix}\right.$$

For an alternative analysis of *dur* see below §7.3.

7.1. More rules for verb forms.

We have now established the general structure of verb morphology. There are, however, several more rules applying to some of the outputs generated in order to account for their systematic phonetic representations. Many of these rules apply only to verb forms, either in the sense that the sequences of items to which they apply do not occur elsewhere, or because they require special limitation to the class of verbs or to some subclass thereof.

Firstly, consider the verbs which exceptionally have stem stress throughout the imperfect tense. There are just ten of these:

riure 'to laugh' has *reia* [rɛ́jə], *reies* [rɛ́jəs],
reia [rɛ́jə], *rèiem* [rɛ́jəm], *rèieu* [rɛ́jə̯w],
reien [rɛ́jən];
caure 'to fall' has *queia* [kɛ́jə] etc.
creure 'to believe' has *creia* [krɛ́jə] etc.
seure 'to sit' has *seia* [sɛ́jə] etc.
treure 'to take out' has *treia* [trɛ́jə] etc.
jeure 'to lie' has *jeia* [ʒɛ́jə] etc.
veure 'to see' has *veia* [bɛ́jə] etc.
dir 'to say' has *deia* [dɛ́jə] etc.
fer 'to do' has *feia* [fɛ́jə] etc.
dur 'to bring' has *duia* [dújə] etc.

Most of these verbs have stems ending in /j/ which is revealed in the gerund, cf. §3.2.1. *Dir* and *riure* – the only two of these verbs with /i/ as root vowel have gerunds *dient* [dién] and *rient* [rién] respectively; a rule deleting /j/ after /i/ applies here, cf §4.5. *Dur* has *duent* [duén] and is the only one of these verbs with /u/ in the root. *Fer* has the gerund *fent* [fén] but has a suppletive conjugation anyway, cf. §6.3. It seems reasonable to suppose, then, that what triggers these exceptional imperfects is just the root-final /j/. Observe also that the root vowels, except for /u/, are all replaced by [ɛ] in these forms.

In order to prevent stress being assigned to the /+i/ of the imperfect tense suffix as is usual, we need a

Verb morphology   131

rule deleting /+i/ between the final /j/ of the root and the
/+j/ of the imperfect suffix, cf. rule (38).

(84) $\begin{bmatrix} -\text{cons} \\ +\text{high} \\ -\text{back} \end{bmatrix} \rightarrow \emptyset \; / \; \begin{bmatrix} -\text{cons} \\ +\text{high} \\ -\text{back} \end{bmatrix} \underline{\hspace{1cm}} \begin{bmatrix} -\text{cons} \\ +\text{high} \\ -\text{back} \end{bmatrix}$

Now, to deal with the fact that non-labial vowels are
replaced by [ɛ] in these forms the following rule is
required, to operate in the environment /____ jj
produced by (84).

(85) $\begin{bmatrix} +\text{syllab} \\ -\text{labial} \end{bmatrix} \rightarrow \begin{bmatrix} +\text{low} \\ -\text{back} \end{bmatrix} \; / \underline{\hspace{1cm}} \begin{bmatrix} -\text{syll} \\ -\text{cons} \\ +\text{high} \\ -\text{back} \end{bmatrix}_2^2$

In II §2.1 and III §4.5, evidence was presented
suggesting that there is a rule deleting /j/ before or after
/i/. A few class I verbs provide further support for this
conclusion, cf. Fabra, 1968a:44. Verbs such as *aboiar* 'to
buoy up', *voleiar* 'to flutter', *esglaiar* 'to scare', whose
roots as revealed in the infinitive, for example, end in
/j/, lose this when /+i/ follows in the present subjunctive;
thus *esglaia* [əzɣlájə] 'scares' (indic.) but *esglaï* [əzɣlái]
'scare' (1 and 3sg pres subj.). Rule (84) also produces
sequences of /j+j/ which are realized phonetically /j/, so
the most general form of the rule we require will delete
/j/ adjacent to a high non-back vowel or glide. This rule
applies after Stress assignment (see §4.5).

(86) $\begin{bmatrix} -\text{syll} \\ -\text{cons} \\ +\text{high} \\ -\text{back} \end{bmatrix} \rightarrow \emptyset \; / \; \begin{bmatrix} -\text{cons} \\ +\text{high} \\ -\text{back} \end{bmatrix}$

As mentioned in §3.2.1, there are four verbs with
underlying root final /w/ in class II. This appears

132   Verb morphology

phonetically as [w] only in the infinitive (and thus also
the derived future tense) and in the 2 and 3sg, and 3pl
pres ind. Thus *cloure* [klówrə] 'to close', *clourà* [kluwrá]
'will close', *clous* [klóws], *clou* [klów], *clouen* [klówən];
and similarly with *raure* 'to scrape', *coure* 'to cook', and
plaure 'to please'. /w/ is deleted when a vowel follows (or
/+g/; see below). Thus *cloem* [kluém] 'we close', *cloïa*
[kluíə] 'I was closing', etc. Note that *clouen* is still
/klɔw+n/ at the stage at which this rule applies. /w/–
deletion applies only to these class II verbs, it appears,
for from class I we have *creuar* [krəwá] 'to cross' with
[w] throughout the paradigm, and similarly *estiuar*
[əstiwá] 'to spend the summer', *pouar* [puwá] 'to draw
water'. But this last verb has an alternative form
poar [puá], *poa* [póə] 'draws water', etc., cf. *pou* [pów]
'well'. This fact suggests that perhaps /w/–deletion
should be restricted on phonetic grounds, rather than on
grounds of morphological class, to capture the difference
between these groups of examples; /w/ is deleted after
low back vowels. The deletion fails to occur before
lexical affixes; so we have *clauer* [kləwé] 'key-ring' from
clau /klaw/ 'key' with the suffix /+er/; similarly
creuer [krəwé] 'cruiser' from /krɛw/ (cf. *creuar* 'to
cross') and /+er/. So the rule is

(87) $\begin{bmatrix} -\text{syll} \\ -\text{cons} \\ +\text{back} \end{bmatrix} \rightarrow \emptyset \Big/ \begin{bmatrix} +\text{syll} \\ +\text{back} \\ +\text{low} \end{bmatrix} \underline{\quad} + \begin{bmatrix} +\text{syllab} \\ -\text{Affix} \end{bmatrix}$

In this form the rule generates *pouar*; the form *poar* can
be seen as a generalization of (87) removing the specification [+low] from the left of the environment.

 The following derivations will illustrate the points of
this section..They correspond to *queia* 'was falling',
traïa 'was betraying' (from *trair* 'to betray'), *plaïa* 'was
pleasing', *esglaï* 'scare' (1 and 3sg pres subj.), and *creui*
'cross' (1 and 3sg pres subj.).

Verb morphology 133

	kaj+i+j+a	trɛ+i+j+a	plaw+i+j+a	asglaj+a+i	krɛw+a+i
rule (84)	kaj +j+a				
rule (85)	kɛj +j+a				
rule (24)				asglaj +i	krɛw +i
rule (74)	kɛ́j +j+a	trɛ+í+j+a	plaw+í+j+a	asgláj +i	krɛ́w +i
rule (86)	kɛ́ +j+a	trɛ+í +a	plaw+í +a	asglá +i	krɛ́w +i
rule (87)			pla +í +a		
other					
rules	kɛ́jə	trəíə	pləíə	əzɣlái	krɛ́wi

7.2. The rules so far presented are not yet quite
sufficient to give us the correct systematic phonetic
representations of all verbs. In the following examples an
asterisk marks forms which, being the output of rules
already mentioned, need further rules to account for their
phonetic realization.

(88) 1sg pres indic.:
(a) */plaw+g/ *plac* 'I please' (and likewise */klɔw+g/
cloc 'I close', */kɔw+g/ *coc* 'I cook', */raw+g/
rac 'I scrape'.)
(b) /kaj+g/ *caic* 'I fall'.
(c) */ʒɛj+g/ *jec* 'I lie' (and likewise */krɛj+g/ 'I
believe', */duj+g/ *duc* 'I bring', etc.).
(d) */mɔv+g/ *moc* 'I move' (and likewise */ɛv+g/
hec 'I get', */bɛv+g/ *bec* 'I drink', etc.).
(e) */kunɛj+g *conec* 'I know' (and likewise
*/a+parɛj+g/ *aparec* 'I appear').

(89) 2sg pres indic.:
(a) /plaw+s/ *plaus* (and likewise /klɔw+s/ *clous*,
/kɔw+s/ *cous*, /raw+s/ *raus*).
(b) */kaj+s/ *caus*.
(c) */ʒɛj+s/ *jeus* (and likewise */krɛj+s/ *creus*,
*/rij+s/ *rius* 'you laugh', */duj+s/ *duus*, etc.).
(d) */mɔv+s/ *mous* (and likewise */ɛv+s/ *heus*,
*/bɛv+s/ *beus*, etc.).

134   *Verb morphology*

(e) /kunɛʃ+ə+s/ *coneixes* (and likewise /a+parɛʃ+ə+s/ *apareixes*).

(90) 3sg pres indic.:
(a) /plaw/ *plau* (and likewise /klɔw/ *clou*, /kɔw/ *cou*, /raw/ *rau*).
(b) */kaj/ *cau*.
(c) */ʒɛj/ *jeu* (and likewise */krɛj/ *creu*, */rij/ *riu*, */duj/ *duu*, etc.).
(d) */mɔv/ *mou* (and likewise */ɛv/ *heu*, */bɛv/ *beu*, etc.).
(e) /kunɛʃ/ *coneix* (and likewise /a+parɛʃ/ *apareix*).

(91) 1pl pres indic.:
(a) /pla+ɛ+m/ *plaem* (and likewise /klɔ+ɛ+m/ *cloem*, /kɔ+ɛ+m/ *coem*, /ra+ɛ+m/ *raem*).
(b) /kaj+ɛ+m/ *caiem*.
(c) /ʒɛj+ɛ+m/ *jaiem* (and likewise /krɛj+ɛ+m/ *creiem*, /rij+ɛ+m/ *riem*, */duj+ɛ+m/ *duem*, etc.).
(d) /mɔv+ɛ+m/ *movem* (and likewise /ɛv+ɛ+m/ *havem*, /bɛv+ɛ+m/ *bevem*, etc.).
(e) /kunɛʃ+ɛ+m/ *coneixem* (and likewise /a+parɛʃ+ɛ+m/ *apareixem*).

(92) 3pl pres indic.:
(a) */plaw+n/ *plauen* (and likewise */klɔw+n/ *clouen*, */raw+n/ *rauen*).
(b) */kaj+n/ *cauen*.
(c) */ʒɛj+n/ *jeuen* (and likewise */krɛj+n/ *creuen*, */rij+n/ *riuen*, */duj+n/ *duen*, etc.).
(d) */mɔv+n/ *mouen* (and likewise */ɛv+n/ *heuen*, */bɛv+n/ *beuen*, etc.).
(e) */kunɛʃ+n/ *coneixen* (and likewise */a+parɛʃ+n/ *apareixen*).

Verb morphology 135

(93) Infinitive:
   (a) /plaw+r+ə/ *plaure* (and likewise /klɔw+r+ə/ *cloure*, /kɔw+r+ə/ *coure*, /raw+r+ə/ *raure*).
   (b) */kaj+r+ə/ *caure*.
   (c) */ʒɛj+r+ə/ *jeure* (and likewise */krɛj+r+ə/ *creure*, */rij+r+ə/ *riure*, etc.).
   (d) */mɔv+r+ə/ *moure* (and likewise */ɛv+r+ə/ *heure*, */bɛv+r+ə/ *beure*, etc.).
   (e) /kunɛʃ+ə+r/ *conèixer* (and likewise a+parɛʃ+ə+r/ *aparèixer*).

We need rules i) converting /j/ to [w] before consonants other than /+g/ and word-finally (89b, 89c, 90b, 90c, 92b, 92c. 93b, 93c), this rule to apply before (86) or underlying /j/ will have been deleted throughout the paradigm of *riure* and *dir* 'to say'; ii) deleting /j/ before /+g/ except after /a/ (88b, 88c); iii) converting /v/ to [w] before consonants and word-finally (88d, 89d, 90d, 92d, 93d); iv) deleting /w/ before /+g/ (88a, 88d); v) inserting [ə] between a consonant and /+n/ (92a–e). Better than i) and ii) would be vi) a rule converting /j/ to [w] before consonants except between /a/ and /+g/ (88b); then iv) applies to more cases.

The rule converting /j/ to [w], then, has the following form (note that parts ii) and iii) resemble dissimilation rules):

(94) $\begin{bmatrix} -\text{syll} \\ -\text{cons} \end{bmatrix} \rightarrow [+\text{back}]$

$$/ \left\{ \begin{array}{l} \underline{} \ \# \\ \underline{} + \begin{bmatrix} -\text{syll} \\ -\text{back} \end{bmatrix} \\ [-\text{back}] \ \underline{} + [-\text{syll}] \end{array} \right\} \text{X} \parallel \text{V} \quad \begin{array}{l} \text{i)} \\ \text{ii)} \\ \text{iii)} \end{array}$$

Alternatively, this may be expressed as:

(95) $\begin{bmatrix} -\text{syll} \\ -\text{cons} \end{bmatrix} \rightarrow [+\text{back}]$

$/ \langle [-\text{back}] \rangle_b \underline{} (+ \begin{bmatrix} -\text{syll} \\ \langle +\text{back} \rangle_a \end{bmatrix} X) \#]_V$

condition: if a, then b.

For the conversion of /v/ to [w] we have a rule whose basic form is:

(96) $\begin{bmatrix} -\text{syllab} \\ +\text{contin} \\ +\text{labial} \\ +\text{voiced} \end{bmatrix} \rightarrow [-\text{cons}] \; / \underline{} \begin{Bmatrix} C \\ \# \end{Bmatrix}$

This rule is in fact of much more general validity than just in these verb forms; it in part accounts for the paradigmatic alternation between [β] and [w]; see V §4 where the rule is discussed in more detail.

In §4.8 above a rule was introduced (rule (61)) to delete certain consonants before /+t/ in irregular participles. This rule can be modified to include the deletion of /w/ before /+g/.

(97) $\begin{bmatrix} -\text{vocal} \\ \langle +\text{coron} \rangle_1 \\ \langle +\text{back} \rangle_2 \end{bmatrix} \rightarrow \emptyset$

$/ \langle [+\text{cons}] \rangle_1 \underline{} + \begin{bmatrix} +\text{obstr} \\ -\text{cont} \\ \langle +\text{back} \rangle_2 \end{bmatrix} X]_V$

Epenthesis of [ə] before /+n/ resembles cases of epenthesis already dealt with by I (19), which I repeat here for convenience.

Verb morphology

(98) $\emptyset \rightarrow [+\text{syll}]$

$$/ \left[\left\{ \begin{matrix} \langle -\text{obstr} \rangle_a \\ +\text{cont} \\ +\text{cons} \end{matrix} \right\} \right] \underline{} + \begin{bmatrix} \langle -\text{obstr} \rangle_b \\ +\text{coron} \\ +\text{cont} \\ +\text{cons} \end{bmatrix} X]_{V, \text{Aux}}$$

condition: if a, then b.

(98) deals with epenthesis before /+s/ and /+r/; epenthesis before /+n/ is more general, since it occurs following any consonant. The alveolars /s/, /r/ and /n/ are all [+coron, −distr]. It is not easy to capture adequately in the usual notation the generalization of epenthesis between all consonants and /+n/, between fricatives or nasals and /+r/, and between fricatives and /+s/. There seem to be two ways of formulating the rule according to the direction in which the condition on the angle brackets is to operate; thus:

(99) $\emptyset \rightarrow [+\text{syll}]$

$$/ \left[\left\langle \left\{ \begin{bmatrix} \left\{ \begin{matrix} -\text{cont} \\ -\text{obstr} \end{matrix} \right\} \\ -\text{nasal} \end{bmatrix} \\ [+\text{nasal}] \end{matrix} \right\}_1 \middle/ a \right\rangle \right] \underline{} + \begin{bmatrix} \langle \left\{ \begin{matrix} -\text{cont} \\ -\text{obstr} \end{matrix} \right\}_1 \rangle_b \\ +\text{coron} \\ -\text{distr} \\ -\text{syll} \end{bmatrix} X]_{V, \text{Aux}}$$

condition: if a, then b.

This seems to be similar from the point of view of rule-evaluation by symbol-count to

(100) $\emptyset \rightarrow [+\text{syll}]$

$$/ \left[\left\langle \left\{ \begin{bmatrix} +\text{obstr} \\ +\text{cont} \end{bmatrix} \middle\langle \begin{bmatrix} -\text{obstr} \\ -\text{cont} \end{bmatrix} \right\rangle_1 \right\} \right\rangle \\ -\text{syllab} \right] \underline{} + \begin{bmatrix} \langle +\text{cont} \rangle_a \\ \langle -\text{obstr} \rangle_1 \\ +\text{coron} \\ -\text{distr} \\ -\text{syll} \end{bmatrix} X]_{V, \text{Aux}}$$

condition: if a, then b.

The similarity between the left and right matrices of (100) is perhaps to some extent more apparent than real, yet it does seem plausible that in the case anyway of /+s/ and /+r/ the purpose of the rule is to break up certain sequences of continuants and sonorants, and this is more evident from the formulation (100) than from (99).

7.3. In §6.3 (verb No. 25) I suggested that the verb *dur* 'to bring' had two suppletive stems: /du/ and /duj/. The argument for the stem /duj/ is based on the fact that this verb has an imperfect *duia*, etc. with recessive stress as have other class II verbs in /—j/ (see §7.1). Nevertheless, if the stem is /duj/ except in the infinitive, as suggested in §6.3, the rules given in §7.1—2 do not account for the occurrence of the gerund *duent* [duén] and the 1 and 2pl pres indic. *duem* [duém], *dueu* [duéw] in place of the expected *[dujén], *[dujém], *[dujéw] respectively. The 2 and 3sg and 3pl are *duus* [dús] or [dúws], *duu* [dú] or [dúw] and *duen* [dúən] respectively (cf. Fabra, 1897:9). This last form must derive from an intermediate /duw+n/, for [ə]–epenthesis occurs only after a consonant; elsewhere we have e.g. *fan* 'they do' from /fa+n/, *són* 'they are' from /so+n/.

It seems as though the grammar must contain a rule deleting /w/ after /u/ which operates after (100). Such a rule would be a generalization of (86) replacing the restriction [—back] with [αback]. Further evidence for such a generalization comes from verbs with labial vowels before /w/ in the root such as *ploure* 'to rain', *coure* 'to cook'; when unstressed the root vowel is reduced as a result of the general rule (II (17)) to [u], and the sequence /uw/ which results is often realized as [u]; thus *plourà* [plurá] /plɔw+r+a/ 'it will rain', *couria* [kuɾíə] /kɔw+r+i+j+a/ 'I would cook'; (pronounciations such as [pləwɾá] are also found; see Fabra, 1897:10).

If we generalize (86) and establish the basic stem of

Verb morphology

dur as /duw/, what follows? The present indicative and gerund are now regular. If (86) modified precedes I (13), which, among other things, deals with epenthesis of [ə] in the environment Cr___#, then the infinitive *dur* is seen to be regular; compare these derivations

	/duw+r/	(*dur*)	/rij+r/	(*riure*)
(94)			riw+r	
(86)m	du + r			
I (13)			riw+r+ə	

Observe that the infinitive *dir* 'to say' can be explained as being derived from the root /dij/ which is idiosyncratically an exception to rule (94), and is thus subject to the modified (86), rather than as exhibiting a suppletive stem /di/ as suggested in §6.3 no. 25. The stem /duj/ is only required specifically in the imperfect of *dur*; this might be the result of a phonological rule w → j / u___+i, for which this verb happens to be the only example, or it might be a case of suppletion like that of *fer* 'to do' with stem /fej/ in the imperfect tense and past participle; in the case of *dur* the choice between /duw/ and /duj/ as the participial stem would be arbitrary.

If /duw/ is the basic stem, this verb may be synchronically related to certain class III compound verbs, e.g. *conduir* 'to drive', *reduir* 'to reduce', *produir* 'to produce', *traduir* 'to translate', etc. The modified version of (86), then, would read as follows:

$$(101) \quad \begin{bmatrix} -\text{syll} \\ -\text{cons} \\ \alpha\text{back} \end{bmatrix} \rightarrow \emptyset \bigg/ \begin{bmatrix} -\text{cons} \\ +\text{high} \\ \alpha\text{back} \end{bmatrix}$$

and the lexical form of *dir* and *dur* (making /duj/ suppletive rather than rule conditioned) would be:

dir 'to say'

$$\begin{matrix} \text{dij} \\ \begin{bmatrix} +\text{Irr Imp} \\ \langle -\text{rule (94)}\rangle_1 \\ \langle -\text{rule (75)}\rangle_2 \\ +\text{II} \\ -\text{A} \end{bmatrix} \end{matrix} \Bigg/ \begin{bmatrix} \overline{\langle -\text{PART}\rangle}_1 \\ \left\langle \begin{bmatrix} +\text{PART} \\ +\text{PRET} \end{bmatrix} \right\rangle_2 \end{bmatrix}$$

dur 'to bring'

$$\begin{Bmatrix} \begin{matrix} \text{duj} \\ \begin{bmatrix} +\text{II} \\ -\text{A} \end{bmatrix} \end{matrix} \Bigg/ \begin{bmatrix} \overline{+\text{PRET}} \\ -\text{PERF} \end{bmatrix} \\ \\ \begin{matrix} \text{duw} \\ \begin{bmatrix} \langle -\text{rule (75)}\rangle \\ +\text{II} \\ -\text{A} \end{bmatrix} \end{matrix} \Bigg/ \begin{bmatrix} \left\langle \overline{\begin{bmatrix} +\text{PART} \\ +\text{PRET} \end{bmatrix}} \right\rangle \end{bmatrix} \end{Bmatrix}$$

CHAPTER IV

Unstressed pronouns

1. The so-called unstressed pronouns correspond to those occurrences of *Pro* dominated by VP and not preceded by a phonological preposition (i.e., if the category *Prep* is present, it dominates a null element at the level of syntactic structure which is the input to the phonological component). A readjustment rule deletes word-boundaries for *Pro* items which have the form of a single consonant, or a vowel, or a consonant followed by a vowel, that is: (C)(V). This readjustment rule is necessary for the correct application of Stress assignment, for the phonetic rules of final-consonant deletion (VII §2, §4) and voicing assimilation (VII §8), and for the phonological rules to be discussed presently, which deal with verb plus pronouns in certain respects as a "word" unit. That is, these pronouns are clitic.

The sample strings *dóna-me'l* 'give it to me' and *me'l dóna* 'gives it to me' can be represented by the following trees:

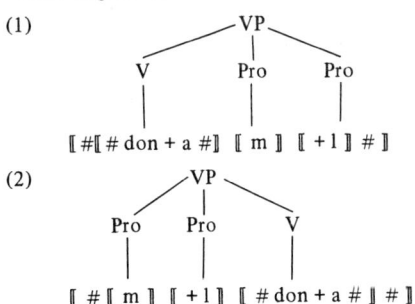

There is not apparently any *phonological* limit to the number of pronouns which may be dominated by VP. The rules I shall give permit sequences of up to seven pronouns (but see below §7.1); that strings of such length do not in fact occur is a result of semantic or syntactic constraints.

2. The pronouns are attached after the imperative, gerund, and infinitive, otherwise before finite verbs. Unlike in Italian, pronouns are not attached to past participles. Rather than their being deleted in this environment, it seems that the syntactic component either prevents *Pro* occurring here, or requires realizable prepositions. Compare, for example, *les ampolles tretes d'allà* 'the bottles taken from there' with *n'hem tret les ampolles* 'we have taken the bottles from there'. With the imperative here I include the so-called third person imperatives ('let him ... ', 'let them ... ', etc.), first person plural imperatives ('let us ... '), and the polite forms used with *vostè, vostès*, which are semantically second person but morphologically third person; the verb forms of all of these are identical with the corresponding persons of the present subjunctive. This is dealt with by the readjustment rule III (11)[1]. Negative imperatives of all kinds have forms identical to those of the present subjunctive throughout, with preposition of unstressed pronouns. The formulation of this condition is a syntactic question which I shall not go into further here, merely pointing out that whatever the deeper structure negative imperatives will not carry the feature [+IMPER] in respect of the rules which follow.

---

[1] III (11) must follow the rule IV (4) determining pronoun position.

Unstressed pronouns 143

2.1. When the category VP in the highest position dominates more than one occurrence of V, ("auxiliary verbs" as generated in III (1), (2), (17), (18) and (19)), the pronouns may be attached optionally either to the finite verb or to the [+INF] form (gerund or participle). The colloquial language gives preference to the former procedure. It is interesting to observe that when infinitivization follows "equi-NP deletion", *Pro*s from the subordinate VP are usually switched to the higher VP which contains the finite V; thus *els hi espero veure* 'I hope to see them there' is preferred to *espero veure'ls-hi*. The effect of this transformation, just as of the one mentioned above relating to auxiliary verbs, is to attach *Pro* to finite verbs wherever possible. There are certain cases in which this transformation is blocked; thus we have *intentaven anar-se'n* 'they attempted to leave' and not **se n'intentaven anar* (cf. Coromines, 1971:275). The constraints may be lexical or syntactic, but there is no reason to suppose they are phonological.

3.1. In giving the phonetic forms of the unstressed pronouns and their combinations, and in presenting the rules generating them, it will be necessary for me to go outside the Standard language which I describe elsewhere. This is because the Standard pronoun system, as prescribed by normative grammarians (whose rules elsewhere broadly correspond to the Standard language as actually spoken by educated persons in Barcelona), is not in my experience used in its complete form by any native speakers, though many people use most of its forms most of the time. There is another system which I shall call "Barcelona colloquial", which, while sharing many forms with the "Standard" language, can best be seen as being generated by distinct rules. The artificiality of the Standard system is sometimes recognized by the normative grammarians who reluctantly "permit" some, at least, of the forms of the other system, (e.g. Fabra, 1968a:62–3). For both correct and incorrect forms see Fabra, 1913; Fabra, 1954:II, 54–86; Fabra, 1968a: 60–3; Badia, 1951:266–75; Badia, 1962:I, 168–214.

This conflict between normative grammar and ordinary usage of the dialect being described does not appear to occur to a significant degree elsewhere affecting phonology or morphology; that is, the prescribed usage always corresponds to the actual practice of at least some speakers. The divergence between prescription and practice is apparent rather in lexis and syntax. In this chapter I shall give rules to account for both "Standard" and "Barcelona colloquial" sets of pronoun forms displayed in Table 1 below. The table gives the forms of single pronouns or groups of two as they occur before or after a consonant or vowel.

3.2. As will be seen, there is not a one-to-one correspondence between the forms of the two systems. The phonetic forms depend, in part at least, on the semantico-syntactic roles of the *Pro* items. These roles are indicated in the table by letters corresponding to case functions; the cases are some of those suggested by Ferrater (1972), deriving from Fillmore (1968), as follows: A = accusative, D = dative, R = reflexive (corresponding notionally to the subject of the Greek "middle voice", or a NP referentially identical to the subject NP but not true accusative), S = subnominal (corresponding to the possessive genitive or Latin "dative of possession"), L = locative, P = partitive. I mention these cases here merely to provide a framework for distinguishing various sets of pronouns.

3.2.1. Note that some examples of apparent D (semantically), in the third person, are represented by *los*, *li* in "Standard", but by *hi* in "Barcelona colloquial",

Unstressed pronouns

when preceded by a case A pronoun. I shall not try
to account for this difference in the rules I give here, but
suppose that the difference results from different
syntactic rules in each dialect. Other examples of
apparently semantic D are realized *hi* in both dialects;
(a syntactic analysis and maybe a deeper semantic
analysis would possibly assign them to L.) For example:

Standard		Barc. coll.
A D		A D
us li presento	'I introduce you to him' =	*us hi presento*
R D		R D
us hi referiu	'you refer to him'	= *us hi referiu*

The correct selection of *Pro* items is a complicated and
interesting area of Catalan syntax worth studying in more
detail that I can give here; for a few suggestions see §7
below.

3.2.2. Note also that in the compound perfect tenses
(*haver* + participle) the participle agrees in form (i.e. is
marked ±F, ±PL and undergoes rules I (9), (14), (15) as do
nouns and adjectives) with a preceding *Pro* /+l/ which is A,
or a preceding /+n/ which is P; cf. Badia, 1962: I, 465–9.
Thus *els hem vistos* 'we have seen them (M)', *n'hem vistes
dues* 'we have seen two of them (F)' , but *els n'hem tret el
motor, de la barca* 'we have taken the motor out of their
boat for them' where *els* is S or D and *n'* is L (ablative).
With regard to *ne* (/+n/) it would be more accurate to say
that the participle agrees with it in respect of gender, but
in number with the *Quant* item to which P is subordinate,
to allow for *de llet, ja li n'he donada* 'I've already given
him some milk' where *Quant* is not realized phonetically
(i.e. is "dummy"), and *d'aquelles pomes, ell n'ha menjades
tres, mentre jo n'he menjada una* (not * . . . *jo n'he
menjades una)* 'he's eaten three of those apples while I've

eaten one (of them)'. Again I shall go no further into this syntactic question.

As will become apparent, rules which generate sequences of two pronouns as in the table will also account for longer sequences. The key forms in the left hand margin are the orthographic "full" forms. The ditto sign indicates that the forms used are identical to those of the group above. The figures refer to the notes which follow the table. [z] is used for final [s]/[z] —voicedness depends on the following segment, cf. VII §8.

Table 1

SE	Standard	Barc. coll.
se	es¹, es² / {s/ʃ}, ze, C—C / s V—V z	es¹, es² / {s/ʃ}, ze, C—C / s V—V z
se vos	C—C zwes / V—V zwes, zns zwes	C—C zwes, zns zwes / V—V zwes, zns
se te	C—C tes / V—V tes	C—C sət / V—V sət
se nos	C—C znes / V—V znes	C—C sənz / V—V znes
se me	C—C mes / V—V mes	C—C səm / V—V səm
R A se los	C—C zles / V—V zelz	³ selzi C—C selzi / V—V selz
R S se los	,, C—C ,, / V—V	⁴ selzi C—C selzi / V—V selzi
A D se los	,, C—C ,, / V—V	⁵ siC—Csi / siV—Vsi
se les	C—C zeles / V—V zeles	C—C zeles / V—V zeles
se lo	C—C les / V—V les	C—C les / V—V les
se la	C—C eles / V—V eles, seles⁶/{ĩ/ũ}	C—C eles / V—V eles

		Standard	Barc. coll.
R S	se li	seli C— —C seli	seli C— —C seli
		seli V— —V seli	seli V— —V seli
A D	se li	,, C— —C ,,	si C— —C si
		,, V— —V ,,	si V— —V si
	se ne	sen C— —C sen	sen C— —C sen
		sen V— —V sen	sen V— —V sen
	se hi	si C— —C si	si C— —C si
		si V— —V si	si V— —V si
	se ho	su C— —C su	su C— —C su
		su V— —V su	su V— —V su

		Standard	Barc. coll.
VOS	vos	uz C— —C buz	uzə², uz⁷ C— —w̯ zə⁸, —C uz
		uz V— —V wz	uz V— —V wzə⁹, —V wz
	vos nos	uzenz C— —C buzenz	uzenz C— —w̯ zenz, —C uzenz
		uzenz V— —V wzenz	uzenz V— —V wzenz
	vos me	uzəm C— —C buzəm	uzəm C— —w̯ zəm, —C uzəm
		uzm V— —V wzəm	uzəm V— —V wzəm
D/R A	vos los	uzəlz C— —C buzəlz	uzəlz C— —w̯ zəlz, —C uzəlz
		uzəlz V— —V wzəlz	uzəlz V— —V wzəlz
R S	vos los	,, C— —C ,,	uzəlzi C— —w̯ zəlzi, —C uzəlzi
		V— —V	uzəlzi V— —V wzəlzi
A D	vos los	,, C— —C ,,	uzi C— —w̯ zi, —C uzi
		V— —V	uzi V— —V wzi

Unstressed pronouns   149

	Standard	Barc. coll.
vos los	zezn C——C buzləz / zezn V——V wzələz	zələz C——C zələz, —C uzzələz / zələz V——V wzələz
vos lo	lezəl C——C buzəl / uzn V——V wzel	lezəl C——C wzəl, —C uzəl / uzn V——V wzel
vos la	uzn/(ĩ/ũ), uzn V——V elezn; elezn C——C buzna / elezn V——V wzlea	elezn C——C w—, elezə, —C uzəli / elezn V——V wzeli
R vos li	uzli C——C buzli / uzli V——V wzli	elezli C——C w zeli, —C uzeli / elezli V——V wzeli
A D vos li	" C——C " / V——V	
vos ne	uzen C——C buzen / uzn V——V wzen	uzen C——C w zen, —C uzen / uzn V——V wzen
vos hi	uzi C——C buzi / uzi V——V wzi	uzi C——C w zi, —C uzi / uzi V——V wzi
vos ho	uzu C——C buzu / uzu V——V wzu	uzu C——C w zu, —C uzu / uzu V——V wzu
TE		
te	tə¹, ət C——C tə / t V——V t	tə¹, ət C——C tə / t V——V t
te nos	tənz C——C tənz / tənz V——V tənz	tənz C——C tənz / tənz V——V tənz
te me	təm C——C təm / təm V——V təm	təm C——C təm / təm V——V təm
R A te los	təlz C——C təlz / təlz V——V təlz	təlz C——C təlz / təlz V——V təlz

150 Unstressed pronouns

		Standard		Barc. coll.
R S	te los	" C――C "		təlziC――C təlzi
		V――V		təlziV――V təlzi
A D	te los	" C――C "		tiC――C ti
		V――V		tiV――V ti
te les		təlazC――C təlaz		təlazC――C təlaz
		tələzV――V tələz		tələzV――V tələz
te lo		təlC――C tal		təlC――C tal
		təlV――V tal		təlV――V tal
te la		tələ⁶ /_ {ĩ/ũ}, tələC――C tale		tələC――C tale
		təlV――V tale		təlV――V tale
R S	te li	təliC――C tali		təliC――C tali
		təliV――V təli		təliV――V təli
A D	te li	" C――C "		tiC――C ti
		V――V		tiV――V ti
te ne		tənC――C tan		tanC――C tan
		tənV――V tan		tanV――V tan
te hi		tiC――C ti		tiC――C ti
		tiV――V ti		tiV――V ti
te ho		tuC――C tu		tuC――C tu
		tuV――V tu		tuV――V tu
NOS		Standard		Barc. coll.
nos		ənzC――C nuz		ənzə², ənzC――N zə⁸, ―C ənz
		ənzV――V nz		ənzə V――V̂ nzə⁹, ―V nz

Unstressed pronouns

R/D A nos los	ənzəlz C__ —C nuzəlz ənzəlz V__ —V nzəlz		ənzəlz C__ —N zəlz, —C ənzəlz ənzəlz V__ —V nzəlz	
R S nos los	" C__ —C " V__ —V		ənzəlzi C__ —N zəlzi, —C ənzəlzi ənzəlzi V__ —V nzəlzi	
A D nos los	" C__ —C " V__ —V		ənzi C__ —N zi, —C ənzi ənzi V__ —V nzi	
nos les	ənzuləz C__ —C nuzləz ənzləz V__ —V nzləz		zələznə C__ —N zələz, —C ənzələz zələznə V__ —V nzələz	
nos lo	ənzəl C__ —C nuzəl ənzl V__ —V nzəl		ənzəl C__ —N zəl, —C ənzəl ənzl V__ —V nzəl	
nos la	ənzlə⁶ / __ {ĩ/ũ} ənzlə C__ —C nuzlə ənzl V__ —V nzlə		elezne C__ —N zələ, —C ənzələ ənzlə V__ —V nzələ	
R S nos li	ənzli C__ —C nuzli ənzli V__ —V nzli		ənzəli C__ —N zəli, —C ənzəli ənzəli V__ —V nzəli	
A D nos li	" C__ —C " V__ —V		ənzi C__ —N zi, —C ənzi ənzi V__ —V nzi	
nos ne	uəznu C__ —C nəznu ənzn V__ —V nzən		ənzəen C__ —N zən, —C ənzən ənzəen V__ —V nzən	
nos hi	ənzi C__ —C nuzi ənzi V__ —V nzi		ənzi C__ —N zi, —C ənzi ənzi V__ —V nzi	
nos ho	uzuə C__ —C nuzu nzuə V__ —V nzu		nzuə C__ —N zu, —C ənzu nzuə V__ —V nzu	

N = [+nasal]

Unstressed pronouns

ME	Standard	Barc. coll.
me	mə¹, əm C– –C me m V– –V m	mə¹, əm C– –C me m V– –V m
R/D A me los	məlz C– –C məlz məlz V– –V məlz	məlz C– –C məlz məlz V– –V məlz
R S me los	„ C– –C „ „ V– –V „	məlzi C– –C məlzi məlzi V– –V məlzi
A D me los	„ C– –C „ „ V– –V „	mi C– –C mi mi V– –V mi
me les	mələz C– –C mələz mələz V– –V mələz	mələz C– –C mələz mələz V– –V mələz
me lo	məl C– –C məl məl V– –V məl	məl C– –C məl məl V– –V məl
me la	mələ⁶/–{ĩ/ũ}, mələ C– –C mələ məl V– –V mələ	mələ C– –C mələ məl V– –V mələ
R S me li	məli C– –C məli məli V– –V məli	məli C– –C məli məli V– –V məli
A D me li	„ C– –C „ „ V– –V „	mi C– –C mi mi V– –V mi
me ne	men C– –C men men V– –V men	men C– –C men men V– –V men
me hi	mi C– –C mi mi V– –V mi	mi C– –C mi mi V– –V mi
me ho	mu C– –C mu mu V– –V mu	mu C– –C mu mu V– –V mu

Unstressed pronouns

LOS	Standard	Barc. coll.
A los	əlz C— —C luz əlz V— —V lz	əlzə², əlz C— —C əlz əlz V— —V̂ lzə⁹, —V lz
S/D los	,, C— —C ,, V— —V	əlzi C— —C əlzi əlzi V— —V lzi
los los	əlzəz C— —C luzəlz əlzəz V— —V lzəlz	,, C— —C ,, V— —V
los les	əlzləz C— —C luzləz əlzləz V— —V lzləz	,, C— —C ,, V— —V
los lo	əlzəl C— —C luzəl əlzl V— —V lzəl	,, C— —C ,, V— —V
los la	əlzlə C— —C luzlə əlzl V— —V lzlə	,, C— —C ,, V— —V
los li	əlzlə⁶/— { ĩ / ũ }, əlzi C— —C luzi əlzi V— —V lzi	,, C— —C ,, V— —V
A L los ne	əlzən C— —C luzən əlzn V— —V lzən	əlzən C— —C əlzən əlzn V— —V lzən
D P los ne	,, C— —C ,, V— —V	əlzəni C— —C əlzəni əlzəni V— —V lzəni
los hi	əlzi C— —C luzi əlzi V— —V lzi	əlzi C— —C əlzi əlzi V— —V lzi
los ho	əlzu C— —C luzu nzu V— —V lzu	,, C— —C ,, V— —V

154   *Unstressed pronouns*

	Standard	Barc. coll.
LES		
les	ləz C — —C ləz ləz V — —V ləz	ləzə[2], ləz C — —C ləz ləz V — —V ləz
les li	ləzi C — —C ləzi ləzi V — —V ləzi	ləzi C — —C ləzi ləzi V — —V ləzi
les ne	ləzən C — —C ləzən ləzən V — —V ləzən	ləzən C — —C ləzən ləzən V — —V ləzən
les hi	ləzi C — —C ləzi ləzi V — —V ləzi	ləzi C — —C ləzi ləzi V — —V ləzi

	Standard	Barc. coll.
LO		
lo	əl C — —C lu l V — —V l	əl C — —C lu l V — —V l
lo li	li C — —C li li V — —V li	li C — —C li li V — —V li
lo ne	lən C — —C lən əln V — —V lən	lən C — —C lən lən V — —V lən
lo hi	li C — —C li li V — —V li	li C — —C li li V — —V li

	Standard	Barc. coll.
LA		
la	lə[6]/ — $\left\{\begin{matrix}\tilde{\text{i}}\\\tilde{\text{u}}\end{matrix}\right\}$,	lə C — —C lə l V — —V lə	lə C — —C lə l V — —V lə
la li	ləj C — —C ləj ləj V — —V ləj	li C — —C li li V — —V li
la ne	lən C — —C lən lən V — —V lən	lən C — —C lən lən V — —V lən
la hi	ləj C — —C ləj	li C — —C li

Unstressed pronouns

	Standard	Barc. coll.
LI		
li	li C — — C li	li C — — C li
	li V — — V li	li V — — V li
li ne	lin C — — C lin	ni C — — C ni
	lin V — — V lin	ni V — — V ni
li ho	liw C — — C liw	li C — — C li
	liw V — — V liw	li V — — V li
li hi	li C — — C li	,, C — — C ,,
	li V — — V li	V — — V
NE	Standard	Barc. coll.
ne	nə¹, en C — — C ne	nə¹, ən C — — C ne
	n V — — V n	n V — — V n
ne ho	¹⁰*nu C — — C *nu	nu C — — C nu
	*nu V — — V *nu	nu V — — V nu
ne hi	ni C — — C ni	ni C — — C ni
	ni V — — V ni	ni V — — V ni
HO	Standard	Barc. coll.
ho	u C — — C u	u C — — C u
	u V — — V w	¹¹aw, u n,we
		aw V — — V n,we
ho hi	li C — — C *li	li C — — C li
	*li V — — V *li	li V — — V li
HI	Standard	Barc. coll.
hi	i C — — C i	¹¹əj, i C — — C i
	i V — — V j	əj, i V — — V j

Notes to Table 1

1. These forms, [sə], [tə], [mə], [nə] are sometimes used in both dialects before a consonant when preceded, for example, by an interrogative adverb, e.g. *com te dius?* alternative to *com et dius?* 'what is your name?'; see below §4.8 for more details.

2. [sə] is optional in both dialects before a verb beginning with [s] or [ʃ], e.g. *se segueix que* 'it follows that...' Barcelona colloquial often inserts [ə] between pronouns terminating in [z] and verbs beginning with [s] or [ʃ].

3. e.g. *se'ls apropia* 'he appropriates them (M)'.

4. e.g. *se'ls queda els diners* 'he keeps their money'.

5. e.g. *s'hi presenta* 'he introduces himself to them'.

6. In "Standard" *la* is [lə] before unstressed [i] or [u]. (This is also true of the definite article *la* in the same environment, see below VII §5.)

7. In "Barcelona colloquial" [əwz] may optionally occur in place of [uz] throughout.

8. In "Barcelona colloquial" *vos* is pronounced [z(ə)] after [w], and *nos* is [z(ə)] after nasals; thus *acosteu-vos* 'come closer' [əkustéwzə], *anem-nos-en* 'lets go' [ənέmzən], *quedant-nos* '(us) remaining' [kəðánzə] with prior /–t/ deletion, or [kəðántənz] with /–t/ deletion applying subsequently; see VII §4.

9. [wzə], [nzə], [lzə] after stressed vowels. This environment arises only in Barcelona colloquial, which has a rule deleting /+r/ (i.e. of infinitives) before more than one consonant; –/+r/ after an unstressed vowel is always deleted in that dialect. Thus *conèixer-los* 'to know them' [kunέʃəlz], *donar-nos* 'to give us' [dunánzə]. (The goal of making verb + pronoun groups paroxytone seems to lie behind many of the rules realizing these forms in Barcelona colloquial.)

10. Normative grammar rejects these combinations: see Fabra, 1968a:73. For *ho + hi* see, however Fabra, 1954:I, 64 and Badia, 1962:I, 180 note 15, I, 199 note 42, where [li] is declared acceptable. Badia, 1962:I, 197 gives no "correct" realization for *ne + ho*; however on page 212 he says: "las formas *en y 'n* pasan a ser *n'* ante *hi* u *ho*:.... *dur-se'n això* 'llevarse esto' > *dur-se-n'ho*". It is quite clear that both *ne + ho* and *ho + hi* can be generated by the rules of syntax and have semantic representations; the spoken language accepts them.

11. The forms [əw] and [əj] seem to be in free variation with [u] and [i] before a verb, when not preceded by another pronoun; thus *hi ha* 'there is' is often [əjá].

Unstressed pronouns   157

4.1. I shall now give what I propose are the underlying
forms of the pronouns and the rules for realizing them
as they appear in Table 1 for "Barcelona colloquial". (3)
gives the underlying forms of the pronouns, linearly
ordered. The rule resembles a subcategorization rule; it
can be regarded as part of the subcategorization of *Pro*.

(3)
$$Pro \rightarrow (+s)\left(+\left\{\begin{bmatrix} w \\ +PL \\ t \end{bmatrix}\right\}\right)\left(+\left\{\begin{bmatrix} n \\ +PL \\ m \end{bmatrix}\right\}\right)\left(+\begin{bmatrix} li \\ \pm PL \end{bmatrix}\right)$$
$$\left(+\begin{bmatrix} 1 \\ \pm F \\ \pm PL \end{bmatrix}\right)\left(+\begin{bmatrix} n \\ \pm F \\ -\text{rule (18)} \end{bmatrix}\right)(+u)(+i+)$$

None of the surface phonetic [ə]s which occur in Table 1
is present, I suggest, at a deeper level. Such vowels appear
after or before the pronoun consonants, or not at all, in
accordance with rules which will be formulated below.

If we suppose that *Pro* items appear to the right of
the verb in the surface syntactic structure, then we need
a transformational readjustment rule to place *Pro* items to
the left of verb forms other than the imperative and
infinitive, as mentioned in §2.

(4)
$$[_V ([_{Aux} X]_{Aux}) Y \begin{bmatrix} -INF \\ -IMPER \end{bmatrix}]_V ([_V Z \begin{bmatrix} +PART \\ +PRET \end{bmatrix}]_V) \; Pro_1 \Rightarrow$$

S.D.   1   2   3
S.C.   3   1   (2)

Aux is mentioned so as to prevent *Pro* from being
inserted in the middle of future forms whose structure is
that generated by III (21).

4.2. The /+s/ of the irregular imperative singular is
deleted before a pronoun in this dialect; thus *digues-li*
[díyəli] 'tell him', *ve-te'l aquí* 'here it is' ('le voici').
Fes and *vés* are exceptions; thus *fes-te enrere*

[féstənrérə] 'get back!', vés-te'n [béstən] 'go away!'.
Perhaps being suppletive forms they have no morpheme
boundary (see below), or they are lexically marked
exceptions to rule (5).

(5)   s → ø / [+IMPER] X +_____#]] [+segment]

Imperatives ending in a consonant other than /n/,
/l/ or /w/ have [ə] added before a pronoun beginning
with a consonant in "Barcelona colloquial", (and
optionally before *hi* or *ho* also). Thus *fuig-ne* [fúʒən]
'run away from it!', *cull-la* [kúʎələ] 'pick it!',
llegeix-lo [ʎəʒɛ́ʃəl] 'read it!', *more't* 'die!', but *pren-lo*
[prɛ́nlu] 'take it!'; cf. Fabra, 1954: II, 78–80.

(6)   ø → +ə

/ [+IMPER] X $\begin{bmatrix} \{+\text{distr}\} \\ \{+\text{cont}\} \\ +\text{cons} \end{bmatrix}$ __ #]] [+segment]

Fes and *vés* are exceptions to this rule too. *Vés-hi*
[bézi] 'go there!' and *fes-ho* [fézu] 'do it!', with
[z] as opposed, for example to *venç-ho* [bɛ́nsu] 'defeat
it!' with [s], seem to indicate that *fes* and *vés* have
final /z/. (There is no other evidence that the second
person singular −*s* is other than unmarked for voice,
though of course it is of little consequence if the
suppletive forms *fes* and *vés* differ in this respect from
the regular paradigm.)

There is, however, another way of approaching this
question. Above I mentioned the fact that [ə] is
optionally inserted before *hi* and *ho*. Thus *fuig-hi* 'run
there!' may be [fúʒəj], *perd-ho* 'lose it!' may be
[pɛ́rðəw]. This kind of alternation is not confined to
imperatives of classes II and III, in fact. Consider the
following alternative forms (Fabra, 1913):

digues-ho 'say it!' [díɣəw] or [díyu} (cf. rule (5))
porta-ho 'bring it!' [pɔ́rtəw] or [pɔ́rtu]

Unstressed pronouns

corre-hi 'run there!' [kórəj] or [kóri]
veure-ho 'to see it' [béwrəw] or [béwɾu]
ofendre-us 'to offend you' [uféndrəws] or [uféndɾus]
seure-hi 'to sit there' [séwrəj] or [séwɾi]

It seems to be the case that deletion of final [ə] which is obligatory before ## followed by unstressed [i] or [u], is optional when one word boundary only intervenes, as in the present examples. Compare the similar phenomenon referred to in note 6 to Table 1. In "Barcelona colloquial", then, we may suppose that [bénsu] is from /bɛns+ə#+u/ with deletion, and likewise [pérðu] is from /pɛrd+ə#+u/. The question of voicedness neutralization does not then concern cases such as these, since it is ordered before final [ə]–deletion. If neutralization does occur across single # in this dialect, *fes* and *vés* can have unmarked final /s/ just like the regular second person suffix, provided they are exceptions to rule (6). When final deletion does not operate, these forms with /i/ or /u/ become subject to sandhi-glide formation; see VII §5.

4.3. As is clear from the table, in "Barcelona colloquial" no sequence of pronouns contains more than one [1] phonetically. When one of the pronouns is 3rd person indirect object plural $\begin{bmatrix} \text{li} \\ +\text{PL} \end{bmatrix}$, the following accusative pronoun $\begin{bmatrix} 1 \\ \pm\text{F} \\ \pm\text{PL} \end{bmatrix}$ receives no phonetic realization. When one of them is the third person indirect object singular, the various forms of the accusative pronoun are realized phonetically in part at least: [əlzi] for $\begin{bmatrix} \text{li} \\ -\text{PL} \end{bmatrix} + \begin{bmatrix} 1 \\ -\text{F} \\ +\text{PL} \end{bmatrix}$, [ləzi] for $\begin{bmatrix} \text{li} \\ -\text{PL} \end{bmatrix} + \begin{bmatrix} 1 \\ +\text{F} \\ +\text{PL} \end{bmatrix}$,

[li] for $\begin{bmatrix} \text{li} \\ -\text{PL} \end{bmatrix} + \begin{bmatrix} 1 \\ -\text{PL} \end{bmatrix}$. Let us suppose that the fundamental basis of the absence of more than one /l/ is a degemination rule of this form:

(7) $\quad 1 \to \emptyset \;/\; \left\{ \begin{matrix} \# \\ + \end{matrix} \right\} \text{l+} \underline{\qquad}$

Then several other rules, if ordered before it, will generate the correct output. To make sure that the accusative /l/ is deleted in the presence of $\begin{bmatrix} \text{li} \\ +\text{PL} \end{bmatrix}$, but the dative /l/ when it is $\begin{bmatrix} \text{li} \\ -\text{PL} \end{bmatrix}$, let us start with a rule switching $\begin{bmatrix} \text{li} \\ -\text{PL} \end{bmatrix}$ to follow accusative /l/:

(8) $\quad \begin{bmatrix} \text{li} \\ -\text{PL} \end{bmatrix} + 1$

$\qquad\qquad 1 \;+\; 2 \;\Rightarrow\; 2 \;+\; 1$

Then (7), which deletes the second /l/ of two, will delete the appropriate one in each case.

4.4. The forms [əlzi] *los* (indirect object), [əlzi] *los* (indirect object) + *ho*, [əlzəni] *los* (indirect object) + *ne*, [ni] *li* + *ne*, [li] *li* + *ho*, indicate that we require a rule switching the /i/ of the /li/ pronoun to final position. Such a rule will correctly "feed" rule (7), producing sequences of /l/ + /l/ from underlying $\begin{bmatrix} \text{li} \\ +\text{PL} \end{bmatrix}$ + /l/. In addition, to account for [ni] corresponding to *li* + *ne* 'of it to him', we need a rule, following (8), to delete /+l/ in just this case. Note that in the case of *los* (indirect object) + *ne* 'of it to them', i.e. + $\begin{bmatrix} \text{li} \\ +\text{PL} \end{bmatrix}$ + /n/, the /l/ is not deleted, nor is accusative /l/ deleted before /+n/ —hence [lən] corresponds to *lo* + *ne* or *la* + *ne*. The rule in question is thus:

(9) $\quad 1 \to \emptyset \: / \: \begin{bmatrix} \\ -PL \end{bmatrix} \: i + n$

This is the last rule that requires /i/ in its original position in the indirect object pronoun. The switching rule mentioned above is:

(10) $\quad \begin{array}{cc} i & \overbrace{(+l)(+n)(+u)(+i+)} \: \rrbracket_{Pro} \\ 1 & 2 \end{array} \Rightarrow \: 2 \quad 1$

If none of the items /+l/, /+n/, /+u/, /+i+/ follows /i/ the rule applies vacuously.

4.5. The sequence *ho + hi* (see note 10 to Table 1) is realized as [li] except when preceded by an /l/ pronoun or /+n/, in which case [i] is the realization. If we have a rule replacing /+u/ by /+l/ before /+i/, then, provided this rule precedes (7), this /l/ is deleted when preceded by /+l/. To deal with the absence of /l/ in the presence of /+n/ there are several possibilities. One is merely to replace /+u/ by zero there; thus:

(11) $\quad u \to \begin{Bmatrix} \emptyset \: / \\ 1 \: / \end{Bmatrix} + \begin{bmatrix} n \\ -\text{rule (18)} \end{bmatrix} \Big\} + \underline{} + i \: X \: \rrbracket_{Pro}$

This method seems quite ad hoc, however. One could make the rule

(12) $\quad u \to 1 \: / \: + \underline{} + i \: X \: \rrbracket_{Pro}$

and try to extend (7) so as to delete /+l/ after either /+l/ or /+n/; in that case, the /+n/ in the environment would still have to be distinguished from the /+n/ corresponding to the 1pl pronoun *nos*, which would hardly make the rule more natural.

If we allow /+u/ before /+i/ to be deleted by the truncation rule III (24), and it seems right that it should do so in order to reduce /+i+i/ to /+i/, then the proper form for (12) will be as follows:

(13) $\quad u \rightarrow 1 \;/\; (+s)(+ \left\{ \begin{matrix} w \\ t \end{matrix} \right\})(+ \left\{ \begin{matrix} n \\ m \end{matrix} \right\}) + \underline{\qquad} +i\; X \;]_{Pro}$

4.6. The rule to insert /+z/ in the plural pronouns *vos, nos* and *los/les* is essentially the same as that introducing the plural morph in nouns and adjectives. The segment introduced here must be voiced rather than unmarked since voicedness is distinctive before +V (as before V), as examples from verb inflection show:

(14) $\quad \emptyset \rightarrow +z \;/\; \left[\begin{matrix} \text{+segment} \\ \text{+PL} \end{matrix} \right] \underline{\qquad}]_{N,\, Pro,\, \bar{A},\, Det}$

Perhaps a more appropriate view than having the plural morph specifically marked because it is so required only in this particular environment, would be along the lines of Stanley, 1971: §7, according to which different affixes would be assigned different boundaries depending on which phonological rules do or do not operate across them. For Catalan, three strengths of boundary might be appropriate: the weakest would be that accompanying inflexional morphs introduced by rule, e.g. plural /+s/, feminine /+ə/, verb inflexions; the next strongest would be those surrounding lexical affixes, which are not subject to truncation. The strongest would surround unstressed "words" (cf. II §6.3) such as the pronouns discussed here, failing to provide the environment for stress assignment, but in other respects operating rather as word boundaries. Such a proposal needs further investigation.

Rule (15), which is in fact part of a more general process of deletion of final stops (cf. VII §4), is mentioned here so that the next rule (16) can correctly account for *quedant-nos* [kəðánzə] '(us) remaining'. It

Unstressed pronouns 163

can optionally apply later instead —after (25)— to account for the variant [kəðántənz].

(15) $\quad t \to \emptyset \ / \ n\underline{\qquad}\# \left\{ \begin{array}{c} [+\text{cons}] \\ \# \end{array} \right\}$

(16) $\quad \left\{ \begin{array}{c} w \\ n \end{array} \right\}_1 \to \emptyset \ / \ \left\{ \begin{array}{c} w \\ [-\text{syll}] \\ +\text{nasal} \end{array} \right\}_1 \#\underline{\qquad} C$

This rule deals with the deletions evidenced in note 8 to Table 1. It must of course follow (14) which "feeds" it by inserting a consonant, /+z/.

4.7. To account for the vowel of the feminine accusative pronouns *la* and *les* (and likewise, in effect, of the feminine definite articles, which have the same form) there is a rule:

(17) $\quad \emptyset \to +\text{ə} \ / \ + \left[\begin{array}{c} 1 \\ +F \end{array} \right] \underline{\qquad} \left\{ \begin{array}{c} \# \\ +C \end{array} \right\}$

As formulated this rule does not apply to /+n/ which is [+F] (see § 3.2.2). However, it is clearly almost identical in effect to I (9) which accounts for feminine [-ə] in nouns and adjectives. It seems preferable to combine these rules as follows —(18)—, merely marking /+n/ [—rule (18)], unless a better solution can be found to the problem mentioned in § 3.2.2. There are indeed many lexical exceptions to this rule, cf. I § 3.2.

(18) $\quad \emptyset \to +\text{ə} \ / \ [+F] \underline{\qquad} \left\{ \begin{array}{c} \# \\ +C \end{array} \right\}$

So far none of the rules of this chapter have referred to stressed vowels. The evidence relevant to their ordering with respect to the stress-assignment rule is that (13) must apply before the Truncation rule III (24), which itself applies before Stress assignment. If

Truncation applied after (18), it would not be necessary to mention C in the braces of (18). Let us suppose, then, that Truncation and Stress assignment apply after (18) but before (21) which mentions stress. We thus need no special rule deleting /+i/ before /+i/, e.g. (after (10)) /+l+i+i/ *li hi* [li].

To provide for the optional form of the 2pl pronoun *vos*: [uz], which alternates with [əwz], (see note 7 to Table 1), we have the rule:

(19) $\begin{bmatrix} +\text{high} \\ +\text{labial} \\ -\text{cons} \end{bmatrix} \underset{\text{opt}}{\rightarrow} [+\text{syll}] / \begin{Bmatrix} C \\ \## \end{Bmatrix} \underline{\quad} C$

The rule is in bleeding order relative to rule (20) which inserts /ə/ which gives syllabicity to pronouns, and thus precedes it. As single # is not mentioned to the left of the environment, (19) does not bleed (21) which deletes final /+r/ in infinitives. (19) is fed by (14), which therefore precedes it.

The first rule giving syllabic structure to unstressed pronouns is this:

(20) ø → ə / C(z) +_____C(z) X]$_{\text{Pro}}$

As a result of this rule a sequence such as /(+s)(+w+z)(+n+z)(+l+z)(+n)/ becomes /(+s)(+əw+z)(+ən+z)(+əl+z)(+ən)/. Similarly /(+s)(+t)(+m)(+l)/ becomes /(+s)(+ət)(+əm)(+əl)/. We require (20) to apply so as not to insert /ə/ before /+z/ in these pronoun sequences. This seems indeed to follow from the principle of interpretation of disjunctive ordering of rules stated by Chomsky & Halle (1968:366), namely: "if rules R_1 and R_2 are disjunctively ordered — R_1 preceding R_2 — and if R_1 applies to the substring Y of a string XYZ but is independent of X and Z, then R_2 may apply to X and Z but not to Y in a stage of the cycle in which R_1 applies. More precisely, if R_1 is the rule A → B/P_____Q, and R_1

Unstressed pronouns

applies to a string XP'A'Q'Y (where P', A', Q' are not distinct from P, A, Q, respectively), converting it to XP'B'Q'Y in the usual manner, then R_2 may apply to a string contained in X or in Y but not to a string that is included in (or, in particular, identical with) P'B'Q'."

That is, the rules should apply in the environments (20a): $C_a z+$____$C_b z$, (20b): $C_a z+$____C_b, (20c): C_a+____$C_b z$, and (20d): C_a+____C_b where $C_b \neq z$. Without this possibility of interpretation the rule would have to be formulated so that the right of the environment explicitly excluded the possibility of /z/, i.e.

(20e) $/C +$____$\begin{bmatrix} -\text{syll} \\ (-\text{obstr}) \\ (-\text{cont}) \end{bmatrix} X]\!] \text{Pro}$

This problem could be avoided and (20) simplified if it were ordered before (14) which inserts /+z/ in plural pronouns. Such an order is not possible, however; (14) in inserting /z/ supplies the environment for (19) to apply converting /w/ to /u/ between consonants — a rule of considerable naturalness. Rule (19) itself "bleeds" (20) inasmuch as the sequences (C)uz which it produces become ineligible as environments for (20).

4.8. To account for the phenomena referred to in note 9 to Table 1 we need a rule deleting infinitive /+r/ at the end of a phonological word, or before a sequence of two consonants beginning a pronoun.

(21) $r \rightarrow \emptyset \;/\; \begin{bmatrix} +\text{syllab} \\ \langle +\text{stress} \rangle_a \end{bmatrix}$ ____ $\#]\!] V \; \langle \begin{Bmatrix} \# \\ CC \end{Bmatrix} \rangle_b$

condition: if a, then b.

Before ## in fact, /+r/ of infinitives is deleted in both dialects as a result of the general final /r/–deletion rule, cf. VII §2. Rule (21) is bled by (20) which splits up consonant sequences, and must therefore be ordered after it; (21) also bleeds (25). (21) does not delete /+r/ in future and conditional forms since as a result of III (21) /+r/ is not there followed by #⟧$_V$ but only ⟧$_{Aux}$.

Rule (22) introduces the vowel of *lo* [lu], e.g. in *donar-lo* [dunárlu] 'to give it', *veient-lo* [bəjénlu] 'seeing it'. Since this rule follows (18) which introduces /ə/ after /+l/ which is [+F], it is not necessary to mention [−F] in the environment here. After (21) has deleted /+r/ after unstressed vowels, (22) will fail to apply in cases like *témer-lo* [téməl] 'to fear him'. (22) also bleeds (25) which therefore follows it.

(22) ø → +u / C # + 1____#

Rule (23), which is optional, deals with the cases referred to in note 2 to Table 1.

(23) ø $\xrightarrow{opt}$ ə / + $\begin{bmatrix} +obstr \\ +cont \\ +coron \end{bmatrix}$ ⟧$_{Pro}$ ⟦# $\begin{bmatrix} +obstr \\ +cont \\ +coron \\ -voice \end{bmatrix}$

Further examples: *ens sent* [ənzəsén] 'he hears us', *els xocava* [əlzəʃukáβə] 'it shocked them'. Rule (23) bleeds (25) which therefore follows it.

For the cases referred to in note 1 to Table 1 we need an optional rule inserting /ə/ after a single consonant pronoun except /+l/ which precedes a verb beginning with a consonant and which follows one of a small list of adverbs. The words after which this process may occur seem to be *tant* 'so much', *quant(s)* 'how much' or 'how many', *com* 'how', *on* 'where' and *quan* 'when'; thus e.g. *tant se val* 'it makes no difference', *tant me fa* 'I don't care', *quants ne vols?* 'how many (of them) do you want?', *com te dius?* 'what is your name?', *com se fa això?* 'how does one do that?', and

similarly *on se fa això?, quan se fa això?* 'where ...?'
and 'when ...?' respectively. The rule, which bleeds
(25) may perhaps be:

(24) $\emptyset \xrightarrow[\text{opt}]{} \mathrm{a} \ / \ \begin{bmatrix} +\text{nasal} \\ -\text{syll} \end{bmatrix} (C)(+z) \# \rrbracket_{\text{Ad}} \begin{Bmatrix} \text{Inter} \\ \text{Quant} \end{Bmatrix}$

$\quad\quad\quad + \begin{bmatrix} +\text{cons} \\ -\text{vocal} \end{bmatrix} \underline{\quad} \# C$

4.9. There are two ways of approaching the formulation of the rule inserting /ə/ after some postverbal single pronouns and before some preverbal pronoun sequences. One is to take separately preverbal and postverbal insertion; then the two parts of the rule are as follows:

(25) $\emptyset \rightarrow \mathrm{a} \ / \ \begin{Bmatrix} \begin{bmatrix} V \\ +\text{stress} \end{bmatrix} \begin{Bmatrix} C_1 \# \\ \#C \end{Bmatrix} C \underline{\quad} \# \\ \begin{Bmatrix} C \\ \# \end{Bmatrix} \# \underline{\quad} C \begin{Bmatrix} \# \\ C \ + \\ \# \ C \end{Bmatrix} \end{Bmatrix}$ i) ii)

Part i) inserts /ə/ after verbs ending in one or more consonants preceded by a stressed vowel (i.e. gerunds, plural imperatives — singular imperatives being 'bled' by rule (6) — and most infinitives), followed by a single consonant pronoun; thus *portar-se* [purtársə] 'to behave oneself', *digueu-me* [diɣɛ́wmə] 'tell me' *traient-ne* [trəjénnə] 'removing some'; or after verbs ending in a stressed vowel, followed by a plural pronoun (*nos, vos,* or *los*). In these cases infinitive /+r/ has been deleted by rule (21). Examples are *donar-nos* [dunánzə] 'to give us', *fer-los* [félzə] 'to make them (M)'. Part ii) inserts /ə/ before single one-consonant pronouns before a verb beginning with a consonant, e.g. *em proposa* [əmprupózə] 'he suggests to me', *el crec* [əlkrέk] 'I believe him';

before plural (two-consonant) pronouns which occur alone before a verb or first in a series; thus *els agafa* [əlzəɣáfə] 'he grasps them', *ens n'ofereix* [ənzənufəɾéʃ] 'he offers us some', *us el recomano* [əwzəlrəkumánu] 'I recommend it to you'. In addition, since part i) has not applied, the structure $\begin{bmatrix} V \\ +\text{stress} \end{bmatrix} C_1 \#CC \begin{Bmatrix} \# \\ + \end{Bmatrix}$ meets the structural description of part ii) for *veient-los* [bəjéntəlz] 'seeing them', *digueu-los* [diɣə́wəlzi] 'tell them' (cf. Fabra, 1954:II, 77).

This formulation of (25) is not wholly satisfactory, since it fails to express the "mirror-image" nature of the rule, especially as it applies to single-consonant pronouns. If we separate these out, the rule applying to them is

(26) $\emptyset \rightarrow \text{ə} \Big/ \begin{Bmatrix} \#\underline{\quad} C \# C \\ C \# C \underline{\quad} \# \end{Bmatrix}$

Here the environment is obviously to be abbreviated by some mirror-image notation. Such a notation is suggested in chapter VII §4.2. The remainder of the rule, dealing with two-consonant pronouns, is not a true mirror-image:

(27) $\emptyset \rightarrow \text{ə} \Big/ \begin{Bmatrix} \begin{bmatrix} V \\ +\text{stress} \end{bmatrix} \#CC\underline{\quad}\# & \text{i)} \\ \begin{Bmatrix} C \\ \# \end{Bmatrix} \# \underline{\quad} CC \begin{Bmatrix} \# \\ + \end{Bmatrix} & \text{ii)} \end{Bmatrix}$

N.B. in part ii) of (25) and (27) the $\begin{Bmatrix} C \\ \# \end{Bmatrix}$ brace on the far left of the environment blocks epenthesis after a verb ending in a vowel; thus /don+a#n+z#/ and not */don+a#ən+z#/. Such a restriction will in fact be unnecessary if the vowel-sandhi rules (cf. VII §5.3) are permitted to delete /ə/ adjacent to a vowel across one #.

4.10. Sample derivations

(5)	kuz # l #	agaf+a+ɛ+m # l #	dig+u+ɛ+s # m+u#	fik+a# li+n+i#
(6)	–F	–F		–PL
(8)	kuzə # l #		dig+u+ɛ # m+u#	
(9)				fik+a# i+n+i#
(10)				fik+a# n+i+i#
(7)				
(13)				
(14)				
(15)				
(16)				
(18)				
(20)				
III(24)		agaf +ɛ+m # l #	dig +ɛ # m+u#	fik+a# n+i #
III(74)	kúzə # l #	agaf +ɛ́+m # l #	díg +ɛ # m+u#	fík+a# n+i #
IV(21)		agaf +ɛ́+m # l+u#		
(22)	[kúzəl]	[ayəfɛ́mlu]	[díyəmu]	[fíkəni]
(23)	*cus-lo*	*agafem-lo*	*digues-m'ho*	*fica-li-n'hi*
(25)	'sew it!'	'let's catch him!'	'tell me it!'	'put some in there for him!'

170 Unstressed pronouns

(5)	#n +n+n#an+a+ɛ+m +PL	ked+a+r+r#t+1 # +F −PL	#s + l +#pɔz+a+b+a +F +PL
(6)			
(8)			
(9)			
(10)			
(7)			
(13)			
(14)	#n+z+n#an+a+ɛ+m		#s + l +z#pɔz+a+b+a +F
(15)	#n+z+ən#an+a+ɛ+m	ked+a+r+r#t +l+ə#	#s +l+ə+z#pɔz+a+b+a
(16)	#n+z+ən#an +ɛ+m	ked+a+r+r#t+əl+ə#	#s+əl+ə+z#pɔz+a+b+a
(18)	#n+z+ən#an +ɛ́+m	ked+á+r+r#t+əl+ə#	#s+əl+ə+z#pɔz+á+b+a
(20)			
III(24)			
III(74)			
IV(21)			
(22)	#ən+z+ən#an +ɛ́+m	[kəðártələ]	[sələspuzáβə]
(23)	[ənzənənɛ́m]	quedar-te-la	se les posava
(25)	ens n'anem 'we're going'	'for you to keep it'	'he put them (F) on'

Unstressed pronouns 171

	# ən+z+ əl+z#ufar +ɛʃ +PL +PL −F	bəw+ɛɹ+ə#l#i+ +F	pɔrt+a+r# n+l # +PL +PL +F
(5)			
(6)			
(8)			
(9)			
(10)			
(7)			
(13)			
(14)	# n+z+ l+z#ufarí+i+eʃ		pɔrt+a+r#n+z# l+z# +F
(15)	# n+z+əl+z#ufari+i+eʃ		pɔrt+a+r#n+z+l+z#
(16)	# n+z+əl+z#ufar +ɛʃ		pɔrt+a+r#n+z+e+l+e#
(18)	# n+z+əl+z#ufar +ɛʃ		pɔrt+a+r#n+z+e+l+e#
(20)			
III(24)			pɔrt+á+r#n+z+e+l+e#
III(74)			pɔrt+á #n+z+e+l+e#
IV(21)		bəw+ɛɹ+ə l i+	
(22)	#ən+z+əl+z#ufar +ɛ́ʃ		
(23)	[ənzəlzufəréʃ]	[béwɾəli]	[purtánzələs]
(25)	*ens els ofereix* 'he offers us them (M)'	*veure-la-hi* 'to see her there'	*portar-nos-les* 'to bring us them (F)'

(5)	#s+əl +i#bɛw −PL −F	kuʎ #t+ 1 +n # −PL −F
(6)		
(8)		kuʎə#t+ 1 +n#
(9)		
(10)		
(7)	# w +u +i#anbi+a+n +PL	
(13)		
(14)	# w + 1 +i#anbi+a+n	
(15)	#w+z+ 1 +i#anbi+a+n	
(16)		
(18)		
(20)	#s+əl +i#bɛw	kuʎə#t+ə1+əyʎ
III(24)	#w+z+əl+i#anbi+a+n	
III(74)	#s+əl +i#bɛ́w	kúʎə#t+ə1+əyʎ
IV(21)	#w+z+əl+i#anbí+a+n	
(22)	#əw+z+əl+i#anbí+a+n	
(23)	[səliβɛ́w]	[kúʌətələn]
	se l'hi veu	cull-te-l'en
(25)	'one sees him there'	'pick it out (for yourself!)'
	[əwzəli (ə) mbíən]	
	us l'hi envien	
	'they send it to you there'	

Unstressed pronouns

(5)	# li + l +n#trɛw+e+n −PL +PL −F	tramɛt+rə# li + l # +PL+PL +F	ked+a+ɛ+w# w + n + l # +PL +PL −PL +F
(6)			
(8)	# l + li +n#trɛw−n−e+n +PL −PL		
(9)	# l + i +n#trɛw+e+n	tramɛt+rə# l +l + i #	
(10)	# l + n +i#trɛw+e+n	tramɛt+rə#l #i+	
(7)			
(13)			
(14)	#l+z+ n +i#trɛw+en	tramɛt+rə# l+z +i#	ked+a+ɛ+w##w+z+n+z+ l #
(15)			ked+a+ɛ+w# +z+n+z+ l
(16)			ked+a+ɛ+w# # e+l+z+
(18)	u+e+w3tri+ ne−e+z+n		ked+a+ɛ+w+3+w+z+ən+z+ e+l+z+
(20)			ked e+3+w#+z+ən+z+ e+l[e+z+
III(24)	#l+z+ən +i#trɛẃw+e+n	tramɛ́lt+rə#l +z +i#	ked e+ɛ́+w+z+ən+z+ e+l[e+z+
III(74)			
IV(21)			
(22)	#əl+z+ən+i#trɛẃw+e+n		
(23)	[əlzənitrɛ́wen] *els n'hi treuen* 'they take them out for him'	[trəmɛ́trəlzi] *trametre'ls-les* 'to send them them'	[kəðɛ́wzənzələ] *quedeu-vos-ens-la* 'keep it (F) (for us)!'
(25)			

(5)		#m + n#baʒ
(6)		
(8)		
(9)		menʒ+a+nt#s + t l #
(10)		+PL
(7)		−F
(13)		
(14)		menʒ+a+nt#s +t +l+z#
(15)		menʒ+a+n #s +t +l+z#
(16)		
(18)		
(20)	#m +ən#baʒ	menʒ+a+n #s+ət+əl+z#
III(24)		
III(74)	#m +ən#báʒ	menʒ+á+n #s+ət+əl+z#
IV(21)		
(22)	[mambátʃ]	[mənʒánsətəls]
(23)	me'n vaig	menjant-se-te'ls
(25)	'I'm going'	'him eating yours up'

N.B. The derivation of *menjant-se-te'ls* shows that, in fact, for the correct application of Stress assignment (III(74)) rule (15), and thus also (16), should be ordered after it. In the order in which these rules appear above, III(74) would incorrectly stress the root.

Unstressed pronouns

5.1. I shall now suggest the form of the rules for pronouns in the "Standard" language, corresponding to the forms recommended by normative grammarians. By the number of each rule I mention the rule of "Barcelona colloquial" to which it most nearly corresponds.

The underlying form of the pronouns is this:

(28)
cf. (3)

$$Pro \rightarrow (+s)\left(+\left\{\begin{bmatrix} v \\ +PL \\ t \end{bmatrix}\right\}\right)\left(+\left\{\begin{bmatrix} n \\ +PL \\ m \end{bmatrix}\right\}\right)\left(+\begin{bmatrix} li \\ \pm PL \end{bmatrix}\right)$$

$$\left(+\begin{bmatrix} l \\ \pm PL \\ \pm F \end{bmatrix}\right)\left(+\left\{\begin{bmatrix} n \\ \pm F \\ -\text{rule (18)} \\ u \end{bmatrix}\right\}\right)(+i+)$$

This differs from rule (3) in that the 2pl pronoun has underlying /v/ to account for the [b] ~ [β] ~ [w] ~ [u] alternations. With this form of rule *ne* and *ho* may not co-occur, (cf. note 10 to Table 1). To exclude *ho* + *hi* too the final part of (28) would read:

$$\left\{\left(+\begin{bmatrix} n \\ \pm F \\ -\text{rule (18)} \end{bmatrix}\right)(+i+) \atop (+u+)\right\} .$$

Rule (4) switching pronouns to preverbal position in certain circumstances applies here in just the same way. Rules (5) and (6) adjusting the form of imperatives when followed by a pronoun are absent from "Standard". The rule transposing *li* (3sg indirect object) after accusative /+l/ is identical in "Standard", viz.

(29) $\begin{bmatrix} li \\ -PL \end{bmatrix}$ + l
= (8)
           1   +   2   ⇒   2   +   1

But the rule for degemination of /l+l/ follows immediately in "Standard", thus deleting /l/ only from the singular indirect object and not from the plural pronoun:

(30)
= (7) $\quad l \rightarrow \emptyset \,/\, \left\{ \begin{matrix} \# \\ + \end{matrix} \right\} \; l \; + \underline{\quad}$

This must be followed by a rule peculiar to this dialect deleting /i/ from the indirect object plural pronoun:

(31) $\left[\begin{matrix} i \\ +PL \end{matrix} \right] \rightarrow \emptyset \,/\, \underline{\quad} X \;]\text{Pro}$

As a result of the operation of (29), (30) and (31), the underlying /+li/ is reduced to /+l/ in the plural, and to /+i/ in the singular when preceded by another /+l/ pronoun.

The rule placing /i/ at the end of the sequence operates in a slightly different way in "Standard", namely, /i/ is moved only when the preceding /l/ has been deleted by (30); after that rule, /i/ is preceded by a morpheme boundary to which the /i/–transposition rule is now sensitive:

(32)
cf. (10) $\quad +i \quad \underbrace{(+n)(+u)(+i+)}_{} \quad]\text{Pro}$
$\qquad\qquad 1 \qquad\qquad 2 \qquad\qquad\qquad \Rightarrow \; 2 \quad 1$

Rule (32) will not shift /i/ in the sequences *li + ho*, nor *li + ne* since it is not directly preceded by a morpheme boundary. Rule (9) is absent from this dialect.

If the sequence *ho + hi* is well-formed, (cf. note 10 to Table 1), then we need a version of rule (13). (33) is the same as this, except that it takes account of the different rule (28), which refers to the pronoun /+v/:

(33)
cf. (13) $\quad u \rightarrow 1 \,/\, (+s)\left(+\left\{ \begin{matrix} v \\ t \end{matrix} \right\} \right)\left(+\left\{ \begin{matrix} n \\ m \end{matrix} \right\} \right) \; +\underline{\quad}+ \; X \;]\text{Pro}$

If the sequences *los* (indirect object) *+ ho + hi* 'it to them there' and *li + ho + hi* 'it to him/her there' are well-formed,

Unstressed pronouns

then the *ho* item will not become /l/ by rule (33) but will be deleted by the truncation rule III (24). That is, the sequences will be realized by [luzi]/[(ə)lzi] and [li] respectively, essentially as in "Barcelona colloquial". As far as I know the normative grammarians do not discuss the realization of these sequences, which seem to be acceptable on semantic and syntactic grounds.

5.2. The rule for plural /+z/ is as before:

(34)
=(14)   ø → +z / [+segment, +PL] _____]N, Pro, A, Det

Rule (15) applies equally in this dialect as part of a more general rule (cf. VII §4) but here has no effect on the form of pronouns so will not be repeated.

For feminine /+ə/ the rule must be slightly differently formulated in "Standard" to deal with *la + hi*: [ləj] rather than [li]. Here the /+ə/ introduced is an exception to the Truncation rule III (24) and must be inserted before /+i/ as well as /+C/. To retain the generality of the rule, a formulation with angle brackets seems most appropriate. Probably the non-deletion of /+ə/ in *la* should be related to the similar phenomenon in the feminine definite article, (cf. VII §5). For the present, I suggest this version of (18).

(35)
cf. (18)   ø → +[ə ⟨−rule III (24)⟩]

/ ⟨+⟩ [⟨1⟩ +F] _____ {+ #} ⟨[V +high]⟩

Now we need a special rule for this dialect, to deal with the forms [buz] *vos*, [nuz] *nos*, [luz] *los* which occur immediately after verb forms ending in a consonant. This will be

(36)   ø → +u / C # C _____ z

This rule is bled by (35) in the case of the feminine plural pronoun *les*; it must precede (37) so as to provide the correct environment for the /v/ → [w] ~ [b] alternations in the *vos* pronoun.

The rule dealing with the realization of /v/ (as [w], [b], or [β]) must be mentioned here, as in this dialect it feeds (40) = (19). The rule is discussed in more detail in V §4. Features other than those specified on the right of the arrow will be supplied by "linking" rules — see chapter VI.

(37) $\begin{bmatrix} \text{+labial} \\ \text{+voiced} \\ \text{+cont} \\ \text{+cons} \end{bmatrix} \rightarrow \begin{bmatrix} \alpha\text{cons} \\ \text{+distr} \end{bmatrix} \ / \underline{\qquad} [\alpha\text{syllab}]$

To account for the form [uz] for *vos*, rule (19) must also be present in this dialect. Here, however, it is not optional, since in preverbal position we have [uz] only, not [əwz]; and it must follow the first epenthesis rule corresponding to (20) to account for *se* + *vos* realized as [səwz] rather than *[suz].

5.3. In this dialect the environment for epenthesis of /ə/ between pronouns is subject to greater restrictions than in "Barcelona colloquial"; in particular, cases of [ə] after [z] are much fewer, and epenthesis is sensitive to whether a following verb begins with a vowel or a consonant. The appropriate modification to (20) would in fact have to be very complicated in order to account for alternations such as *nos* + *lo* + *ne*: [ənzlən#C] ~ [ənzəln#V] ~ [nzlən##].

A neater solution is to let (20) apply as before;

(38)   ø → ə / C(z) + $\underline{\qquad}$ C(z)X⟧$_{\text{Pro}}$
= (20)

and then to delete /ə/, where required, by rule (39):

(39)   ə → ø / ⟦$_{\text{Pro}}$ X $\left\{\begin{bmatrix} z \\ l \\ -F \end{bmatrix}\right\}$ $\underline{\qquad}$ C (#)V

Unstressed pronouns 179

This rule cannot be incorporated into (38) as an exception, since its environment is sensitive to vowels introduced by (38); that is, it is critically ordered after (38). The rules which the schema of (39) abbreviates are themselves ordered by the usual convention; that is, first with C#V to the right of the environment bar, then with CV. So we have these derivations.

	n+z+ l+ n #C	n+z+ l+ n #V	V# n+z+ l+ n ##
(38)	n+z+əl+ən#C	n+z+əl+ən#V	V#n+z+əl+ən##
(39i)		n+z+əl+ n#V	
(39ii)	n+z+ l+ən#C		V#n+z+l+ən##

[−F] is mentioned in rule (39) to avoid deletion of /ə/ in feminine pronouns. For *lo + ne* before a verb beginning with a vowel, these rules derive /##l+n#V/, which is subject to the "Standard" version of (25). Rule (39) also deletes /ə/ from /C#ləni##/ (*lo + ne + hi*). This /ə/ will be replaced through the appropriate form of (25) to give [C#ləni##]; /ə/ is correctly deleted from the sequence /V#ləni##/ giving [V#lni##].

Corresponding to (19) we now have

$$(40) = (19) \quad \begin{bmatrix} +\text{high} \\ +\text{labial} \\ -\text{cons} \end{bmatrix} \rightarrow [+\text{syll}] \quad / \left\{ \begin{matrix} C \\ \## \end{matrix} \right\} \underline{\quad} C$$

In "Standard" the angle bracket conditions on (21) are not applicable; the final /+r/ of infinitives is deleted only before ## whether the preceding vowel is stressed or not. So we have

$$(41) \quad \text{cf. (21)} \qquad r \rightarrow \emptyset \quad / \underline{\quad} \##$$

"Standard" has rule (22), which deals with the form [lu] : *lo*, in the same form. Here it is not critically ordered with respect to (41) but must precede (45) (= (25)).

$$(42) = (22) \qquad \emptyset \rightarrow +u \quad / \ C\# \ l \underline{\quad} \#$$

As mentioned in note 2 to Table 1, in "Standard" /ə/ is inserted before verbs beginning with /s/ or /ʃ/ only after the /+s/ pronoun, not after /+z/; so here we have:

(43)
cf. (23) $\emptyset \xrightarrow[\text{opt}]{} \text{ə} / + \begin{bmatrix} +\text{obstr} \\ +\text{cont} \\ +\text{coron} \\ -\text{voiced} \end{bmatrix}$ ——⟧Pro⟦ # $\begin{bmatrix} +\text{obstr} \\ +\text{cont} \\ +\text{coron} \\ -\text{voiced} \end{bmatrix}$

(44)
= (24) $\emptyset \xrightarrow[\text{opt}]{} \text{ə} / \begin{bmatrix} +\text{nasal} \\ -\text{syll} \end{bmatrix}$ (C)(+z) # ⟧Ad $\begin{Bmatrix} \text{Inter} \\ \text{Quant} \end{Bmatrix}$

$+ \begin{bmatrix} +\text{cons} \\ -\text{vocal} \end{bmatrix}$ ——#C

Corresponding to rule (25) we have a similar rule here, but which is not sensitive to stress in the verb, and from which strings of the form #⟧$_V$ CC# are bled away by (36) and (38). So we have:

(45)
cf. (25) $\emptyset \rightarrow \text{ə} / \begin{Bmatrix} \text{C\#C} \underline{\quad} (\text{C X}) \# \\ \begin{Bmatrix} \text{C} \\ \# \end{Bmatrix} \# \underline{\quad} \text{C} \begin{Bmatrix} \text{C} \begin{Bmatrix} + \\ \# \end{Bmatrix} \\ \# \text{ C} \end{Bmatrix} \end{Bmatrix}$ i)
ii)

If, as before, we extract the mirror-image part as (26), the remainder is now

(46)
cf. (27) $\emptyset \rightarrow \text{ə} / \begin{Bmatrix} \text{C\#C}\underline{\quad}\text{C} \\ \begin{Bmatrix} \text{C} \\ \# \end{Bmatrix} \# \underline{\quad} \text{CC} \begin{Bmatrix} + \\ \# \end{Bmatrix} \end{Bmatrix}$

The parenthesis (C X) in part i) of rule (45) is to permit re-epenthesis in the case of /C#lni#/ mentioned above.

5.4. The following sample derivations for the "Standard" language take the same lexical forms as in the "Barcelona colloquial" examples (§4.10), and illustrate how different systematic phonetic representations are derived.

Unstressed pronouns

	kuz # l # −F	agaf+a+ɛ+m # l # −F	dig+u+ɛ+s# m+u#	fik+a# li+n+i# −PL
(29)				
(30)				
(31)				
(32)				
(33)				
(34)				
(35)				
(36)				
(37)				
(38)				
(39)				
(40)				
III(24)	kúz # l #	agaf +ɛ+m # l #	dig +ɛ+s# m+u#	
III(74)		agaf +ɛ́+m # l #	díg +ɛ+s# m+u#	
IV(41)	kúz #l+u#	agaf +ɛ́+m #l+u#		fík+a# li+n+i#
(42)	[kúzlu]	[ayəfɛ́mlu]	[díyəzmu]	[fíkəlini]
	cus-lo	*agafem-lo*	*digues-m'ho*	*fica-li-n'hi*
	'sew it!'	'let's catch him!'	'tell me it!'	'put some in there for him!'

Unstressed pronouns

(29)	# n +n#an+a+ɛ+m +PL	ked+a+r#t+ l # +F −PL	#s+ l #pɔz+a+b+a +F +PL
(30)			
(31)			
(32)			
(33)			
(34)	#n+z+n#an+a+ɛ+m	ked+a+r#t+ l+ə# +F	#s+ l +z#pɔz+a+b+a +F
(35)			#s+ l+ə+z#pɔz+a+b+a +F
(36)	#n+z+ən#an+a+ɛ+m		
(37)	#n+z+ n#an+a+ɛ+m		
(38)		ked+a+r#t+əl+ə# +F	#s+əl+a+z#pɔz+a+b+a +F
(39)	#n+z+ n#an +ɛ+m		
(40)	#n+z+ n#an +ɛ+m		
III(24)	#n+z+ n#an +έ+m	ked+á+r#t+əl+ə#	#s+əl+ə+z#pɔz+á+b+a
III(74)	#n+z+ n#an +έ+m		
IV(41)			
(42)	#ən+z+n#an +έ+m		
(45)	[ənznanέm] *ens n'anem* 'we're going'	[keðártələ] *quedar-te-la* 'for you to keep it (F)'	[sələspuzáβə] *se les posava* 'he put them (F) on'

Unstressed pronouns

	# n + l #ufar+i+eʃ +PL +PL −F	bəw+rəə # l +i# +F	pɔrt+a+r# n + l # +PL +PL +F
(29)			
(30)			
(31)			
(32)			
(33)			
(34)	#n+z+l+z #ufar+i+eʃ	bəw+rəə#l+e+i# +F	pɔrt+a+r#n+z+l+z# +F
(35)			pɔrt+a+r#n+z+l+e+z# +F
(36)			pɔrt+a+r#n+u+z+l+e+z# +F
(38)	#n+z+ə+l+z#ufar+i+eʃ		pɔrt+a+r#n+u+z+ə+l+ə+z# +F
(39)	#n+z+ə+l+z#ufar +eʃ		pɔrt+a+r#n+u+z+ l+ə+z#
(40)	#n+z+ə+l+z#ufar +éʃ		
III(24)			
III(74)		bə́w+rə+#l+ə+i	pɔrt+á+r#n+u+z+ l+ə+z#
IV(41)			
(42)			
(45)	#ən+z+ə+l+z#ufar +éʃ		
	[ənzəlzufəréʃ]	[béwrəlai]	[purtárnuzləs]
	ens els ofereix	*veure-la-hi*	*portar-nos-les*
	'he offers us them'	'to see her there'	'to bring us them (F)'

(29)	#s+ + l +i#bɜw −PL −F	# v +u +i#anbi+a+n +PL	kuʎ #t+ l +n# −PL −F
(30)			
(31)			
(32)			
(33)			
(34)		# v +l +i#anbi+a+n +PL	
(35)		#v+z+l +i#anbi+a+n	
(36)			
(37)	#s+əl +i#bɜw	#w+z+l +i#anbi+a+n	kuʎ #t+əl+n#
(38)		#w+z+əl+i#anbi+a+n	
(39)		#w+z+ l+i#anbi+a+n	
(40)		#u+z+ l+i#anbi+a+n	
III(24)			
III(74)			
IV(41)	#s+əl +i#bɜ́w	#u+z+ l+i#anbí+a+n	kúʎ #t+əl+n#
(42)	[səliβɜ́w] *se l'hi veu* 'one sees him there'	[uzli(ə)mbíən] *us l'hi envien* 'they send it to you there'	[kúʎtələn] *cull-te-l'en* 'pick it out (for yourself)!'
(45)			

(29)	# li + l +n#trɛw+e+n tramɛt+rɛ# li + l #
−PL +PL   +PL +PL
−F   +F
(30)	# l + li +n#trɛw+e+n
+PL −PL
(31)	# l + i +n#trɛw+e+n tramɛt+rɛ# l + l #
−PL   +PL +PL
+F
(32)	# l + n i+#trɛw+e+n
(33)	#l+z+ n i+#trɛw3ti+e+n tramɛt+rɛ#l+z+ l+z+ #
+F
(34)	#l+z+ n i+#trɛw3ti+e+n tramɛt+rɛ#l+z+l+e+z#
(35)	u+e+w3ti+e+n
(36)	
(37)	#l+z+ən i+#trɛw3ti+e+n tramɛt+rɛ#l+z+el+e+z#
+F
(38)	#l+z+ n i+#trɛw3ti+e+n tramɛt+rɛ#l+z+ l+e+z#
(39)	
(40)	
III(24)	
III(74)	#l+z+ n i+#trɛ́w+e+n tramɛ́t+rɛ#l+z+ l+e+z#
IV(41)	
(42)	#əl+z+n +i#trɛ́w+e+n [trəmɛtrəlzles]
[əlznitrɛ́wen]   trametre'ls-les
els n'hi treuen   'to send them them (F)'
'they take them out for
him'
(45)	

186   *Unstressed pronouns*

(29)	ked+a+ɛ+w# v + n + l # +PL +PL −PL +F	##m +n#baʒ	menʒ+a+nt#s+ t + l # +PL −F	
(30)				
(31)				
(32)				
(33)				
(34)	ked+a+ɛ+w#v+z +n+z + l # +F		menʒ+a+nt#s+ t +l+z#	
(35)	ked+a+ɛ+w#v+z +n+z +l+ e+l+ #			
(36)	ked+a+ɛ+w#v+u+z+n+z+l+ e+ #			
(37)	ked+a+ɛ+w#b+u+z+n+z+l+ e+ #			
(38)	ked+a+ɛ+w#b+u+z+ən+z+əl+e+#	#m+ən#baʒ	menʒ+a+nt#s+ə+t+əl+e+z#	
(39)	ked+a+ɛ+w#b+u+z+ən+z+ l+e+#			
(40)				
III(24)	ked +ɛ+w#b+u+z+ən+z+ l+e+#			
III(74)	ked +ɛ́+w#b+u+z+ən+z+ l+e#	#m+ən#báʒ	menʒ+ɑ́+nt#s+ə+t+əl+z #	
IV(41)				
(42)	[kəðέwβuzənzle]	[mambátʃ]	[mənʒánsətels]	
(45)	*quedeu-vos-ens-la*	*me'n vaig*	*menjant-se-te'ls*	
	'keep it (F) (for us)!'	'I'm going'	'him eating yours up'	

6. Rules in this chapter, specifically (34) = (14), (35) = (18) and (44ii) = (25ii) will also generate correct forms of the definite article from the underlying
$\begin{bmatrix} 1 \\ \pm F \\ \pm PL \end{bmatrix}$ —giving the same forms as for the pre-verbal /+l/ pronoun. Thus we have M singular: /əl#C/, /l#V/; M plural: /əlz#/; F singular /lə#C/, /l(ə)#V/; F plural: /ləz#/.

7.1. The early rules in the sequence for both dialects, which readjust the form and order of the pronouns (rules (8), (9), (10), (7), (13); (29)–(33)) are made necessary by the form of the rewrite rules (3) and (28) which introduce the segmental form of the pronouns. As formulated these rules also permit, incorrectly, the cooccurrence of accusative *lo/los/la/les* with *ho*. This could be avoided by putting /+u/ in disjunctive braces with /+l/ and switching it to a position after /+n/ by another readjustment rule. But a different approach to "spelling-out" based on a deeper analysis in terms of semantic/syntactic features might avoid some of the problems caused by the specified linear sequence of phonological items in (3) and (28). In the following paragraphs I shall suggest some rules which would be required in such an approach for "Barcelona colloquial".

7.2 The person and number features will be [+1P], [+2P], [+3P], [±PL], together with [I] (= impersonal) and [Δ] (= a pronoun corresponding to an embedded sentence or unspecified [+3P], which is typically realized by *ho* when accusative). The case functions (cf. § 3.2) are indicated by these symbols:

    A = accusative
    D = dative

R = reflexive
S = subnominal
P = partitive
Ab = ablative
C = comitative
L = locative

I will suppose that [i] which appears to correspond to semantic "dative" in certain circumstances (see § 3.2.1) is L syntactically; (possibly it has undergone a special readjustment rule such as D → L / A___).

The following "lexical insertion" rules are ordered with respect to each other, and replace (3), (7)–(10) and (13). Commas indicate disjunction between the symbols they separate linearly. The rules are not to be evaluated by the usual symbol-count evaluation measure; I do not know what evaluation measure might be appropriate for rules of this sort. Maybe one which valued highly a grammar in which each function received a distinct realization?

(47) $\left\{\begin{bmatrix} +3P \\ A \end{bmatrix}, \begin{bmatrix} +3P + PL \\ D, S \end{bmatrix}\right\} \rightarrow +l \;/\; \underline{\qquad} \rbrack_{Pro}$

This rule (47) inserts accusative *lo/los/la/les* and dative *los*.

(48) $[P, Ab] \rightarrow +n \;/\; \underline{\qquad} \rbrack_{Pro}$

This rule (48) introduces *ne*; if (47) has applied, /+n/ follows /+l/.

(49) $\left\{\begin{matrix} [C, L] \\ \begin{bmatrix} +3P, \Delta \\ D, S \end{bmatrix} \end{matrix}\right\} \rightarrow +i \;/\; \underline{\qquad} \rbrack_{Pro}$

Rule (49) accounts for *hi* (after /+n/ if (48) applies, after /+l/ if (47) applies) in comitative/locative function

Unstressed pronouns

(all persons), and third person or "dummy" dative or subnominal, corresponding to the [i] of [li],

(50) $\left\{ \begin{bmatrix} +3P \\ D, S \end{bmatrix} \\ \begin{bmatrix} \Delta \\ A \end{bmatrix} \right\} \rightarrow +l \;/\; [\!\![\; \underline{\quad} +V \;]\!\!]_{Pro}$

In a sense, (50) is a key rule in this approach, since it inserts /+l/ for dative *li*, and *l'hi* corresponding to *li + ho*, only when (49) has applied and (47) and (48) have not: this is the point of the brackets [[...]] and +V in the environment. Rule (50) ordered in this way deals with most of the phenomena mentioned in §§ 4.3 and 4.4.

(51) $\begin{bmatrix} +1P \\ R,A,D,S \end{bmatrix} \rightarrow \left\{ \begin{array}{l} +m \;/\; [\!\![\;_{Pro} \begin{bmatrix} \overline{-PL} \end{bmatrix} \\ +n \;/\; [\!\![\;_{Pro} \begin{bmatrix} \overline{+PL} \end{bmatrix} \end{array} \right\}$

(52) $\begin{bmatrix} +2P \\ R,A,D,S \end{bmatrix} \rightarrow \left\{ \begin{array}{l} +t \;/\; [\!\![\;_{Pro} \begin{bmatrix} \overline{-PL} \end{bmatrix} \\ +w \;/\; [\!\![\;_{Pro} \begin{bmatrix} \overline{+PL} \end{bmatrix} \end{array} \right\}$

(53) $\left\{ \begin{bmatrix} +3P, I, \Delta \\ R \end{bmatrix} \\ \begin{bmatrix} I \\ A, D, S \end{bmatrix} \right\} \rightarrow +s \;/\; [\!\![\;_{Pro} \underline{\quad}$

(54) $\begin{bmatrix} \Delta \\ -segm \end{bmatrix} \rightarrow +u \;/\; \underline{\quad}]\!\!]_{Pro}$

Rule (54) introduces /+u/ as the last in a sequence only if Δ has not previously been spelt out segmentally (by (49), (50) or (53)). The problems mentioned in § 4.5 are in this way dealt with quite simply.

These lexical insertion rules which, being ordered, are

sensitive to phonetic environments, would not be permitted in a grammar which separated components strictly, linking the syntactic and phonological components by readjustment rules (cf. Chomsky & Halle, 1968: 9–10, 371–2; Hurford, 1971: 6). It is not clear, however, that the separation of components, or of levels, within a grammar has a sound theoretical basis. A unified grammar which would permit rules such as (47)–(54) may, it seems, capture generalizations which a "component" grammar is obliged to ignore.

CHAPTER V

Problems in underlying representations

1. The representation of phonetic [r].

Phonetically [r] in Catalan is, as in Castilian, a voiced apico-alveolar multiple flap; (cf. Barnils, 1933:89ff, 168; Badia, 1962:93; Harris, 1969:46ff). It is longer and more tense than [ɾ] which is a voiced apico-alveolar single flap; (cf. Barnils, 1933:168; Badia, 1962:91). Alarcos (1953) includes /r/ as a unit phoneme distinct from /ɾ/ as does Badia (1965a:277–84), both without discussion. Badia (1973a:154) states: "Nous acceptons volontiers qu'il existe une opposition phonologique entre /r/ et /rr/, et refusons de considérer l'*r* multiple /rr/ comme une composition de /r/ + /r/ ..." Badia's data (1965a: loc. cit.) reveal, nevertheless, the strange distribution of [r] and [ɾ].

At the beginning of a morpheme only [r] occurs, e.g. *romà* [rumá] 'Roman', *preromà* [prərumá] 'pre-Roman'. Between vowels [r] is opposed to [ɾ] e.g.

vara [báɾə] 'rod' *barra* [bárə] 'bar'
mira [míɾə] 'looks' (V) *mirra* [mírə] 'myrrh'
vari [báɾi] 'varied' *barri* [bári] 'suburb'

Before a consonant only [r] occurs: *forma* [fórmə] 'shape', *part* [párt], *forn* [fórn] 'oven', *cors* [kɔ́rs] 'hearts'. (In finding [r] rather than [ɾ] before consonants I differ from Badia, and follow rather Mascaró (1972:48–9) and

Barnils (1933:97), and, apparently, Arteaga (1915:24), where preconsonantal and final [r] (Arteaga's symbol) is distinguished both from the initial and post-sonorant sound, represented [r̄], and from the intervocalic and post-flap, represented [ɹ]. In the study of Barnils the average number of vibrations in preconsonantal [r] as pronounced by the two experimental subjects was 3.1.)

After stops, /f/ and glides —and also after the voiced fricative allophones of /b/, /d/ and /g/— we have only [ɾ], e.g. *prim* [prím] 'thin', *teatre* [teátɾə] 'theatre', *franc* [fráŋ] 'free', *aire* [ájɾə] 'air', *cabra* [káβɾə] 'goat'. After /n/ or /l/ only [r] occurs, e.g. *honra* [ónrə] 'honour', *folro* [fólru] 'lining'. The only example of /sr/ or /zr/ I can find is *Israel* [izɾəél] or [iɾəél]—evidently a non-native word which violates a morpheme structure rule. /ʎr/, /mr/, /ɲr/, /ʃr/, /ʒr/, /vr/ do not occur within morphemes. When these sequences occur with **intervening morpheme boundary, that is, mostly in** infinitive forms of verbs, epenthesis of /ə/ occurs (I (19)) or /v/ → [w] operates.

At the end of a phonetic word Mascaró and I (unlike Badia, 1965a:280; 1962:91–3) find only [r] normally, though with fewer vibrations than elsewhere, e.g. *amor* [əmór] 'love', *regular* [rəɣulár], *cor* [kɔ́r] 'choir'. Barnils's examples (1933:97) are of no value here; of his word-final examples he says (98): "els exemples reproduïts no són, doncs, corrents en la llengua, sinó que han estat pronunciats a imitació dels normals en el dialecte de Mallorca [examples of /–rr#/ —M.W.] i per completar la distribució sil·làbica de la consonant". This final [r] reappears as [ɾ] when followed by a suffix morpheme beginning with a vowel, e.g. *amorós* [əmuɾós] 'amorous', *regularitzar* [rəɣuləridzá] 'to regularize', *coral* [kuɾál] 'choral'; just as does the final underlying /r/ which is deleted before a following # or +C (cf. VII §2), e.g. *clar* [klá] 'clear (M)', *clara* [kláɾə] 'id (F)', *claror* [kləɾó] 'light'. So it does not seem to be the case that an underlying phonological difference between /r/ and /ɾ/ will explain the difference between words which undergo final /r/–deletion and those which do not. In conclusion, then, [r] and [ɾ] are in phonological opposition only intervocalically. [r] is related to [ɾ] in being longer and more tense, just as geminate consonants are related to simple ones, cf. *bella* [béʎə] 'beautiful (F)', *vetlla* [béʎ:ə] 'eve, staying awake' *revela* [rəβélə] 'reveals', *es rebel·la* [ərəβél:ə] 'rebels' (V); *suma* [súmə] 'sum', *summe* [súm:ə] 'supreme'; see below §7. Geminates (long consonants) occur phonetically only between vowels; that is, if final in the Underlying Representation they undergo vowel epenthesis (cf. I (13)). The case of [r] is, it seems to me, essentially the same; that is, I propose that intervocallic [r] derives from underlying /rr/ according to the rule which converts $C_i C_i$ to

$$\begin{bmatrix} C_i \\ +\text{tense} \\ +\text{long} \end{bmatrix}$$ (V (26)). Underlying morpheme-final /rr/ is realized [rə]; thus *esquerre* [əskɛ́rə] /skɛrr/ 'left', cf. *esquerrà* [əskərá] /skɛrr+an/ 'of the left'.

A rule specific to /r/ is required so as to account for the other occurrences of phonetic [r] in statable environments; thus we have, following /ə/–epenthesis (I (13)), and final /r/–deletion where applicable:

(1) $\begin{bmatrix} -\text{syll} \\ +\text{vocal} \\ +\text{cont} \end{bmatrix} \rightarrow \begin{bmatrix} +\text{tense} \\ +\text{long} \end{bmatrix} / \begin{cases} \#\# \underline{\hspace{1em}} \\ \underline{\hspace{1em}} \#\# \\ \begin{bmatrix} +\text{cons} \\ -\text{obstr} \end{bmatrix} \underline{\hspace{1em}} \\ \underline{\hspace{1em}} (\#) \, C \end{cases}$ i) ii) iii) iv)

Parts i) and ii) of the environment of rule (1) are

"mirror images" and thus suitable for abbreviation. (#) is mentioned in part iv) so as to account for cases of infinitive /+r/ which is realized [r] before #C, that is, before an unstressed pronoun beginning with a consonant (see chapter IV), e.g. *estimar-lo* [əstimárlu] 'to love him'. In fact, by parts iii) and iv) of the rule both segments of underlying /rr/ become [+tense, +long] and will undergo the general degemination rule (V (26)).

This approach, namely, having underlying /r/ and /rr/ with a distribution like that of other sonorants, but subject to rule (1), seems to me to account for the unusual distribution of [r] and [ɾ] in the simplest and most revealing way. The alternative requires an additional phoneme being added to the inventory, which would be defined by distinctive features not otherwise used in underlying representations, and a number of specific morpheme structure restrictions which would include proscribing both /rr/ and /ɾɾ/ and initial and final /ɾ/.

2. The glides [j] and [w].

Alarcos (1953:139–40) and Lleó (1970:38–40) state that [j] and [w] are not phonemes but predictable variants of /i/ and /u/ following a vowel. Badia (1965a: passim) accepts /j/ and /w/ as phonemes without discussion of their relationship to /i/ and /u/. Badia (1973a:144–51, 154–5) accepts the phonemic status of /j/ and /w/ but is hesitant about assigning to them the sounds at the ends of falling diphthongs. He does not consider cases like those mentioned below, in which a falling diphthong is in opposition to disyllabic V-i or V-u, which seem to me to make the assignment of the various allophones quite straightforward.

In any case, the position is not the simple one that Alarcos and Lleó propose. There is indeed a rule converting high vowels to glides after stressed vowels

Problems in underlying representations 195

(cf. Lleó, 1970:39). I refer to it at I §2.6. This rule has the form

(2)
= I(8) $\begin{bmatrix} -\text{cons} \\ +\text{high} \end{bmatrix} \rightarrow [-\text{syllab}] \Big/ \begin{bmatrix} +\text{syllab} \\ +\text{stress} \end{bmatrix} \underline{\quad} X]_{N,A}$

and accounts for e.g. *fluid* [flújt] /flu+id/, *laic* [lájk] /la+ik/, *trapezoide* [tɾəpəzɔ́jðə] /trepɛz+ɔida/ 'trapezoid', *europeu* [əwɾpéw] /awɾɔp+ɛ+u/ 'European (M)', *impiu* [impíw] /in+pi+u/ 'impious (M)', *menyspreu* [mɛ̀ɲspɾéw] /mɛɲs+pre+u/ 'scorn' (N).
Verb forms are exceptions to this rule, thus we have e.g. *menyspreo* [mɛ̀ɲspɾéu] /mɛɲs+pre+u/ 'I scorn', *envio* [əmbíu] /an+bi+u/ 'I send', *enviïs* [əmbíis] /an+bi+i+s/ 'you send' (2sg pres subj.). Note that although verbs have intermediate forms different from those of nouns and adjectives, namely /mɛɲs+pre+a+u/, /an+bi+a+i+s/, etc., rule (2) depends on previous stress assignment, which must itself follow Truncation; hence (2) must be restricted to non-verbs.

Let us make the following suppositions which are necessary if the statement "/i/ becomes [j] and /u/ becomes [w] in the environment after a vowel" (Lleó, 1970:39) is to be taken at all seriously.

(a) Stress is marked in the lexicon for oxytone and paroxytone words. This is necessary to distinguish e.g. *raima* [rájmə] 'ream' from *raïma* [rəímə] 'picks grapes' (if URs are /ráim(+ə)/ and /raím(+a)/ respectively); *roina* [rójnə] 'drizzle' from *roïna* [ruínə] 'mean (F)', *ruïna* [ruínə] 'ruin'.

(b) Underlying /ɔ/ or /o/ does not become [w], i.e. glide formation occurs before vowel reduction, which converts unstressed /ɔ/ and /o/ to [u]. Thus *teoria* [təuɾíə] not *[təwɾíə] cf. *teòric* 'theoretical', that is, *teoria* 'theory' will have underlying /taɔr+ij+ə/; *caos* [káus] 'chaos' /kaɔ+s/, cf. *caòtic* 'chaotic'; *crúor* [kɾúur], cf. *cruorina* [kɾuuɾínə] 'cruorin'. In fact we could assign to /ɔ/ or /o/ all phonetic syllabic [u] after a vowel which is not in a paradigmatic relation with [ú]; thus *harmònium* [ərmɔ́niu̯m], *dionisíac* [diu̯nizíək] 'Dionysiac', *pleonasme* [pləu̯názmə] 'pleonasm', *triumvirat* [triu̯mbirát] 'triumvirate', would have the URs /armɔ́niom/, /dioniz+íak/, /plaonásm/ and /trion+bir+át/ respectively.

(c) A vowel which has been stressed at some stage of derivation is resistant to glide formation (i.e. word stress is subject to cyclic rules including stress deletion). This would deal with *veïnat* [bəinát] /baín+át/ 'neighbourhood', cf. *veí* [bəí] 'neighbour'; *llaüter* [ʎəuté] /ʎaút+ér/ 'maker of *llaüts*' [ʎəúts] 'dinghies', and presumably, *nihilisme* [niilízmə] /niíl+ísm/ 'nihilism'.

(d) An intervening morpheme boundary prevents glide formation when the previous vowel is unstressed, i.e. glide formation must explicitly exclude + from its left environment, an unnatural exclusion by the principle of interpretation for + proposed by Chomsky & Halle (1968a:364), which principle is elsewhere confirmed in this study by the Catalan evidence. Thus *deïtat* [dəitát] /dé+itát/ 'deity', *reunió* [rəunió] /ra+un+ión/ 'reunion', *fluïdesa* [fluiðézə] /flú+id+έz+ə/ 'fluidity' (see *fluid* above), *laïcitzar* [ləisidzá] /lá+ik+ítz+á+r/ 'to laicize'.

There remain, however, some examples which can only be accounted for by the wholly arbitrary application of one or other of these conditions; e.g. *trapezoidal* [−ui−], cf. *trapezoide* [−ɔ́j−]. The suffixes *−oide, −oïdal* are not rare, and there is no reason to analyse them as /ɔ+ida/, /ɔ+ida+al/; cf. also *apaïsat* [−əi−] 'horizontally rectangular', *caïnita* [−əi−] 'cainite', *cuneïforme* [−əi−] 'cuneiform', *zoïsita* [−ui−] 'zoisite'. Technical words like these are not hard to find in the dictionary; positing a morpheme boundary before /i/ in each case would be quite ad hoc.

Problems in underlying representations

Consider also the following groups of words:

(3) (a) *iode* [jóðə] 'iodine' (b) *hiat* [iát] 'hiatus'
    iambe [jámbə] 'iambus' *hiena* [iɛ́nə] 'hyaena'
    iaia [jájə] 'granny' *hieràtic* [iərátik] 'hieratic'
    iogurt [juɣúrt] 'yogurt' *hialí* [iəlí] 'hyaline'
    iot [jót] 'yacht' *ió* [ió] 'ion'
    iuca [júkə] 'cassava' *ionosfera* [iunusférə] 'ionosphere'

No amount of juggling with the conditions mentioned above can account for the fact that the words in (3a) begin with [j] and those in (3b) with [i], if there is only one underlying /i/.

The fact is that suppositions a), c) and d) are not required on any other grounds than to distinguish between glides and high vowels. c) requires a cyclic word-stress rule for which there is no other evidence which I have been able to discover, and a) requires stress to be marked lexically in a large number of morphemes whose stress pattern is predictable if we accept /j/ and /w/; in particular, it requires lexically marked stress in verb stems, which is not only unnecessary on other grounds, but indeed contrary to fact. Compare the following examples:

(4) (a) *cuina* [kújnə] 'kitchen, cookery': UR /kúin+ə/?? *cuina* [kújnə] 'cooks' (V): UR/kúin+ə/??
    (b) *ruïna* [ruínə] 'ruin': UR/ruín+ə/?? *arruïna* [əruínə] 'ruins' (V): UR/a+ruín+a/??
    (c) *càrrega* [kárəɣə] 'load': UR /kárrɛɡ+ə/?? *carrega* [kərɛ́ɣə] 'loads' (V): UR/ ?? /
    (d) *evidència* [əβiðɛ́nsiə] 'evidence': UR/abidɛ́nsi+ə/ *evidencia* [əβiðənsíə] 'evidences' (V): UR/ ?? /

Examples (4a) and (4b) require lexically marked stress in the verb forms in order to account for [j] in (4a) but not (4b). Examples (4c) and (4d) cannot, if verb and noun have the same stem, have correct lexically marked stress on the verb but must undergo a verb-stress rule which ignores any stress already marked.

In short, lexically marked stress is required in a large

number of cases merely to distinguish post-vocalic [i] and [u] from [j] and [w]; an otherwise unmotivated cyclic stress rule is required for the same purpose, and many words must be assigned internal + on a purely ad hoc basis. The correct solution is, I believe, the obvious one indicated by the opposition between initial [j] and [i] in examples (3); that is, /j/ and /w/ have phonemic status, and phonetic [j] and [w], including the second part of falling diphthongs, correspond to underlying /j/ and /w/, with a few exceptions. Some of these are accounted for by rule (2), which must exclude verbs in order to distinguish e.g. *menyspreu* [mɛ̀ɲspréw] 'scorn'(N) from *menyspreo* [mɛ̀ɲspréu] 'I scorn', both /mɛɲs+pre+u/.

Other examples of vowels and glides in paradigmatic alternation are, e.g. -

(5) (a) *fluida* [flújðə] 'fluid (F)' *fluïdesa* [fluiðézə] 'fluidity'
    (b) *laic* [lájk] *laicitzar* [ləisidzá] 'to laicize'
    (c) *druida* [drújðə] 'druid' *druïdessa* [druiðésə] 'druidess'
                                     druïdisme [druiðízmə] 'druidism'
    (d) *–oide* [–ójðə] '–oid' *–oïdal* [–uiðál] '–oidal'
cf. (e) *buida* [bújðə] 'empty (F)' *buidesa* [bujðézə] 'emptiness'
                                       buidar [bujðá] 'to empty'

Examples (5a) and (5b) clearly contain the unstressed suffixes $-id-$, $-ic-$, cf. *vàlida* [báliðə] 'valid (F)' : *val* 'is valid'; *històric* [istɔ́rik] 'historic' : *història* 'history'. We can suppose *druida* to have a similar structure to *fluida*. Then /+id/ and /+ik/ block the Major stress rule and trigger the Minor stress rule II (16). They then undergo rule (2) when a stressed vowel precedes but not otherwise. *–oide* and *–oidal* can be dealt with likewise if their underlying form is $\genfrac{}{}{0pt}{}{/+\text{ɔ ida}/}{+E}\ \genfrac{}{}{0pt}{}{/+\text{ɔida+al}/}{+E}$ cf. II§2.2–2.4. Example (5e) naturally has no internal boundary and undergoes the Major stress rule.

3. Labiovelar phonemes /k^w/ and /g^w/.

Discussing /u/ and [w] Lleó (1970:40) suggests establishing "underlying labialized velar phonemes /k^w/ and /g^w/. Evidence for this solution lies in the fact that the only glide found before a syllabic nucleus in Catalan is [w] and that it appears only when preceded by a velar consonant". More accurately, glides do not occur in the environment C_V, except when the consonant is /k/ or /g/; then the glide is /w/. (Glides do, of course, occur between vowels, and as we have seen /j/ occurs morpheme-initially; there are no examples of initial /w/.) This curious fact of distribution would require no little complication of the morpheme-structure rules, so Lleó's suggestion is attractive. In fact, there is more evidence in favour of it. Consider the following groups of nouns and adjectives in their Msg, Mpl, and Fsg forms.

(6)(a) *sec, secs, seca* 'dry'
heroic, heroics, heroica 'heroic'
blavenc, blavencs, blavenca 'bluish'
(b) *inic* [iník], *inics* [iníks], *iniqua* [iníkwə] 'wicked'
oblic, oblics, obliqua [uβlíkwə] 'oblique'
propinc, propincs, propinqua [pɾupíŋkwə] 'neighbouring'
ventríloc, ventrílocs, ventríloqua [bəntɾílukwə] 'ventriloquist'
(c) *innocu, innocus, innòcua* [innɔ́kuə] 'harmless'
vacu, vacus, vàcua [bákuə] 'empty'
conspicu, conspicus, conspícua [kunspíkuə] 'conspicuous'
(d) *groc, grocs, groga* [gɾɔ́ɣə] 'yellow'
feixuc, feixucs, feixuga 'heavy'
antic, antics, antiga 'ancient'
(e) *ambigu, ambigus, ambigua* [əmbíɣwə] 'ambiguous'
exigu, exigus, exigua [əgzíɣwə] 'exiguous'
contigu, contigus, contigua [kuntíɣwə] 'contiguous'

There are no cases of alternations of [–Vk] ~ [–Vywə]
or of [–V́ɣu] ~ [–V́ɣuə]. Type (6a) clearly has
underlying /–k/; type (6c) has /–ku/; Type (6d) has /g/.
If (6b) and (6e) had underlying /–kw/ and /–gw/
respectively, as required for the phonetic form of the
feminine, we should be obliged to allow for final post-
consonantal glides –after velars only– in the morpheme
structure rules; these sequences would also be exceptions
to the final /ə/ epenthesis rule; i.e. we should expect
/–kw#/ and /–gw#/ to be realized [–kwə] and [–ɣwə]
respectively by I (13). These apparent anomalies are
resolved by positing unit phonemes /k^w/ and /g^w/ which
are [+obstr, –cont, +back, +labial]. Then we require
rules which de-labialize /k^w/ finally or before a consonant,
convert /g^w/ to [gu] in the same environment, and
convert /k^w/ and /g^w/ to /kw/ and /gw/ elsewhere. Thus

(7) $\begin{bmatrix} +\text{cons} \\ +\text{back} \end{bmatrix} \rightarrow [-\text{labial}] \Big/ \begin{bmatrix} \overline{-\text{voice}} \end{bmatrix} (C) \#$

(8) $\begin{bmatrix} +\text{cons} \\ +\text{back} \\ +\text{labial} \end{bmatrix} \emptyset \langle (C) \# \rangle \Rightarrow [-\text{labial}] \begin{bmatrix} +\text{labial} \\ +\text{high} \\ -\text{cons} \\ \langle +\text{syllab} \rangle \end{bmatrix}$
123123

If # were also [–syllab], then instead of the angle
brackets we could say ... [αsyllab] ⇒ ... [αsyllab]. Or
(8) could just convert C^w to Cw, and a rule like IV (19)
would convert /w/ to [u] except when adjacent to a vowel.

4. The phoneme /v/.

The only occurrences of phonetic [v] in the
dialect studied are those derived from /f/ by the voicing
assimilation rule, cf. VII §8; *baf desagradable*
[bávðəzəɣrəðábblə] 'unpleasant fumes'. However, there is

Problems in underlying representations 201

substantial evidence in favour of the existence of underlying /v/; cf. Lleó, 1970:33–5; Badia, 1973b:191. Consider these examples:

(9)(a) 1 *xop* (M) [ʃóp], *xopa* (F) [ʃópə] 'soaked'
UR / –p –/
2 *llop* [ʎóp] 'wolf', *lloba* [ʎóβə] 'she-wolf'
UR /–b–/
3 *blau* (M) [bláw], *blava* [bláβə] 'blue'
4 *geliu* (M) [ʒəlíw], *geliua* [ʒəlíwə] 'icy'
UR /–w–/

(b) 1 *esquerp* (M) [əskérp], *esquerpa* [əskérpə]
'unsociable' UR /–rp–/
2 *corb* (M) [kórp], *corba* [kórβə] 'curved'
UR /–rb–/
3 *serf* (M) [sérf], *serva* [sérβə] 'serf'

(c) 1 *ajup* [əʒúp] 'bends', *ajupint* [əʒupín]
'bending' UR /–p–/
2 *rep* [rép] 'receives', *rebent* [rəβén] 'receiving'
UR /–b–/
3 *mou* [mów] 'moves', *movent* [muβén]
'moving'
4 *clou* [klów] 'closes', *cloent* [kluén] 'closing'
UR /–w–/

The forms numbered 3 require a root-final segment which is not /p/, /b/ or /w/, and which is realized [f] / C_ $\left\{ \begin{matrix} \# \\ C \end{matrix} \right\}$, [w] / V_ $\left\{ \begin{matrix} \# \\ C \end{matrix} \right\}$, and [β] elsewhere. /v/ is the obvious candidate, not least as it fills an odd gap in the phoneme inventory; otherwise, /f/ is the only obstruent without a voiced counterpart. I propose, then, to assign to /v/ all cases of alternating [w] ~ [β] and [f] ~ [β]. The realization rule will have the following form, (cf. III §7.2):

202   *Problems in underlying representations*

(10) $\begin{bmatrix} +\text{cons} \\ +\text{cont} \\ +\text{labial} \\ +\text{voice} \end{bmatrix} \rightarrow \left\{ \begin{matrix} [+\text{distr}] \;/\underline{\quad}\; [+\text{syllab}] \\ \begin{bmatrix} -\text{cons} \\ u-\text{obstr} \\ u+\text{high} \\ u+\text{back} \\ u-\text{anter} \\ u+\text{distr} \end{bmatrix} \Big/ \begin{Bmatrix} V \\ \# \end{Bmatrix} - \begin{Bmatrix} C \\ \# \end{Bmatrix} \end{matrix} \right\} \begin{matrix} \text{i) } v \rightarrow \beta \;/\underline{\quad}\; V \\ \\ \text{ii) } v \rightarrow w \end{matrix}$

Observe that it is not formally necessary to mention the features with *u* (=unmarked) to the right of the arrow in ii). Those changes are consequent upon the change to [−cons], and will be dealt with by a redundancy rule, or "linking" rule, i.e. a rule which changes redundant features whenever the conditions apply. Parts i) and ii) must of course be disjunctively ordered. Note that no additional rule will be required to convert /v/ to [f] in *serf*; this is dealt with by the voicing assimilation rule as it applies to obstruent continuants; that is, [f] occurs before voiceless consonants and **utterance-finally**.
The mention of # in part ii) is just to allow this rule to include the effect of rule IV (37), which accounts for the forms of the *vos* pronoun [βus] ∼ [us]. This is the only item in which /v/ is revealed as underlying an initial consonant.

5. Affricates.

Are the affricates [ts], [dz], [tʃ], [dʒ] to be considered unit phonemes or assigned to /t-s/, /t-z/, /t-ʃ/, /t-ʒ/ respectively? Alarcos (1953:139) takes the latter position: "tampoco son fonemas los sonidos africados [ts], [dz] alveolares y [tʃ], [dʒ] prepalatales, los cuales son o realización del conjunto de dos fonemas (/t/+/s/, /t/+/z/; /t/+/ʃ/, /t/+/ʒ/) o variante 'enfática' de los sonidos fricativos correspondientes". (This second possibility is relevant only to final /ʒ/, → [tʃ], [dʒ] in the dialect studied here.) Badia (1965a:298–321) takes the

Problems in underlying representations 203

former view, except with regard to [ts] which derives always from /t+s/ —with intervening morpheme boundary (306).

5.1. For [ts] Badia's arguments are conclusive: [ts] can always be assigned on morphological grounds to /t+s/ or /d+s/. Thus *rets* [réts] 'you (sg) render' /rɛt+s/ where /+s/ is the 2sg morph; likewise *ets* [éts] 'you (sg) are' /et+s/; *xicots* [ʃikɔ́ts] 'boys' /ʃikɔt+s/ where /+s/ is the plural morph. *Tsar* [tsár] and its derivatives need not worry us; it is obviously a non-native word and a unique exception to the morpheme-structure rules insofar as it begins with /ts–/. It is unremarkable for foreign words to be exceptions to morpheme-structure rules, and indeed to other phonological rules. Badia's conclusion, that only [ts] of the affricates is diphonemic leaves his structure unbalanced, as he is well aware: "nogensmenys, el magnífic cub de les vuit sibilants no sembla pas ésser, en el català d'avui, una realitat des d'un punt de vista funcional i significatiu" (298). Let us consider the evidence with regard to the other three affricates.

5.2. Distribution. Affricates never occur in initial position; the only exceptions are *tsar* (see above) and *txec* 'Czech' whose non-native status is obvious. The only other segment which does not occur in initial position is /w/. Affricates are never in opposition to fricatives after a consonant; other obstruent non-continuants occur after all consonants except /ʎ/, /ɲ/, /ʃ/, /ʒ/. Of the coronal fricatives, /s/ and /z/ may be preceded by /w/, /r/, /l/, /n/, /m/, /p/, /k/, and /ʃ/ and /ʒ/ may be preceded by /w/, /r/, /l/ or /n/. The restriction to [+syllab] before unit /dz/, /tʃ/, /dʒ/ would be quite anomalous. [dz] does not occur word-finally at the phonetic level. It is followed, if not by /+u/ or F /+ə/ (e.g. *gotzo* (M), *gotza* (F) [gódzu], [gódzə] 'corpulent') by epenthetic /ə/: thus *dotze* [dódzə] 'twelve', *tretze* [trédzə] 'thirteen', *setze* [sɛ́dzə] 'sixteen'.

If the underlying representation is /t-z/, /t-ʃ/, /t-ʒ/, (/t/ here representing an appropriately unmarked obstruent stop), these restrictions on distribution cease to be anomalous and correspond to morpheme-structure rules that are required anyway, e.g. that after an initial obstruent stop a [+vocalic] segment follows; or that /z/, /ʃ/ and /ʒ/ do not occur in groups of more than two consonants, and /ʃ/ and /ʒ/ are preceded only by /w/ or [+coronal].

5.3. Badia is mistaken in the belief that there is no evidence for dividing [dʒ] on morphological grounds. He says (1965a:318): "debades cercaríem, doncs, dins els significats dels exemples adduïts abans, la més petita relació de parentiu que pogués suggerir als catalano-parlants que ... *tj* [i.e. [dʒ] –M.W.] és un so compost de /t/ + /ʒ/". This conclusion arises merely because Badia does not adduce the relevant examples, which are:

(11)(a)   *metge* [médʒə] 'doctor', cf. *mèdic* [mɛ́ðik] 'medical'
         jutge [ʒúdʒə] 'judge', cf. *judicar* [ʒuðiká] 'to judge'
         petja [pédʒə] 'tread', cf. *pedal* [pəðál] 'pedal'
(b)   *heretge* [ərédʒə] 'heretic', cf. *herètic* [ərɛ́tik] 'heretical'

There is at least the possibility of separating out /d+ʒ/ in group (11a) and /t+ʒ/ in (11b), in as much as [−ik] and [−ál] are readily interpreted as common suffixes.

5.4. A rule converting /t/ or /d/ followed by /s/, /z/, /ʃ/ or /ʒ/ to an affricate is needed anyway (cf. Badia, 1965a:318). Thus

Problems in underlying representations 205

potser [putsé] 'maybe', /pɔd##se+r/ 'may be'
vuit cerveses [bújtsərβézəs] 'eight beers'
   /bujt##sarbɛz+ə+s/
aquest zero [əkédzɛ́ru] 'this zero' /akɛst##zɛru/
set zulús [sédzulús] 'seven Zulus' /sɛt##zulur+s/
tornat ximple [turnátʃimplə] 'gone stupid'
   /torn+a+d ##ʃinpl/
tot xop [tótʃóp] 'soaked through' /tot##ʃop/
adjuntar [ədʒuntá] 'bring together' /ad+ʒunt+a+r/
petit jardí [pətídʒərðí] 'little garden'
   /patit##ʒardin/

5.5. Badia's other arguments can be summarized under four headings:

(a) [dz], [tʃ], [dʒ] are of "rendiment normal" especially compared with [ts] (302, 314). This is neither here nor there as far as the unit phoneme question is concerned. The rarity of [ts] except where it is from /t+s/ or /d+s/ is just a curious fact of Catalan.

(b) There is no morphological evidence for /t+z/ → [dz], /t+ʃ/ → [tʃ], or /t+ʒ/ → [dʒ]. This is false in the case of [dʒ] — see above. For the rest we may observe the rarity of morphemes with initial /z−/ (two and a half pages in Fabra, 1968b, as opposed to 88 for initial *s−*, plus 21 and a half for initial *ce−, ci−* (/s/)), and the relative rarity of those with initial /ʃ/, (nine and a half pages in Fabra, 1968b, as opposed to 20 and a half for /ʒ/: nine and a half *j−*, and 11 *ge−, gi−*). There are no suffixes beginning with /z/, /ʃ/ or /ʒ/ that I can find, except possibly as in (11) above, and the only prefixes ending in /t/ or /d/ are /ad+/, cf. *adherent ~ inherent,* and /sot+s+/, cf. *sota* 'under'; *sots-diaca* 'subdeacon'. The lack of dimorphemic examples for /tz/, /tʃ/ is therefore not especially surprising.

(c) (312, 315) French and Castilian etymological

equivalents of Catalan words with [dz], [tʃ] have single phonemes corresponding. These facts are irrelevant. The grammar of Catalan is not dependent on the grammars of similar or historically related languages.

(d) The graphic attempts of the semi-literate reveal no awareness of the composite nature of affricates. This is as irrelevant as the previous point. When a person is ignorant of Catalan orthography, he will of course do the best he can with whatever orthography is more familiar to him, whether or not it is adequate phonetically, let alone phonemically. If arguments from orthographic practice carry any weight at all, then the fact that Catalan has traditionally represented its affricates by digraphs with *t* as the first member: *tz* for [dz], *tx* for [tʃ], *tg/tj* for [dʒ] may well carry more weight than the attempts made by those whose spelling habits are those corresponding to another language — Spanish — with a rather different phonemic system.

It is perhaps worth pointing out, nevertheless, that the argument in favour of a diphonemic solution for [tʃ], [dʒ] is less strong than for [ts], [dz]. For while /–tz/ is always followed by a vowel, as accounted for by the epenthesis rule I (13), which supplies /ə/ after certain two-consonant sequences, /tʃ/ and /tʒ/ are not always followed by a vowel even though other cases of /Cʃ/, /Cʒ/ require it, (cf. I §4). N.B. /–Cs/ requires no support vowel. Consider these examples.

(12) a) *fetitxe* 'fetish', cf. *fetitxisme* 'fetishism'
       reprotxe 'reproach', cf. *reprotxar* 'to reproach'
   b) *esquitx* 'splash', cf. *esquitxar* 'to splash'
       capritx 'caprice', cf. *capritxos* 'caprices'
   c) *viatge* 'journey', cf. *viatjar* 'to travel'
       jutge 'judge', cf. *jutjar* 'to judge'
   d) *lleig* [ʎétʃ] 'ugly' (Msg), cf. *lletges* [ʎédʒəs] 'ugly' (Fpl)

desig [dəzítʃ] 'desire', cf. *desitjar* [dəzidʒá] 'to desire'

In fact only /tz/ unfailingly has a following vowel, and these cases are not common, for apart from *dotze, tretze, setze* mentioned above there is perhaps only *sutze* 'dirty', an archaism not used spontaneously in the language being described.

The arguments based on distribution, the need for a smaller phoneme inventory, and the necessity, in any case, for an affrication rule I find conclusive, bearing in mind the overall simplicity of the description. I think the correct solution is to exclude the affricates /tʃ/, /tʒ/ from the operation of the epenthesis rule; consequently *fetitxe, viatge,* etc. will have a final vowel in the UR. The morpheme structure rules will permit /Cs#/, /Cz#/, /Cʃ#/, /Cʒ#/.

The affrication rule, after deletion of boundaries, will look like this:

$$(13) \quad \begin{bmatrix} +\text{obstr} \\ +\text{coron} \\ -\text{cont} \end{bmatrix} \begin{bmatrix} +\text{obstr} \\ +\text{coron} \\ +\text{cont} \end{bmatrix} \Rightarrow \quad \emptyset \quad \begin{bmatrix} -\text{cont} \\ +\text{del. rel} \end{bmatrix}$$
$$\quad\quad\quad 1 \quad\quad\quad\quad 2 \quad\quad\quad\quad\quad 1 \quad\quad\quad 2$$

6. Geminate obstruents.

Consider the following groups of words containing obstruents followed by /l/.

(14) (a) [–V́kl–] *nucli* 'nucleus' [–V́pl–] *rèplica*
    xucla 'sucks'

   (b) [–klXV́–] *aclarir* 'to clarify' [–plXV́–] *suplert* 'supplied'
    nuclear *replà* 'landing'
    xuclar 'to suck'

(15) (a) [–V́ɣl–] *sigla* [–V́βl–] *bíblia* 'Bible'
    ègloga 'eclogue'

(b) [−ɣlXV́−] *seglar* 'secular'   [−βlXV́−] *reblert* 'filled in'
              negligent   *problema* 'problem'
              jeroglífic 'hiero-   *oblit* 'forgetfulness'
              glyphic'

(16) (a) [−V́ggl−] *segle* 'century'   [−V́bbl−] *poble* 'people'
                   regla 'rule'   *doble* 'double'
                                                 estable 'stable'
                                                 possible
                                                 públic

(b) [−gglXV́−] *Iglésies* (surname) [−bblXV́−] *poblet* 'village'
              = *iglésies* vulgar   *població* 'settlement'
              form for *esglésies*   *doblar* 'to double'
              'churches'   *establert* 'established'
              joglar 'minstrel'   *fibló* 'sting'
              arreglar 'arrange'

For both the velar and labial groups there are examples of voiceless stop + /l/, voiced fricative + /l/, and voiced geminate stop + /l/, both before and after the accented vowel, (cf. Badia, 1951:196, 216; Badia, 1962:I, 72, 74, 101, 103). There is vacillation between pronunciations of type (14) and (16) in certain words: *xucla*, *xuclar* may be heard [ʃúgglə], [ʃugglá], and in vulgar Barcelonese it is common to unvoice the geminates in (16). Neologisms tend to be assigned to types (14) or (15) according to the spelling; that is to say, in effect according to the Castilian model, where −*pl*−, −*cl*− are always [−pl−], [−kl−], and −*bl*−, −*gl*− always [−βl−], [−ɣl−]. However, there does not seem to be a sound basis for saying that classes (14) and (15) consist only of neologisms and (16) only of traditional "inherited" words. There is, at any rate, it seems, an unstable situation in Barcelona, with a tendency to reduce the tripartite opposition to a simple one of two types: [−pl−], [−kl−] or [−ppl−], [−kkl−] versus [−βl−], [−ɣl−]. The problem is how to represent these groups phonemically. The solution which accords best with the naturalness condition would assign [−pl−] to /pl/, [−βl−] to /bl/ and [−bbl−] to /tbl/ (where /t/ represents a maximally unmarked obstruent stop). A disadvantage of this is that it complicates the morpheme-structure rules, which have to allow geminate /b/ and /g/ (/tb/, /tg/) only before /l/, though it is true there are a few other examples of [−bb−], e.g. *obvi* [ɔ́bbi] 'obvious' (to be analysed /ɔb+bi/?), *futbol* [fubbɔ́l] 'soccer'. An alternative might be to distinguish [−ɣl−], [−βl−] words from [−ggl−] and [−bbl−] words by means of a minor rule geminating /g/ and /b/ in certain words marked [+rule (17)]; geminate consonants ([+tense]) would not be subject to the spirantization rule, which affects voiced stops between vocalic segments and some others (see VII § 10), making them fricatives: [ɣ], [β], [ð]. The minor rule in question would be:

(17) $\begin{bmatrix} +\text{obstr} \\ -\text{cont} \\ +\text{voice} \end{bmatrix} \rightarrow \begin{bmatrix} +\text{tense} \\ +\text{long} \end{bmatrix} / \text{V} \underline{\hspace{1cm}} \begin{bmatrix} -\text{obstr} \\ -\text{cont} \\ +\text{vocal} \end{bmatrix}$

In this work I have adopted the former solution, though with no great commitment.

7. Geminate sonorants.

A few examples of geminates have been treated above, § 1, § 6. Here we are concerned with [n:], [m:], [l:] and [ʎ:] which normally I shall represent [nn], etc. These sounds are phonetically distinct from simple consonants, in being, I suggest, [+tense, +long]. Examples are:

(18) [−nn−] *perenne* 'perennial'
              cotna 'rind'
              ètnic 'ethnic'

(19) [−mm−] a) *summe* (M), *summa* (F) 'supreme'
                gemma 'gem'
                gamma
             b) *atmosfera* 'atmosphere'
                ritme 'rhythm'

      logaritme 'logarithm'
      cadmi 'cadmium'

(20) [−ll−] *atlas*
      cel·la 'cell'
      putxinel·li 'puppet'
      atleta 'athlete'
      til·la 'tila'
      col·legi 'college'

(21) [−ʎʎ−] *motllo* 'mould'
      vetlla 'waking'
      ametlla 'almond'
      espatllar 'to spoil'
      rutllar 'to go well'

Note that in examples (19b) the pronunciation [−dm−] may be heard in careful speech.

  Rather than set up underlying segments using the distinctive features [tense] or [long], features not otherwise used to distinguish segments at that level, it seems obvious to posit a sequence of two underlying segments, of which the first is the appropriate archiphoneme. Thus [nn] would correspond to underlying $/\begin{bmatrix} -\text{cont} \\ +\text{coron} \\ -\text{vocal} \end{bmatrix} n/$, where $\begin{bmatrix} -\text{cont} \\ +\text{coron} \\ -\text{vocal} \end{bmatrix}$ is the same as the class /n, t, d/. [mm] would be $/\begin{bmatrix} -\text{cont} \\ -\text{high} \\ -\text{vocal} \end{bmatrix} m/$, where $\begin{bmatrix} -\text{cont} \\ -\text{high} \\ -\text{vocal} \end{bmatrix}$ is the same as the class /n, m, p, b, t, d/*. [ll] would be $/\begin{bmatrix} -\text{cont} \\ +\text{coron} \end{bmatrix} l/$, where $\begin{bmatrix} -\text{cont} \\ +\text{coron} \end{bmatrix}$

---

*For the pronunciation [−dm−], [+coron, +obstr] would have to be specified, and optionally, [−assimilation rule].

is the same as the class /l, n, t, d/; and [ʎʎ] would be
/[–syllab] ʎ/. One may observe that the redundancy
rules specifying the remaining features of the first
segment are very similar to the assimilation rules
required converting members of those classes defined by
the above matrices into consonants identical to the
following /n/, /m/, /l/, or /ʎ/ when a boundary intervenes,
except that /n##l/ is not realized [ll], and that
only /t/ and /d/ are wholly assimilated to a following
/ʎ/. Apparently, /t/ is the least marked of all consonants,
so at the deepest level may be represented merely
[–syllabic]. In this case, the redundancy rule specifying
C as /ʎ/ /____ ʎ would be equivalent in effect to the
marking rule and assimilation rule which together
realize /t##ʎ/ as [ʎʎ]. Examples of this geminate
assimilation across boundaries are:

(22) [–nn–] *adnascent* /ad+nas+ent/
 fet nou 'made new' /fe+t##nɔv/
(23) [–mm–] (a) *submergir* 'to submerge'
  /sub+marʒ+i+r/
  immergir 'to immerse' /in+marʒ+i+r/
  cap mariner 'no sailor'
  /kap##mar+in+er/
 (b) *sotmetre* 'to submit'
  admetre 'to admit'
  set mariners 'seven sailors'
(24) [–ll–] *tot l'any* 'all year'
 demà passat l'altre 'three days hence'
(25) [–ʎʎ–] *et lleves* 'you get up'
 ha portat llet 'has brought milk'

A further argument for positing a sequence of two
consonants in the UR of geminates is the fact that like
certain other sequences of two consonants, the geminates
cannot appear finally at the phonetic level; that is, they
are subject to epenthesis rules. In particular, [nn]

resembles /mn/, /kn/ in this respect; [mm] resembles /km/; [ll] resembles /bl/, /gl/, etc. — all are sequences of non-continuants. There are a few exceptions, all of [ll], where instead of final [–lə] we have [–l]. For examples see I §4. As suggested there, these words may be subject to a rule of the form $l \rightarrow \emptyset \;/\; l\underline{\quad}(C)\;\#$.

We have already mentioned briefly (§1) a rule reducing two identical consonants to one long one, when discussing [r]. Within the present theory there is no obviously simple way to formulate the notion "identical segment". The only way is to mention all the possible features with different Greek-letter variables; thus, for identical consonants:

$$\begin{bmatrix} -\text{syllab} \\ \alpha \text{ vocal} \\ \beta \text{ conson} \\ \gamma \text{ obstr} \\ \delta \text{ cont} \\ \epsilon \text{ labial} \\ \zeta \text{ high} \\ \eta \text{ back} \\ \theta \text{ voiced} \\ \iota \text{ anter} \\ \kappa \text{ coron} \\ \lambda \text{ distr} \\ \mu \text{ nasal} \end{bmatrix} \begin{bmatrix} -\text{syllab} \\ \alpha \text{ vocal} \\ \beta \text{ conson} \\ \gamma \text{ obstr} \\ \delta \text{ cont} \\ \epsilon \text{ labial} \\ \zeta \text{ high} \\ \eta \text{ back} \\ \theta \text{ voiced} \\ \iota \text{ anter} \\ \kappa \text{ coron} \\ \lambda \text{ distr} \\ \mu \text{ nasal} \end{bmatrix}$$

This is patently absurd in terms of any appropriate evaluation measure. I suggest the following notation: that [αDF], [αDF] (DF = distinctive feature) be used when segments have identical feature values except for those which may be otherwise specified. Our rule, after boundary deletion, will be:

$$(26) \quad \begin{bmatrix} \alpha\text{DF} \\ -\text{syll} \end{bmatrix} \quad \begin{bmatrix} \alpha\text{DF} \\ -\text{syll} \end{bmatrix} \Rightarrow \begin{bmatrix} \alpha\text{DF} \\ -\text{syll} \\ +\text{tense} \\ +\text{long} \end{bmatrix}$$

In fact, this is over general, since /ss/, /zz/, /ff/, /ʃʃ/ are simplified without being tensed. There being no straightforward way to exclude them from rule (26), one solution is an additional rule — see below, however, VII §3, §11. The additional rule would be:

(27) $\begin{bmatrix} +\text{obstr} \\ +\text{cont} \end{bmatrix} \rightarrow \begin{bmatrix} -\text{tense} \\ -\text{long} \end{bmatrix}$

For those cases where "correct usage" prescribes a geminate but vulgar or colloquial speech offers a simple consonant, e.g. *novel·la* 'novel', *col·lecció* 'collection', *setmana* 'week', rather than an optional or stylistically determined reduction rule applying only in certain words, I suggest distinct URs for each dialect, e.g. "correct" /nubɛtl+ə/ → [–ll–] vulgar /nubɛl+ə/ → [–l–] and so on. Indeed the reverse effect is not unknown, e.g. *ametlla* 'almond': "correct" [əmɛ́ʎʎə], vulgar [əmmɛ́ʎʎə]. The solution is the same, viz. URs /amɛtʎ+ə/, /atmɛtʎ+ə/ in the two dialects respectively.

8. The vowel [ə].

It is well known that Catalan has seven vowel phonemes: /i/, /e/, /ɛ/, /a/, /ɔ/, /o/, /u/, and that /e/, /ɛ/, /a/ are neutralized as [ə], /ɔ/, /o/, /u/ as [u] when unstressed. (Cf. Fabra, 1897:6–8; Roca, 1971:103–6; Cerdà, 1972, passim; Badia, 1970b:124–9; 1973a:138–44.) Badia (1965b and 1973a:143–4) puts forward the view that /ə/ is phonemic in certain monosyllables. He concludes (1973a:144): "Entre *jo sé que dibuixa* [kə] 'je sais qu'il dessine' et *jo sé què dibuixa* [kɛ] 'je sais ce qu'il dessine', la seule différence est encore l'alternance kə/kɛ. Il est hors de doute que tout cela nous oblige à accorder une valeur de différenciation phonologique au son /ə/". He presents (1965b:81–8) thirty-four examples of what he claims are minimal pairs in support of his view. The great majority of these are unstressed pronouns, which in our view have no vowel at all in underlying representations (see chapter IV); in the definite article *el/la/els/les* also I suggest that the vowel [ə] is introduced by an epenthesis rule (IV §6). The remaining examples are just these: the prepositions *a, amb, de, en, per; En,* the masculine "personal" article; *que,* relative pronoun or conjunction; and the uncommon forms of the feminine possessive adjective *ma* 'my', *ta* 'your', *sa* 'his/her/its'. We could add the 2sg and 3sg and 3pl of the present tense of the perfect auxiliary; *has* [əs], *ha* [ə], *han* [ən], cf. III §1.2.5.

These verb forms have underlying /a/; a readjustment rule (III (22)), operating in a syntactically specified context, deletes #, thereby preventing stress assignment. In the possessive adjectives the underlying form will be /m/, /t/, /s/ (compare the unstressed pronouns); feminine [−ə] is supplied by I (9). The masculine personal article *En* which appears before proper names beginning with a consonant, e.g. *En Jaume* 'James', will, like the other articles, have a single consonant /n/ underlying; [ə] is inserted as with the other articles.

If we can show that the lack of stress in *a, amb, de, en, per* and *que* can be predicted without the use of ad hoc devices, Badia's problem will have disappeared. The other prepositions which are monosyllabic at a stage before stress-assignment are *fins* 'until', *dins* 'within', *vers* 'towards', *des* 'since', *entre* 'among' /entr/. What we need is a rule to delete #, such as:

$$(28) \quad \# \rightarrow \emptyset \ / \ [_{Prep} \ \# \ (C) \ V \left(\begin{bmatrix} -syll \\ -obstr \end{bmatrix} ([-cont]) \right) \underline{\quad}$$

Note that the stressed monosyllabic prepositions contain either an obstruent continuant or more than two consonants after the vowel. Without # stress assignment is blocked.

Problems in underlying representations

It remains to distinguish *que* [kə] from *què* [kɛ́].
The former is a conjunction 'that', and a relative pronoun 'who', 'which'; the latter is an interrogative pronoun, and a relative pronoun only after prepositions. This syntactic distinction is sufficient to distinguish them so that # is deleted after *que*. Badia's difficulties in respect of the phonological analysis of these words arise from his not considering syntactic information.

CHAPTER VI

Between underlying representations and the input to the phonological rules

1.1. In Generative Phonology we require the lexical representation to consist of segmental matrices containing no more information than the minimum amount necessary to distinguish each formative unambiguously, cf. Chomsky & Halle, 1968:164–77, 380–9. That is, no information is to be included in lexical representations which can be supplied by some rule. As Chomsky & Halle say (166): "the lexicon specifies only idiosyncratic features of lexical entries, omitting all those that can be determined by general rules."

1.2. The output of the phonological rules – the systematic phonetic representation – should consist of sequences of matrices specified for all distinctive features relevant for an adequate description of perceptual reality. The features will be characterized by integer or ± variables. (Chomsky & Halle, 1968:5, 25, 164, 293ff.)

1.3. The phonological rules, including "readjustment" rules which give phonetic shape to underlying formatives which may be abstract, must apply to sequences of matrices so specified that in the case of any rule it must be unambiguous whether that rule applies or does not apply to any given sequence. That is, if any matrix enters the phonological component unspecified, for example, with respect to [voiced], there must be no rule mention-

ing [voiced] in its structural description (on the left of
the arrow or in the environment) before a rule specifying
[voiced] has operated. This is essentially Chomsky &
Halle's condition (147) (1968:384); it is less rigorous than
that proposed by Stanley (1967:395) who would have all
matrices fully specified before any phonological rules
operate.

Stanley's requirement can perhaps best be met by
making the "input to the phonological component"
fully specified, but partially unmarked, in the sense to
be discussed below, so that little cost will attach to
rules altering features which had to be specified only to
meet Stanley's condition. For example, this would be
the case for Catalan formatives ending in obstruents;
when word-final, phonetic voicedness of obstruents is
determined by what follows. Where paradigmatic evidence
does not reveal a final obstruent to be voiced or voiceless
in its underlying form, e.g. in *cap* 'any', *res* 'anything',
rather than entering the phonological component with
final segments unspecified for voice, such items will
have the unmarked value [u−voiced] in the underlying
final segment. But consequently, we want no cost to
attach to a rule in respect of its switching this [−voice]
to [+voice] before the appropriate voiced segments.

Similarly, instead of having in the underlying
representation a back non-labial vowel unspecified for
the feature [low] which will be specified [+low] (/a/)
or [−low] (/ə/) only after the stress-assignment rule has
applied, the marking rules will specify it as [u+low];
the conversion to [−low] when unstressed we should
like to regard as costless.

Stanley's requirement should be relaxed in respect
of certain features which are not distinctive at all at
the level of underlying representations; in our case
[±stress], [±long], [±tense], [±del. rel]. In Catalan
these are phonetic realization features whose

specification in part depends on the prior operation of readjustment rules and other phonological rules. [±lateral] is also a low-level phonetic feature; it could be specified at any stage, but any but a very late specification would facilitate specious simplifications in other rules by permitting the expression of dubious natural classes (cf. Wheeler, 1972). Chomsky & Halle's "condition (147)" can be accepted for these features. Provided that when they are specified anywhere they are specified everywhere, e.g. by an "elsewhere" statement, the unfortunate consequence of "condition (147)" will be avoided, namely, the necessity of examining a large class of derivations to discover whether the grammar is well formed.

Throughout the phonological component binarism is a requirement for distinctive features just so as to avoid indeterminacy of rule application. The features must be + or −, with no third possibility just because any rule either does or does not apply to any matrix sequence. Only at a stage when the output can be an input to no further rule with the feature in its structural description can + or − be replaced by integers.

1.4. In Chomsky & Halle (1968:412, 415, etc.) marking conventions alone fill in all the blanks in minimally specified matrices. One of the several aims their theory of markedness tries to achieve is to provide a means of evaluating phonological rules so that some rules are more highly valued than others (401), that is, some rules are more "natural" and thus should be less costly in the evaluation of the grammar. The same aim is stated by Schane (1973:111−20). I believe that this is the proper function of a theory of markedness; it seems to me that, as a consequence, the use of marking conventions as the sole blank-filling device cannot be accepted.

We want our grammar to value as more natural, for

example, a rule assimilating /n/ in position of articulation to following obstruents than a rule assimilating /m/ or /ɲ/; if /n/ is less marked than /m/ or /ɲ/ then a rule converting unmarked features to marked features in phonetic environments is the type of rule we want to have low cost. Or a rule converting /l/ to /ł/ before [+back] segments and to /ʎ/ befcre [+high, −back] segments should be relatively less costly than, say, a rule converting /l/ to [+labial] or [+nasal] before segments with those features. Let us suppose, then, that a rule changing u features on the left of the arrow to m features is the type of rule which we want to be less costly. It is clear that not all redundant features can be u features, for /l/ is clearly redundantly [−labial] and [−nasal], yet we specifically do not want to give a low value to rules changing such features in this case. Similarly vowels and sonorants are redundantly [+voiced], but a rule devoicing them would be rather unnatural in any environment. It is indeed true that in some cases the decision on which features are the redundant ones is arbitrary (cf. Bar-Hillel, 1957:326−7), but, for example, if liquids were lexically specified [−nasal], they could be redundantly [+vocalic], and thus liable to improbable assimilations at low cost according to an evaluation metric which took redundant as equivalent to unmarked.

I have tried to devise a system of rules and conventions applicable to Catalan such that certain segments enter the phonological rules with features specified + or −, and also distinguished as unmarked − meaning, among other things, "naturally assimilable"; I represent such features as $[u \pm DF]$; the others will be $[m \pm DF]$. There does not seem to be much point in proposing a system which has m, u, + and − as independent symbols any of which may occur in underlying lexical matrices, as is done in Chomsky & Halle (1968:409, 412). m and u are essentially indices of an evaluation measure for matrices and rules, and need not replace + and − which have a quite different function.

I do not think rules of the kind I put forward below can be universal as Chomsky & Halle (1968:403) and Schane (1973:113) propose. In part, this is because the simple and well-motivated formulation of Context-free Redundancy (CFR) rules and Marking (Mk) rules depends on what distinctions are required in the phonemic systems of particular languages, and on what features are required to formulate oppositions at the underlying level.

S.R. Anderson (1971:145) is led to a similar conclusion: "it seems we are once again led to language particular formulations of marking conventions, or at least of the kind of facts they were designed to handle". Various facts lead Sommerstein in the same direction. He says, (1973:87): "what we really want to say is that where length is distinctive and tenseness redundant the unmarked vowel is short; where tenseness is distinctive and length redundant, the unmarked vowel is tense (and incidentally long). This is a problem already noted in connection with voicing by Postal (1968:184−5), that the unmarked value of the same feature in the same environment may be different according as the feature is distinctive or redundant in that environment"; and more conclusively (1973:115): "the better solution, then, is to concede that not all features in all contexts are covered by universal marking conventions; rather, there are some universal conventions, and other cases in which different languages can assign markedness in different ways." In what follows, some suggestions along these lines will be put forward.

There is a sense, also, in which rules converting marked features to unmarked features are natural; cf. Schane, 1973:117; Cairns, 1969:865. These define neutralizations which are not assimilations in the

ordinary sense; thus the Catalan vowel-reduction rules
II (17), (25), which convert labial vowels to [u] and
other non-high vowels to [ə] when unstressed,
resulting in an unstressed vowel system /i ə u/ as
opposed to the stressed vowels /i e ɛ a ɔ o u/, are natural
in that they result in a "simpler" vowel system, (cf.
Haiman, 1972; Schane, 1973:119). Similarly, voicedness
neutralization of obstruents in word-final position is
"natural" at least in the sense of being a frequent
phenomenon in languages; cf. Postal, 1968:184. This
seems to be a quite different kind of naturalness from
that which converts u features to m features. Tentatively,
I suggest that relatively low value be assigned to rules
of the form:

(1) $\quad [u \pm DF_i] \rightarrow [m \pm DF_i] \;/\; \begin{bmatrix} +\text{segment} \\ \pm DF_i \end{bmatrix}$

(2) $\quad [m \pm DF_j] \rightarrow [u \pm DF_j] \;/\; X \begin{bmatrix} - \\ Y \end{bmatrix} Z$

condition: X, Z are null or [−segment]

Rule (1) corresponds to an assimilation or dissimilation
rule; (2) to a rule of neutralization with non-segmental
environment. Note that (1) and (2) resemble diachronic
rule types of conditioned and isolative change
respectively.

2.1. The following Table I indicates how the
various segments are marked in the lexicon in their
maximally distinctive positions, (e.g. a morpheme-
initial vowel, or a morpheme-final single consonant).
Segments less specified than these will receive further
specification by morpheme-structure rules. For
Catalan there will be no rules specifying [low] for
consonants or [anterior], [coronal], or [distributed] for
vowels, since such specifications would allow improper

VI TABLE 1
Lexical specification of segments in maximally distinctive positions.

	i	e	ɛ	a	ɔ	o	u	j	w	l	ʎ	r	n	m	ɲ	p	b	t	d	k	g	kʷ	gʷ	f	v	s	z	ʃ	ʒ
syllabic	+	+	+	+	+	+	+	−	−	−	−	−	−	−	−	−	−			−		−	−	−	−	−	−	−	−
vocalic	+	+	+	+	+	+	+	−	−	+	+	+	−	−	−														
conson								−	−	+	+	+	+	+	+	+	+	+	+	+	+	+	+	+	+	+	+	+	+
obstruent																+	+	+	+	+	+	+	+	+	+	+	+	+	+
contin													−	−	−														
nasal													+	+	+														
labial									+					+	−	+	+					+	+	+	+				
voiced	+	+	+	+	+	+	+		+	+	+	+	+	+	+		+		+		+		+		+		+		+
low			+	+																									
high	+	−	−		−	−	+																						
back	−	−			+	+	+		+											+	+	+	+						
anterior																													
coronal																													
distrib																													
	2	3	3	1	3	3	2	2	3	3	4	3	2	3	4	2	3	1	2	2	3	3	4	3	4	2	3	3	4

natural classes (cf. **Wheeler**, 1972, and also Sampson, 1970:600n). Consequently those features must always be mentioned in conjunction with [+syllabic] or [−syllabic], or with some feature specification corresponding to a subclass of those classes, (e.g. [+cons] or [+obstr] as subclasses of [−syllabic]), in the formulation of phonological rules; this is necessary to determine whether a rule applies or not (see § 1.3). The features specified in the table may, when appropriate, be written [m±DF].

2.1.1. Specifying segments as in Table 1 gives four degrees of relative markedness for underlying segments in maximally distinctive positions:

    Least marked (1 feature): a, t
                  (2 features): i, u, j, n, p, d, k, s
                  (3 features): e, ɛ, o, ɔ, w, l, r, m, b,
                                  g, k^w, f, z, ʃ
    Most marked (4 features): ʎ, ɲ, g^w, v, ʒ

This very roughly corresponds to a classification by degrees of assimilability. Rules of type (1) we might expect to apply assimilating segments to those of equal rank or higher, but not lower; rules of type (2) we might expect to neutralize a segment in the direction of one of equal rank or lower, not higher. Are the lower ranked segments, perhaps, the most readily deletable? These observations on the hierarchy given by the table suggest that the marking there may be along the right lines. For further discussion see below, § 2.3.

2.2. Context-free redundancy (CFR) rules. The function of CFR rules given here is to fill in redundant features which are not unmarked. They are unordered, i.e. the block of rules reapplies until no further features are added. As they stand these rules are not language-universal; e.g. CFR(26) ([−obstr] → [+voiced]) is not appropriate for a language having underlying /h/, or voiceless liquids (e.g. Welsh). Some of the rules, however, are clear candidates for universality, e.g. [+obstr] → [−vocal], or [−cont] → [+cons].

Tentatively we may suppose that there is in general linguistic theory a list of CFR rules; some of them, e.g. [+high] → [−low] would be obligatory in the grammar of any natural language — they could be seen as part of the definition of the distinctive features. Other CFR rules would be available. No cost would attach to the presence of such a rule in the grammar of a language, but a certain cost might be attached to the absence of available CFR rules. The consequence of this evaluation measure would be to assign least cost to the simplest phoneme inventories. Possibly a rule such as (26) [−obstr] → [+voiced] should be broken down into components, e.g. [+nasal] → [+voiced], [+syllabic] → [+voiced], [+vocalic] → [+voiced], [−conson] → [+voiced]. That is, there might be a hierarchy of such rules, such that if a language fails to have any given rule it must also fail to have the rules preceding it in order, rather in the manner of the universal sequence redundancy rules (neutralization rules) proposed by Cairns (1969:875). Thus in the following hierarchy:

1 [−obstr] → [+voiced]
2 [+vocalic] → [+voiced]
3 [−cons] → [+voiced]
4 [+syllab] → [+voiced]

these implications would hold: if not 2, then not 1; if not 3, then not 2; if not 4, then not 3.

By the rules which follow I indicate with U which of them may in fact be obligatory (universal) CFR rules.

CFR(1) $\begin{bmatrix} +\text{syll} \\ -\text{high} \end{bmatrix}$ → [+vocal]   U

Between UR's and the input to P-rules   225

CFR(2) $\begin{bmatrix} +\text{cons} \\ -\text{obstr} \\ -\text{nasal} \end{bmatrix} \rightarrow [+\text{vocal}]$ U

CFR(3) $[+\text{obstr}] \rightarrow [-\text{vocal}]$ U

CFR(4) $\begin{bmatrix} -\text{syll} \\ +\text{nasal} \end{bmatrix} \rightarrow [-\text{vocal}]$ U

These rules limit the possible classes of liquids, e.g. (3) and (4) exclude obstruent liquids and nasal liquids respectively.

CFR(5) $\begin{bmatrix} -\text{syll} \\ +\text{vocal} \end{bmatrix} \rightarrow [+\text{cons}]$ U

CFR(6) $[+\text{obstr}] \rightarrow [+\text{cons}]$ U

CFR(7) $[-\text{cont}] \rightarrow [+\text{cons}]$ U

CFR(8) $[-\text{voiced}] \rightarrow [+\text{cons}]$

CFR(9) $[+\text{syll}] \rightarrow [-\text{cons}]$

CFR(10) $\begin{bmatrix} +\text{cont} \\ -\text{obstr} \\ -\text{vocal} \end{bmatrix} \rightarrow [-\text{cons}]$ U?

A language with voiceless vowels or glides would lack (8); one with syllabic nasals or liquids would lack (9); (10) is perhaps universal.

CFR(11) $[-\text{cons}] \rightarrow [-\text{obstr}]$

This is universal if, e.g. /h/, /ʔ/ are not [+obstruent].

CFR(12) $[+\text{vocal}] \rightarrow [-\text{obstr}]$ U

CFR(13) $[+\text{nasal}] \rightarrow [-\text{obstr}]$

(13) is not universal if obstruent nasals occur, which seems to be the case; e.g. some Spanish dialects have phonetic [x̃], Celtic languages have, or had, [ṽ].

CFR(14) $[-\text{cons}] \rightarrow [+\text{cont}]$

Languages with /ʔ/ lack CFR (14).

CFR(15) $\begin{bmatrix} +\text{obstr} \\ -\text{distr} \end{bmatrix} \rightarrow [+\text{cont}]$

CFR(16) $[+\text{nasal}] \rightarrow [-\text{cont}]$

CFR(17) $\begin{bmatrix} +\text{obstr} \\ +\text{distr} \\ \{-\text{high}\} \\ \{-\text{coron}\} \end{bmatrix} \rightarrow [-\text{cont}]$

CFR(18) $\begin{bmatrix} +\text{vocal} \\ -\text{syll} \end{bmatrix} \rightarrow [-\text{nasal}]$ U

This rule excludes nasal liquids.

CFR(19) $[+\text{cont}] \rightarrow [-\text{nasal}]$

CFR(20) $\begin{bmatrix} -\text{cons} \\ +\text{back} \\ +\text{high} \end{bmatrix} \rightarrow [+\text{labial}]$

CFR(21) $\begin{bmatrix} +\text{anter} \\ -\text{coron} \\ -\text{syll} \end{bmatrix} \rightarrow [+\text{labial}]$ U?

CFR(22) $\begin{bmatrix} +\text{syll} \\ -\text{back} \end{bmatrix} \rightarrow [-\text{labial}]$

CFR(23) $\begin{bmatrix} -\text{syll} \\ +\text{vocal} \end{bmatrix} \rightarrow [-\text{labial}]$ U

CFR (23) excludes labial liquids.

CFR(24) $\begin{bmatrix} -\text{syll} \\ +\text{coron} \end{bmatrix} \rightarrow [-\text{labial}]$

Only a language with **labialized** coronals would lack CFR (24).

CFR(25) $\begin{bmatrix} +\text{high} \\ -\text{back} \end{bmatrix} \rightarrow [-\text{labial}]$

CFR(26) $[-\text{obstr}] \rightarrow [+\text{voiced}]$

CFR(27) $\begin{bmatrix} +\text{syll} \\ +\text{high} \end{bmatrix} \rightarrow [-\text{low}]$ U

CFR(28) $\begin{bmatrix} -\text{syll} \\ +\text{back} \end{bmatrix} \rightarrow [+\text{high}]$

CFR(29) $\begin{bmatrix} +\text{syll} \\ +\text{low} \end{bmatrix} \rightarrow [-\text{high}]$ U

CFR(30) $\begin{bmatrix} +\text{cons} \\ +\text{labial} \\ -\text{back} \end{bmatrix} \rightarrow [-\text{high}]$

Languages with palatalized labials lack CFR (30).

CFR(31) $\begin{bmatrix} -\text{syll} \\ +\text{vocal} \\ +\text{cont} \end{bmatrix} \rightarrow [-\text{high}]$

CFR(32) $\begin{bmatrix} +\text{labial} \\ -\text{cons} \end{bmatrix} \rightarrow [+\text{back}]$

CFR(33) $\begin{bmatrix} +\text{cons} \\ +\text{cont} \end{bmatrix} \rightarrow [-\text{back}]$

CFR(34) $\begin{bmatrix} +\text{cons} \\ -\text{obstr} \\ -\text{coron} \\ +\text{high} \end{bmatrix} \rightarrow [-\text{back}]$

CFR(35) $\begin{bmatrix} +\text{cons} \\ +\text{labial} \\ -\text{high} \end{bmatrix} \rightarrow [-\text{back}]$

CFR(36) $\begin{bmatrix} +\text{cons} \\ +\text{labial} \\ -\text{back} \end{bmatrix} \rightarrow [+\text{anter}]$

A language with labialized apico-alveolars or palatals would lack CFR (36).

CFR(37) $\begin{bmatrix} +\text{high} \\ -\text{syll} \end{bmatrix} \rightarrow [-\text{anter}]$

CFR(38) $\begin{bmatrix} -\text{syll} \\ +\text{vocal} \\ +\text{cont} \end{bmatrix} \rightarrow [-\text{anter}]$

CFR(39) $\begin{bmatrix} -\text{syll} \\ +\text{vocal} \\ +\text{cont} \end{bmatrix} \rightarrow [+\text{coron}]$

CFR(40) $\begin{bmatrix} +\text{cons} \\ +\text{high} \\ +\text{cont} \end{bmatrix} \rightarrow [+\text{coron}]$

CFR(41) $\begin{bmatrix} +\text{labial} \\ -\text{syll} \end{bmatrix} \rightarrow [-\text{coron}]$

CFR(42) $\begin{bmatrix} +\text{high} \\ -\text{back} \\ -\text{obstr} \\ -\text{syll} \end{bmatrix} \rightarrow [-\text{coron}]$

CFR(43) $\begin{bmatrix} +\text{high} \\ +\text{obstr} \\ -\text{cont} \end{bmatrix} \rightarrow [-\text{coron}]$

A language with pre-palatal plosives would lack CFR (43).

CFR(44) $\begin{bmatrix} +\text{labial} \\ +\text{obstr} \\ \alpha\,\text{cont} \end{bmatrix} \rightarrow [-\alpha\,\text{distr}]$

The effect of CFR (44) is to make labial plosives bilabial and labial fricatives labiodental.

CFR(45) $\begin{bmatrix} -\text{syll} \\ +\text{high} \end{bmatrix} \rightarrow [+\text{distr}]$

Table 2 shows the features which have been supplied by the CFR rules starting from the marked features

VI TABLE 2
Specification of segments after CFR rules

	i	e	ε	a	ɔ	o	u	j	w	l	ʎ	r	n	m	ɲ	p	b	t	d	k	g	kʷ	gʷ	f	v	s	z	ʃ	ʒ
syllabic	+	+	+	+	+	+	+	−	−	−	−	−	−	−	−	−	−	−	−	−	−	−	−	−	−	−	−	−	−
vocalic	+	+	+	+	+	+	+	−	−	+	+	+	−	−	−	−	−	−	−	−	−	−	−	−	−	−	−	−	−
conson	−	−	−	−	−	−	−	−	−	+	+	+	+	+	+	+	+	+	+	+	+	+	+	+	+	+	+	+	+
obstruent																								+	+	+	+	+	+
contin	+	+	+	+	+	+	+	−	−	+	+	+	−	−	−	−	−	−	−	−	−	−	−	+	+	+	+	+	+
nasal	−	−	−	−	−	−	−	−	−	−	−	−	+	+	+	−	−	−	−	−	−	−	−	−	−	−	−	−	−
labial	−	−	−	−	+	+	+	−	+	−	−	−	−	+	−	+	+	−	−	−	−	+	+	+	+	−	−	−	−
voiced	+	+	+	+	+	+	+	+	+	+	+	+	+	+	+	−	+	−	+	−	+	−	+	−	+	−	+	−	+
low	−	−	+	+	+	−	−																						
high	+	−	−	−	−	−	+	+	+	−	−	−								+	+	+	+						
back	−	−	−	+	+	+	+	−	+											+	+	+	+						
anterior								−	−	+	−	+	+	+	−	+	+	+	+	−	−	−	−	+	+	+	+	−	−
coronal								−	−	+	+	+	+	−	+	−	−	+	+	−	−	−	−	−	−	+	+	+	+
distrib								−	+	−	+	−			+	−	−							−	−			+	+

illustrated in Table 1, before any Marking rules have applied.

2.3. Markedness and marking rules

I should like to justify briefly the marking of segments as in Table 3, and propose some rules and conventions which in addition to the CFR rules just given will specify blanks.

2.3.1. I propose that /a/ (=/ə/) should be the least marked vowel. It is the vowel introduced by epenthesis rules (I (13), (19), (20)); it is the vowel most readily deleted (in syntactic phonetic environments), and is the archiphoneme of /e/, /ɛ/ and /a/ when unstressed; that is to say, I regard the change of $\begin{bmatrix} -\text{labial} \\ -\text{high} \end{bmatrix}$ vowels to /ə/ when unstressed as basically a change of m features to u features. The marking rules will make this least-marked vowel [+low] on general grounds favouring /i/, /a/, /u/ as the optimal unmarked vowel system (cf. Haiman, 1972); it will become [−low] only when the stress-assignment rule does not assign stress to it. See below under Marking rule (8) for further observations.

The next least-marked vowels will be /i/ and /u/; /u/ is introduced in a morphophonologically motivated epenthesis rule (I (15)) and is the archiphoneme of labial vowels, i.e. [+labial] → [+high] will be a $m → u$ change; /i/ is marked to the same degree as /u/ on account of holding a similar place in the vocalic system. I make /i/ and /u/ [u +vocalic] in order to reflect the relative naturalness of changes such as /i/ → /j/, /u/ → /w/. (Similarly /j/, /w/ are [u −vocalic].) The remaining four vowels are marked with three features in the UR.

Of the glides I have made /j/, $\begin{bmatrix} -\text{syll} \\ -\text{cons} \\ u-\text{labial} \end{bmatrix}$, less marked than /w/, $\begin{bmatrix} -\text{syll} \\ -\text{cons} \\ +\text{labial} \end{bmatrix}$, on the grounds that

Catalan has a rule converting /j/ → /w/ (III (95)) but not vice versa; however, this may not necessarily be appropriate — perhaps they should be equally marked.

Of the liquids, I think it is appropriate for /ʎ/ and /r/ to have no unmarked features inasmuch as they undergo no assimilations. Catalan has no /ʎ/ → /j/ or /ʎ/ → /ʒ/ rules; languages which have, ought perhaps to allow such rules to be relatively costless, i.e. to give /ʎ/ a certain degree of unmarkedness. /l/ should remain [u−back, u−distr] to take account of the relative naturalness of /l/ → /ł/ (backness assimilation) or /l/ → /l'/ (partial palatal assimilation).

The most marked of nasals is /ɲ/ which undergoes no assimilations. The least marked is /n/, which is assimilated "naturally" to following labials, velars, dentals, and (partially) palatals; therefore it should be at least [u−back, u−labial, u−distr, u−anterior] −/n/ is also the most deletable nasal. /m/ should be [u+distr] at least, so that /m/ → [m̥] before /f/ counts as natural.

/s/ and /z/ are perhaps to be the least marked of obstruent continuants; they are the most deletable, and assimilable to following dentals (thus [u−distr, u−anterior]). All the voiced obstruents are marked [m+voiced], making the unvoicing of utterance-final obstruents a m → u change. Among the obstruent stops /t/, /d/ are least marked, being the most deletable and most assimilable, (e.g. to following /l/, /ʎ/, /n/, /m/, /p/, /k/, /ʃ/, /s/, /z/); and /p/, /b/ are next least marked, being occasionally deletable (finally after /n/) and assimilable to following /n/, /m/. /k/ and /g/ are slightly more marked than /p/ and /b/ respectively, and /k^w/ and /g^w/ are most marked.

2.3.2. The Marking rules (more strictly they are "unmarkedness" rules) which follow are to be interpreted in the following way: they are ordered with respect to each other, and after each has applied the block of CFR rules reapplies (unordered). Only the features supplied by the Marking (Mk) rules themselves have "unmarked value"; all the others are marked. It is in this way that "unmarked" is restricted from being equivalent to "redundant" to what I have suggested is its proper value in indicating formally the relative naturalness of phonological rules. These Marking rules have no special claim to universal status as they stand, though it may be that they follow in a universally natural way from the actual phoneme system of Catalan. Thus one might conceive of an algorithm to derive Mk rules for a language from the phoneme inventory plus the CFR rules.

Marking rules:

Mk(1) $[u \text{ obstr}] \rightarrow [u+\text{obstr}]$

Mk(2) $[u \text{ cont}] \rightarrow [u-\text{cont}]$

Mk(3) $\begin{bmatrix} u \text{ nasal} \\ -\text{syllab} \end{bmatrix} \rightarrow [u-\text{nasal}]$

Mk(4) $[u \text{ voiced}] \rightarrow [u-\text{voiced}]$

Mk(5) $[u \text{ labial}] \rightarrow [u-\text{labial}]$

Mk(6) $\begin{bmatrix} u \text{ coron} \\ -\text{syllab} \end{bmatrix} \rightarrow [u+\text{coron}]$

Mk(7) $\begin{bmatrix} u \text{ back} \\ \alpha \text{syllab} \end{bmatrix} \rightarrow [u\alpha\text{back}]$

Mk(8) $\begin{bmatrix} u \text{ low} \\ +\text{syll} \end{bmatrix} \rightarrow \left\{ \begin{matrix} [u-\text{low}] \\ [u+\text{low}] \end{matrix} \right. \Bigg/ \left\{ \begin{matrix} [\overline{+\text{labial}}] \\ [\overline{-\text{back}}] \end{matrix} \right\}$

Perhaps this rule should rather make [*u* low] into
[*u*−low] everywhere, thus making the specification of
the least marked vowel correspond to mid /ə/ rather
than low /a/. It would make sense if generally /ə/ were
the least marked unstressed vowel, and /a/ the least
marked stressed vowel. We expect a language with
stressed /ə/ to have also unstressed /ə/, but not
necessarily conversely; and we expect a language with
unstressed /a/ to have stressed /a/, but not necessarily
conversely. Possibly, then, marking rules for non-high
central vowels should be linked in some way to the
specification of stress.

Mk(9)   [*u* high] → [*u*αhigh] / $\left[\overline{-\alpha \text{ cons}} \right]$

Mk(10) $\begin{bmatrix} u \text{ vocal} \\ \alpha \text{syllab} \end{bmatrix}$ → [*u*αvocal]

Mk(11) $\begin{bmatrix} u \text{ anter} \\ -\text{syllab} \end{bmatrix}$ → $\left\{ \begin{matrix} [u\text{+anter}] \\ [u-\text{anter}] \end{matrix} \middle/ \begin{bmatrix} -\text{cont} \\ +\text{obstr} \end{bmatrix} \right\}$

Mk(12) $\begin{bmatrix} u \text{ distr} \\ -\text{syllab} \\ \alpha \text{anter} \end{bmatrix}$ → [*u*αdistr]

Table 3 shows the full feature specification of Catalan
phonemes, with the exception of features supplied by late
phonological rules (e.g. [stress], [tense], [del. rel],
[lateral]). The unmarked features are indicated with *u*.
Features which were still unspecified in Table 2 and are not
themselves specified by Mk rules will have been supplied
by CFR rules, which apply in a block after each Mk rule.

2.4. Linking.

The CFR and Mk rules also act as linking rules (cf.
Chomsky & Halle, 1968:419−35; Sommerstein, 1973:

VI TABLE 3
Full feature specification of Catalan phonemes.

	i	e	ε	a	ɔ	o	u	j	w	l	ʎ	r	n	m	ɲ	p	b	b	t	d	k	g	kʷ	gʷ	f	v	s	z	ʃ	ʒ
syllabic	+	+	+	+	+	+	+	−	−	−	−	−	−	−	−	−	−	−	−	−	−	−	−	−	−	−	−	−	−	−
vocalic	u+	+	+	+	+	+	u+	u−	u−	+	+	+	−	−	−	−	−	−	−	−	−	−	−	−	−	−	−	−	−	−
conson	−	−	−	−	−	−	−	−	−	+	+	+	+	+	+	+	+	+	+	+	+	+	+	+	+	+	+	+	+	+
obstruent	−	−	−	−	−	−	−	−	−	−	−	−	−	−	−	+	+	+	+	+	+	+	+	+	+	+	+	+	+	+
contin	+	+	+	+	+	+	+	+	+	+	+	+	−	−	−	u+	u+	u+	u+	u+	u+	u+	u+	u+	+	+	+	+	+	+
nasal	−	−	−	−	−	−	−	−	−	−	−	−	−	+	+	+	u−	u−	u−	u−	u−	u−	u−	u−	u−	−	−	−	−	−	−
labial	−	−	−	u−	−	−	−	u−	−	−	−	−	−	+	−	+	+	u−	u−	u−	u−	u−	+	+	+	+	−	−	−	−
voiced	+	+	+	+	+	+	+	+	+	+	+	+	+	+	+	u−	+	u−	+	u−	+	u−	+	u−	+	u−	+	u−	+	u−
low	u−	u−	+	+	+	u−	u−	u+	+	u−	+	u−	−	u−	+															
high	u+	−	−	−	−	−	u+	u−	+	u−	+	u−	−	−	+															
back	−	−	−	−	+	+	+	−	u−	−	−	+	u−	−	+															
anterior										−	u−					+	+	+	u+	u+	−	−	−	−	+	+	+	+	−	−
coronal										+	u+					−	−	−	u+	u+	−	−	−	−	−	−	+	+	+	+
distrib																+	+	u+	u+	u+	+	+	+	+	−	−	u−	u−	+	+

91–109), subject to the following conventions concerning the interpretation of phonological rules.

(a) CFR rules apply to the segments resulting from P-rule application; they can be seen as changing some marked and unmarked features of the segment on the left of the arrow into others which are marked.

(b) any *m* feature of the original segment not changed by the P-rule itself or the CFR rules is transferred to the output segment in the usual way.

(c) any remaining features are supplied by the Mk rules (to which the CFR rules link, if necessary, as in § 2.3.2).

(d) a linking convention applies either to all or to none of the segments formed by a given rule (Chomsky & Halle, 1968:431). "Rule" here must be understood as meaning each rule abbreviated by a rule-schema with Greek letter variables; otherwise no CFR rule could link to a P-rule output with e.g. [αhigh], since necessarily CFR rules for [+high] will not be applicable to the [−high] output. Possibly all abbreviatory schemas should be expanded when this convention operates. In addition, it seems right for obligatory (universal) CFR rules to apply to any matrix whatever. That is, such rules should constrain grammars so that no rule produces impossible segments.

Observe that linking conventions have the effect of changing *m* features to other *m* features, *u* features to other *u* features and *u* features to *m* features, but not *m* features to *u* features. This is the result we want to achieve. Allowing linking to change *m* features to other *m* features makes the device rather powerful. If it were thought inappropriate to permit this, a version of condition (b):

(b') any *m* feature of the original segment not changed
by the P-rule is transferred to the output segment:
could apply before condition (a). Consequently, to
achieve the same output in a given case, the P-rule
would need to mention all the *m* features to be changed.
*Consider the following examples:

The rule changing /v/ to /w/ (V (10)) can have the
form:

(3) $\begin{bmatrix} -\text{syllab} \\ +\text{labial} \\ +\text{cont} \\ +\text{voice} \end{bmatrix} \rightarrow$ [−cons] / in certain environments.

When conditions (a), (b) and (c) apply, in that order, the
matrix to the right of the arrow,

$\begin{bmatrix} -\text{syllab} \\ +\text{labial} \\ +\text{cont} \\ +\text{voice} \\ -\text{cons} \end{bmatrix}$, becomes

[*m*−obstr] by CFR (11) (a change of *u*DF
　　　　　　　　　　　　　　　　　to *m*DF),

[*m*+high] by CFR (28)
[*m*+back] by CFR (32)   (changes of *m*DF
[*m*−anter] by CFR (37)　　　　to *m*DF);
[*m*+distr] by CFR (45)

and by (b), $\begin{bmatrix} m-\text{vocal} \\ m-\text{nasal} \\ m-\text{coron} \end{bmatrix}$ is carried over to the output segment.

---

*Another consequence of these linking conventions is
that all P-rules have as output a segment or segments
identical to those in the phoneme inventory, unless the
P-rule specifies otherwise explicitly.

Between UR's and the input to P-rules 237

If the weaker convention is applied, i.e. (b'), (a), (c) in that order, then (3) would have to be replaced by (4):

(4) $\begin{bmatrix} -\text{syllab} \\ +\text{labial} \\ +\text{cont} \\ +\text{voice} \end{bmatrix} \rightarrow \begin{bmatrix} -\text{cons} \\ +\text{back} \\ +\text{high} \\ -\text{anter} \\ +\text{distr} \end{bmatrix} / \quad \ldots$

The stronger condition (a), (b), (c) is to be preferred until counter-evidence appears.

The rule assimilating /t/ or /d/ totally to a following /l/ or /ʎ/ (cf. VII § 9.1) can be expressed thus:

(5) $\begin{bmatrix} -\text{cont} \\ -\text{nasal} \\ -\text{labial} \\ -\text{back} \end{bmatrix} \rightarrow \begin{bmatrix} +\text{vocal} \\ \alpha\text{high} \end{bmatrix} / \underline{\quad} (\#(\#)) \begin{bmatrix} +\text{vocal} \\ -\text{cont} \\ \alpha\text{high} \end{bmatrix}$

Rule (5) has two possible outputs, as follows, and the CFR and Mk rules apply as indicated:

(i) $\begin{bmatrix} -\text{cont} \\ -\text{nasal} \\ -\text{labial} \\ -\text{back} \\ +\text{vocal} \\ +\text{high} \end{bmatrix}$
[−obstr] by CFR (12)
[+voiced] by CFR (26)
[−anter] by CFR (37)
[−coron] by CFR (42)
[+distr] by CFR (45)

[ʎ]

(ii) $\begin{bmatrix} -\text{cont} \\ -\text{nasal} \\ -\text{labial} \\ -\text{back} \\ +\text{vocal} \\ -\text{high} \end{bmatrix}$
[−obstr] by CFR (12)
[+voiced] by CFR (26)
[u+coron] by Mk (6)
[u−anter] by Mk (11)
[u−distr] by Mk (12)

[l]

Let us suppose further that features specified on the right of the arrow in P-rules have m value, and that those specified on the left carry over the m or u values they had previously; then the /l/ which is the output of (5) will be [u−back] just as is underlying /l/, and thus with the same cost changeable to [+back] in the appropriate environments, as the facts indicate. However, this means that we would have as an output of (5) a kind of /l/ which is [u−cont], [u−nasal] and [u−labial], and a kind of /ʎ/ which is all that and also [u−back]; the implication is that a change of these feature values in assimilatory environments would be natural (and moreover, somehow more natural than such a change of original /l/ or /ʎ/). We want to avoid such a consequence if we can. This can be done **by interpreting condition (a) so that the CFR rules apply to the output features which are those on the right of the arrow plus those specified on the left which are not changed in the P-rule itself**, so as to alter the markedness value from [uDF] to [mDF]. Thus to the outputs i) and ii) of (5) CFR (18) applies, making them both [m−nasal]; CFR (23) makes them both [m−labial] and CFR (34) makes i) = /ʎ/ [m−back]. There is no obvious way of making them [m−cont].

The rule assimilating /p/, /b/, /t/, or /d/ in nasality to a following /m/ or /n/ can be expressed thus:

(6) $\begin{bmatrix} -\text{cont} \\ -\text{back} \\ -\text{vocal} \end{bmatrix} \rightarrow [+\text{nasal}] \;/\; \underline{\quad} \; (\#(\#)) \begin{bmatrix} +\text{nasal} \\ -\text{high} \end{bmatrix}$

Rule (6) has two possible outputs, to which linking applies thus:

(i) $\begin{bmatrix} m-\text{cont} \\ u-\text{back} \\ m-\text{vocal} \\ m+\text{nasal} \end{bmatrix} u \rightarrow m$ by CFR (16)
[m−obstr] by CFR (13)
[m+voiced] by CFR (26)
[u−labial] by Mk (5)

[u+coron] by Mk (6)
[u−high] by Mk (9)
[u−anter] by Mk (11)
[u−distr] by Mk (12)
/n/

(ii) $\begin{bmatrix} m-\text{cont} \\ m-\text{back} \\ m-\text{vocal} \\ m+\text{nasal} \end{bmatrix}$ $u \rightarrow m$ by CFR (16)
$u \rightarrow m$ by CFR (35)

[m−obstr] by CFR (13)
[m+voiced] by CFR (26)
$\begin{bmatrix} m+\text{labial} \\ m-\text{high} \\ m+\text{anter} \\ m-\text{coron} \\ m+\text{distr} \end{bmatrix}$ m DFs carried over

/m/

The /n/ which is output of rule (6) is identical to underlying /n/, and will undergo labial assimilation if the following nasal is /m/, as does original /n/, changing [u−labial], [u−anterior] and [u−distr]. Condition (d), it seems from this example, should constrain only convention (a), not (b) or (c). It will be so interpreted henceforth.

3. Morpheme-structure rules.

3.1.1. The rules which are proposed in this section correspond in essence to what have received various names in other works, e.g. "lexical redundancy rules" (Chomsky & Halle, 1968; Cairns, 1969); "phonotactic rules" (Bladon, 1970); "sequence redundancy rules" (Schane, 1973); "a phonological base" (Sampson, 1970); and "morpheme-structure rules" (e.g. Sommerstein,

1973). Feature redundancy in isolated matrices I have already dealt with by means of Context-free Redundancy rules. The other functions of the kinds of rules presented in the works referred to are firstly, to deal with sequence redundancy: that is to specify blanks in matrices when feature value is predictable on the basis of surrounding matrices in lexical formatives. This is a contribution to minimizing the specification of lexical representations. To take a well known example, morpheme-initial preconsonantal /s/ need only be specified [+segment] in the lexicon. An unmarked initial segment is [−syllabic] anyway, and when no other feature is specified an initial consonant will be assigned the feature [+contin] when a [−vocalic] segment follows. Mk and CFR rules will specify the remaining features of /s/.

The second function of morpheme-structure rules is to express that part of a speaker's competence by which he knows what are possible phonological sequences in his language, i.e. the kind of competence by which an English speaker knows that /blik/ is possible while */bnik/ is not; cf. Sommerstein, 1973:110−13. The rules can also be seen as conditions for well-formedness of lexical representations, just as in syntax phrase-structure rules generate all and only the well-formed deep structures.

Thirdly, the morpheme-structure rules are intended to be an integral part of the grammar, playing a significant role in the evaluation of the grammar as a whole, in the way proposed by Sampson (1970). He says (590): "The relative simplicity of the phonological base will count toward the over-all evaluation measure of the entire grammar; that is, a language with a symmetrical set of underlying phonological matrices, and therefore a simple phonological base, will in that respect be less complex, in a psychologically real way, than a language with a less symmetrical set of underlying phonological matrices."

3.1.2. The approach I offer to the formulation of morpheme-structure rules for Catalan includes the notion that sequences cannot be adequately generated by a finite-state device, but require rules of a phrase-structure type, which derive the structure of syllables from an arbitrary initial symbol. This is the view of Fudge (1969: 260) and of Sampson (1970:603) as also of Bladon (1970) to whose article I owe part of the inspiration for my own proposals. He says (96): "I feel there is a good deal of evidence, and there is also a scholastic precedent, to suggest that a phonotactic model which recognizes positions in a structure is operationally the simpler and descriptively the more satisfactory".

The actual "phonotactic rules for Old Provençal" which Bladon offers (107ff.) are in my view unacceptable as they stand for two reasons: the form of his rules is far from maximally simple – notably, their expression in terms of unit phonemes rather than distinctive features obscures most of the real generalizations – and, secondly, he avoids directionality at the cost of arbitrariness in the order of rules. Though one might not follow the tentative suggestion of Chomsky & Halle (1968:386) that MS rules apply simultaneously, surely any rule ordering proposed must be well-motivated by the facts of the language in question. In effect, Bladon accounts for initial groups of three consonants by first specifying the first (/s/), and the third (/l/ or /r/) and then listing the consonants that can appear between them. This is open to the same criticism of directionality as he himself puts forward (96), for what he claims, effectively, is that only certain consonants can follow initial /s/, and only certain consonants can precede /l/ or /r/ in initial groups. There is no clear motivation for making this statement rather than, for example, that of consonants in initial groups, only certain ones can be preceded by /s/, or followed by /r/ or /l/.

I myself do not see how directionality can be avoided

except at the cost of failing to express what significant generalizations there are. However, it seems to me that if we adopt the approach which regards segment sequences as structured, we can attempt to state MS rules in which directionality is relatively well motivated. Though positive conditions and negative conditions can formulate some (though not all) sequence restrictions, and avoid the problem of directionality, it is hard to see how they can be effectively integrated into a grammar; cf. Bladon, 1970:99–102.

3.2. Let us consider informally the possible segment sequences of Catalan morphemes. The source of the less obvious examples given in this chapter is the *Diccionari General de la Llengua Catalana* (Fabra, 1968b), and the *Diccionari de la Rima* (Ferrer Pastor, 1956).

3.2.1. There are sequences of two vowels, e.g. *aeri* [əɛɾi] 'aerial', *amoïnar* [əmuiná] 'to bother', but not, apparently, of more than two. Probably there are no sequences of two identical underlying vowels: *oolita* [uulítə] 'oolite' possibly has the UR /uɔ+lit+a/, cf. *oòspora* [uɔ́spuɾə] 'oosperm'.[1]

3.2.2. A morpheme may begin with a vowel, or any consonant except /w/. Badia (1965:235n and passim) affirms that initial /w/ is possible in Catalan; but he gives no example, and I know of none either, so it is hard to see what his affirmation means.

3.2.3. A morpheme may begin with these groups:
pr br tr dr kr gr fr
pl bl   kl gl fl

---

[1]*nihilisme* 'nihilism', and other words with the same stem, e.g. *anihilar* 'annihilate', offer what seems to be a unique counter-example.

Between UR's and the input to P-rules   243

There are no other initial groups of /Cr/ or /Cl/, except possibly /sl/, for which see below.

3.2.4. I have earlier (I §7) discussed the epenthesis of [ə] before morpheme initial /sC/. It is not always evident from paradigmatic relationships when an initial [ə] before [sC] is epenthetic and when present in the UR. Here are some paradigms revealing initial /sC/:

> *perspirar* 'to perspire', *transpirar* 'to transpire', *inspirar* 'to inspire', *expirar* 'to expire' (/spir+a+r/ with prefixes /par+/, /tranz+/, /in+/, /aks+/).
> *conspicu* 'conspicuous', *perspicu* 'perspicuous' (/+spiku/ with prefixes /par+/, /kun+/).
> *instil·lar* 'to instil', *destil·lar* 'to distil' (/stitl+a+r/ with prefixes /in+/, /da+/).
> *constituir* 'to constitute', *substituir* 'to substitute', *instituir* 'to institute' (/stitu+i+r/ with prefixes /kun+/, /sub+/, /in+/).

In many cases, however, there is no evidence of this kind, and initial /sC/ is established on the basis of economy of lexical representations. In addition to /st−/ and /sp−/ there are:

> /sb/, e.g. *asbest* 'asbestos'
> ?/sd/: no clear example, though /sdr/ appears (see §3.5.1)
> /sk/, e.g. *escala* 'stair'
> /sg/, e.g. *esgarriar-se* 'to get lost'
> /sk^w/, e.g. *esquadra* 'squadron'
> /sg^w/, e.g. *esguard* 'regard'

Further support for this general approach to groups of /sC/ where C is an obstruent stop will appear in the discussion of internal groups. It is doubtful whether initial /sf/, /sl/, /sm/, /sn/ should be permitted. In *hemisfèric* 'hemispherical' [ɛmisfɛ́rik], cf. *esfèric* 'spherical', the structure would be /#ɛmi##asfɛr+ik#/ where the internal ##, necessary to account for the two accents, may account also for the deletion of unstressed /a/. /sm/ occurs in e.g. *esmalt* 'enamel'; /sl/ and /sn/ are extremely rare in any position: we have e.g. *eslora* 'length of ship', *esnob* 'snob'. As we shall see, in internal positions these sequences are never preceded by another consonant, which implies that a syllabic division always occurs between the two members of the sequence. Many cases of phonetic [əsC−] contain the prefix /as+/, and thus have UR /#as+C−/.

3.2.5. Some "exceptional" two-consonant initial sequences occur in words of foreign origin (mostly Greek), such as /mn/, /pn/, /kn/, /pt/, /kt/, /bd/, /ft/, /ps/, /ks/, /ts/, /tʃ/; almost the only such morphemes in normal use (i.e. outside specialized scientific terminology) are /psɛwdɔ+/ 'pseudo−', /psik+/ 'psych−' and /pnɛwma+/ 'pneuma−'; and certain Castilianisms, e.g. [tʃíste] or [tʃístu] 'joke'. I believe the correct solution is for these morphemes to be lexically marked as exceptions to MS rules; consequently their matrices must be so specified that CFR and Mk rules will fill in all the blanks.

3.2.6. Some groups of three initial consonants (/sCr/ or /sCl/) are revealed by paradigmatic evidence as in § 3.2.4, e.g.

> *estrènyer* 'to squeeze', *constrènyer* 'to constrain' (/strɛɲ+r/ with prefix /kun+/)
> *estrat* 'stratum', *substrat* 'substratum' (/strat/ with prefix /sub+/)
> *escriure* 'to write', *inscriure* 'to inscribe', *subscriure* 'to subscribe', etc.

Other cases may be:

Between UR's and the input to P-rules   245

?/spr/: no example found.
/sbr/, e.g. *esbroncar* 'to criticize'
/sdr/, e.g. *esdrúixol* 'proparoxytone'
/sgr/, e.g. *esgrimir* 'to fence'
/spl/, e.g. *espluga* 'cave'
/sbl/, e.g. *esblaimar-se* 'to turn pale'
/skl/, e.g. *esclerosi* 'sclerosis'
/sgl/, e.g. *esglai* 'fright'

It will be observed that these groups of three consonants are just those resulting from a combination of the possibilities in § 3.2.3 and § 3.2.4; thus it seems intuitively well-motivated to say that */stl/ and */sdl/ do not occur *because* */tl/ and */dl/ do not occur, or that */+sfr/, */+sfl/ do not occur *because* */+sf/ does not occur. That is, /+sC$_i$l/, /+sC$_i$r/ occur only if /+sC$_i$/, and either /+C$_i$l/ or /+C$_i$r/ respectively occur. That is, C$_i$ is somehow primary or basic in determining possible sequences. This suggests to me that an MS statement of this kind, in which directionality is not wholly arbitrary, is possible:

A single initial C is not /w/; if there is an obstruent stop, it may be preceded by one C which is /s/; if there is an obstruent which is [+anter] or [+back] it may be followed by /r/, and if it is [−coron] it may be followed by /l/.

In order to have a suitable framework for the discussion of internal/final groups, I shall express the facts referred to so far in terms of phonological base rules — these are like phrase-structure rules, and the terminal symbols are distinct items of the phoneme inventory — and sequence-redundancy (SR) rules, which may specify features necessary for the correct subsequent application of CFR and Mk rules, or express neutralizations stating that in certain sequences only the unmarked of two possible feature values occurs. Some of these rules will apply vacuously to well-formed sequences, but exceptional morphemes will have to be marked as exceptions to them.

3.3. In these rules which follow, accounting for morpheme-initial sequences, M, the initial symbol, stands for morpheme; On corresponds to "onset", C and V to consonant ([−syllabic]) and vowel ([+syllabic]) respectively. CFR and Mk rules link to these rules, supplying some of the features mentioned in MS (5) and (6). The structure of morpheme-initial sequences can be illustrated like this:

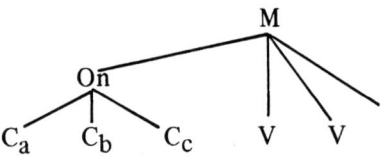

MS (1)   M → + (On) V (V) ...

This is part of the rule generating the structure of complete morphemes which will be given later.

MS (2)   On → $(C_a) C_b (C_c)$

MS (3)   V → $\left\{ \begin{bmatrix} +syll \\ -back \end{bmatrix} , \begin{bmatrix} +syll \\ -high \\ -back \end{bmatrix} , \begin{bmatrix} +syll \\ +low \\ -back \end{bmatrix} , \right.$

$\left. [+syll] , \begin{bmatrix} +syll \\ +labial \\ +low \end{bmatrix} , \begin{bmatrix} +syll \\ +labial \\ -high \end{bmatrix} , \begin{bmatrix} +syll \\ +labial \end{bmatrix} \right\}$

In fact, [+syll] need only be specified when + or V precedes; elsewhere it will be supplied by SR (1).

MS (4) C_b → $\left\{ \begin{bmatrix} -syll \\ -cons \end{bmatrix} , \begin{bmatrix} -syll \\ -cons \\ +labial \end{bmatrix} , \begin{bmatrix} -syll \\ +vocal \\ -cont \end{bmatrix} , \right.$

$$\left\{\begin{bmatrix}-\text{syll}\\+\text{vocal}\\-\text{cont}\\+\text{high}\end{bmatrix}, \begin{bmatrix}-\text{syll}\\+\text{vocal}\\+\text{cont}\end{bmatrix}, \begin{bmatrix}-\text{syll}\\+\text{nasal}\end{bmatrix}, \begin{bmatrix}-\text{syll}\\+\text{nasal}\\+\text{labial}\end{bmatrix},\right.$$

$$\begin{bmatrix}-\text{syll}\\+\text{nasal}\\-\text{labial}\\+\text{high}\end{bmatrix}, \begin{bmatrix}-\text{syll}\\+\text{labial}\end{bmatrix}, \begin{bmatrix}-\text{syll}\\+\text{labial}\\+\text{voiced}\end{bmatrix}, [-\text{syll}],$$

$$\begin{bmatrix}-\text{syll}\\+\text{voiced}\end{bmatrix}, \begin{bmatrix}-\text{syll}\\+\text{back}\end{bmatrix}, \begin{bmatrix}-\text{syll}\\+\text{back}\\+\text{voiced}\end{bmatrix}, \begin{bmatrix}-\text{syll}\\+\text{labial}\\+\text{back}\end{bmatrix},$$

$$\begin{bmatrix}-\text{syll}\\+\text{labial}\\+\text{back}\\+\text{voiced}\end{bmatrix}, \begin{bmatrix}-\text{syll}\\+\text{cont}\\+\text{labial}\end{bmatrix}, \begin{bmatrix}-\text{syll}\\+\text{cont}\\+\text{labial}\\+\text{voiced}\end{bmatrix}, \begin{bmatrix}-\text{syll}\\+\text{cont}\end{bmatrix},$$

$$\left.\begin{bmatrix}-\text{syll}\\+\text{cont}\\+\text{voiced}\end{bmatrix}, \begin{bmatrix}-\text{syll}\\+\text{cont}\\+\text{high}\end{bmatrix}, \begin{bmatrix}-\text{syll}\\+\text{cont}\\+\text{high}\\+\text{voiced}\end{bmatrix}\right\}$$

MS rules (3) and (4) rewrite as the phoneme inventory of Catalan, with feature values specified as in Table 1. [−syll] in fact need only be specified when C_a is present; otherwise, after +, it will be supplied by SR (1). All the terminal symbols of MS rules (3) and (4) are of course [+segment].

MS (5) $C_a \rightarrow \begin{bmatrix}m+\text{segment}\\u \text{ syllab}\\u \text{ cont}\\u \text{ voiced}\end{bmatrix} \Big/ \underline{\qquad} \begin{bmatrix}+\text{obstr}\\-\text{cont}\end{bmatrix}$

The unmarked features here will be specified by a sequence redundancy rule.

248   *Between UR's and the input to P-rules*

$$\text{MS (6)} \quad C_c \rightarrow \begin{Bmatrix} \begin{bmatrix} m\text{+segment} \\ m\text{−syll} \\ m\text{+cont} \\ u \text{ vocal} \end{bmatrix} \Big/ \begin{bmatrix} \text{+obstr} \\ \text{+anter} \\ \text{+back} \end{bmatrix} \underline{\quad} & \text{i)} \\ \begin{bmatrix} m\text{+segment} \\ m\text{−syll} \\ m\text{−cont} \\ u \text{ vocal} \\ u \text{ high} \end{bmatrix} \Big/ \begin{bmatrix} \text{+obstr} \\ \text{−coron} \end{bmatrix} \underline{\quad} & \text{ii)} \end{Bmatrix}$$

SR rules will specify the [vocalic] and [high] values. As a result of MS (6) these groups are defined as well formed:

+pr +br +tr +dr +kr +gr +k^{W}r +g^{W}r +fr +vr
+pl +bl   +kl +gl +k^{W}l +g^{W}l +fl +vl

Some of these will be excluded by SR rules.

3.4.1. Sequence Redundancy (SR) rules.

Some of these SR rules correspond to certain of Chomsky & Halle's marking conventions which have restricted environments, and give preference to universal syllable structures, as discussed by Cairns (1969).

$$\text{SR (1)} \quad [u \text{ syll}] \rightarrow \begin{Bmatrix} [m\text{−syll}] \ / \ + \ [\overline{\text{+segm}}] \\ [m\alpha\text{syll}] \ / \ [-\alpha\text{syll}] \ [\overline{\text{+segm}}] \end{Bmatrix}$$

This rule allows CV(CV)* sequences to be unmarked for [syllabic] in the lexicon; a morpheme-initial vowel will be marked [+syllabic] and the second and subsequent segments in sequences of vowels or consonants will also be lexically marked. SR (1) is a universal rule, and thus of no cost to the grammar of a particular language. SR (2) is also, if we follow Cairns (1969), part of universal grammar, in that it prefers stop + liquid to other morpheme-initial sequences.

Between UR's and the input to P-rules 249

SR (2) $\begin{bmatrix} u \text{ vocal} \\ -\text{syllab} \end{bmatrix}_c \rightarrow [m\text{+vocal}]$

Consequently morphemes beginning with e.g. /pl/, such as *platja* 'beach' will have lexical entries like this:

$+ \begin{bmatrix} +\text{segment} \\ +\text{labial} \end{bmatrix} \begin{bmatrix} +\text{segment} \\ -\text{syllab} \\ -\text{cont} \end{bmatrix} [+\text{segment}] \ldots$

to which SR, CFR and Mk rules will apply to specify other features.

SR (3) $[u \text{ cont}]_a \rightarrow [m\text{+cont}]$

SR (3) makes an initial consonant in C_a position /s/, when linked to CFR and Mk rules. Note that without SR (3) $\begin{bmatrix} -\text{syllabic} \\ u \text{ contin} \end{bmatrix}$ would be specified as /t/ by CFR and Mk rules; clearly SR rules apply first.

3.4.2. Now let us deal with further restrictions on initial groups. How is the absence of */vr/, */vl/ to be accounted for? There are many possibilities: we could say that the opposition /v/ ~ /f/ was neutralized before liquids, or that the opposition /v/ ~ /b/ or /v/ ~ /w/ was neutralized before liquids, or that the opposition between liquids and vowels was neutralized after /v/, or that $C_a \rightarrow$ ø after /v/. It will be recalled that /v/'s allophones overlap entirely with those of /b/, /w/ or in one case /f/, and its underlying presence is revealed only when morpheme-final, by paradigmatic alternations (see V § 4). In one case only can we postulate it elsewhere. The second person plural unstressed pronoun has underlying /v/ (see IV § 5.1), and it seems appropriate to relate this to the stressed pronouns *vós* [bós] 'you' (polite) and *vosaltres* [buzáltrəs] 'you (pl)'. There is no reason to postulate its presence anywhere else in this dialect, though it is present in other dialects where its allophones are [v] and [w]. Even in other dialects, however, there are no examples of [vl] or [vɾ] at the systematic phonetic level. When a morpheme boundary intervenes, /v+r/ is realized as [wɾ], (see III §7.2). So perhaps the most appropriate way of formulating the fact that the sequences */vr/, */vl/ do not occur is to say that the opposition /v/ ~ /w/ is neutralized before liquids; thus:

SR (4) $\begin{bmatrix} -\text{syllab} \\ +\text{labial} \\ +\text{voice} \\ +\text{cont} \end{bmatrix} \rightarrow [-\text{cons}] \ / \underline{\quad} \begin{bmatrix} -\text{syll} \\ +\text{vocal} \end{bmatrix}$

In the case of the absence of */k^{w}r/, */k^{w}l/, */g^{w}r/, */g^{w}l/ the problem is similar. Underlying /k^w/ and /g^w/ are revealed as distinct from e.g. /k/, /g/ only morpheme-finally and before vowels (and, I shall suggest below, after vowels in some cases). In $C_b C_c$ position we could say, for example, that the opposition between labial and non-labial velars was neutralized before liquids, or that the opposition between liquids and vowels was neutralized after labial velars, or that $C_c \rightarrow \emptyset$ after them. The first of these alternatives is perhaps the most natural, so let us say:

SR (5) $\begin{bmatrix} +\text{cons} \\ +\text{back} \end{bmatrix} \rightarrow [u-\text{labial}] \ / \underline{\quad} \begin{bmatrix} -\text{syll} \\ +\text{vocal} \end{bmatrix}$

For the absence of initial /w/ we can have the rule

SR (6) $\begin{bmatrix} -\text{cons} \\ -\text{syll} \end{bmatrix} \rightarrow [u-\text{labial}] \ / \ + \underline{\quad}$

3.5. Now I would like to show that medial and final consonant groups can be explained as just those occurring initially, optionally preceded by one consonant, which I refer to as C_d. That is, medial/final groups are $((C_d)(C_a)$

Between UR's and the input to P-rules   251

C_b (C_c)). There does not seem to be any difference
between possible medial and possible final groups.
This is not surprising if we consider that the restrictions
are essentially in terms of the structure of the syllable,
which structure is partially repeated in a polysyllabic
morpheme. The full form of MS (1) is, one might
propose, as follows, allowing for morphemes of a length
of at least one and not more than three underlying
syllables. Note that underlying syllables are not identical
to syllables at the systematic phonetic level, since the
P-rules introduce epenthetic syllabic vowels, nor does the
possible division between syllables (indicated here with a
vertical line) always correspond with the syllabification
principles of normative grammar or metrical theory.

MS (1') $M \rightarrow (On) V (_1 (_2 (_3 C_d)_3 \mid On)_2 (_4 V(_5 (_6 (_7 C_d)_7 \mid On)_6 (_8 V(_9 (_{10} C_d)_{10} On)_9)_8)_5)_4)_1$

The expansion of this rule gives the following possibilities:

$$(On)\, V \left(\left\{ \begin{array}{c} On \\ C_d On \\[4pt] \left\{ \begin{array}{c} V \\ OnV \\ C_d OnV \end{array} \right\} \end{array} \left(\left\{ \begin{array}{c} On \\ C_d On \\[4pt] V \\ On\ V \\ C_d On\ V \\[4pt] V \quad On \\ V C_d On \\[4pt] OnV \quad On \\ C_d OnV \quad On \\[4pt] OnV C_d On \\ C_d OnV C_d On \end{array} \right\} \right) \right\} \right)$$

MS (1′) wrongly permits a sequence of three vowels; this can be blocked by a SR rule:

SR (7) [+segment] → [−syll] / VV _____

3.5.1. Let us now consider in detail the medial and final consonant groups which these rules are to permit. Firstly, those groups appearing in initial position also occur elsewhere. MS rules (2), (4), (5) and (6) also account for these, and the occurrence of /w/. It hardly seems necessary to give examples of morphemes with single medial or final consonants, as they are so frequent; but where possible I shall give examples illustrating the other possibilities, trying to avoid examples where the presence of a morpheme boundary might be justified.

Of these groups identical to initial groups I have found no examples of /sgl/, /sbl/, /sgr/, /sbr/, /sdr/. This is rather curious, and the regularity: /s $\begin{bmatrix} -\text{cont} \\ +\text{voice} \end{bmatrix}$ $\begin{bmatrix} -\text{syllab} \\ +\text{vocal} \end{bmatrix}$ / is perhaps not fortuitous. If these sequences were not of the structure $C_a C_b C_c$ but of $C_d C_b C_c$ they would be excluded by MS (1′) from initial but not from medial or final position. This makes more sense in terms of the $C_d O n$ structure I have suggested. Consequently, the examples of § 3.2.6, *esbroncar, esdrúixol, esgrimir, esblaimar-se, esglai* and others like them would have underlying initial vowels, and we could state a further restriction on $C_a C_b C_c$ sequences:

SR (8) C_b → [u−voiced] / C_a _____ C_c

It remains a curious fact that there appear to be no examples of /s $\begin{bmatrix} +\text{obstr} \\ -\text{cont} \\ +\text{voiced} \end{bmatrix}$ $\begin{bmatrix} -\text{syllab} \\ +\text{vocal} \end{bmatrix}$ / after a stressed vowel, and thus not finally either, though in any case the sequences are rather rare. They are in addition never preceded by another consonant, a fact which favours the $C_d C_b C_c$ interpretation. Furthermore, since /sb/, /sd/, /sg/, /sg^w/ are not themselves ever preceded by a consonant, it is likely that what in § 3.2.4 were proposed as examples of initial / s $\begin{bmatrix} -\text{syll} \\ +\text{voice} \end{bmatrix}$ / have in fact an underlying initial vowel. I can find no clear case of paradigm alternation showing any of the words with [əzβ−], [əzɣ−], [əzɣw−], themselves not uncommon, to have an underlying initial consonant. This being so we can generalize SR (8) as follows:

SR (9) C_b → [u−voiced] / C_a _____

That is, / s $\begin{bmatrix} -\text{syllab} \\ +\text{voiced} \end{bmatrix}$ / sequences are more appropriately to be assigned the structure $C_d C_b$.

Examples of the other two-consonant sequences which are identical to initial sequences are:

/pl/:   *rèplica* [−pl−]
/bl/:   *bíblia* [−βl−] 'Bible'
/kl/:   *nucli* [−kl−] 'nucleus'
/gl/:   *ègloga* [−ɣl−] 'eclogue'
/fl/:   *xufla* 'chufa'

/pr/:   *lepra* 'leprosy'
/br/:   *llibre* 'book'
/tr/:   *teatre* 'theatre'
/dr/:   *vidre* 'glass'
/kr/:   *dimecres* 'Wednesday'
/gr/:   *llàgrima* 'tear'
/fr/:   *sofre* 'sulphur'

/sp/:   *dèspota* 'despot'
/st/:   *agost* 'August'

/sk/: *buscar* 'to look for'
/sk^W/: *pasqua* 'religious festival'

/spl/: *nespla* (a fruit, similar but, according to a native informant, not identical to *nespra* 'medlar')
/skl/: *xisclar* 'to scream'

/spr/: *vespre* 'evening'
/str/: *frustrar* 'to frustrate'
/skr/: no example found; I suppose this to be fortuitous.

3.5.2. Other sequences of two consonants.

Recall that by MS (4) C_b not adjacent to another C can be any one of 22 consonants. On what grounds do I propose that in two-consonant groups other than those mentioned in § 3.5.1 the second consonant is to be identified as C_b — the axial or basic C — and the first as a facultative preposed C? Well, here in C_b position 19 out of the 22 can appear, all except /j/, /w/ and /ɲ/. Before them, a consonant is one of only 12, of which several also appear before $C_a C_b$, $C_b C_c$, or $C_a C_b C_c$, i.e. the groups specified in § 3.5.1, which are a subset of initial groups. So it seems most economical to account for medial and final groups by the rules already needed for initial groups, with additional constraints to account for the preposed C_d. Table 4 opposite shows groups of two consonants which occur, as $C_d C_b$. See V § 7 for the 'archiphonemic' representation of geminates.

The only sequence in which /ɲ/ occurs is /ɲs/; in two words only: *prenys* [pɾéɲs] 'pregnant', but cf. *prenyada* id., i.e. *prenys* is to be analysed /preɲ+s/; and *menys* [méɲs] 'less', presumably /mɛɲ+s/ where /+s/ is perhaps an adverbial suffix which may be seen also in *més* 'more', *gens* 'any', *abans* 'before', *llavors* 'then', etc.

VI Table 4.
C_dC_b sequences

C_b \ C_d	j	w	l	r	n	m	p	t	k	k^w	f	s
l		wl	(tl)	rl				tl				sl
ʎ			(tʎ)					tʎ				
r	jr	wr	lr	rr	nr							
n	jn	wn	ln	rn	(tn)	(pm)	pn	tn	kn			sn
m	jm	wm	lm	rm	(tm)	(pm)	pm	tm	km	k^wm		sm
p	jp	wp	lp	rp	np	(np)						
b	jb	wb	lb	rb	nb	(nb)	(tb)	tb				sb
t	jt	wt	lt	rt	nt	mt	pt		kt		ft	
d	jd	wd	ld	rd	nd	md	pd		kd			sd–
k	jk	wk	lk	rk	nk	(nk)						
g	jg	wg	lg	rg	ng	(ng)		tg–	(tg)			sg
k^w					nk^w	(nk^w)						
g^w	jg^w				ng^w	(ng^w)						sg^w
f		wf	lf	rf	nf	(nf)						sf
v		(wb)	(lb)	rv	(nb)	(nb)						
s	js	ws	ls	rs	ns	ms	ps	ts	ks	k^ws		
z	jz	wz	lz	rz	nz	mz		tz	kz			
ʃ		wʃ	lʃ	rʃ	nʃ	(nʃ)		tʃ				
ʒ		wʒ	lʒ	rʒ	nʒ	(nʒ)	pʒ	tʒ				

The groups /kʷm/ and /kʷs/ require some comment. As stated above, medial/final groups may consist of initial groups preceded by one consonant. There are very few exceptions indeed to this principle, all of which, I would claim, are non-native words (as is the case with initial /mn–/, /bd–/, etc, though the examples here are yet rarer) except for e.g. *auxili* [əwksíli] 'assistance', *bauxita* [bəwksítə] 'bauxite', *augment* [əwgmén] 'increase', *zeugma* [zɛ́wgmə] ; *auxili, augment* and their compounds are not at all uncommon. I should like to suggest that /kʷs/, /kʷm/ underlie [–wks–] and [–wgm–] respectively. Since we already need a rule realizing /kʷ/ as [kw] before a vowel (cf. V § 3), it seems not an extravagant proposal that /kʷ/ should be realized [wk] ([wg] by voicedness assimilation) before a consonant. Examples of the other exceptions follow, whose foreignness is, I hope, apparent.

/nkt/ : *sanctus*
/rks/ : *marxisme* 'Marxism' (I have heard the Catalanizing pronunciation [mərʃízmə])
/rtz/ (or /rts/?) *hertzià* 'Hertzian'
/wtʃ/ : *gautxo* 'gaucho'
/nkst/ : *tungstè* 'tungsten'
/nkstr/: *angstrom* 'Angstrom'

There follow examples illustrating the groups in Table 4.

/jl/ : *rail* [rájl], a unique example, of doubtful native status since it is an exception to the final [ə]–epenthesis rule. I can see no principle behind the absence of the sequence. Note that there are no examples of /jkʷ/ or /jf/.
/jr/ : *boira* 'mist'
/jn/ : *eina* 'tool'

Between UR's and the input to P-rules

/jm/	:	*esblaimar-se* 'to turn pale'
/jp/	:	*naip* 'playing card', a unique example; it is doubtful if this word is proper to the dialect described; *carta* is usual.
/jb/	:	*copaiba* ("aromatic herb used in medicine, etc.")
/jt/	:	*beneita* 'silly (F)'
/jd/	:	*buida* 'empty (F)'
/jk/	:	*mosaic*
/jg/	:	*enraigar* 'to start'
/jg^w/	:	*aigua* 'water'
/js/	:	*faiçó* 'shaping, shape'
/jz/	:	*faisà* 'pheasant'
/wl/	:	*taula* 'table'
/wr/	:	*heura* 'ivy'
/wn/	:	*llauna* 'tin can'
/wm/	:	*reuma* 'rheumatism'
/wp/	:	*pauperisme* 'pauperism'
/wb/	:	*gaubar-se* 'to be glad'
/wt/	:	*flauta* 'flute'
/wd/	:	*viuda* 'widow'
/wk/	:	*meuca* 'whore'
/wg/	:	*euga* 'mare'
/wf/	:	*nyaufar* 'to dent'
/ws/	:	*glauci* (flower of genus glaucium)
/wz/	:	*nàusea*
/wʃ/	:	*rauxa* 'whim'
/wʒ/	:	*greuge* 'grudge'
/lr/	:	*folrar* 'to line'
/ln/	:	*balneari* 'spa'
/lm/	:	*oftàlmic* 'ophthalmic'
/lp/	:	*palpar* 'to feel'
/lb/	:	*calba* 'bald (F)'
/lt/	:	*multa* 'fine'
/ld/	:	*falda* 'lap'

/lk/	:	*remolcar* 'to tow'
/lg/	:	*alga* 'seaweed'
/lf/	:	*escalfar* 'to heat'
/ls/	:	*falsa* 'false (F)'
/lz/	:	*colze* 'elbow'
/lʃ/	:	*Elx* 'Elche' (toponym); *bolxevic* 'bolshevik' (only two examples found)
/lʒ/	:	*àlgebra*
/rl/	:	*parlar* 'to speak'
/rr/	:	*barri* 'district'
/rn/	:	*carn* 'meat'
/rm/	:	*terme* 'term'
/rp/	:	*extirpar* 'to extirpate'
/rb/	:	*herba* 'grass'
/rt/	:	*morta* 'dead (F)'
/rd/	:	*corda* 'string'
/rk/	:	*barca* 'boat'
/rg/	:	*llarga* 'long (F)'
/rf/	:	*orfe* 'orphan'
/rv/	:	*serf* [sérf] / *serva* [sérβə] 'serf' – a unique example for revealing underlying /v/ **postconsonantally.**
/rs/	:	*farsa* 'farce'
/rz/	:	*esmorzar* 'to have breakfast'
/rʃ/	:	*xarxa* 'net'
/rʒ/	:	*verge* 'virgin'
/nr/	:	*conreu* 'cultivation'
/np/	:	*pàmpol* 'lampshade'
/nb/	:	*tombar* 'to turn'
/nt/	:	*càntir* 'pitcher'
/nd/	:	*agenda* 'diary'
/nk/	:	*trencar* 'to break'
/ng/	:	*fangós* 'muddy'
/nk^w/	:	*propinqua* 'neighbouring (F)'
/ng^w/	:	*bilingüe* 'bilingual'

Between UR's and the input to P-rules

/nf/	:	*triomf* 'triumph'
/ns/	:	*llançar* 'to throw'
/nz/	:	*bronze*
/nʃ/	:	*manxa* 'bellows'
/nʒ/	:	*diumenge* 'Sunday'
/mt/	:	*comte* 'earl'
/md/	:	*lambda*, a unique example, unless we accept *ambdós* 'both', which is doubtless rather a compound of some element with *dos* 'two'.
/ms/	:	*premsa* 'press'
/mz/	:	*zumzejar* 'to hover'
/pn/	:	*solemne* 'solemn', *hipnosi* 'hypnosis'
/pm/	:	*gemma* 'gem'
/pt/	:	*dubte* 'doubt'
/pd/	:	*súbdit* 'subject'
/ps/	:	*copsar* 'to catch'
/pʒ/	:	*objecte* 'object'
/tl/	:	*atleta* 'athlete'
/tʎ/	:	*espatlla* 'shoulder'
/tn/	:	*ètnic* 'ethnic'
/tm/	:	*atmosfera* 'atmosphere'
/tb/	:	*obvi* 'obvious', *futbol* 'soccer'
/tg/	:	no example, though /tgl/ occurs – see below.
/ts/	:	*lletsó* 'dandelion' – sole example; perhaps a compound: /ʎet+son/ ?
/tz/	:	*setze* 'sixteen'
/tʃ/	:	*esquitxar* 'to splash'
/tʒ/	:	*calitja* 'haze'
/kn/	:	*signar* 'to sign'
/km/	:	*enigma*
/kt/	:	*acte* 'act'
/kd/	:	*maragda* 'emerald'

/ks/	:	*sexe* 'sex'
/kz/	:	*èczema; exacte* 'exact'
/k^{w}m/	:	*augment* 'increase'
/k^{w}s/	:	*auxili* 'assistance'
/ft/	:	*diftèria* 'diphtheria'
/sl/	:	*eslora* 'length of hull'
/sn/	:	*esnob* 'snob'
/sm/	:	*prisme* 'prism'
/sb/	:	*bisbe* 'bishop'
/sd/	:	no example found, though /sdr/ occurs.
/sg/	:	*pelasga* 'Pelasgian (F)'
/sg^w/	:	*esguard* 'regard'

Groups of three consonants of structure $C_d C_b C_c$:

/wtr/	:	*neutre* 'neutral'
/lbr/	:	*cualbra* (a fungus)
/ltr/	:	*filtre* 'filter'
/ldr/	:	*boldró* 'patch of corn growing higher than the rest'
/lkr/	:	*fulcre* 'fulcrum'
/rpr/	:	*porpra* 'purple'
/rbr/	:	*marbre* 'marble'
/rtr/	:	*murtra* 'myrtle'
/rdr/	:	*ordre* 'order'
/rkl/	:	*cercle* 'circle'
?/rgr/	:	*burgrave*
/npl/	:	*omplir* 'to fill'
/npr/	:	*sempre* 'always'
/nbl/	:	*semblar* 'to seem'
/nbr/	:	*membre* 'member'
/ntr/	:	*entrar* 'to enter'
/ndr/	:	*mandra* 'laziness'
/nkl/	:	*oncle* 'uncle'

Between UR's and the input to P-rules

/nkr/	:	*pollancre* 'poplar'
/ngl/	:	*ungla* 'finger-nail'
/ngr/	:	*congru* 'congruous'
/nfl/	:	*pamflet* 'pamphlet'
/nfr/	:	*infra-*

/ptr/	:	*ceptra* 'sceptre'
/tbl/	:	*poble* 'people'
/tgl/	:	*segle* 'century'
/ktr/	:	*elèctric*

/sbr/	:	*esbroncar* 'to criticize'
/sbl/	:	*esblaimar-se* 'to turn pale'
/sdr/	:	*esdrúixol* 'proparoxytone'
/sgr/	:	*esgrimir* 'to fence'
/sgl/	:	*esglai* 'fright'

Groups of three consonants of structure $C_d C_a C_b$:

/wsp/	:	*auspici* 'auspice'
/wst/	:	*holocaust*
/wsk/	:	*auscultar* 'to listen through a stethoscope'

/nst/	:	*instint* 'instinct'
?/nsk/	:	*lansquenet* – a non-native word? cf. *sànscrit* below
/pst/	:	*abstemi* 'abstemious'
/psk/	:	*obscur* 'dark'
/ksp/	:	*expiar* 'to expiate'
/kst/	:	*text*

Groups of four consonants $C_d C_a C_b C_c$:

/wstr/	:	*claustre* 'cloister'
/nstr/	:	*monstre* 'monster'
/nskr/	:	*sànscrit* 'Sanskrit'
/pstr/	:	*abstrús* 'abstruse'
/kstr/	:	*extra-*

3.5.3. The expansion of C_d is:

MS (7) $C_d \rightarrow \left\{ [-\text{cons}], \begin{bmatrix} -\text{cons} \\ +\text{labial} \end{bmatrix}, \begin{bmatrix} +\text{vocal} \\ -\text{cont} \end{bmatrix}, \right.$

$\begin{bmatrix} +\text{vocal} \\ +\text{cont} \end{bmatrix}, [+\text{nasal}], \begin{bmatrix} +\text{nasal} \\ +\text{labial} \end{bmatrix}, [+\text{labial}], [+\text{segm}],$

$\left. [+\text{back}], \begin{bmatrix} +\text{back} \\ +\text{labial} \end{bmatrix}, \begin{bmatrix} +\text{cont} \\ +\text{labial} \end{bmatrix}, [+\text{cont}] \right\}$

These are the 12 distinct consonants which can appear in C_d position. SR (1) will supply [−syll] in every case.

3.5.4. What we want to achieve now with sequence redundancy rules is to exclude from well-formedness as many as possible of the non-occurring sequences. If a sequence cannot be excluded by a rule of any generality, however, I shall suppose that we have a case of an "accidental gap". So, of two-consonant sequences, /jk^w/, /pz/, /pʃ/, /lv/, /k^{w}t/ may be "accidental gaps".

The following SR rules give specifications on which the Mk rules can apply to produce fully specified matrices. They do not therefore state the assimilations which P-rules also generate, e.g. /mf/ → [m̫f] ; /sd/ → [z̫d] ; /ng/ → [ŋg], etc., since, as discussed previously, no cost is to be attached to change of u features in assimilation rules, and it is unnecessary to repeat rules having the same effect. The result is that these rules do not generate matrices distinct from items of the phoneme inventory (MS (3), (4)).

We can exclude */jf/, */jv/, */jʃ/, */jʒ/, */kf/, */kv/, */kʃ/, */kʒ/ by this rule:

SR (10) $\begin{bmatrix} +\text{obstr} \\ +\text{cont} \end{bmatrix} \rightarrow \begin{bmatrix} u \text{ labial} \\ u \text{ high} \end{bmatrix} \Big/ \begin{bmatrix} -\text{syll} \\ +\text{high} \\ -\text{labial} \end{bmatrix} \underline{}$

Between UR's and the input to P-rules 263

For the absence of */nl/ and */ml/, and indeed of */nʎ/, */mʎ/, we have

SR (11) $[-\text{syll}] \rightarrow [u \text{ nasal}] \Big/ \underline{\quad} \begin{bmatrix} -\text{syll} \\ +\text{vocal} \\ -\text{cont} \end{bmatrix}$

To exclude all consonants before /ʎ/ other than maximally unmarked /t/ we have

SR (12) $[-\text{syll}] \rightarrow \begin{bmatrix} u \text{ vocal} \\ u \text{ cons} \\ u \text{ cont} \\ u \text{ nasal} \\ u \text{ labial} \\ u \text{ voiced} \\ u \text{ high} \\ u \text{ back} \end{bmatrix} \Big/ \underline{\quad} \begin{bmatrix} -\text{syll} \\ +\text{vocal} \\ +\text{high} \end{bmatrix}$

/tʎ/ will become /ʎʎ/ by a phonological assimilation rule. As /ɲ/ occurs in no consonant groups we have a rule

SR (13) $[+\text{segm}] \rightarrow [+\text{syll}] \Big/ \begin{bmatrix} -\text{syll} \\ +\text{nasal} \\ +\text{high} \end{bmatrix}$

Consonant + glide sequences must be excluded:

SR (14) $[-\text{syll}] \rightarrow [+\text{cons}] \;/\; [-\text{syll}] \underline{\quad}$

A number of obstruent + fricative sequences can be excluded by

SR (15) $[+\text{obstr}] \rightarrow \begin{bmatrix} \langle +\text{anter} \rangle \\ \alpha\text{cont} \end{bmatrix} \Big/ \underline{\quad} \begin{bmatrix} +\text{obstr} \\ +\text{cont} \\ \langle +\text{high} \rangle \\ \alpha\text{labial} \end{bmatrix}$

This excludes */kʃ/, */kʒ/, */kʷʃ/, */kʷʒ/, */fʃ/, */fʒ/, */sʃ/, */sʒ/, (*/ʃʃ/, */ʃʒ/), */pf/, */pv/, */tf/, */tv/, */kf/,

*/kv/, */k^Wf/, */k^Wv/, */fs/, */fz/, (*/ʃs/, */ʃz/), */ss/, */sz/; the parenthesized groups are excluded by MS (7) anyway, /sf/ is permitted by this rule.

*/fn/, */fm/, */fp/, */fb/, */fd/, */fk/, */fg/, */fk^W/, */fg^W/, */ff/, */fv/ can be excluded by

SR (16) $\begin{bmatrix} +\text{obstr} \\ +\text{cont} \end{bmatrix} \rightarrow [u\ \text{labial}] / \underline{\qquad} \begin{bmatrix} -\text{vocal} \\ \{-\text{coron}\} \\ \{+\text{voiced}\} \end{bmatrix}$

Various stop sequences can be excluded by SR (17), namely */kp/, */kb/, */kk/, */kg/, */kk^W/, */pp/, */pb/, */pk/, */pg/, */pk^W/, */pg^W/.

SR (17) $[-\text{cont}] \rightarrow \begin{bmatrix} u\ \text{labial} \\ u\ \text{back} \end{bmatrix} / \underline{\qquad} \begin{bmatrix} +\text{obstr} \\ -\text{coron} \end{bmatrix}$

Formulated in this way, SR (17) also excludes */pf/, */pv/, */kf/, */kv/, */k^Wf/, */k^Wv/, */mp/, */mb/, */mk/, */mg/, */mk^W/, */mg^W/, */mf/, */mv/ as we require, i.e. before [−coron] only unmarked non-continuants occur.

Further examples of neutralization between labial and non-labial velars can be dealt with by SR (18), which incorporates the neutralization expressed in SR (5).

SR (18) $\begin{bmatrix} +\text{cons} \\ +\text{back} \end{bmatrix} \rightarrow [u\ \text{labial}] / \underline{\qquad} \begin{bmatrix} -\text{syll} \\ +\text{coron} \\ +\text{voiced} \end{bmatrix}$

This excludes */k^Wl/, */k^Wr/, */k^Wn/, */k^Wd/, */k^Wz/, */k^Wʒ/. To account for the absence of some groups with /k^W/ or /g^W/ as the second member we have

SR (19) $\begin{bmatrix} -\text{syll} \\ -\text{obstr} \end{bmatrix} \rightarrow \begin{bmatrix} -\text{vocal} \\ u\ \text{labial} \end{bmatrix} / \underline{\qquad} \begin{bmatrix} -\text{syll} \\ +\text{back} \\ +\text{labial} \end{bmatrix}$

*/wk^W/, */wg^W/, */lk^W/, */lg^W/, */rk^W/, */rg^W/, */mk^W/, */mg^W/ are excluded by this rule. By SR (20) */tk^W/,

*/tg^W/, as well as other obstruent + labiovelar sequences (which are also dealt with by other rules) are prohibited:

SR (20) $\begin{bmatrix} -\text{syll} \\ +\text{obstr} \end{bmatrix} \rightarrow \begin{bmatrix} +\text{cont} \\ u \text{ labial} \\ u \text{ high} \end{bmatrix} / \underline{\qquad} \begin{bmatrix} -\text{syll} \\ +\text{back} \\ +\text{labial} \end{bmatrix}$

To permit only /rv/ from /Cv/ groups we can say

SR (21) $[-\text{syll}] \rightarrow \begin{bmatrix} +\text{vocal} \\ +\text{cont} \end{bmatrix} / \underline{\qquad} \begin{bmatrix} +\text{obstr} \\ +\text{cont} \\ +\text{labial} \\ +\text{voiced} \end{bmatrix}$

For the absence of */mʃ/, */mʒ/, */mr/ the rule is

SR (22) $[+\text{nasal}] \rightarrow [u \text{ labial}] / \underline{\qquad} \begin{bmatrix} -\text{syll} \\ \{+\text{high}\} \\ \{+\text{vocal}\} \end{bmatrix}$

As nasality is not distinctive before nasals we can say

SR (23) $[-\text{syll}] \rightarrow [u \text{ nasal}] / \underline{\qquad} \begin{bmatrix} -\text{syll} \\ +\text{nasal} \end{bmatrix}$

By this rule */mn/, */nn/, */mm/, */nm/ are excluded. We can exclude */tt/, */td/ thus:

SR (24) $\begin{bmatrix} +\text{obstr} \\ -\text{cont} \end{bmatrix} \rightarrow [-\text{coron}] / \underline{\qquad} \begin{bmatrix} +\text{obstr} \\ -\text{cont} \\ +\text{coron} \end{bmatrix}$

Further rules are subject to diminishing returns; it is perhaps preferable to regard the following sequences as accidental gaps: /jk^W/, /pz/, /pʃ/, /tp/, /tk/, /sr/. In each case the sequence is paired by an existing but rare one: /jg^W/, /ps/, /pʒ/, /tb/, /tg/, /sl/ respectively, so the fortuitous absence of the other member of each pair is not improbable. /k^{W}t/ is also admitted.

3.5.5. The MS and SR rules already given greatly limit the possible three and four-consonant sequences. In addition, further limitations are expressed in the following rules. Of the glides, only /w/ occurs before two or more consonants, so we can say

SR (25) $\begin{bmatrix} -\text{syll} \\ -\text{cons} \end{bmatrix} \rightarrow [+\text{labial}] / \underline{\qquad} \text{CC}$

Furthermore, in three or four-consonant sequences /w/ is followed only by /t/ or /s/, so

SR (26) $[-\text{syll}] \rightarrow [u \text{ cons}] / \underline{\qquad} \begin{bmatrix} -\text{syll} \\ -\text{coron} \end{bmatrix} \text{C}$

This rule allows only /wtr/ and /wsC/. We have no */lsC/, */rsC/, */lfC/ or */rfC/, so

SR (27) $[-\text{syll}] \rightarrow [u \text{ vocal}] / \underline{\qquad} \begin{bmatrix} -\text{syll} \\ +\text{cont} \end{bmatrix} \text{C}$

There is no */lCl/. There is not much reason for preferring the neutralization of either the first or the third consonant, but if the MS rules are ordered, it is more appropriate to say

SR (28) $\begin{bmatrix} -\text{syll} \\ +\text{vocal} \end{bmatrix} \rightarrow [+\text{cont}] / \underline{\qquad} \text{C} \begin{bmatrix} +\text{vocal} \\ -\text{cont} \end{bmatrix}$

Only the unmarked nasal occurs in CCC sequences:

SR (29) $\begin{bmatrix} -\text{syll} \\ +\text{nasal} \end{bmatrix} \rightarrow [u \text{ labial}] / \underline{\qquad} \text{CC}$

In order to exclude several stop + stop + liquid sequences we have the rule

Between UR's and the input to P-rules 267

SR (30) [+obstr] → [+cont]

$$/\underline{\quad\quad} \left\{ \begin{bmatrix} +\text{obstr} \\ -\text{cont} \\ -\text{coron} \\ -\text{voiced} \end{bmatrix} \quad\quad\quad\quad \text{i)} \\ \begin{bmatrix} -\text{cont} \\ +\text{voiced} \end{bmatrix} \begin{bmatrix} -\text{syll} \\ +\text{vocal} \\ +\text{cont} \end{bmatrix} \quad \text{ii)} \right\}$$

Part i) of this rule excludes */tp/, and */tk/, which I suggested above might be seen as accidental gaps; but excluding them by rule accounts for the absence of */tpr/, */tpl/, */tkr/, */tkl/, without further rules. Part ii) excludes */pbr/, */pdr/, */pgr/, */tbr/, */tdr/, */tgr/, */kbr/, */kdr/, */kgr/; */ftC/ can be excluded by adapting SR (16) which deals with cases of /fC/:

SR (31) $\begin{bmatrix} +\text{obstr} \\ +\text{cont} \end{bmatrix}$ → [u labial]

$$/\underline{\quad\quad} \left\{ \begin{bmatrix} -\text{vocal} \\ -\text{coron} \\ +\text{voiced} \end{bmatrix} \quad \right\} \\ \quad\quad\quad\quad C \quad\quad C$$

To exclude */tsC/:

SR (32) $\begin{bmatrix} -\text{syll} \\ +\text{coron} \end{bmatrix}$ → [−obstr] $/\underline{\quad\quad}$ $\begin{bmatrix} +\text{obstr} \\ +\text{cont} \end{bmatrix}$ C

Having expressed this rule thus, we are permitted to exclude */psp/, */ksk/, while admitting /ksp/, /kst/, /pst/, /psk/, by SR (33):

SR (33) $\begin{bmatrix} +\text{obstr} \\ -\text{cont} \end{bmatrix}$ → $\begin{bmatrix} -\alpha\text{back} \\ -\beta\text{labial} \end{bmatrix}$

$$/\underline{\quad\quad} \begin{bmatrix} +\text{obstr} \\ +\text{cont} \end{bmatrix} \begin{bmatrix} -\text{cont} \\ -\text{coron} \\ \alpha\text{back} \\ \beta\text{labial} \end{bmatrix}$$

The following sequences have not been excluded, though no clear examples of their occurrence within morphemes have been found. I suggest they may be accidental gaps: /lpr/, /lgr/, /rkr/, /rpl/, /rbl/, /rgl/, /sfr/, /sfl/, /kʷtr/, /wskʷ/, /nsp/, /nskʷ/, /wspr/, /wskr/, /nspr/, /pskr/, /kspr/.

There are also a few redundancies in VC(C) sequences, with regard to [± low] in the vowel. It appears that /er[−labial]/, /eʒ/, /enk/, /eng/ do not occur[1] (though there is one example of /engʷ/, namely *llengua* [ʎéŋgwə] 'tongue'); nor do /oj/, /oll/, /oʎʎ/; nor /ɔɲ/, /ɔʃ/. No rules of very great generality account for these facts — the form of such rules might be, firstly, for /e/ ~ /ɛ/ neutralization:

SR (34) $\begin{bmatrix} +\text{syll} \\ -\text{back} \\ -\text{high} \end{bmatrix} \rightarrow [+\text{low}]$

$/\underline{} \left\{ \begin{matrix} \begin{bmatrix} -\text{syll} \\ +\text{nasal} \end{bmatrix} & \begin{bmatrix} -\text{syll} \\ +\text{back} \\ -\text{labial} \end{bmatrix} \\ \begin{bmatrix} -\text{syll} \\ +\text{vocal} \\ +\text{cont} \end{bmatrix} & \begin{bmatrix} -\text{syll} \\ -\text{labial} \end{bmatrix} \\ \begin{bmatrix} +\text{obstr} \\ +\text{cont} \\ +\text{high} \\ +\text{voiced} \end{bmatrix} & \end{matrix} \right\}$

The geminates /ll/ and /ʎʎ/ are rare enough to make the absence of /o/ before them possibly fortuitous; for the

---

[1] N.B. there seem to be only two morphemes with /e/ before /l/, namely, *feltre* 'felt' and *ela* '(letter) L'.

remainder we have

$$\text{SR (35)} \quad \begin{bmatrix} +\text{syll} \\ +\text{labial} \\ -\text{high} \end{bmatrix} \rightarrow \left\{ \begin{array}{l} [-\text{low}] \Big/ \underline{\qquad} \begin{bmatrix} +\text{obstr} \\ +\text{cont} \\ +\text{high} \\ -\text{voiced} \end{bmatrix} \\ \\ [-\alpha\text{low}] \Big/ \underline{\qquad} \begin{bmatrix} -\text{obstr} \\ -\text{vocal} \\ +\text{high} \\ -\text{back} \\ \alpha\text{cons} \end{bmatrix} \end{array} \right\}$$

To exclude sequences of two identical vowels (cf. § 3.2.1), it seems that the only simple formulation is in terms of a negative condition, such as

$$\text{SR (36)} \quad * \begin{bmatrix} +\text{syll} \\ \alpha\text{DF} \end{bmatrix} \begin{bmatrix} +\text{syll} \\ \alpha\text{DF} \end{bmatrix}$$

Finally, to deal with voicedness neutralization — obstruents are voiced before voiced non-liquid consonants, voiceless before voiceless ones, we have the rule

SR (37) $[+\text{obstr}] \rightarrow [u-\text{voiced}] \; / \underline{\qquad} [-\text{vocal}]$

The correct value for the systematic phonetic representation will be supplied by the assimilation P-rule VII (51).

CHAPTER VII

Further phonological rules

1. There is a well known rule in Catalan which deletes word-final /n/ in some circumstances; cf. Lleó, 1970:7–8, 15, 23; Badia, 1973b: 188–9, 196; Brasington, 1972. Lleó expresses the rule informally as follows (68): "/n/ preceded by a stressed vowel is deleted before a word boundary". However, as we shall see, this rule not only has many exceptions in cases where /n/ is not deleted, but it also fails to account for all the cases where /n/ is deleted. I shall propose a rule that at least accounts for all cases of deletion.

Consider the following paradigms (in standard orthography):

(1) (a) Cases of deletion /V́__#

__#	__+ə(F)	__+s#	derivatives:__+V−
pla 'flat'	*plana*	*plans*	*planer* 'level'
camí 'path'		*camins*	*caminar* 'to walk'
català 'Catalan'	*catalana*	*catalans*	*catalanisme* 'Catalanism'
té 'has'		*tens* 'you have'	*tenir* 'to have'

(b) deletion /V̆__(+C) #

orfe 'orphan'	*òrfena*	*orfes*	*orfenesa* 'orphanhood'
jove 'young'		*joves*	*jovenet* 'young (dimin.)'
home 'man'		*homes*	*homenia* 'manliness'
freixe 'ash tree'		*freixes*	*freixeneda* 'ash plantation'

Further phonological rules

	___#	___+ə(F)	___+s#	derivatives: ___+V−
	marge 'bank'		*marges*	*margener* 'bank builder'
	terme 'limit'		*termes*	*termenar* 'to put limits'
	orgue 'organ'		*orgues*	*orguener* 'organ-builder'
	ase 'ass'		*ases*	*asenet* 'little ass'
	rave 'radish'		*raves*	*ravenar* 'radish field'

(2) Regular non-deletion (/C___#, etc.)

	___#		___+s#	derivatives
	carn 'meat'		*carns*	*carnisser* 'butcher'
	forn 'oven'		*forns*	*forner* 'baker'
	diürn 'diurnal'	*diürna*	*diürns*	*diürnal* 'book of hours'

(3) Exceptional non-deletion
    (a) "proclitics" −/n/ is deleted only before some major syntactic boundary, not, for example, within [$_{NP}$X___Y]$_{NP}$ where Y ≠ ø.

	___+ə	___+s	___#]$_{NP}$, etc.
un d'ells 'one of them'	*una*	*uns*	*tot és u* 'it's all one' *són vint-i-ú* 'there are 21 of them'
algun d'ells 'some one of them'	*alguna*	*alguns*	*algú* 'someone'
cadascun d'ells 'each one of them'	*cadascuna*		*cadascú* 'each' (Pro)
bon dia 'good day'	*bona*	*bons*	*el temps és bo* 'the weather is good'
ben fet 'well done'		(*bens* 'goods')	*has fet bé* 'you've done right'

    (b) non-deletion /V́___#

___#	___+ə	___+s	derivatives: ___+V−
segon 'second'	*segona*	*segons*	
pregon 'deep'	*pregona*	*pregons*	*pregonesa* 'deepness'
roman 'remains' (V)		*romans* (2sg)	*romanem* 'we remain'
ton 'shears' (V)		*tons* (2sg)	*tonem* 'we shear'
encén 'lights' (V)		*encens*	*encenem* 'we light'
entén 'understands' (V)		*entens*	*entenem* 'we understand'

___#	___+ə	___+s#	derivatives: ___+V―
depèn 'depends'		depens	depenem 'we depend'
ofèn 'offends'		ofens	ofenem 'we offend'
ven 'sells'		vens	venem 'we sell'
respon 'responds'		respons	responem 'we respond'
fon 'melts'		fons	fonem 'we melt'
plan		plans (pl)	planejar 'to make plans'
nan 'dwarf'	nana	nans	
(c) non-deletion /V̆___(+C) #			
orígen 'origin'		orígens	originar 'to originate'
exàmen 'exam'		exàmens	examinar 'to examine'
òrgan 'organ (biol)'		òrgans	orgànic
		créixens 'cress'	criexenera 'cress bed'

Nouns and adjectives of type (1a) are very common, though only two verbs (and their compounds) undergo /−n/ deletion, *tenir* 'to have' and *venir* 'to come', cf. III §6.1, nos 1 and 2. Nine verbs and their compounds are exceptions; see under (3b). Brasington (1972:108) discusses, among other proposals, a rule-feature switching rule whereby a major rule for nouns and adjectives may become a minor rule for verbs. Such an approach has in its favour the fact that *venir* and *tenir* are exceptional anyway in their morphological behaviour. The rule would be

(4)   [u rule (7)] → [−αrule (7)] / $\left[\overline{\alpha \text{Verb}} \right]$

The forms under (1b) are not taken into account for the formulation of /n/−deletion by Lleó, who explicitly rejects (1970:56) the UR /ɔman/ for *home* 'man' in the modern Barcelona dialect. Observe that /n/ is also deleted before /+s/ in these cases where an unstressed vowel precedes. Examples (2) show that deletion does not occur when /n/ is preceded by a consonant.

In the (3a) examples deletion apparently occurs in some syntactic environments and not in others. Tenta-

Further phonological rules 273

tively, I would suggest it occurs only when no other item within the NP or VP follows; that is, for these words

(5)   n → ø / ___ #]$_{NP, VP}$

Rule (5) would be a minor rule applying to a subset of the exceptions to the major /n/–deletion rule. It is not clear whether *quin/quina/quins/quines*? 'which?' can be brought within the scope of this rule; rather, it seems improbable, unless in *quin va ser?* 'which one was it?' some dummy element is present at the stage of the application of (5) so that the /n/ of *quin* does not immediately precede the NP symbol. Similarly *un* is often an exception to (5), e.g. *n'he perdut un* 'I've lost one of them'. Maybe here *un* is Quant with a pronoun following at some stage of the derivation; *u* might have a different syntactic analysis. The last example, anyway, would be evidence against a proposal for dealing with the cases of (3a) by boundary adjustment to distinguish these cases from those subject to the major rule, e.g. by reducing a series of #s to one # (after stress-assignment) just in the case where a member of the categories N, V, A, or Ad followed within the same NP or VP.

The number of exceptions under (3b) and (3c) seems not to be a high proportion of morphemes in /–n/. Ferrer Pastor (1956) gives 74 distinct morphemes; some of these (e.g. *gran* 'large', cf. *grandíssim* 'very large'; *tan* 'so much', cf. *tanta* id. (F)) clearly are not examples of underlying /–n/. For many of the others there is in fact no paradigmatic evidence for underlying final /–n/ rather than /–nt/ or /–nd/, and many are certainly foreign to Barcelona Standard. Note also that *origen – originar*, *examen – examinar* undergo a vocalic alternation which is typical of "learned" words, cf. *índex – indicar* 'to indicate'. There may be a readjustment rule making nouns marked [+learned] exceptions to the /n/–deletion rule, viz.

(6) [+learned] → [−rule (7)]

Obviously /n/−deletion precedes final stop deletion, otherwise the /n/ of *calent* [kəlén] ← /kalent/, cf. *calenta* (F) [kəléntə], 'hot' would be deleted, giving *[kəlé]. In fact, the great majority of cases of final [−n] at the phonetic level derive from underlying /−nt/ or /−nd/.

In the following isolated examples the /n/ which appears in certain members of the paradigm is probably not to be regarded as part of the stem, but as an arbitrary suffix; or, the stems with and without /n/ are suppletive.

___#	___+ə	___+s	derivative:
rei 'king'	*reina* 'queen'	*reis*	*reial* 'royal'
heroi 'hero'	*heroïna* 'heroine'	*herois*	*heroisme* 'heroism'

The final /n/−deletion rule can now be expressed as follows:

$$(7) \quad \begin{bmatrix} +\text{nasal} \\ +\text{coron} \end{bmatrix} \rightarrow \emptyset \Big/ \left\{ \begin{array}{l} \begin{bmatrix} +\text{syll} \\ -\text{stress} \end{bmatrix} \underline{\quad} +C \\ [+\text{syll}] \underline{\quad} \# \end{array} \right\}$$

or alternatively:

$$(8) \quad \begin{bmatrix} +\text{nasal} \\ +\text{coron} \end{bmatrix} \rightarrow \emptyset \Big/ \begin{bmatrix} +\text{syllab} \\ \langle -\text{stress} \rangle_b \end{bmatrix} \underline{\quad} \langle +C \rangle_a \#$$

condition: if a, then b.

Rule (8) contains fewer features and formalizes the generalization that deletion occurs only after vowels, but the condition on angle-brackets is intuitively a rather clumsy device, presumably not very highly valued in the evaluation measure for rules.

Further phonological rules 275

We want to prevent (8) from applying to the /–n/ which is the third person plural morph in verbs. (8) cannot precede the rule inserting /+n/ since the latter must precede stress assignment (unless the /+n/ insertion is separated from that of the other person/number morphs /+m/, /+w/), while (8) must follow stress-assignment. Probably the /+n/ inserted carries the marker [–rule (8)]. It is not adequate to rely on rule (4) since in *venir* and *tenir* only the /–n/ of the root is deletable, the 3pl present forms being *venen*, *tenen*. Alternatively (8) could be restricted so that it applied only to /n/ not preceded by a morpheme boundary.

This exceptional treatment of 3pl /+n/ is resolved in the "vulgar" speech of Barcelona by restructuring the suffix as /+nt/. This results in imperative forms such as *facin-ho* [fásintu] rather than [fásinu] 'do it' (2pl polite), *vagin-hi* [báʒinti] rather than [báʒini] 'let them go there', with final /t/ preserved before the vowel-initial unstressed pronouns, as occurs normally after the gerund in /+nt/, e.g. *anant-hi* [ənánti] 'going there'.

2. The deletion of /r/ word-finally or before /+s/ is discussed by Lleó (1970:24–5) and Badia (1973b:188, 196–7). The effect of this rule is very widespread due to the frequency of /–r/ suffixes, e.g. in infinitives, or with /+er/, /+dor/ (agentive and adjectival suffixes). Some paradigms revealing underlying /r/ are as follows:

(9)	___#	___+s (Mpl)	___+ə (F)	derivatives:
	darrer 'last' [dəré]	*darrers* [dərés]	*darrera* [dərérə]	*endarrerir* 'to get behind' [əndərərí]
	clar 'clear' [klá]	*clars* [klás]	*clara* [klárə]	*claredat* 'clarity' [klərəðát]
	dur 'hard' [dú]	*durs* [dús]	*dura* [dúrə]	*duresa* 'hardness' [duɾézə]
	sencer 'whole' [sənsɛ́]	*sencers* [sənsɛ́s]	*sencera* [sənsɛ́rə]	
	obrer 'worker' [uβré]	*obrers* [uβrés]	*obrera* [uβrérə]	*obrerisme* 'working class politics' [uβrərízmə]

276 *Further phonological rules*

___#	___+s(Mpl)	___+ə (F)	derivatives:
pastor 'shepherd' [pəstó]	*pastors* [pəstós]	*pastora* [pəstórə]	*pastoral* [pəsturál]
peixater 'fishmonger' [pəʃəté]	*peixaters* [pəʃətés]	*peixatera* [pəʃətérə]	*peixateria* 'fishmonger's' [pəʃətəríə]
millor 'better' [miʎó]	*millors* [miʎós]		*millorar* 'to improve' [miʎurá]
deutor 'debtor' [dəwtó]	*deutors* [dəwtós]	*deutora* [dəwtórə]	
flor 'flower' [flɔ́]	*flors* [flɔ́s]		*floral* [flurál]
dolor 'pain' [duló]	*dolors* [dulós]		*dolorós* 'painful' [dulurós]
campanar 'belltower' [kəmpəná]	*campanars* [kəmpənás]		*campanaret* 'little b.-t.' [kəmpənəɾɛ́t]
color 'colour' [kuló]	*colors* [kulós]		*acolorit* 'coloured' [əkuluɾít]
plor 'weeping' [plɔ́]	*plors* [plɔ́s]		*plorar* 'to weep' [plurá]
olor 'smell' [uló]	*olors* [ulós]		*olorar* 'to smell' [ulurá]
carrer 'street' [kəré]	*carrers* [kərés]		*carreró* 'alley' [kərəɾó]

agrair 'to thank' [əɣɾəí] *agrairé* 'I shall thank' [əɣɾəiɾé]   *agrair-l'hi* 'to thank him for it' [əɣɾəírli]
pensar 'to think' [pənsá] *pensaria* 'I would think' [pənsəɾíə]   *pensar-ho* 'to think it' [pənsáɾu]

On this evidence we can set up a rule deleting /r/ as follows:

(10) $\begin{bmatrix} -\text{syllab} \\ +\text{vocal} \\ +\text{cont} \end{bmatrix} \rightarrow \emptyset \ / \ \underline{\quad} (+C) \#\#$

The environment /___ ## ensures non-deletion in infinitive + pronoun groups, and similarly in the preposition *per* 'by, through' which must in any case be followed by only one # to prevent stress being assigned to it. Thus *per ells*

Further phonological rules

/#par#eʎ+s##/ [pəréʎs] 'by them'. There are, however, many exceptions to (10), many more than to (8), partly because some common suffixes are exceptions, e.g. /+ar/ — adjectival suffix, /+or/ — forming abstract nouns from verb roots. Examples are (all with [−r] ← /−r#/, [−rs] ← /−r+s#/):

(11) Adjectives: *familiar, particular, futur* 'future', *auster* 'austere', *sever* 'severe', *sincer* 'sincere', *car* 'dear', *pur* 'pure'.

(12) Abstract nouns: *amor* 'love', *favor* 'favour', *honor* 'honour', *sabor* 'flavour'

(13) Deverbative abstracts with zero suffix: *sospir* 'sigh' (cf. *sospirar* 'to sigh'), *conjur* 'conspiracy' (cf. *conjurar* 'to conspire'), *gir* 'turn' (cf. *girar* 'to turn'), *atur* 'stoppage' (cf. *aturar* 'to stop'), *enyor* 'longing' (cf. *enyorar* 'to miss').

(14) Other nouns: *cor* 'heart', *cor* 'choir', *mar* 'sea', *acer* 'steel', *or* 'gold', *far* 'lighthouse', *tresor* 'treasure', *llar* 'hearth', *bar, atzar* 'chance', *motor*.

(15) One verb, the only one with root-final /r/ and no suffix: *mor* 'dies', *mors* 'you (sg) die'.

There seem to be few principles lying behind these exceptions. Observe that some abstract nouns apparently similar to group (12) undergo deletion, e.g. from group (9), *dolor, color, olor*. Perhaps the only generalization to be made is that /+ar/ (adjectival suffix) never has deletion, and /+er/ (adjective or noun suffix) and /+dor/ (adjective or noun suffix) always have. Many lexical items must therefore be marked [−rule (10)].

In chapter IV (note 9 to Table 1; rule IV (21)), I discussed some other cases of /−r/ deletion in infinitives in "Barcelona colloquial". In this dialect, in addition to rule (10) as above, a rule deletes /r/ sometimes when only one # follows, that is, before pronouns; and always in infinitives which become paroxytone by [ə] —epenthesis.

2.1. The /r/–deletion rule, in deleting /r/ before # or +C, allows us to consider the possibility that all polysyllabic words ending in a stressed vowel (thus apparent exceptions to stress assignment) which are not revealed by paradigmatic alternation to have underlying /–n/ have in fact underlying final /r/, even though no alternating form exists which reveals this /r/ phonetically, such words are:

sofà, pl. *sofàs* 'sofa'; *taranna*̀, pl. *taranna*̀s 'character'; *ximpanzé*, pl. *ximpanzés* 'chimpanzee'; *quinqué*, pl. *quinqués* 'oil lamp'; *comitè*, pl. *comitès* 'committee'; *cafè*, pl. *cafès* 'coffee'; *bisturí*, pl. *bisturís* 'scalpel'; *monestir* [munəstí] pl. *monestirs* [munəstís] 'monastery'; *dominó*, pl. *dominós* 'cape for disguise'; *bambú*, pl. *bambús* 'bamboo'.

Cafè, it is true, offers us the derived form *cafeter* [kəfəté] 'coffee-seller', showing an exceptional [t] infix; this remains exceptional, whether or not /kafɛr/ is the UR of the root. The UR /kafɛt/ would require a special rule of /–t/ deletion. *Esquí*, pl. *esquís* 'ski', with a derived verb *esquiar* [əskiá] 'to ski' which shows no sign of internal /r/, is not a counter-example to this proposal, or to the stress-assignment rule if the UR is monosyllabic /ski/. I have not examined *all* the vowel-final oxytone words which lack positive paradigmatic evidence to show underlying /–n/ or /–r/, in order to discover whether the derivatives of any of them reveal clearly the absence of a final consonant in the root (a dictionary which classified words under their roots would facilitate such a task). On the hypothesis that there are no such words we can conclude that the only exceptions to the

Further phonological rules

stress-assignment rule are those which carry the stress on the syllable before that stressable by the general rule. In the case of polysyllabic adverbs and conjunctions with stressed final vowels (having no related /——+s forms), the choice between /–n/ and /–r/ in the UR must remain arbitrary. However, in the case of the pronouns *això* 'this', and *allò* 'that', the apparently related *daixonses*, *dallonses* 'thingummy, whatsit' would indicate underlying /n/ rather than /r/.

3. /s/, /z/ are deleted before a word beginning with /s/, /z/, /ʃ/, /ʒ/, or /r/, cf. Badia, 1951:101; Mascaró, 1972:43. Thus:

els sastres [əlsástrəs] 'the tailors'
dues zones [dùəzónəs] 'two zones'
als jardins [əlʒərðíns] 'in the gardens'
més ximple [mèʃímplə] 'sillier'
dos rals [dòráls] '50 cts' ('two "rals"')
les reaccions [lərɛəksións] 'the reactions'

The rule can be stated thus:

(16) $\begin{bmatrix} +\text{obstr} \\ +\text{cont} \\ +\text{coron} \\ -\text{high} \end{bmatrix} \rightarrow \emptyset \;/\; \underline{\quad} (\#(\#)) \begin{bmatrix} -\text{syll} \\ +\text{cont} \\ +\text{coron} \end{bmatrix}$

Alternatively, this process can be seen as, first, an assimilation

$s \rightarrow \int \;/\; \underline{\quad} \# \begin{Bmatrix} \int \\ 3 \end{Bmatrix}, \; s \rightarrow r \;/\; \underline{\quad} \# r\text{:}$

(17) $\begin{bmatrix} +\text{obstr} \\ +\text{cont} \\ +\text{coron} \\ -\text{high} \end{bmatrix} \rightarrow \begin{bmatrix} \alpha\text{high} \\ \beta\text{vocal} \\ \gamma\text{tense} \end{bmatrix} \Big/ \underline{\quad}\#_0 \begin{bmatrix} -\text{syll} \\ +\text{cont} \\ +\text{coron} \\ \alpha\text{high} \\ \beta\text{vocal} \\ \gamma\text{tense} \end{bmatrix}$

The outputs, [ʃ#ʃ], [ʃ#ʒ], [r#r] are subject to voicing assimilation ([ʃ#ʒ] → [ʒ#ʒ]), and then to V (26), (27) which degeminate, and make /s/, /ʃ/ and /ʒ/ [−tense, −long]. But see below, §11, for another solution. For those speakers who delete /ʃ/ also, before /r/ (*el mateix ratolí* [əlmətèrətulí] 'the same mouse'), instead of [−high] in the left matrix we would have an anglebracket condition [⟨ +high ⟩ ₐ] with [⟨ −obstr ⟩ ᵦ] in the right-hand matrix, and the condition: if a, then b. This rule applies after final stop deletion (see below), thus: *l'he vist riure* [lèβìríwɾə] 'I've seen him laugh', *un agost xafogós* [unəɣòʃəfuɣós] 'a sweltering August'.

4. The deletion of final stops applies (not in exactly the same way) in these three groups: (18a) /−nt/, /−nd/, /−np/, /−nb/, /−lt/, /−ld/, (18b) /−rt/, /−rd/, /−st/, (18c) /−nk/, /−ng/. The rule is discussed by Lleó (1970: 25−9) and by Mascaró (1972:12ff.).

4.1. In group (18a) the root-final stop is deleted in word-final position or before /+s/, thus:

(18a)

____#	____##V	__+s(Mpl)	____+V
content 'happy' [kuntén]	*content i* 'h. and..' [kuntén i]	*contents* [kunténs]	*contenta* (F) [kunténtə]
fecund 'fertile' [fəkún]	*fecund i* 'f. and..' [fəkún i]	*fecunds* [fəkúns]	*fecunda* (F) [fəkúndə]
llamp 'lightning' [ʎám]	*llamp i* 'l. and..' [ʎám i]	*llamps* [ʎáms]	*llampar* 'to strike by lightning' [ʎəmpá]
tomb 'turn' [tóm]	*tomb i* 't. and..' [tóm i]	*tombs* [tóms]	*tombar* 'to turn' [tumbá]
alt 'tall' [ál]	*alt i* 't. and..' [ál i]	*alts* [áls]	*alta* (F) [áltə]

Rule (19) accounts for these phonemena (after assimilation of unmarked nasals to the point of articulation of following consonants has applied).

Further phonological rules 281

(19) $\begin{bmatrix} +\text{obstr} \\ -\text{cont} \\ +\text{anter} \end{bmatrix} \rightarrow \emptyset\ /\ [-\text{cont}]\underline{\quad}(C)\ \#\ \begin{Bmatrix} C \\ \# \end{Bmatrix}$

Mentioning two ## in the environment, we can account for some anomalous exceptions in the case of /nt/. Consider:

vint-i-un [bìntiún] 'twenty-one'
Sant Andreu [sàntəndɾéw] 'St Andrew'
veient-ho [bəjéntu] 'seeing it'
anant-hi [ənánti] 'going there'
on és? [òntés] 'where is it?'
quant era? [kwàntéɾə] 'how much was it?'

In the case of gerunds followed by unstressed pronouns only one # will intervene anyway; the other words must undergo a minor rule which has the effect of deleting # in some environments. What is not clear, however, is how the environments can be defined. It will not work to say "before a vowel within the same NP or VP" for we have *vint hores* [bìnɔ́ɾəs] 'twenty hours', *el Sant Imperi* [əlsànimpéɾi] 'the Holy Roman Empire'. Perhaps we can do little more than give a list, e.g.

(20) $\#\rightarrow\emptyset/\ \begin{Bmatrix} \text{sant}\underline{\quad}][\#\text{ V X }]_{\text{Proper name}} \\ \text{bint}\underline{\quad}]\ [\ i\ ] \\ \begin{Bmatrix}\text{ont}\\ k^w\text{ant}\end{Bmatrix}\underline{\quad}][\ \#\text{V} \end{Bmatrix}$

4.1.1. Brasington (1973) points out that some speakers sometimes pronounce an audible stop transition between a nasal or /l/ and a following sibilant which is homorganic with the preceding sonorant. This occurs irrespective of whether there is an underlying stop. Thus *calents* [kəléns] (besides [kəléns]) 'hot' (Mpl) /kalent+s/, *alts* [álts] (besides [áls]) 'tall' (Mpl) /alt+s/, *blancs* [bláŋks] (besides [bláŋs]) 'white' (Mpl) /blank+s/, *prims* [prímps] (besides [príms]) 'thin' (Mpl) /prim+s/, *mans* [mánts] (besides [máns]) 'hands' /man+s/. We could add, for example, *menja* [mén'd'ʒə] (besides [mén'ʒə]) 'eats'. To express the fact that "homorganic stops are optional between nasal or lateral and sibilant" he proposes a new notational convention

(21) OPT X ⟷ ø / Y ___ Z

(More generally we could represent the schema as

(22) A ⟷ B / Y ___ Z

since it is necessarily optional. This device is of somewhat limited applicability: it is usable whenever an opposition between A and B which, except when either is ø, are underlying segments (or possibly distinct segments at some intermediate stage) is neutralized in a certain environment, and either may be realized by either.) Though there is something to be said in general for an abbreviatory device with this purpose, it is not clear that it provides much of a simplification in the present case, since we need pure deletion rules anyway − (19) and others − to delete stops between sonorants and ##, and the deletion rule for velars is different from the rule for anterior consonants. The optional rule for stop insertion would look something like this (after boundary deletion):

$$
(23) \quad \emptyset \xrightarrow[\text{opt}]{} \begin{bmatrix} +\text{obstr} \\ -\text{cont} \\ \alpha\text{labial} \\ \beta\text{coron} \\ \gamma\text{anter} \\ \delta\text{distr} \\ \left\{\langle \epsilon\text{high}\rangle\right\} \\ \text{ʃback} \\ -\text{back} \\ \eta\text{voiced} \end{bmatrix} \Bigg/ \begin{bmatrix} -\text{syll} \\ -\text{obstr} \\ -\text{cont} \\ \alpha\text{labial} \\ \beta\text{coron} \\ \gamma\text{anter} \\ \delta\text{distr} \\ \epsilon\text{high} \\ \left\langle \begin{matrix} \text{ʃback} \\ +\text{nasal} \end{matrix} \right\rangle \end{bmatrix} \underline{\qquad} \begin{bmatrix} +\text{obstr} \\ +\text{cont} \\ +\text{coron} \\ \eta\text{voiced} \end{bmatrix}
$$

Further phonological rules 283

Here the inserted stop agrees in voicing with the following sibilant — this could be dealt with by the general voicing assimilation rule. The angle brackets prevent the insertion of a velarized alveolar stop after velarized [ł] (cf. §6.4) since rule (23) can normally be expected to apply after various assimilations of sonorants to their environments.

4.1.2. The other use Brasington proposes for the ⟷ notation (29–33) seems to me fundamentally different. It is as a context-free redundancy rule dealing with reciprocal implication of the kind $\begin{bmatrix} +\text{vocal} \\ -\text{cons} \end{bmatrix} \longleftrightarrow [+\text{syllab}]$. I have suggested above (chapter VI) that context-free redundancy rules may be universals; as such, abbreviations for them would have no theoretical significance. They would not be subject to the evaluation measure for grammars. On the contrary, they would themselves be part of the evaluation measure.

4.2. In the second group (18b) (/–rt/, /–rd/, /–st/, – there is no example of /–sd/) the stop is deleted only before a consonant. Lleó (1970:27, and note) claims that /t/ and /d/ are deleted after /r/ as after /n/ and /l/ except "in a very stilted style". This observation conflicts with my own experience (and apparently Badia's (1951:112)). Indeed not only is [t] pronounced here, but it can also often be heard in words to which it does not belong in the UR, e.g. *mar* [márt] 'sea', *car* [kárt] 'dear', *or* [ɔ́rt] 'gold'. These "vulgar" forms would not be heard in any careful, let alone stilted, style of speech. It is true that in rapid speech the [t] is not pronounced before a phrase or sentence boundary. This would be a special rule of "allegro" style (cf. Harris, 1969:6–8 for this use of musical terminology). Examples:

284   Further phonological rules

		/rt/	/rd/	/st/
──	‖	*fort* [fɔ́rt] 'strong'	*verd* [bért] 'green'	*trist* [trı́st] 'sad'
──	+V	*forta* [fɔ́rtə] ,, (F)	*verdura* [bərðúrə] 'greens'	*trista* [trı́stə] ,, (F)
──	##V	*fort i musculat* [fɔ́rt i muskalát] 'strong and muscular'	*verd especial* [bért əspəsiál] 'special green'	*trist o alegre* [trı́st o léɣrə] 'sad or happy'
──	+s	*forts* [fɔ́rs] 'strong' (Mpl)	*verds* [bérs] 'green' (Mpl)	(*tristos* [trı́stus] 'sad' (Mpl))
──	##C	*fort xàfec* [fɔ̀r ʃáfək] 'heavy squall'	*verd fosc* [bèr fósk] 'dark green'	*trist deure* [trìz ðéwrə] 'sad duty'

The rule can be expressed thus:

(24) $\begin{bmatrix} +\text{obstr} \\ -\text{cont} \\ +\text{coron} \end{bmatrix} \rightarrow \emptyset \Big/ \begin{bmatrix} +\text{cons} \\ +\text{cont} \end{bmatrix} \underline{\quad} \Big[\langle x\text{WB} \rangle_b \Big]_1 \Big[\begin{matrix} -\text{syll} \\ \langle +\text{vocal} \rangle_a \end{matrix} \Big]$

condition: if a, then b.
(WB = word boundary)

The purpose of the condition is to exclude the case of *perdre* [pérðrə] /pɛrd+r/ from the operation of the rule. If the rule could be ordered after the vowel epenthesis rule I (13) however, (and it must anyway come after initial vowel epenthesis I (20) so as to prevent deletion of /t/, /d/ before initial /sC/), it could be expressed in the following way:

(25) $\begin{bmatrix} +\text{obstr} \\ -\text{cont} \\ +\text{coron} \end{bmatrix} \rightarrow \emptyset \Big/ \begin{bmatrix} +\text{cons} \\ +\text{cont} \end{bmatrix} \underline{\quad} \Big\{ \begin{matrix} C \quad \# \\ \# \, (\#) \, C \end{matrix} \Big\}$

The notation here on the right of the environment does not adequately express the generalization "before a consonant which is either preceded or followed by a word boundary", which is equivalent to "before a word boundary which is either preceded or followed by a consonant". I wish to suggest a notation for this kind of sequential disjunction, viz. ⟨A B⟩ which is to be interpret-

Further phonological rules

ed: either AB or BA, where A, B, represent one or more symbols; thus in the present case the environment is

(26) $\quad / \begin{bmatrix} +\text{cons} \\ +\text{cont} \end{bmatrix}$ ____ $\widehat{(\# (\#) \quad C)}$

This notation might, if required, be extended to abbreviate discontinuous disjunction, thus $\widehat{A \cup X \cup B}$ which is to be interpreted: either AXB or BXA. It is also possible with this notation to express ordering in the disjunction. We can adopt the convention that the abbreviation is expanded first in the sequential order as written. Thus

$\widehat{A \cup B}$ = $\begin{Bmatrix} AB \\ BA \end{Bmatrix}$ (disjunctive) and $\widehat{B \cup A}$ = $\begin{Bmatrix} BA \\ AB \end{Bmatrix}$

This notation allows a clearer expression for "either before or after" statements, for which a notation was proposed by Bach (1968) and modified by S.R. Anderson (1971:92ff.). Thus X → Y / $\widehat{A \_\_\_ B}$ expands to
i) X → Y / A ____B, and ii) X → Y / B'____A'. If A and B are sequences of symbols, A = $a_1, a_2, \ldots a_n$, B = $b_1, b_2, \ldots b_m$ then / $\widehat{A \_\_\_ B}$ would normally be interpreted i) / $a_1, a_2, \ldots a_n$ ____ $b_1, b_2, \ldots b_m$
ii) / $b_1, b_2, \ldots b_m$ ____ $a_1, a_2, \ldots a_n$

If however we wish to restrict this kind of notation to strict "mirror-image" environments, we can dispense with the "double twiddle" $\frown\frown$ and express thus:
X → Y / $\widehat{A \_\_\_ B}$, which expands to
i) X → Y / $a_1, a_2, \ldots a_n$ ____ $b_1, b_2, \ldots b_m$
ii) X → Y / $b_m, b_{m-1}, \ldots b_2, b_1$ ____ $a_n, a_{n-1}, \ldots a_2, a_1$

This "mirror-image only" interpretation seems intuitively the correct one, that is, the other interpretation does not seem to capture any significant generalization. The right hand side of (26), strictly interpreted, expands to

(i) ___ #(#)C, i.e. _____ $\left\{ \begin{array}{l} \#\# \text{ C} \\ \# \text{ C} \end{array} \right\}$

(ii) ___ C (#) #, i.e. _____ $\left\{ \begin{array}{l} \text{C } \#\# \\ \text{C } \# \end{array} \right\}$

The double twiddle ⌒⌣ remains available for non-mirror-image expansions if required. Anderson's device, which consists of replacing the usual environment slash by % is not adequate to deal with the type of environment in rule (25).

4.3. The issue of stop deletion in the groups (18c) /nk/ (→ [ŋk]) and /ng/ (→ [ŋg]) is mentioned by Badia (1951:110): "Cuando el grupo de *n* + velar queda final ante pausa, no se articula la velar, pero sí la *n*, tan velarizada como en los demás casos: *blanc* [bláŋ], *sang* [sáŋ]; pero si no queda final hay que **distinguir:** a) *n* + velar + vocal: se articula la velar, generalmente sonorizada si no lo era: *blanc i negre* [blàŋg-i néɣɾə], *sang i fetge* [sàŋg-i fédʒə]; b) *n* + velar + consonante: se articula la velar, asimilándose, en su caso, a la sonoridad de la consonante siguiente, pero con tendencia a perder el punto de articulación por poco que quepa su asimilación: *blancs* [bláŋks], *blancs o verds* [blàŋgz-o βɛ́rts], *sangtraït* [sàn̪tɾəít] (y también [sàn̪tɾəít])." Badia is corrected by Coromines (1971:248): "*Blanc i negre* i *sang i fetge* es pronuncien més sovint amb [−k] que amb [−g]; ningú no pronuncia [bláŋks] sinó [bláns] (ni els valencians i balears, que solen dir [bláŋk] en el singular)." See also Lleó, 1970:28. In these groups the stop is deleted except when a vowel follows (ignoring boundaries). In fact, I have also heard a voiceless stop before a pause, as in −*Quants n'hi ha?* −*Cinc.* [síŋk] 'How many are there?'

Further phonological rules   287

'Five'. So perhaps the presence of ‖ in the rule should be optional.

__‖	*sang* [sáŋ] 'blood' ([sáŋk])	*blanc* [bláŋ] 'white' (M) ([bláŋk])
__+V	*sangonós* [səŋgunós] 'bloody'	*blancor* [bləŋkó] 'whiteness'
__#V	*sang a les venes* [sàŋkələz βénəs] 'blood in one's veins'	*blanc i negre* [bláŋkinéɣrə] 'black and white'
— C	*sang freda* [sàɲfɾέðə] 'cold blood'	*blancs o blaus* [bláɲzoβláws] 'white or blue' (Mpl)

Rule (27) is then

(27)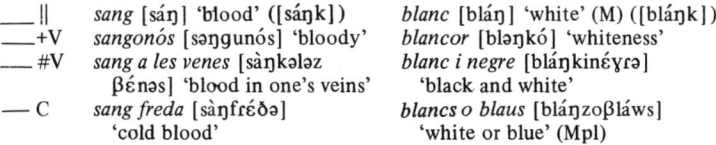

The distinct environments do not permit us to collapse rules (19), (25) and (27) as Lleó (1970:29) attempts to do, ignoring the differences. It would perhaps not be surprising if at a future stage of the language the rules were simplified so as to delete stops between homorganic consonantal sonorants or continuants and word-final or word initial consonants.

5. Vowel sandhi: contacts between vowels across word boundaries.

Some discussion and exemplification of these sandhi phenomena can be found in Fabra, 1897:12–13; Badia, 1951:111–2, 114–7; Badia, 1973a:121–30, 144–9; and Solà, 1973:82–4. The rules I shall present are those appropriate, in my experience, for normal spontaneous colloquial speech, and also, as it happens, for the "correct" recitation of metrical verse. In a formal, declamatory reading style it is possible to make no elisions of [ə], and (even more formally) no glide-formation of /i/, /u/. There is also a pronunciation, probably reading-influenced, where [ə] is not deleted after [i] or [u] and a rising diphthong occurs. Cf. Badia, 1973a:124. Speaking of unstressed [i] he says: " Quand la voyelle suivante n'est pas accentuée, la prononciation la plus normale pratique la réduction de toute la syllabe en [i]; *a mi em sembla* 'moi, il me semble' [ə-mim], *si et diu això* 's'il te dit ceci' [sit] ... Un type d'élocution plus calme maintient l'hiatus: [ə-mi-əm], [si-ət]. Mais, entre ces deux extrêmes, il n'est pas rare d'entendre précisément la prononciation diphtonguée: [ə-mjəm], [sjət]. Il existe un vers d'une chanson populaire (*a tu qui et treurà* 'toi, qui va te faire (danser)', de *L'Hereu Riera*) qui permet soit la prononciation que j'ai appelée normale [ə-tu-kit-], soit la prononciation incorrecte avec la diphtongue [ə-tu-kjət-], mais qui, à cause du rythme de la chanson, ne pourrait être prononcée de la façon correcte [sic, M.W.] [ə-tu-ki-ət], parce que, dans ce cas, il y aurait une syllabe de trop."

Aramon (Badia & Straka, 1973:177) replies pertinently to this and similar points made by Badia (loc. cit.):
"... dans mon enfance ... lorsqu'on lisait les textes des chansons populaires, on les lisait en ancienne graphie, dans laquelle elles étaient publiées. Mais quand l'orthographe de l'Institut a supprimé la possibilité d'écrire les pronoms *m* (= *me*), *t* (= *te*), *l* (= *lo*), etc., ajoutés aux mots terminés en voyelle, autres que les verbes – par exemple à la fin de *qui, jo,* etc., qu'on devait écrire *qui em, jo et* et prononcer [ki m], [ʒɔ t] –ceux qui ne savaient pas très bien l'orthographe et n'avaient pas l'habitude de réciter ont commencé à prononcer *quiem, joet,* ce qui était une prononciation tout à fait inexplicable en catalan.

"M. Badia à cité la prononciation [ə mjəm] dans *a mi em sembla.* Je crois que c'est la prononciation de ceux qui savent lire, mais qui ne connaissent pas exactement les règles de lecture ...

"Il est possible de faire entendre l'*e* s'il y a un arrêt: *a mi, em sembla;* sinon, cette combinaison aboutit à [ə mim sɛmblə]. Je crois que la langue écrite dans

Further phonological rules 289

l'orthographe de l'Institut a eu une grande influence sur ceux qui ne connaissent pas bien la grammaire quant aux prononciations comme [twets], car la prononciation normale est, comme on sait bien, non pas [twets] mais [tu ets] ou en prononciation rapide [tuts]."
Let us then consider what occurs in spontaneous speech when vowels come into contact across #. The examples are divided into four groups, the last three in the order corresponding to that of the rules which account for them.

(A) V́ # (#) V́ : no change

no éreu vós? 'was it not you?' [nò érəw . . .]
vindrà ella 'she will come' [bindrà éʎə]
així ha de ser 'that must be' [əʃɔ̀ àðə sé]

There are exceptions only when the second word is *ets* 'you (sg) are', or *és* 'is' (cf. Badia, 1973a:128–9), e.g.

tu ets aquí? 'you're here?' [túdzəkí]
no és veritat 'it's not true' [nòzβəritát]
el senyor és amb vós 'the Lord is with you' [əlsəɲòzəm . .]

To deal with this exception we must suppose a special rule of this form:

(28) $\begin{bmatrix} +\text{syllab} \\ -\text{low} \\ -\text{labial} \\ +\text{stress} \end{bmatrix} \rightarrow \emptyset \;/\; \begin{bmatrix} +\text{syllab} \\ +\text{stress} \end{bmatrix}$ # (#) ___ (t) s #

(B) (a) V#i#V, V#u#V; (b) ‖#i#V, ‖#u#V: glide formation.

This rule is optional; in (a) the effects of non-application are shown second. The application of glide formation is the more usual, in my experience. In fact, it will be more appropriate to say that rule (29) may optionally apply after (31) ([ə] –deletion), in which case (29) will be bled of [ə]s for its environment, and will apply only to cases like *ni ho era*.

(a) V#i#V

comença i acaba 'begins and ends' [–səjək–], [–sik–]
jo hi anava 'I was going there' [ʒɔ̀jən–], [ʒɔ̀jn–]
encara hi és 'it's still there' [–rəjés]
tu hi entens? 'do you know about it?' [tújən–], [tújn–]

V#u#V

porta-ho a casa 'take it home' [–təwək–], [–tuk–]
ni ho era 'nor was it' [nìwérə]
no ho havia fet 'he hadn't done it' [nòwəβíə–], [nòwβíə–]
tu ho havies fet 'you had done it'? [tùwəβíəs]
(→ [tùəβíəs] : see below), [tùwəβíəs]
(→ [tùβíəs])

(b) ‖#i#V

I aquell dia 'And that day' [jəkéʎ–]
Hi havia 'There was' [jəβíə], cf. *N'hi havia* 'There was some' [niβíə]

‖#u#V

Ho he fet 'I've done it' [wèfét]
Ho anava a fer 'I was going to do it' [wənàβə–]

The rule for these cases is

(29) $\begin{bmatrix} -\text{cons} \\ +\text{high} \end{bmatrix} \rightarrow [-\text{syll}] \bigg/ \left\{ \begin{matrix} \| \\ V* \end{matrix} \right\} \#_1 \underline{\quad\quad} \#_1 V$
*optional

Further phonological rules 291

Note that this rule is a bleeding rule with respect to [ə]-deletion below.

(C) (a) V́ # ə; (b) V̌ # ə; (c) ə # V́; (d) ə # V̌ deletion of [ə] occurs.

(a) V́ # (#) ə

a mi em sembla 'it seems to me' [əmìm–]
sortir a veure 'to go out and see' [–tìβéwɾə]
va escriure 'he wrote' [báskɾíwɾə]
tu en tens 'you have some' [tùnténs]
es va posar a examinar 'he began to examine' [–puzàgzəmi–]

(b) V̌ # (#) ə

sense esperar 'without waiting' [sènsəspəɾá]
ha estat 'has been' [əstát]   } = ə #(#) V̌
torna a entrar 'comes in again' [tòrnəntɾá]
vingui a visitar-nos 'come and visit us' [bìŋgiβiz–]
carro enorme 'huge cart' [kàrunórmə]
començo a animar-me 'I am beginning to cheer up' [–mènsunimár–]

(c) ə# (#) V́

aquesta illa 'this island' [əkèstíʎə]
massa obvi 'too obvious' [màsɔ́bbi]
una àguila 'an eagle' [unáɣilə]
força útil 'very useful' [fɔ̀rsútil]
per a ells 'for them' [pəɾéʎs]

(d) ə# (#) V̌ (see also under (b))

primera imatge 'first image' [–èɾimá–], [–èɾəjmá–]
ella ho sap 'she knows it' [èʎusáp], [èʎəwsáp]
una altra ocasió 'another occasion [àltɾukə–], [áltɾəwkə–]
veure-hi clar 'to be able to see clearly' [bɛ̀wɾiklá], [bɛ̀wɾəjklá]

Deletion of [ə] is optional here (cf. IV §4.3 for other examples such as *porta-ho* 'bring it' [pɔ́rtu] or [pɔ́rtəw]). That is, optionally, glide formation (32) applies before (31) to examples like these. The order (31) (32) is more likely when only one # comes between.

In the Standard language *la* (F definite article or F pronoun) is an exeption to [ə]–deletion when unstressed /u/ or /i/ follows, or a few other listed words, thus:

la impossibilitat 'the impossibility' [ləjm−]
la unitat 'unity' [ləwn−]
la invito 'I am inviting her' [ləjm−]
la utilitzo 'I use it (F)' [ləwt−]
la ira 'anger' [ləírə]
la una 'one o'clock' [ləúnə]

This exception can be expressed thus:

(30) ⟦+lə⟧$_{Det, Pro}$ → [−rule (31)] / ___ ⟦# $\begin{Bmatrix} \begin{bmatrix} +syll \\ +high \\ -stress \end{bmatrix} \\ ira \\ una \\ host \\ etc. \end{Bmatrix}$

This rule is not commonly applied in spontaneous speech except in *la una* [ləúnə]. Rule (31) ([ə]–deletion) is:

(31) $\begin{bmatrix} +syll \\ -stress \\ -high \end{bmatrix}$ → ø / ⌢ #$_1$ V

When expanded as suggested above (§4.2) rule (31) will, when applied to *começo a animar-me,* by the first sub-

Further phonological rules

rule delete [ə] before [ə], and by the second, the remaining [ə] after [u]. However, if we accept Chomsky & Halle's (1968:366) interpretation for disjunctive rule ordering (see above IV §4.7), it seems that the second application of the rule as it stands is blocked. Consequently the rule will have to be specified as iterative.

(D) (a) $\begin{Bmatrix} i \\ u \end{Bmatrix}$ # (#) V́ : no change

va dir-ho ell 'he said it' [−ðìɾuéʎ]
Josep i Anna 'J. and A.' [ʒuzɛ̀piánnə]
el principi era 'the beginning was' [−sìpiéɾə]
el toro entra 'the bull comes in' [−tɔ̀ɾuéntɾə]

(D) (b) V́ # (#) $\begin{Bmatrix} \breve{i} \\ \breve{u} \end{Bmatrix}$; (c) lə # $\begin{Bmatrix} \breve{i} \\ \breve{u} \end{Bmatrix}$;

(d) $\begin{Bmatrix} \breve{i} \\ \breve{u} \end{Bmatrix}$ # (#) $\begin{Bmatrix} \breve{i} \\ \breve{u} \end{Bmatrix}$: glide formation occurs.

(b) V́ # (#) $\begin{Bmatrix} \breve{i} \\ \breve{u} \end{Bmatrix}$

anar i venir 'to come and go' [ənàjβəní]
va ofendre 'he offended' [bàwféndɾə]
té interès 'has interest' [tèjntəɾɛ́s]
tu ho saps 'you know it' [tùwsáps] (→ [tùsáps])
qui hi va ser? 'who was there?' [kíjβàsé] (→ [kíβàsé])

(c) lə # $\begin{Bmatrix} \breve{i} \\ \breve{u} \end{Bmatrix}$ (see above)

la idea 'the idea' [ləjðéə]
la utilitzo [ləwtilídzu]

(d) $\begin{Bmatrix} \breve{i} \\ \breve{u} \end{Bmatrix}$ # (#) $\begin{Bmatrix} \breve{i} \\ \breve{u} \end{Bmatrix}$

dir-t'ho humilment 'to say it to you humbly' [−tuwmil−] (→ [−tum−])

comenci-ho 'begin it' [kuménsiw]
acabo interessant-me 'I end up getting interested'
[−áβujntə−]
que torni immediatament 'let him come back immediately' [−tórnijm−] (→[−nim−])

To account for these phenomena we have the glide-formation rule (32). (For glide formation within words, cf. V §2.)

(32) $\begin{bmatrix} -\text{cons} \\ +\text{high} \\ -\text{stress} \end{bmatrix} \rightarrow [-\text{syll}] \,/\, V\, \#_1 \rule{1cm}{0.4pt}$

Finally we need a rule to account for the optional high diphthong simplification — see above for examples of /uw/ → [u], /ij/ → [i], and see also III §4.5, §7.1, §7.3, where we have also [dús] 'you bring', [dú] 'he brings', [dúən] 'they bring' from /duw+s/, /duw/, /duw+n/ respectively, and [plurá] from intermediate /pluwrá/. More precisely, in view of the verb forms, we should say that simplification is obligatory before a vowel, and optional elsewhere. In its most general form the rule is:

(33) $\begin{bmatrix} -\text{syllab} \\ -\text{cons} \\ \alpha\text{labial} \end{bmatrix} \rightarrow \emptyset \,\Big/\, \begin{bmatrix} +\text{syllab} \\ +\text{high} \\ \alpha\text{labial} \end{bmatrix} \#_0 \rule{1cm}{0.4pt} \,{}^*V$

*optional restriction

6. Assimilation of point of articulation (cf. Badia, 1951:96−113).

The consonants which undergo assimilation are those which I have suggested above (chapter VI) are less marked, namely, the dentals and alveolars: /l/, /n/, /t/, /d/, /s/, /z/. Labial non-continuants (/m/, /p/, /b/) undergo assimilation of the feature [distributed] for which /m/, at least,

Further phonological rules

is unmarked, when a labiodental (/f/) follows. /r/, which is alveolar, undergoes no assimilation in point of articulation, nor, apparently, is it the environment for any. It is conceivable that /t/ and /d/ might be alveolar before /r/ ([r] or [ɾ]) as they are before other alveolars, but I have seen no statement that this is so in Catalan, nor has my ear observed it.

The exclusion of /r/ from such rules seems quite natural, though in the feature system being used in this work /l/, /n/, /t/, /d/, /s/, /z/ are not a natural class but

only $\begin{bmatrix} +\text{coron} \\ -\text{high} \\ \begin{Bmatrix} -\text{cont} \\ +\text{obstr} \end{Bmatrix} \end{bmatrix}$ It seems to be that in this respect,

and some others, the feature system I am using is not quite adequate for representing natural classes, and a revision might be along the lines suggested by Zwicky (1972:277). Zwicky observes that English and other languages reveal a hierarchy of segments of the kind: 1 Vowels, 2 Glides, 3 [r], 4 [l], 5[n], 6[m], 7[ŋ], 8 Fricatives, 9 Plosives, and that any sequence of adjacent members is a natural class.

One possible way of representing such a hierarchy is set out in the table below (Table 1). Two new distinctive features are suggested: [plosive], the meaning of which is evident, and [approximant] which groups together non-low glides (e.g. [j], [w], [ʍ], [ɥ]) and [r] sounds. The term approximant is used in something like this sense in Abercrombie, 1967, and, with a slightly different definition, in Ladefoged, 1971. It corresponds to what are sometimes called "frictionless continuants"; for our purpose, a precise articulatory or acoustic definition is less important than the classificatory purpose. If non-low glides and [r]−sounds are not in fact a natural class, then there will be no point in looking for physical definitions. Glides are [+vocalic] here; this makes the table more symmetrical. For example, glides then differ by one feature only, out of [syllabic], [vocalic] and [consonantal] from the classes either side of them, namely, vowels and liquids. Observe that the feature [nasal] need not be used to establish these major classes, except to define a class [−nasal]. In the table V = vowels, G = glides, N = nasals ([n], [m], [ŋ]) not distinguished for this purpose. The internal hierarchy among nasals is rather a question of markedness.) Fr = fricatives, Pl = plosives.

VII TABLE 1

	V	G	r	l	N	Fr	Pl
syllab	+	−	−	−	−	−	−
vocal	+	+	+	+	−	−	−
cons	−	−	+	+	+	+	+
obstr	−	−	−	−	−	+	+
cont	+	+	+	−	−	+	−
plosive	−	−	−	−	−	−	+
approx	−	+	+	−	−	−	−

Adjacent natural classes can now be defined as follows:

V + G: [−cons], G + r: [+approx], r + l: $\begin{bmatrix}+\text{vocal}\\+\text{cons}\end{bmatrix}$, l + N:

$\begin{bmatrix}-\text{obstr}\\-\text{cont}\end{bmatrix}$, N + Fr: $\begin{bmatrix}-\text{vocal}\\-\text{plos}\end{bmatrix}$, Fr + Pl: [+obstr]; V + G + r:

$\begin{bmatrix}+\text{vocal}\\+\text{cont}\end{bmatrix}$, G + r + l: $\begin{bmatrix}-\text{syll}\\+\text{vocal}\end{bmatrix}$, r + l + N: $\begin{bmatrix}+\text{cons}\\-\text{obstr}\end{bmatrix}$,

l + N + Fr: $\begin{bmatrix}-\text{syll}\\-\text{plos}\\-\text{approx}\end{bmatrix}$, N + Fr + Pl: [−vocal];

Further phonological rules 297

V + G + r + l: [+vocal], G + r + l + N: $\begin{bmatrix} -\text{syll} \\ -\text{obstr} \end{bmatrix}$,

r + l + N + Fr: $\begin{bmatrix} +\text{cons} \\ -\text{plos} \end{bmatrix}$, l + N + Fr + Pl: $\begin{bmatrix} -\text{syll} \\ -\text{approx} \end{bmatrix}$;

V + G + r + l + N: [−obstr], G + r + l + N + Fr: $\begin{bmatrix} -\text{syll} \\ -\text{plos} \end{bmatrix}$,

r + l + N + Fr + Pl: [+cons]; V + G + r + l + N + Fr: [−plos],
G + r + l + N + Fr + Pl: [−syll].

In addition, the following non-adjacent classes can be expressed naturally:

r + Fr: $\begin{bmatrix} +\text{cons} \\ +\text{cont} \end{bmatrix}$, V + Fr: $\begin{bmatrix} +\text{cont} \\ -\text{approx} \end{bmatrix}$, V + l: $\begin{bmatrix} +\text{vocal} \\ -\text{approx} \end{bmatrix}$,

N + Pl: $\begin{bmatrix} -\text{vocal} \\ -\text{cont} \end{bmatrix}$; l + N + Pl: [−cont], G + r + Fr:

$\begin{bmatrix} -\text{syll} \\ +\text{cont} \end{bmatrix}$, V + l + N: $\begin{bmatrix} -\text{obstr} \\ -\text{approx} \end{bmatrix}$; V + G + r + Fr: [+cont],

V + l + N + Fr: $\begin{bmatrix} -\text{plos} \\ -\text{approx} \end{bmatrix}$; V + l + N + Fr + Pl:

[−approx].

Of these, the classes including vowels with certain consonants as [−approx] seem in fact rather unnatural. Probably, therefore, we should make [approx] subordinate to [−syllab] only, to avoid these false natural classes. (For such restrictions cf. Wheeler, 1972:93.)

In formulating the rules of this chapter I use the more conventional feature system. The suggestions presented here are meant to show that the binary distinctive feature approach is capable of dealing with the type of classification we require in a straightforward way, without, as far as I can see, permitting falsely simple expression of unnatural classes.

6.1. Assimilation to labials, Examples:

n/__p	*mon pare* 'my father' [mumpárə]
	impossible [impusíbblə]
n/__b	*un bon violí* 'a good violin' [umbɔ́mbiulí]
	convenir 'to agree' [kumbəní]
*t/__p	*aquest període* 'this period' [akɛ̀ppəríuðə]
*t/__b	*permet viure* 'allows to live'
	[pərmɛ̀bbíwrə]
	advers 'adverse' [əbbɛ́rs]
n/__m	*bon minyó* 'good boy' [bɔ́mmiɲó]
	immodest [immuðést]
*t/__m	*al costat meu* 'at my side' [əlkustàmméw]
	admetre 'to admit' [əmmɛ́trə]
n/__f	*enfilar-se* 'to climb' [əɱfilársə]
	tan fresc 'as fresh' [tàɱfrɛ́sk]
m/__f	*volem fer* 'we want to do' [bulɛ̀ɱfé]
*p/__f	*rep fredament* 'receives coldly'
	[rɛ̀pfrɛ̀ðəmén]
	capficat 'worried' [kàpfikát]
*t/__f	*aquest fenomen* 'this phenomenon'
	[əkɛ̀pfənɔ́mən]

Of these assimilations, those marked with an asterisk may fail to occur in very careful speech; the others (all of sonorants) are obligatory. In the case of p/__f and t/__f affrication is consequent upon assimilation in point of articulation; that is, affrication applies, as we shall see, to an obstruent stop + fricative sequence which already have as many features as possible in common. The rule of labial assimilation is as follows (34), assuming that the rule realizing /k^W/, /g^W/ as sequences of two segments has already operated. Note that it is not necessary to mention [coronal] or [anterior] to the right of the arrow since their values are supplied by linking.

(34) $\begin{bmatrix} -\text{vocal} \\ -\text{cont} \\ -\text{high} \\ -\text{obstr}* \end{bmatrix} \rightarrow \begin{bmatrix} +\text{labial} \\ \alpha\text{distr} \end{bmatrix} \Big/ \underline{\qquad} \#_0 \begin{bmatrix} +\text{cons} \\ +\text{labial} \\ \alpha\text{distr} \end{bmatrix}$

*add this restriction for "largo" style.

If the interpretation of Linking Condition (d) (VI §2.4) is right, then [−vocal] need not be mentioned to the left of the arrow; CFR rule (23) will prevent labial liquids being generated. CFR rule (36) links to supply [+anterior] and CFR (41) to supply [−coron].

6.2. Alveolar assimilation. Examples:

t/__s	*plats* 'plates' [pláts] ([ts] = alveolar affricate)
	tot sencer 'whole' [tòtsənsέ]
t/__z	*setze* 'sixteen' [sέdzə]
	aquest zero 'this zero' [əkὲdzέru]
t/__l	See below, §9.1. [−ll−]
t/__n	See below, §9.2. [−nn−]

The rule is:

(35) $\begin{bmatrix} -\text{cont} \\ +\text{coron} \end{bmatrix} \rightarrow [-\text{anter}] \Big/ \underline{\qquad} \#_0 \begin{bmatrix} \{-\text{cont}\} \\ \{+\text{obstr}\} \\ -\text{anter} \\ +\text{coron} \end{bmatrix}$

Since all the input segments to this rule are [u±distr], linking brings Mk (12) into operation, supplying [u−distr] to all the outputs. Rule (35) also makes /t/, /d/ [−anter] before palatals, which is right and simplifies the expression of (36).

6.3. Partial palatal assimilation.

/n/ and /l/ become palatalized [n'], [l'] before /ɲ/, /ʎ/, /ʃ/, /ʒ/; that is, they become [+high] but not [−coron]. Cf. Badia, 1951:106–7: "En contacto con una consonante palatal siguiente la alveolar *n* retrotrae su punto de articulación hasta hacerse prepalatal . . . Sin embargo no llega a confundirse nunca con la [ɲ]" − similarly for /l/. Examples:

n/__ʃ	*manxa* 'bellows'	[mán'ʃə]
	tan ximple 'so silly'	[tàn'ʃímplə]
n/__ʒ	*engendrar* 'to engender'	[ən'ʒəndɾá]
	ton germà 'your brother'	[tun'ʒərmá]
n/__ʎ	*enllestir* 'to complete'	[ən'ʎəstí]
	fent lletres 'making letters'	[fèn'ʎétɾəs]
n/__ɲ	*un nyeu-nyeu* 'a hypocrite'	[un'ɲɛ̀wɲɛ́w]
l/__ʃ	*el xoc* 'the crash'	[əl'ʃɔ́k]
l/__ʒ	*àlgebra*	[ál'ʒəβɾə]
	vol jugar 'wants to play'	[bɔ̀l'ʒuɣá]
l/__ʎ	*cal llevar-se* 'one must get up'	
		[kàl'ʎəβársə]
l/__ɲ	*el nyanyo* 'the lump'	[əl'ɲáɲu]

Thus we have:

(36) $\begin{bmatrix} -\text{cont} \\ +\text{coron} \end{bmatrix} \rightarrow [+\text{high}] \Big/ \underline{\qquad} \#_0 \begin{bmatrix} +\text{cons} \\ +\text{high} \\ -\text{back} \end{bmatrix}$

Convention (d) (VI §2.4) prevents CFR (42) and (43) from linking to this rule (36) and making all the outputs [−coron], since neither CFR rule applies to all the outputs of (36), but only to the [−obstr] and [+obstr] classes respectively. CFR rules (37) and (45) do link, however, to make the output [−anter] and [+distr]. Rule (36) also palatalizes /t/ and /d/ before /ʃ/, /ʒ/, /ʎ/, and /ɲ/. This is certainly right in the first three cases − it is part of the affrication of /t−ʃ/, /d−ʒ/, and the total assimilation of /t−ʎ/. It is probably right for /ɲ/ too;

morphemes beginning with /ɲ/ are few and occur rarely, which makes it hard to discover spontaneous examples. Mascaró (1972:27) accepts /t #ɲ/ → [ɲɲ].

6.4. Velar assimilation. Examples

l/__k	*solc* 'furrow' [sóɫk]
	arrel quadrada 'square root' [ərɛ̀ɫkwəðɾáðə]
l/__g	*algú* 'someone' [əɫɣú]
	abril gris 'grey April' [əβɾìɫɣɾís]
n/__k	*blanc* 'white' [bláŋ]
	Sant Carles 'St Charles' [sàŋkárləs]
n/__g	*vengui* 'let him sell' [béŋgi]
	un gros 'a fat man' [uŋgɾɔ́s]
t/__k	*adquirir* 'to acquire' [əkkiɾí]
	aquest camí 'this road' [əkɛ̀kkəmí]
t/__g	*s'ha fet gran* 'has grown big' [səfèggɾán]

The rule of velar assimilation can be expressed as:

(37) $\begin{bmatrix} -\text{labial} \\ -\text{cont} \\ -\text{high} \\ \langle +\text{vocal} \rangle \end{bmatrix} \rightarrow \begin{bmatrix} +\text{back} \\ \langle -\text{distr} \rangle \end{bmatrix} / \underline{\quad} \#_0 \begin{bmatrix} +\text{cons} \\ +\text{back} \end{bmatrix}$

Linking applies (CFR (28), (37)) to make the changed segment [+high] and [−anterior]. By convention (d) CFR (43), which mentions [+obstr], fails to apply, leaving the outputs [+coron]; this is right for [ɫ] which is, I suggest, [+coron, +high, +back, −anter]. The angle brackets are to prevent CFR (45) applying after CFR (28) and making [ɫ] [+distr], which it seems it should not be, since the primary point of articulation for [ɫ] remains the same as for [l], namely, apico-alveolar. However, velarization of /l/ takes place in other environments as well (§ 6.7), and a better generalization is achieved by excluding /l/ from

302 Further phonological rules

the present assimilation rule, as it was excluded from (34). So we have rather,

(38) $\begin{bmatrix} -\text{vocal} \\ -\text{cont} \\ -\text{high} \end{bmatrix} \rightarrow \begin{bmatrix} +\text{back} \\ -\text{coron} \end{bmatrix} / \underline{\quad} \#_0 \begin{bmatrix} +\text{cons} \\ +\text{back} \end{bmatrix}$

Linking (CFR (28), (37), (45)) supplies [−anter], [+high], [+distr], but CFR (43) fails as it stands to supply [−coron] which is therefore mentioned in the rule. I suspect that an additional CFR rule is appropriate, such as

CFR (46) $\begin{bmatrix} -\text{vocal} \\ +\text{back} \end{bmatrix} \rightarrow [-\text{coron}]$

It seems natural for velar plosives and nasals to be [−coron], while a velarized lateral might normally be [+coron], i.e. maintain contact with the front of the tongue.

6.5. Dental assimilation. Examples:

n/__t	*contreu* 'contracts' (V) [kuntréw]	
	ven taronges 'sells oranges' [bèn̪tərɔ́n'ʒəs]	
n/__d	*endemà* 'next day' [ən̪dəmá]	
	un dia 'one day' [un̪díə]	
l/__t	*galta* 'cheek' [ga̪ltə]	
	el tap 'the cork' [ə̪ltáp]	
l/__d	*voldrà* 'will want' [bu̪ldrá]	
	mal de cap 'headache' [mà̪ldəkáp]	
s/__t	*llest* 'clever' [ʎést̪]	
	vas tenir 'you had' [bàs̪təní]	
s/__d	*desdir* 'to go back on one's word' [dəz̪ðí]	
	des de 'since' [déz̪ðə]	

The rule is:

Further phonological rules 303

(39) $\begin{bmatrix} \{+obstr\} \\ \{-cont\} \\ +coron \\ -high \end{bmatrix}$ → [+anter]/___ #₀ $\begin{bmatrix} -syll \\ +coron \\ +anter \end{bmatrix}$

Mk (12) links, supplying [+distr].

6.6. How do these assimilation rules (34)–(39) relate to the stop-deletion rules (19), (25), (27)?

Labial and velar assimilation (34), (38), must apply before stop deletion, otherwise the unmarked nasal in e.g. /ʎanp/, /blank/ will not become [m] and [ŋ] respectively, and we would generate *[ʎán] *[blán] in place of [ʎám], [bláŋ]. However, it seems that these rules must also apply after stop deletion. Thus

Sant Miquel 'St Michael' [sàmmikél] /–nt#m–/
quant vols? 'how much do you want?' [kwàmbóls] /–nt#b–/
tan fresc 'as fresh' [tàɱfrɛ́sk] /–nt#f–/
fent camí 'making (his) way' [fèŋkəmí] /–nt#k–/
vint gossos 'twenty dogs' [bìŋgósus] /–nt#g–/

Dental assimilation (39) does not apply before stop deletion; we have

decent || [dəsén] not *[dəsén̪]
posant-les 'putting them (F) on' [puzánləs] not *[puzán̪ləs]
molt bé 'very well' [mòɫβé] not *[mòɫ̪βé]
alt 'tall' [áɫ] not *[áɫ̪]
solts 'loose (Mpl)' [sɔ́ɫs] not *[sɔ́ɫ̪s]
ho he vist fer 'I've seen it done' [wèβìsfé] not *[wèβìs̪fé]

In order to bring these rules together, it will in fact be preferable not to regard stop deletion as a unitary phenomenon which intervenes between various kinds of assimilation, but rather to account for the difference with regard to dental assimilation by separating out the deletion of dentals. If this occurs first, then assimilation of coronals to the point of articulation of following consonants, then deletion of final labial or velar stops, the phenomena mentioned in this section will be adequately dealt with. And in fact my rule (19) is inaccurate, since it deletes labial stops not only after nasals but also after /l/, whereas we have in fact *calb* 'bald' [kálp], cf. *calba* (F) [kálβə]; *talp* 'mole' [tálp], *talps* (pl) [tálps]. We have already seen that stop deletion operates differently in different environments in a way that makes conflation of the rules problematic. On the other hand, we should like to bring together as many as possible of the rules assimilating points of articulation. We can do this if we deal at one time only with the coronals /l/, /n/, /t/, /d/, /s/, /z/, leaving aside the assimilations of underlying labials to following labio-dentals, and also, as I suggested above, the velarization of /l/.

Taking first, then, the deletion of /t/ and /d/ we have rule (40). The condition excludes deletion after /s/ or /r/ utterance-finally or when a vowel-initial word follows.

(40) $\begin{bmatrix} +\text{obstr} \\ -\text{cont} \\ +\text{coron} \end{bmatrix} \rightarrow \emptyset \ / \ \begin{bmatrix} -\text{syll} \\ +\text{coron} \\ \langle -\text{cont} \rangle_b \end{bmatrix} \underline{\qquad} \left\{ \begin{matrix} \# \\ +C \end{matrix} \right\} \# \left\langle \begin{Bmatrix} V \\ \| \end{Bmatrix} \right\rangle_a$

condition: if a, then b.

The assimilation rule is (41): /n/, /t/, /d/ undergo total assimilation to following labials and velars. /l/, /s/, /z/, together with /n/, /t/, /d/ undergo alveolar, dental, and palatal assimilation.

(41) $\begin{bmatrix} \{+obstr\} \\ \{-cont\} \\ -labial \\ -back \\ -high \\ \langle -cont \rangle \\ \langle -vocal \rangle_a \end{bmatrix} \rightarrow \begin{bmatrix} \langle \alpha labial \rangle_b \\ \langle \beta back \rangle_b \\ \gamma distr \\ \delta high \\ \epsilon anter \end{bmatrix} / \underline{\qquad} \#_o \begin{bmatrix} \left\{ \begin{matrix} \langle \alpha labial \rangle_b \\ \langle \beta back \rangle_b \end{matrix} \right\} \\ \begin{bmatrix} -labial \\ -back \end{bmatrix} \\ \gamma distr \\ \delta high \\ \epsilon anter \\ \{+obstr\} \\ \{-cont\} \end{bmatrix}$

condition: if a, then b.

Rule (41) is iterable in the sense proposed by Sommerstein (1973:104). That is, it can reapply to its own output. We can think of a rule normally proceeding to scan a string of matrices for sequences which meet its structural description, on which the change stated by the rule then operates. The scanning process then moves on to the next rule. An iterable rule takes again the strings which are its output and reapplies until no sequence meets its structural description, or until the rule applies vacuously. CFR rules (41), (46) link to (41) making labials and velars [−coronal], but CFR (42) does not link to palatal assimilation since it refers only to [−obstr] segments, and is thus prevented from applying by linking condition (d).

Rule (42) deletes final labial or velar plosives — labials word-finally or /___+C, and velars except when a vowel-initial word follows.

(42) $\begin{bmatrix} +obstr \\ -cont \\ \langle +anter \rangle_b \end{bmatrix} \rightarrow \emptyset / \begin{bmatrix} -vocal \\ -cont \end{bmatrix} \underline{\qquad} \left\{ \begin{matrix} \# \\ +C \end{matrix} \right\} \# \left\langle \left\{ \begin{matrix} V \\ \| * \end{matrix} \right\} \right\rangle_a$

condition: if a, then b.
*optional

The option permits *cinc* [síŋk] utterance-finally. Lastly, distributedness assimilation for labials is as follows:

(43) $\begin{bmatrix} +\text{cons} \\ +\text{labial} \end{bmatrix} \rightarrow [-\text{distr}] / \underline{\hphantom{xx}} \#_0 \begin{bmatrix} +\text{cons} \\ -\text{labial} \\ -\text{distr} \end{bmatrix}$

6.7. We have seen above (§6.4) some examples of the velarization of /l/ before /k/ or /g/. /l/ is also velarized after back vowels. Badia describes the Catalan /l/ in the following terms (1951:102–3): "Aun cuando su articulación sea efectivamente alveolar, el postdorso de la lengua, retrayéndose, forma, en la pronunciación de la *l* una amplia zona de resonancia en la parte velar de la cavidad bucal, de suerte que el efecto producido por la *l* catalana es de un sonido velar; advertido desde ahora ese carácter accidental de la alveolar *l*, no haremos ninguna distinción entre las demás alveolares, a no ser en el caso de articulación implosiva, en que el efecto velar predomina por el conjunto de su articulación; por lo demás, los sonidos vecinos acentúan o atenúan la velaridad de la caja de resonancia de la *l,* que aparece menos velarizada en contacto con vocales palatales, por ejemplo, que con vocales de las series media y posterior."

(110): "llamamos, pues, *l* velar a la articulación implosiva precedida de vocal de las series media (*a*, vocal neutra, etc.) o velar (*o, u*); también lo es, precedida de cualquier vocal, pero seguida de consonante velar. El ápice de la lengua toma contacto con el paladar anterior, (en un punto algo posterior a los alvéolos dentarios), y el postdorso adopta una posición parecida a la de la articulación de la vocal velar [u]."

A detailed phonetic study would reveal, I think, the precise hierarchy of velarity in the Catalan /l/; the factors influencing velarity seem to be, from the least velarizing to the most, environments consisting of preceding or following: 1) front non-low vowels, 2) front low vowel /ɛ/, 3) back vowels; and environments

Further phonological rules 307

consisting of a following: 1) non-back consonant, 2) phrase boundary, 3) back consonant. That is, there is a continuum from the least velarized /l/ between front non-low vowels, e.g. *militar* 'military', *milers* 'thousands', and the most velarized /l/ between a back vowel and a back consonant, e.g. the first *l* in *calcular* [kəłkulá] 'to calculate'. At a surface level of description where binary feature values are replaced or supplemented by integers, these degrees of velarity would correspond to integral values of [+back] and [−back]. Where should we draw the line? We could say that all /l/'s preceded by back vowels should be [+back] of some kind. This would be simple, i.e. /l/ → [+back] / $\begin{bmatrix} V \\ +back \end{bmatrix}$ $\#_0$ ——— but it seems from observation that /l/ is not particularly velar in fact after a back vowel before a non-low front vowel, thus *alimentar* [əlimən tá] 'to nourish', *vendre-li* [béndrəli] 'to sell to him'. That is, in environments like this /l/ is rather in a state of equilibrium between the pulls of the preceding back and following front vowels, being possibly rather less velarized than, e.g.

/ i ——— $\begin{bmatrix} +syll \\ +back \end{bmatrix}$ as in *vila* 'town', *quilo* 'kilo'. As an approximation, then, I propose the following rule:

(44) $\begin{bmatrix} +vocal \\ -cont \\ -high \end{bmatrix}$ → $\begin{bmatrix} +back \\ -distr \end{bmatrix}$ / $\left\{ \begin{matrix} [+back] \underline{\quad} \#_0 \ [+cons] \\ [+syll] \ \#_0 \underline{\quad} \#_0 \left\{ \begin{matrix} [+back] \\ \| \end{matrix} \right\} \end{matrix} \right\}$

This rule should apply after degemination (cf. V § 7) of /ll/ so that [lː] may undergo the same kind of velarization as /l/. We have *tot l'any* [tòɫːáɲ] 'the whole year', *molt líquid* [mòɫːíkit] 'a lot of liquid'. If (44) applied before degemination we should get these derivations from intermediate forms:

308   Further phonological rules

by   /tól##l#áɲ/   /mól##líkit/
(44) [tół l áɲ]   [mół líkit]

and degemination would in fact be blocked.

6.8. There follow some sample derivations illustrating the rules of this section.

	molt bonic	molts trossos	molt ximple	molt car
	'very pretty'	'many pieces'	'very silly'	'very dear'
(40)	mólt buník	mólt+s trósus	mólt ʃínplə	mólt kár
(41) 1.	mól buník	mól +s trósus	mól ʃínplə	mól kár
(41) 2.		mól +s̪ trósus	mól' ʃímplə	
(42)		mól̪ +s̪ trósus		
(43)				
(44)	mół buník	mół̪ +s̪ trósus		mół kár

	molt amable	fent música	fent drames	fent llits
	'very kind'	'making music'	'making plays'	'making beds'
(40)	mólt əmábblə	fént múzikə	fént dɾáməs	fént ʎit+s
(41) 1.	mól əmábblə	fén múzikə	fén dɾáməs	fén ʎit+s
(41) 2.		fém múzikə	fén̪ dɾáməs	fén' ʎit+s
(42)				
(43)				
(44)	mół əmábblə			

	fent gresca	fent fosc	camp gran	volem fer
	'making uproar'	'getting dark'	'large field'	'we want to do'
(40)	fént gɾéskə	fént fósk	kánp gɾánd	bulém fé
(41) 1.	fén gɾéskə	fén fósk	kánp gɾán	
(41) 2.	féŋ gɾéskə	fém̪ fósk		
(42)			kám gɾán	
(43)				bulém̪ fé
(44)				

Further phonological rules 309

	capſicat	sang freda	vol jugar	aquest zero
	'worried'	'cold blood'	'wants to play'	'this zero'
(40)		káp+fikát	sáng fréðə	ból ʒuyá	əkɛ́t zɛ́ru
(41)			sáŋg fréðə	ból' ʒuyá	əkɛ́t̬ zɛ́ru
(42)			sáŋ fréðə		
(43)		káp+fikát			
(44)					

7. Affrication of final /ʒ/. As is well known, underlying /ʒ/, /tʒ/ and /tʃ/ are neutralized in word-final position as a prepalatal affricate whose voicing depends on that of the following segment, cf. Badia, 1965a:313–15. Here are some examples:

/bɔʒ/ *boig* 'mad' [bɔ́tʃ]
/bɔʒ+ə/ *boja* 'mad (F)' [bɔ́tʃ]
/bɔʒ+arij+ə/ *bogeria* 'madness' [buʒəríə]

/raʒ/ *raig* 'trickle' [rátʃ]
/raʒ+a+r/ *rajar* 'to trickle' [rəʒá]
/raʒ#da#bin/ *raig de vi* 'trickle of wine' [ràdʒ ðə βí]

/baʒ/ *vaig* 'I go' [bátʃ]
/baʒ+i/ *vagi* 'go' (1, 3sg pres subj) [báʒi]
/baʒ#a#kaz+ə/ *vaig a casa* 'I'm going home' [bàdʒ ə kázə]

The rule accounting for this phenomenon must precede voicedness assimilation; otherwise we should have the following incorrect derivation

/əl#mateʃ#ɔman/   *el mateix home* 'the same man'
Voicing   mateʒ
Affric^n matedʒ
*[əlmətèdʒ ɔ́mə]   instead of   [əlmətèʒ ɔ́mə]

310   *Further phonological rules*

/ʒ/ could be affricated directly, becoming [−cont, +del. rel], but then, being [−cont] it would be an exception to the voicing assimilation rule, non-continuant obstruents (stops) being otherwise voiceless before a word beginning with a vowel. Great difficulties would also arise with the spirantization rule (cf. § 10) which affects /b/, /d/, and /g/ after continuants. These difficulties can be avoided by making the affrication follow from the insertion of a stop, /t/, i.e. the least marked consonant. The affrication itself is dealt with by the general affrication rule, see below § 11. The insertion rule is thus:

(45) ø → [−syll] / ___ $\begin{bmatrix} +\text{obstr} \\ +\text{cont} \\ +\text{high} \\ +\text{voiced} \end{bmatrix}$ (+C) #

This rule is ordered before the assimilations of § 6 (rule (41)), so that the inserted /t/ undergoes the same palatal assimilation as underlying /t/.

8. **Voicedness assimilation.** Obstruents always take their voicedness from immediately following consonants; across word-boundaries before vowels continuants are voiced, non-continuants unvoiced; affricates behave like continuants in this respect so it is best for this rule to operate while affricates are still represented as sequences of stop + continuant (cf. V § 5). In utterance-final (or phrase-final) position obstruents are unvoiced. Cf. Fabra, 1897:15−16. Here are some examples illustrating the same stems in different environments:

(46)   / ___+V : no assimilation.
    (a) /sab+ɛ+r/ *saber* 'to know' [səβέ]
    (b) /ad+ar+i+r/ *adherir* 'to adhere' [əðərí]
    (c) /fe+t+ə/ *feta* 'made (F)' [fétə]
    (d) /ʎarg+ə/ *llarga* 'long (F)' [ʎáryə]

Further phonological rules 311

(f) /serv+ə/ serva 'serf (F)' [sérβə]
(g) /kaz+u+s/ casos 'cases' [kázus]
(h) /es+r/ ésser 'to be' [ésə]
(i) /mateʃ+ə/ mateixa 'same (F)' [mətéʃə]
(j) /skitʃ+a+r/ esquitxar 'to splash' [əskitʃá]
(k) /mitʒ+ə/ mitja 'half (F)' [míʤə]

(47) / ___ {#/+} [−syllab / +voiced]

(a) sap riure 'knows how to laugh' [sàbríwrə]
(b) admetre 'to admit' [ədmétrə] or [əmmétrə]
(c) m'ha fet llegir 'has made me read' [məfèʎʎəʒí]
(d) llarg de cames 'long-legged' [ʎàrgdəkáməs]
(e) buf d'aire 'puff of air' [bùvðájrə]
(f) serf de 'serf of' [sérvðə]
(g) cas notable 'notable case' [kàznutábblə]
(h) és veritat 'it is true' [èzβəɾitát]
(i) mateix nom 'same name' [mətèʒnóm]
(j) esquitx gran 'big splash' [əskìʤyrán] or
   [−ʤgɾ−]
(k) migdia 'midday' [miʤðíə]

(48) / ___ {#/+} [−voiced]

(a) sap cantar 'knows how to sing' [sàpkəntá]
(b) adscriure 'to ascribe' [ətskríwrə]
(c) s'ha fet xafogós 'has become sultry' [səfètʃəfuyós]
(d) llarg camí 'long road' [ʎàrkkəmí]
(e) buf calent 'warm puff of air' [bùfkəlén]
(f) serf tímid 'timid serf' [sèrftímit]
(g) cas terrible 'terrible case' [kàstəríbblə]
(h) és fals 'it is false' [èsfáls]
(i) mateix so 'same sound' [mətèʃsó]
(j) esquitx petit 'little splash' [əskìtʃpətít]
(k) mig cru 'half raw' [mìtʃkɾú]

312   Further phonological rules

(49) /____ # V

(a) *sap explicar* 'knows how to explain' [sàpəkspliká]
(b) ————
(c) *fet anar* 'made to go' [fètəná]
(d) *llarg any* 'long year' [ʎàrkáɲ]
(e) *buf enorme* 'enormous puff' [bùvənórmə]
(f) *serf ancià* 'old serf' [sèrvənsiá]
(g) *cas optimístic* 'optimistic case' [kàzuptimístik]
(h) *és horrible* 'it's horrible' [èzuríbblə]
(i) *mateix home* 'same man' [mətèʒómə]
(j) *esquitx alt* 'high splash' [əskiʤál]
(k) *mig any* 'half a year' [miʤáɲ]

(50) /____ ‖

(a) *sap* 'knows' [sáp]
(b) ————
(c) *fet* 'made' [fét]
(d) *llarg* 'long' [ʎárk]
(e) *buf* 'puff' [búf]
(f) *serf* [sérf]
(g) *cas* 'case' [kás]
(h) *és* 'is' [és]
(i) *mateix* 'same' [mətéʃ]
(j) *esquitx* 'splash' [əskítʃ]
(k) *mig* 'middle' [mítʃ]

Voicing assimilation can be expressed in the following way:

(51) [+obstr] →
iterable
$$\left\{ [\alpha\text{voiced}] \Big/ \left\{ \begin{array}{l} \underline{\quad} \#_0 \langle \# \rangle_b \begin{bmatrix} \alpha\text{voiced} \\ +\text{cons} \\ \langle +\text{vocal} \rangle_a \end{bmatrix} \\ [\overline{\alpha\text{cont}}] \quad \#_1 \quad [-\text{cons}] \end{array} \right. \right.$$
$$[-\text{voiced}] \quad / \underline{\quad} \#_1 \|$$

condition: if a, then b.

Further phonological rules 313

As /kw/ does not become [gw] I have expressed part i) in terms of [+cons] rather than [−syllabic]. I have no clear evidence on whether stops are normally voiced before initial /j/, there being few examples of initial /j/ words. The rule predicts e.g. *aquest iot* 'this yacht' [əkɛ̀t jɔ́t] (vacuously by part ii)) rather than [əkɛ́d jɔ́t] which would come from part i) with [−syll] in place of [+cons]. Observe that this rule follows those realizing labiovelars as two segments (V (7) and (8)), otherwise final /gʷ/ will be neutralized for voice, becoming identical to /kʷ/ instead of being realized as /gu/. Note that (51) is iterable, i.e. it reapplies to its own output. So, for example, for *text difícil* 'difficult text' we obtain the following derivation:

	/tékst##difísil/
Rule (40)	téks ##difísil
Rule (41)	téḵs ##difísil
Rule (51) 1.	tékz̲ ##difísil
Rule (51) 2.	tégz̲ ##difísil
Spirantization	tégz ##ðifísil

or for *discs antics* 'old records':

	/dísk+s##antík+s/
Rule (51) 1.	dísk+z##antík+s
2.	dísg+z##antík+s
3.	dízg+z##antík+s

The complicated nature of part i) of the rule is to exclude voicing assimilation before /+r/, e.g. *batre* 'to strike' /bat+r/, *permetre* 'to allow' /par+mɛt+r/. Voicing assimilation in internal /Cr/ and /Cl/ is of course also excluded. The rule must allow for other cases of assimilation across +, as example (48b) shows. Cf. also *substituir* [supstituí] 'to substitute', compared with *subratllar* [subrəʎʎá] 'to underline'.

9.1. Lateral assimilation. Examples of this phenomenon were given in V §7. Here are a few more:

aquest llum 'this lamp' /akɛt##ʎum/ [əkèʎʎúm]
dit llarg 'long finger' [dìʎʎárk]
ha posat límits 'has set limits' [əpuzàllímits]
fet lògic 'logical fact' [fèllɔ́ʒik]

A form of this rule was used as an example in VI §2.4. We can now see that as expressed it is not quite correct, since by it underlying /l/ and /ʎ/ are altered; examples in §6.3 of this chapter show that /l/ undergoes only partial palatal assimilation to a following /ʎ/ and, in fact, /ʎ/ is not assimilated at all. The correct form is

(52) $\begin{bmatrix} -\text{cont} \\ -\text{vocal} \\ -\text{labial} \\ -\text{back} \end{bmatrix} \rightarrow \begin{bmatrix} +\text{vocal} \\ \alpha\text{high} \end{bmatrix} / \underline{\qquad} \#_0 \begin{bmatrix} -\text{cont} \\ +\text{vocal} \\ \alpha\text{high} \end{bmatrix}$

The remaining features of [l] and [ʎ] are supplied by linking, which operates in the following way:

(i) $\begin{bmatrix} -\text{cont} \\ -\text{labial} \\ -\text{back} \\ +\text{vocal} \\ +\text{high} \end{bmatrix}$ *m* by CFR (23)
   m by CFR (34)

[*m*+cons]   by CFR (7)
[*m*−obstr]   by CFR (12)
[*m*−nasal]   by CFR (18)
[*m*+voiced]   by CFR (26)
[*m*−anter]   by CFR (37)
[*m*−coron]   by CFR (42)
[*m*+distr]   by CFR (45)
[*m*−syll]   carried over

[ʎ]

Further phonological rules 315

(ii) $\begin{bmatrix} -\text{cont} \\ -\text{labial} \\ -\text{back} \\ +\text{vocal} \\ -\text{high} \end{bmatrix}$ *m* by CFR (23)

[*m*+cons] by CFR (7)
[*m*−obstr] by CFR (12)
[*m*−nasal] by CFR (18)
[*m*+voiced] by CFR (26)
[*m*−syll] carried over
[*u*+coron] by Mk (6)
[*u*−anter] by Mk (11)
[*u*−distr] by Mk (12)

[1]

9.2. Nasal assimilation. A rule similar to the one above assimilates anterior obstruent stops to following nasals. Examples were given in V § 7. By (41) /t/ and /d/ have already become labial before /m/, for fairly rapid speech, at least − see rule (34). When this labial assimilation does not occur, nasalization does not occur either. Thus in careful speech we have e.g. *admetre* [ədmétrə] 'to admit', *tot millor* [tòd miʎó] 'all better'; similarly in careful speech we have *abnegació* [əbnəɣəsió] 'abnegation', *cap novetat* [kàb nuβətát] 'no change'; in rapid speech [əmnəɣəsió], [kàm nuβətát]. In fairly rapid speech /g/ becomes [ŋ] before nasals (especially /n/, within words −cf. Coromines (1973:248): "és poc freqüent [fɔ̀ŋnów] per [fɔ̀gnów] *(foc nou)*, i [dɔ́ŋmə] *(dogma)* molt rar". In my experience, though, [dɔ́ŋmə] is by no means unusual.) Examples:

digne 'worthy' [díŋnə]
tècnic 'technician' [téŋnik]
pragmàtic [prəŋmátik]

316 *Further phonological rules*

Allowing [dɔ́ŋmə] but not *[fɔ̀ŋnɔ́w] the rule is:

(53) $\begin{bmatrix} -\text{vocal} \\ -\text{cont} \end{bmatrix} \rightarrow [+\text{nasal}] \Big/ \begin{bmatrix} \overline{(\alpha\text{labial})^*} \\ \langle+\text{back}\rangle_a \end{bmatrix} \#_0^{\langle o \rangle} b \begin{bmatrix} -\text{syll} \\ +\text{nasal} \\ (\alpha\text{labial})^* \end{bmatrix}$

condition: if a, then b.
*restriction for careful speech

10. Sprirantization of /b/, /d/, /g/. These phonemes are realized as [β], [ð], [ɣ] respectively, in environments which, as we shall see, are not so simple to describe as Badia implies. He says (1962:74): "[β] ... es la articulación normal de *b* o *v* en todos los casos en que no ocupe posición inicial absoluta ni siga a consonante nasal." (81): "[ð] ... es la articulación normal de la *d* en todos los casos en que no se encuentre como inicial absoluta, ni precedida de *n, m, l.*" (105): "[ɣ] ... es la articulación normal de *g* (+ *a, o, u*) o *gu* (+ *e, i*) en todos los casos en que no ocupe posición inicial absoluta ni siga a consonante nasal." Similar statements are found in Badia, 1951:97, 100, 109, though note that in this earlier work Badia is slightly more accurate, with regard to [ɣ] only, since he states the position as above, concluding " ... ni siga a consonante nasal ni oclusiva" (109). Here are examples of the distribution of these allophones:

/b/ → [β]:

/V __V	*acaba* 'ends', *va veure* 'saw' [bàβéwrə]
/Gl __V	*gaubança* 'rejoicing', *noi beneit* 'stupid boy'
/Liq __V	*estalvis* 'savings', *barba* 'beard', *mar bonic* 'attractive sea', *molt bèstia* 'very stupid' [mòɫβéstiə]

Further phonological rules   317

/Fr __ V	bisbe 'bishop' [bízβə], mateix vaixell 'same ship' [mətèʒβəʃéʎ]
/Affr __ V*	vàig voler 'I wanted' [bàʤβulé] or [bàʤbulé] tots vius 'all alive' [tòdzβíws] or [tòdzbíws]
/V __ Liq	bíblia 'Bible' [bíβliə], moixó blau 'little blue bird' pebre 'pepper', la brisa 'the breeze'
/Gl __ Liq	rei blanc 'white king', nou brot 'new shoot'
/Liq __ Liq	marbre 'marble', cualbra 'toadstool', far blanc 'white lighthouse', molt breu 'very short', vol blasmar 'wants to blame', ull brilliant 'shining eye'
/Fr __ Liq	és blau 'is blue', fotògraf brillant 'brilliant photographer' [futɔ̀ɣrəvβriʎán]
/Affr __ Liq*	veig branques 'I see branches' [bèʤβráŋkəs] or [bèʤbráŋkəs], aquests blens 'these wicks' [əkèdzβléns] or [əkèdzbléns]

/b/ → [b]:

/Nasal __	canvi 'change', tan violent 'so violent', any vinent 'next year'
/Pl __	advent [əbbén] /ad+ben+t/, probable [pruβábblə] /probatbl/, aquest blat 'this wheat' [əkèbblát], poc viu 'with little life' [pɔ̀gbíw]
/ ǁ __	Basta! 'Enough!'
/ __ [+obstr]	capdavall 'bottom' [kàbdəβáʎ], objecte 'object' [ubʒéktə], cap zona 'no zone' [kàbzónə], sap

318 Further phonological rules

/___ $\begin{Bmatrix} \# \\ + \end{Bmatrix}$ [r] *demanar* 'knows how to ask'
[sàbdəməná]
subratllar 'to underline'
[subrəʎʎá] /sub+ratʎ+a+r/, *cap raó*
'no reason' [kàbrəó]

/___ # $\begin{Bmatrix} ʎ \\ l \end{Bmatrix}$ *qui-sap-lo* 'extremely' [kìsáblu]
/ki##sab#l+u/, *cap llum* 'no light'
[kàbʎúm]

/d/ → [ð]:

/V___V   *ferida* 'wound', *la dona* 'the woman'
/Gl___V   *viuda* 'widow', *avui dia* 'nowadays'
/Liq ___V   *absurda* 'absurd (F)' [əpsúrðə]
far de St Sebastià 'lighthouse of S. S.'
/Fr ___V   *agost de 1914* 'August 1914'
[əɣòzðə−], *calaix de sastre* 'rag-bag' [kəlàʒðə−]
/Affr___V*   *vaig decidir* 'I decided'
[bàʤðəsiðí] or [bàʤdəsiðí]
grapats de sorra 'handfuls of sand'
[grəpàʣðə−] or [grəpàʣdə−]
/V___ Liq   *lladre* 'thief', *de drames* 'of plays'
/Gl ___Liq   *nou drap* 'new cloth', *noi drogadicte* 'young drug-addict'
/r___ Liq   *ordre* 'order', *mort dramàtica* 'dramatic death'
/Fr___Liq   *mateix drac* 'same dragon', *més dràstic* 'more drastic'
/Affr___Liq*   *vaig dreçar* 'I straightened'
[bàʤðrəsá] or [bàʤdrəsá], *tots drets* 'all upright' [tòʣðréts] or [tòʣdréts]

Further phonological rules

/d/ → [d]:

/Nasal ____   *gendre* 'son-in-law', *any de* 'year of'

/Pl ___   *un xic difícil* 'a bit difficult' [unʃigdifísil] *pot defensar* 'can defend' [pɔ̀ddəfənsá] /pɔd##dafɛns+a+r/

/ ‖ ___   *Déu meu!* 'Good God!'

/ ___ [+obstr]   *dotze* 'twelve' [dódzə], *pot guarir* 'can cure' [pɔ̀dgwəɾí], *pot jugar* 'can play' [pɔ̀ʤuyá]

/ ___ { #/+ } [r]   *ha posat rodes* 'has put wheels on' /a#pɔz+a+d##rɔd+ə+s/

N.B. / { 1/ʎ } ___   *caldre* 'to be necessary' [káɫdrə], *vol demanar* 'wants to ask', *gall dindi* 'turkey'

/g/ → [ɣ]:

/V ___ [−cons]   *amaga* 'hides', *la garantia* 'the guarantee', *he guanyat* 'I've won' [èɣwəɲát]

/Gl ___ [−cons]   *euga* 'mare', *noi golós* 'greedy boy' *aigua* 'water'

/Liq ___ [−cons]   *colgar* 'to bury', *amarga* 'bitter (F)', *vol guiar* 'wants to guide' [bɔ̀ɫɣiá], *cor galant* 'gallant heart', *el gual* 'the ford' [əɫɣwáɫ]

/Fr ___ [−cons]   *mes guix* 'more chalk', *mateix gol* 'same goal', *els guants* 'the gloves' [əɫzɣwáns]

/Affr ___ [−cons]   * *vaig gosar* 'I dared' [bàʤɣuzá] or [bàʤguzá], *aquests gandalls* 'these lazybones' [əkɛ̀dzɣəndúɫs] or [−dzg−], *tots guardats* 'all

320   Further phonological rules

	kept' [tòdʐɣwərðáts] or [−dʐgw−]
/V __ Liq	ègloga 'eclogue', alegre 'cheeful', la glòria 'glory', la granota 'the frog'
/Gl __ Liq	rei gloriós 'glorious king', nau gran 'nave'
/Liq __ Liq	mar gris 'grey sea', no val gran cosa 'isn't worth a great deal', mar glaçat 'frozen sea', vol glucosa 'wants glucose'
/Fr __ Liq	els grans 'the adults', desglaçar 'to unfreeze', peix gros 'big fish'
/Affr __ Liq*	aquests glops 'these mouthfuls' [əkédʐylóps] or [−dʐgl−], vaig gratar 'I scratched' [bàdʒɣrətá] or [−dʒgr−]

/g/ → [g]:

/Nasal __	sangonós 'bloody', camp gran 'big field' [kàmgɾán]
/Pl __	aquest gos 'this dog' [əkèggós], segle 'century' [ségglə] /setgl/, drap gastat 'used cloth' [dɾàbgəstát]
/ ‖ __	Guaita! 'look!'
/ __ [+obstr]	examinar 'to examine' [əgzəminá], maragda 'emerald', llac gelat 'frozen lake' [ʎàgʒəlát], regla 'rule' [régglə] /retgl+ə/ → /reggl+ə/
/ __ [r]	antic repte 'old challenge'
/ __ # {1, ʎ}	groc llampant 'bright yellow'

Observe that the dental case differs from the others, in

Further phonological rules 321

that "spirantization" does not occur after /l/, or /ʎ/. Note too that spirantization occurs in each case before [r], but not before [r|. The free variation between stops and fricatives after affricates is best seen, in my view, as an optional variation in rule ordering. Spirantization will occur when the affrication rule follows it; otherwise the affricate, being [−cont], is no longer a proper part of the environment for spirantization, though with this ordering, i.e. 1) affrication, 2) spirantization the latter rule must be formulated to prevent its operating on the affricates themselves. When spirantization precedes affrication (−this ordering seems the more usual−), the rule is thus:

(54) $\begin{bmatrix} +\text{obstr} \\ +\text{voiced} \end{bmatrix} \rightarrow [+\text{cont}]$

$/ \left\{ \begin{matrix} [+\text{cont}] \\ \langle [+\text{vocal}] \rangle \end{matrix} \right\} \#_0 \left[\overline{\langle -\text{coron} \rangle} \right] \left\{ \begin{matrix} \#_0 \begin{bmatrix} -\text{cons} \end{bmatrix} \\ \begin{bmatrix} +\text{vocal} \\ -\text{tense} \end{bmatrix} \end{matrix} \right\}$

When spirantization follows affrication, we will have on the left of the environment slash:

(55) $\begin{bmatrix} +\text{obstr} \\ +\text{voiced} \\ -\text{cont} \\ -\text{del. rel} \end{bmatrix} \rightarrow \begin{bmatrix} +\text{cont} \\ +\text{del. rel} \end{bmatrix}$

Because of the convention "a linking rule applies either to all or to none of the segments formed by a given rule", (see above VI § 2.4), CFR(44) does not link to (54) and make [β] [−distr], i.e. [v], since CFR (44) specifically applies to labials only. Rule (54) is ordered after the rules previously mentioned in this chapter.

11. Affrication. The form of the affrication rule I shall propose will also deal with the reduction of /s##s/,

322 Further phonological rules

/z##z/, /ʃ##ʃ/, and /ʒ##ʒ/ to [s] [z], [ʃ], and [ʒ] respectively, cf. Fabra, 1897:19. Some of the examples of /ʃ##ʃ/ and /ʒ##ʒ/ are from underlying /s##ʃ/, /s##ʒ/, with assimilation by VII (17) or (41). Here are some examples:

/pf/, /tf/; see above, §6.1, §6.6, for the rules dealing with the assimilation in point of articulation in these cases. I repeat the examples here:

rep fredament 'receives coldly' [rɛ̀p̪fɾɛ̀ðəmén]
capficat 'worried' [kə̀p̪fikát]
aquest fenomen 'this phenomenon' [əkɛ̀p̪fənɔ́mən]

/ts/, /dz/; see above §6.2, for the assimilation in point of articulation here, and V §5.

plats 'plates' [pláts]
tot sencer 'complete' [tòtsansɛ́]
setze 'sixteen' [sédzə]
tots a l'hora 'all at once' [tòdzəlɔ́ɾə]

/tʃ/, /dʒ/; see above §6.3, and V §5. See also VII §7.

tornat xerraire 'become a chatterbox' [turnàtʃəɾájɾə]
boig 'mad' [bɔ́tʃ] ← /bɔdʒ/ ← /bɔʒ/
viatge 'journey' [biádʒə]
et nét juga 'the grandson is playing' [ə̝lnèdʒúyə]

/ff/ : *buf fort* 'strong puff' [bùfɔ́rt]

/ss/, /zz/; see above §3.
els sastres 'the tailors' [ə̝lsástɾəs]
dues zones 'two zones' [dùəzɔ́nəs]

/ʃʃ/, /ʒʒ/
mateix xiscle 'same scream' [mətèʃísklə]
coneix Joan 'knows John' [kunɛ̀ʒuán]

We can simplify the formulation of the affrication rule by

Further phonological rules

making it follow the rule which introduces the feature [delayed release], which itself follows the spirantization rule (54). It is

(56) $\begin{bmatrix} +\text{obstr} \\ \alpha\text{cont} \end{bmatrix} \rightarrow [\alpha\text{del. rel}]$

Then the affrication rule can be expressed thus

(57) iterative $\begin{bmatrix} +\text{obstr} \\ \alpha\text{cont} \\ \beta\text{labial} \\ \gamma\text{distr} \\ -\text{back} \end{bmatrix}$ $\#_0$ $\begin{bmatrix} +\text{obstr} \\ +\text{cont} \\ \beta\text{labial} \\ \gamma\text{distr} \end{bmatrix}$

$\quad\quad\quad 1 \quad\quad\quad\quad 2 \quad\quad 3 \;\Rightarrow\; \emptyset \;\; 2 \;\; \begin{bmatrix} 3 \\ \alpha\text{cont} \end{bmatrix}$

The [γdistr] specification prevents alteration of /ʃ##s/, /ʒ##z/. Since the second original segment, being [+cont] is [+del. rel], this feature is transferred to the output segment. The rule is iterative as the following derivations show; (as is normal, the expansion of the schema of (57) with #'s is taken before that without).

(58) *tots sencers* 'all whole'
/tot+s##sansɛr+s/
tót+s##sənsé +s   Stress, vowel reduction,
                        r-deletion, (41)
tót ##sənsé +s   Rule (57) 1.
tó ##tsənsé +s   Rule (57) 2.
[tòtsənsés]

(59) *posats junts* 'put together'
/pɔz+a+d +s ##ʒunt+s/
puz+á+d +s ##ʒún +s   Stress, vowel reduction,
                        stop deletion
puz+á+d +ʃ ##ʒún +s   VII rule (17)
puz+á+d'+ʒ ##ʒún +s   Rule (51) (also (41))

324   *Further phonological rules*

      puz+á+d'   ##ʒún +s   Rule (57) 1.
      puz+á   ## ǰún +s   Rule (57) 2.
     [puzàǰúns]

(60) *assaigs xilens* 'Chilean essays'
     /asaʒ +s##ʃilɛn+s/
     əsáʒ +s##ʃilén+s   Stress, vowel reduction
     əsáʒ +ʃ ##ʃilén+s   VII rule (17)
     əsátʒ+ʃ##ʃilén+s   Rule (45)
     əsát'ʃ+ʃ ##ʃilén+s   Rule (51) (also (41))
     əsát'ʃ ##ʃilén+s   Rule (57) 1.
     əsát'   ##ʃilén+s   Rule (57) 2.
     əsá   ##ʧilén+s   Rule (57) 3.
     [əsàʧiléns]

12. As a result of assimilation rules of various kinds (V (1), VII (17), (41), (43), (51), (52), (53); see also V §7 on geminates in underlying representations), we now have the following sequences of two identical consonants: /rr/, /ll/, /ʎʎ/, /mm/, /nn/, /pp/, /bb/, /tt/, /dd/, /gg/. Phonetically these are not sequences of two consonants each with its own release, but are long tense consonants. This fact is formulated in rule (61), which replaces the tentative version V (26), V (27) having now been replaced by VII (57).

(61) $\begin{bmatrix} +\text{cons} \\ \alpha \text{DF} \end{bmatrix}$ $\#_0$ $\begin{bmatrix} +\text{cons} \\ \alpha \text{DF} \end{bmatrix}$ $\begin{bmatrix} +\text{tense} \\ +\text{long} \end{bmatrix}$

        1   2   3   ⇒   ø   2   3

Bibliography

The works listed are those referred to in the text. The abbreviations are those of the Permanent International Committee of Linguists, which appear in the annual *Bibliographie Linguistique*. Utrecht-Antwerp.

Abercrombie, D. (1967). *Elements of General Phonetics*. Edinburgh.
Alarcos Llorach, E. (1953). 'El sistema fonemático del catalán.' *Archivum* 3, 135–46.
Alcover, A. M. & Moll, F. de B. (1929–33). *La flexió verbal en els dialectes catalans*. 4 fascicles. (Extrets de l'*Anuari de l'Oficina Romànica de Lingüística i Literatura*, 1929–32).
Anderson, S. R. (1971). *West Scandinavian Vowel Systems and the Ordering of Phonological Rules*. Bloomington, Indiana.
Arteaga Pereira, J. (1904). 'Spécimen catalan d'après la prononciation normale . . . ' *Le Maître phonétique* 9, 118–23.
  (1908). 'Ullada general a la fonètica catalana.' *Actes del primer congrés internacional de la llengua catalana*. Barcelona. 445–65.
  (1915). *Textes catalans avec leur transcription phonétique*. Barcelona.
Bach, E. (1968). 'Two proposals concerning the simplicity metric in phonology.' *Glossa* 2, 128–49.

Badia i Margarit, A. M. (1951). *Gramática histórica catalana*. Barcelona.
(1962). *Gramática catalana*. 2 vols. Madrid.
(1965a). 'Problemes de la commutació consonàntica en català.' *Boletim de Filologia* 21, 213–335.
(1965b). 'Función significativa y diferencial de la vocal neutra en el catalán de Barcelona.' *RFE* 48, 79–95.
(1966). 'Predominio de las vocales abiertas e y o en el catalán de Barcelona.' *RFE* 49, 315–20.
(1970a). 'Les oppositions phonologiques ɛ/e et ɔ/o du catalan dans les rimes des poètes modernes.' *Actele celui de-al XII-lea Congres Internaţional de Lingvistică şi Filologie Romanică*. Bucharest. I, 341–75.
(1970b). 'Les vocals tòniques "e" i "o" en el català de Barcelona: Assaig d'anàlisi fonològica de la situació actual.' *ER* 12, 119–73.
(1970c). 'L'alternance sourde/sonore dans les réalisations de /s/ en catalan.' *Phonétique et Linguistique Romanes. Mélanges offerts à M. Georges Straka*. Lyon-Strasbourg. I, 32–42.
(1973a). 'Phonétique et phonologie catalanes.' In Badia & Straka, eds., 1973: 115–79.
(1973b). 'Morpho-syntaxe catalane.' In Badia & Straka, eds., 1973:181–237.
Badia i Margarit, A. M. & Straka, G., eds. (1973). *La Linguistique Catalane: actes du colloque international . . . 1968*. Paris.
Bar-Hillel, Y. (1957). 'Three methodological remarks on "Fundamentals of Language".' *Word* 13, 328–35.
Barnils, P. (1933). 'Estudis Fonètics [1911–32].' *Anuari de l'Oficina Romànica de Lingüística i Literatura* 6, 3–178.
Bladon, R. A. W. (1970). 'Phonotactics in a generative grammar of Old Provençal.' *TPhS* 1970, 91–114.

Brame, M. K., ed. (1972). *Contributions to Generative Phonology.* Austin.

Brasington, R. W. P. (1972). 'The treatment of exceptions in phonology.' *Lingua* 29, 101–119.

(1973). 'Reciprocal rules in Catalan phonology.' *JL* 9, 25–33.

Cairns, C. E. (1969). 'Markedness, neutralization and universal redundancy rules.' *Lg* 45, 863–85.

Cerdà i Massó, R. (1970). 'L'estructura vocàlica del català comú modern.' *ER* 12, 179–213.

(1972). *El timbre vocálico en catalán.* Madrid.

Chomsky, N. & Halle, M. (1968). *The Sound Pattern of English.* New York.

Coromines, J. (1971). *Lleures i converses d'un filòleg.* Barcelona.

Daniels, W. J. (1971). 'Greek-letter variables and the Russian šžc class.' *LIn* 2, 416–8.

Di Pietro, R. J. (1965). 'Los fonemas del catalán.' *RFE* 48, 153–8.

Fabra, P. (1897). 'Étude de phonologie catalane.' *Revue Hispanique* 4, 5–30.

(1913). 'Els mots àtons en el parlar de Barcelona.' *Butlletí de Dialectologia Catalana* 1, 1–17; 2, 1ff.

(1954). *Converses filològiques.* 10 vols. Barcelona.

(1968a). *Gramàtica Catalana.* (4th edition.) Barcelona.

(1968b). *Diccionari General de la Llengua Catalana.* (5th edition.) Barcelona.

Ferrater, G. (1972). 'Llengua Catalana II.' Course of lectures, Barcelona University Faculty of Arts, 1971–2.

Ferrer Pastor, F. (1956). *Diccionari de la rima.* Valencia.

Fillmore, C. J. (1968). 'The case for case.' In *Universals in Linguistic Theory,* eds. E. Bach & R. Harms. New York. 1–90.

Fudge, E. C. (1969). 'Syllables.' *JL* 5, 253–86.

Haiman, J. (1972). 'Phonological targets and unmarked structures.' *Lg* 48, 365–77.

Harms, R. T. (1968). *Introduction to Phonological Theory*. Englewood Cliffs, N.J.
Harris, J. W. (1969). *Spanish Phonology*. Cambridge, Mass.
Hill, K. C. & Nessly, H. (1973). Review of Chomsky & Halle, 1968. *Linguistics* 106, 57–121.
Hoard, J. E. (1972). 'Naturalness conditions in phonology, with particular reference to English vowels.' In Brame, ed., 1972: 122–54
Hurford, J. R. (1971). 'The state of phonology.' *Linguistics* 71, 5–42.
Lacerda, A. de, & Badía Margarit, A. (1948). *Estudios de fonética y fonología catalanas*. Madrid.
Ladefoged, P. (1971). *Preliminaries to Linguistic Phonetics*. Chicago.
Lightner, T. M. (1972). *Problems in the Theory of Phonology: I Russian and Turkish Phonology*. Edmonton, Alberta.
Lleó, C. (1970). *Problems of Catalan Phonology*. University of Washington: Studies in Linguistics and Language Learning 8. Seattle.
Mascaró, J. (1972). *Fonologia Catalana: Processos segmentals i ordenació cíclica*. Unpublished tesi de llicenciatura, University of Barcelona Faculty of Arts.
Matthews, P. H. (1972). *Inflectional Morphology*. Cambridge.
Phelps, E. (1972). 'Catalan vowel reduction – alpha, braces or angled brackets?' *LIn* 3, 246–9.
Postal, P. (1968). *Aspects of Phonological Theory*. New York.
Renat i Ferris, G. (1933). *La conjugació dels verbs en valencià*. Castelló de la Plana.
Roca Pons, J. (1970). 'Morfologia verbal catalana.' *ER* 12, 227–54.
(1971). *Introducció a l'estudi de la llengua catalana*. Barcelona.

Bibliography

Saltarelli, M. (1970a). 'Fonologia generativa dell'algherese.' *Actele celui de-al XII-lea Congres Internaţional de Lingvistică şi Filologie Romanică*. Bucharest. I, 311–14.

(1970b). *A Phonology of Italian in a Generative Grammar*. The Hague.

Sampson, G. (1970). 'On the need for a phonological base.' *Lg* 46, 586–627.

Schädel, B. (1908). *Manual de fonètica catalana*. Cöthen.

Schane, S. A. (1968). *French Phonology and Morphology*. Cambridge, Mass.

(1973). *Generative Phonology*. Englewood Cliffs, N.J.

Smith, N. V. (1973). *The Acquisition of Phonology*. Cambridge.

Solà, J. (1973). 'Orthographe et grammaire catalanes.' In Badia & Straka, eds., 1973: 81–100.

Sommerstein, A. H. (1973). *The Sound Pattern of Ancient Greek*. Publications of the Philological Society 23. Oxford.

Stanley, R. (1967). 'Phonological redundancy rules.' *Lg* 43, 393–436.

(1971). *Boundaries in Phonology*. Bloomington, Indiana.

Stockwell, R. P. & Macaulay, R. K. S., eds., (1972). *Linguistic Change and Generative Theory*. Bloomington, Indiana.

Stockwell, R. P., Schachter, P. & Partee, B. H. (1973). *The Major Syntactic Structures of English*. New York.

Teixidor, J. (1970). *El retaule del flautista*. Barcelona.

Vallès, E. (1931). *Lliçons de gramàtica catalana*. Barcelona.

Vogt, E. (1971). 'Catalan vowel reduction and the angled bracket notation.' *LIn* 2, 233–7.

Wang, W. S. -Y. (1968). 'Vowel features, paired variables and the English vowel shift.' *Lg* 44, 695–708.

Wheeler, M. W. (1972). 'Distinctive features and natural classes in phonological theory.' *JL* 8, 87–102.

Zwicky, A. M. (1970). 'Greek-letter variables and the Sanskrit *ruki* class.' *LIn* 1, 549–54.

(1972). 'Note on a phonological hierarchy in English.' In Stockwell & Macaulay, eds., 1972: 275–301.